MW00942345

From Inkwell to Internet

Internet

90 Years of Teaching Business Administration at Johns Hopkins University (1916–2006)

Peter B. Petersen
Johns Hopkins Carey Business School
Where business is taught with humanity in mind.

iUniverse, Inc.
New York   Bloomington

From Inkwell to Internet
90 Years of Teaching Business Administration at Johns Hopkins University (1916–2006)

iUniverse books may be ordered through booksellers or by contacting:

iUniverse
1663 Liberty Drive
Bloomington, IN 47403
www.iuniverse.com
1-800-Authors (1-800-288-4677)

ISBN: 978-0-595-52478-5 (pbk)
ISBN: 978-0-595-51211-9 (cloth)
ISBN: 978-0-595-62531-4 (ebk)

Printed in the United States of America

iUniverse rev. date: 2/20/2009

To my loving wife, Jan, on our 53rd anniversary;
our three sons, John, Bill, and Jim;
their wives, Charlotte, Melissa, and Amy;
their children, John and Ellie; Matthew, Will, and Jack;
and Kate, Julie, and Eric, and to our great-grandchildren;
who will extend our love into the 22nd century

Contents

Appendices

Acknowledgments

This account of 90 years of teaching Business Administration at Johns Hopkins University needs to acknowledge the efforts of many people. In fact, before this subject was taught formally, it was covered as a part of other programs in different schools throughout the university. One individual personally involved was Henry L. Gantt, who, as a major follower of Frederick W. Taylor in the scientific management movement and a Hopkins graduate in 1880, occasionally presented free lectures in the evening on how to improve efficiency and effectiveness in the workplace. (One of his lectures, given on April 14, 1916, is described in Appendix A.) Then, a program launched during Academic Year 1916–1917 became the first identifiable predecessor of the Business Division. Concurrent with this first business program, titled Evening Courses in Business Economics, Alexander Graham Christie in the School of Engineering headed Night Courses for Technical Workers. In fact, Dr. Christie became the focal point for many decades for the subject of efficiency and effectiveness in industry. In what is now the Krieger School of Arts and Sciences, Dr. William O. Weyforth, Associate Professor of Political Economics, and Dr. Leslie W. Baker, Professor of Accounting, were major figures in teaching Business Administration during the late 1920s and early 1930s.

Recognition goes to Dr. Howard Cooper, Professor of Accounting, for recovering the fumble made by Dean Edward

Hawkins in 1953. Also to be recognized are Dr. Cooper's longtime secretary Ms. Angela Lavarello and Ms. Mary Levin, who began her 48 years with Hopkins in 1923 and retired as executive secretary to the dean in 1971. During the 1950s, 1960s, and 1970s, major contributors of time and energy to develop two graduate-level degree programs were Robert H. Roy, Professor and Dean of the School of Engineering; Charles D. Flagle, Professor and Director of the Department of Health Policy and Management in the School of Hygiene and Public Health; and John P. Young, Professor of Operations Research and Professor of Health Services in the School of Hygiene and Public Health.

Appreciation and acknowledgment are also expressed to the three deans (Evening College and Summer Session, School of Continuing Studies, and School of Professional Studies in Business and Education), who were most helpful in the support that they gave me when I was a member of the Business Division—Roman J. Verhaalen, Stanley C. Gabor, and Ralph Fessler. Absent from this report is a discussion of their actions and accomplishments, but hopefully some researcher a decade or two from now, when enough time has passed for an objective report, will present their story. Nevertheless, the lengthy chronology at the ending of this report provides a comprehensive portrayal of their work.

Special thanks is extended to Jim Gillispie, head of the Government Publications/Maps/Law Library, whose wizardry in revitalizing long-forgotten maps can be seen on these pages.

On a day-by-day basis, I owe the most gratitude to my assistant, Margaret Criscione, who has been working with me since 1995. She is the most efficient and productive person I know and also has the ability to pay attention to detail. A wife and the mother of seven children, she currently manages to homeschool the oldest four and deal with me long-distance via the Internet and telephone. We are accustomed to working together while located far apart, in different time zones. In fact, we have not seen each other since 1999. What means a lot to me is that she has a good disposition and can keep her cool in fast-moving situations. For me, her presence on the Internet makes research fun. Thanks, Margaret.

Preface

In some families, one spouse is a "pack rat" who saves everything, and the other throws away everything that no longer has any immediate value. Such is the case in my family: I hang on to things, and my dear wife of over 53 years throws away almost everything that has no apparent immediate value. Consequently, the vast amounts of data contained in this report owe their survival to my clandestine hoarding of cardboard boxes containing old reports and countless clippings of information ranging from trivia to important historical facts. Although this compilation started on August 31, 1979, when Dr. Frederic H. Glade turned over the Division of Administration and Business to my stewardship, my collection efforts have continued since my departure from the division on June 30, 2006. At the beginning, my attention focused on the division's major degree offered in 1979, which was the Master of Administrative Science (MAS) (see Appendix B for details). For my next 10 years as director of the division, the number of MAS degrees awarded each year at commencement increased—from 89 in 1979 to 400 in 1990. It seems that from the very start I became attached to the degree program, including its students and part-time faculty. In fact, I became smitten with one motivation technique being taught: namely, intrinsic motivation, in which the person being motivated internalizes the task and in one form sees it as a manifestation of himself or herself. I had taken the bait, and I would not leave until the age of 73.

The work on this report started in July 2006, immediately following my departure, and concluded in November 2008. Significant in the timing is that a major event concerning the teaching of Business Administration at Hopkins occurred on December 4, 2006, when the Trustees of Johns Hopkins University approved the separation of the business and education programs to create two separate schools. A generous gift of $50 million from William P. Carey, a trustee emeritus of Hopkins, made this financially possible. Furthermore, the Carey Business School was launched on January 1, 2007, with a $100 million funding plan, with the additional money to be raised from other donors (see Appendix C for details). As a result of this fortunate development, this historical report will cover the entire 90-year history of teaching Business Administration at Hopkins, concluding with the start of the Carey Business School on January 1, 2007. Hopefully, many years from now, when people look back on the decades of splendid work by the Carey Business School, where the teaching of Business Administration is advanced to a higher level, they will also have information available about 90 years of teaching the subject prior to the establishment of the Carey Business School.

Peter B. Petersen, DBA
Professor Emeritus,
Department of Management
Carey Business School
Johns Hopkins University
November 1, 2008

Introduction

From time to time, attempts at documenting the history of Johns Hopkins University are conducted, often by departing faculty or senior administrators. This reporting effort about one particular division is conducted by a person who got very much involved starting on August 31, 1979, when the division was small (myself and a half-time secretary). I thoroughly enjoyed being immersed in the day-to-day activities until my departure on June 30, 2006. Although the history of the Business Division is fairly clear from 1953 to 2006, it is sparse prior to 1953. Essentially, in 1953, the Hopkins Business programs moved from the Faculty of Philosophy (now known as the Krieger School of Arts and Sciences) to McCoy College. Shifting from both a full- and part-time program to strictly a part-time program, practically all the full-time faculty moved to other parts of the university or departed altogether. One notable exception, Dr. Howard E. Cooper, Jr., directed the part-time business programs within McCoy College. He also continued to teach accounting and later became associate dean of the school, a position he held until he retired in 1969. Also in

1969, Dr. Frederic H. Glade, Jr., became director of the Division of Administration and Business and served in this capacity for 10 years. I followed Glade for the next decade when the late 1980s brought a tremendous amount of growth in terms of students, faculty, staff, and facilities. This rapid growth caused an abundance of turbulence. In fact, as an illustration of personnel turbulence, there were 13 directors for the Business Division, in contrast with the Education Division, which had only two directors during the same 27 years (1979–2006). Starting in about 1998, the Business Division had as many as 19 to 21 full-time members of its own faculty. Its numerous part-time faculty consisted of an excellent group of people, including some who were also full-time faculty at Hopkins or elsewhere. However, most of the part-time faculty consisted of skilled practitioners in their respective disciplines, holding at least a master's degree in their field or specialty. Understandably, the vast majority of the classes were taught by part-time faculty.

This historical report, although focusing on the Business Division[1] or whatever that element was called over the years, also considers what two other elements were concurrently doing. One other element is the School of Professional Studies in Business and Education, or whatever that element was called over the years. The second element is the Education Division and its other designations. Accordingly, this report mainly covers the Business Division but also includes, when appropriate, its sister unit Education and its next-higher element, the School of Professional Studies in Business and Education.

---

1 As one might expect, the Graduate Division of Business and Management has had many names. In fact, in 1979, it was called the Division of Administration and Business. To simplify discussions in day-to-day activities, members often call the unit the "Business Division." That practice will continue from time to time in this report. All of this changed on January 1, 2007, when the unit moved to a higher level as the Carey Business School.

The Business–Engineering Connection

In the three decades spanning the start of the 20th century (1885–1915), Frederick W. Taylor (1856–1915) and his scientific management movement enjoyed a period of popularity in business and industry. Focusing on the work of efficiency experts, many captains of industry wanted to learn more about the scientific management claim by Harrington Emerson that "the Eastern Railroads could save a million dollars a day by using scientific management" (Wren, 1987, p. 119). Taylor's position as the president of the American Society of Mechanical Engineers during 1906 added some level of credibility to their claims of having effective cost-cutting production methods. Significant in all this is that the early advocates and pioneers of good business practices, including scientific management, emerged from the field of engineering, rather than business administration. Consequently, one could argue that academic business administration programs gained their early ideas from engineers. Like other colleges and universities, during the early decades of the 20th century a similar outpouring of information came from the Johns Hopkins University School of Engineering.

Although the historical records of business programs at Hopkins are scant for the first half of the 20th century, comments made in 1984 by Robert H. Roy, last dean of the Johns Hopkins

University School of Engineering, provide an insight into the
extent of the School of Engineering's involvement in what are now
considered traditional business school subjects. When Robert Roy
was a student in the School of Engineering (1925–1928), working
toward a degree "in Mechanical Engineering, the Chairman and
Professor of Mechanical Engineering was Alexander Graham
Christie"[2] (Petersen, 1984, p. 16). Although he enrolled in a four-
year baccalaureate program focusing on mechanical engineering,
Rob Roy entered the university as a sophomore because of his
earlier high school academic preparation and subsequently finished
his bachelor's degree in three years. In addition to participating in
courses at Hopkins such as steam turbine design, power plant
calculations, heat engines, and internal combustion engines, he
took one course from Christie,[3] called Industrial Organization
and Contracts. In the text, written by Dexter Kimball, there was
something about the work that Taylor had done. The book covered
[Taylor's] pig iron loading experiments … the Gantt Chart and
something about … wage incentives (Petersen, 1984, p. 17).

"The Harrington Emerson Organization was then in existence.
[Furthermore, Robert Roy indicated that there] were incentive
plans: the Charles Bedeau plan, the Halsey Premium Plan, the
Emerson Efficiency Plan, Gantt's Task and Bonus plan, and the
Taylor Differential Piece Rate" (Petersen, 1984, p. 17). In addition,
Dean Roy stated, "all of these were in use [in business and industry]
around the country" (Petersen, 1984, p. 16). Today one would expect
that contemporary topics (such as these in 1928) would be covered
in business administration courses. Instead, at Hopkins, they were
covered at the time in the School of Engineering.

---

2 Alexander Graham Christie continues to be remembered at Hopkins as a
professor who blazed a trail in his field, mechanical engineering, and who also
championed the new field of production management and a wider approach
known as scientific management.
3 Professor Christie's personal books, donated to the Engineering School's
library, were transferred to the Milton S. Eisenhower Library when departmental
collections were consolidated on the Homewood Campus. His books, now integrated throughout the MSE collection, represent the finest collection of business
administration and management books (circa 1900 –1950) located in the State of
Maryland.

A Brief History of Teaching Business Administration at Hopkins, 1916–2006[4]

Daniel Coit Gilman (1831–1908), who had studied at Yale and in Europe prior to being selected as the first president of Johns Hopkins University, "cast the new institution in the mold of the European research university" (Schmidt, 1986, p. 6). President Gilman's European approaches included "an emphasis on teaching laboratories, student research, and the seminar method" (Macksey, 1976, p. 5). Although several older U.S. institutions such as Harvard and Yale had "a growing interest in postgraduate education ... all remained basically collegiate in character and none had yet identified advanced study and serious research as its primary goals" (Macksey, 1976, p. 1). This would all change as Johns Hopkins University became "the first American institution to stress advanced study—the first true university in the modern sense in the United States" (Schmidt, 1986, p. 6). In October 1876, Johns Hopkins University opened its doors to students

---

4 Occasionally, writers of proposals and reports need a short summary of the history of teaching Business Administration at Hopkins. From personal experience, I found that they need it both quickly and briefly. Although a short 90-year history could be difficult to produce, three versions are attempted. The longest version is here, in the body of the text, and a short version and an even shorter version are included in Appendixes D and E, respectively.

3

"in a modest collection of buildings located at North Howard and Little Sharps streets" (Macksey, 1976, p. 5) in the northern portion of downtown Baltimore.[5] President Gilman quickly became a respected and popular member of the Baltimore community. His practicality and outgoing personality helped the university thrive in a somewhat traditional and rather reserved city. Even after his retirement in 1901, Gilman enjoyed interacting with members of the Baltimore community, who reciprocated by seeking his council and involvement on important matters of civic concern. For example, after the Great Baltimore Fire of 1904, "Gilman was called upon to lead numerous meetings of city officials and business leaders and along with other prominent members of the community helped Baltimore snap back from this tragedy" (Petersen, 2004, p. 173). More specifically, in one of his major tasks for the city, he was chairman of the Burnt District Commission, charged with rebuilding Baltimore after 70 blocks of downtown Baltimore had been destroyed by fire. It was this sort of involvement that encouraged the close working relationships between Hopkins and the city of Baltimore.

From the very beginning, President Gilman welcomed members of the community to free evening lectures covering a wide range of timely and relevant topics, including practical matters dealing with commerce and industry. One popular but sometimes controversial speaker at these evening lectures at Hopkins was Henry L. Gantt (a graduate of the class of 1880), who had become a major follower of Frederick W. Taylor and was a key participant in the scientific management movement.[6] Members of the business community enjoyed Gantt's discussions about efficiency and the value of the manufacturing approach of finding the one best way to do things, but they often disagreed with his negative opinions of the financial

5 Although nothing seems to remain of these buildings, this site is located across the street from the Maryland Historical Society, at the corner of North Howard and West Monument Streets. More specifically, the location of this site, in terms of today's road net, is on the northwest corner and southwest corner of North Howard and West Monument Streets.
6 Gantt eventually invented the Gantt Chart, used to display a temporal comparison. The Gantt Chart was also used in the 1950s as the foundation for PERT and then, a century after its inception, in a software package bearing his name.

community and his overreliance on engineers to run industrial production (Petersen, 1986, pp. 128–132). What with people such as Gantt, the audiences at those evening Hopkins lectures had much to discuss about popular topics. Charles H. Sumwalt, in commenting about a forthcoming lecture by Gantt at Hopkins, included a discussion of the topic and a joke about Gantt's singing ability. "A note received this morning from H. L. Gantt states that he will lecture next Friday evening April 14, 1916, at Hopkins. The subject will be Industrial Leadership. He promises to introduce some radical innovations—if only he doesn't sing" (Petersen, 1984, p. 200).

Beyond lecturing at Hopkins, Gantt gained an excellent reputation in Baltimore as well as at the national level. In fact, he was considered as a candidate for the position of the president of Johns Hopkins University. An article in the June 14, 1913, Baltimore *Sun* "suggests that the Hopkins trustees consider the qualifications of Mr. Gantt for the presidency of the university, calling attention to his special fitness for the task of organizing—the new Department of Engineering just being born" (Petersen, 1984, p. 199).

In 1916, Hopkins started offering evening courses in business economics to part-time students who were employed during the day. This event became the first identifiable predecessor of today's Business Division as engineers took the lead in teaching and applying their approaches for efficient and effective management. Hopkins' new program in business economics would grow, mature, and eventually take the lead in teaching good practices in both leadership and management; however, during the World War I era engineers were the dominant force in management consulting. For example, when America entered World War I, Gantt applied his sophisticated management approaches to solving the problems of a crowded and clogged Port of New York. Heading the Emergency Fleet Corporation, he helped speed America's war supplies to Europe. As before, he shared his sound management approaches with his colleagues back at Hopkins. Then, in February 1919, the year of his death, Gantt also assisted the economic development of Baltimore by accompanying several professors from the Johns Hopkins School of Engineering "working on a proposal to conduct an extensive study of Baltimore's port. The purpose of their study

[was] to improve the port so that the 'masters of industry' and the 'great shipping interests' will be attracted" (Petersen, 1984, p. 199).

The field of Business Administration emerged and expanded in American colleges and universities during the early 1920s. Although only a few colleges and universities had academically focused programs prior to this decade, expansion of businesses during these Roaring Twenties called for educated young professionals and potential leaders in commerce and industry. Johns Hopkins University met this need by a natural expansion of President Gilman's earlier efforts. His prior emphasis for business people on practical business methods rather than on lofty theories produced graduates long after his death who could be employed and quickly provide genuine value to a firm.

As advocates of teaching business administration in America promoted an expansion of business programs, other forces sought to protect the teaching of more traditional academic disciplines. These early actions in the 1920s are unclear; however, the discovery in 2006 of several news articles from 1926 reveals an attempt to consolidate the business programs of the University of Maryland and Johns Hopkins University.

In February 1926, the Baltimore *Evening Sun* reported, "The Johns Hopkins University will take over the School of Business Administration of the University of Maryland ... beginning next October [1926]." Furthermore, those students who have completed two years (or more) of work will finish their program at Johns Hopkins University but will receive their Bachelor of Science degree at the University of Maryland. Conversely, students who have completed less than two years at the University of Maryland will complete their program at Johns Hopkins University and also receive their Bachelor of Science degree from Hopkins. The agreement was reached by Dr. Albert F. Woods, President, University of Maryland, and Dr. F. J. Goodnow, President, Johns Hopkins University.

Also in February 1926, the *Baltimore American* reported that "effective with the Academic Year 1926–1927, the University of Maryland, will discontinue academic and business courses and the work will be taken over by Johns Hopkins University through its College for Teachers and Evening Courses in Business Economics." In addition, the *Baltimore American* reported that "instruction in accounting by the Johns Hopkins Evening Courses in Business Economics will be broadened to make it the equivalent to the courses now offered by the University of Maryland School of Business Administration." What is unknown is the extent to which this overall agreement with the University of Maryland was implemented. However, some evidence that an active undergraduate business program existed at the time at Hopkins is the fact that Chi Chapter of Delta Sigma Pi (a business fraternity) permanently moved to Hopkins from the University of Maryland during the 1926 fall semester (see Appendix F for details). As additional material becomes available the Hopkins–University of Maryland connection should be revealed further.

Within the field of Business Administration during the 1920s, accounting was a particularly popular subject. Indeed, it was the sort of subject that might qualify a graduate for a job, or perhaps a career. Then, in 1928, Howard Cooper arrived at Hopkins to spend the next 41 years. In fact, he became a favorite professor, who taught accounting to many future leaders and fiscal chiefs.

The Great Depression (1929–1940) had an impact on academia throughout America, and Hopkins was no exception, with fewer enrollments and the early conclusion of some ongoing grants and other forms of fiscal support. For example, in the School of Engineering, Night Courses for Technical Workers had been fully supported by business and industry and had existed as a separate corporation, but it could now no longer be afforded as many companies fought for their own survival and the other companies faced an uncertain future. Fortunately, these fiscal requirements were taken over by Hopkins and were fully supported.

Although Evening Courses in Business Economics were situated in the Department of Political Economy, the Hopkins budget for Academic Year 1936–1937 showed them for the first time as a separate unit. Then, in Academic Year 1941–1942, Dr. Howard E. Cooper (who continued teaching accounting) was also appointed Director of Evening Courses in Business Economics. The number of students enrolled in accounting courses expanded until the entry of the United States into World War II. Although programs in business administration continued during the war, they had fewer students and also experimented with accelerated but much shorter programs. The war effort was paramount, and the university did all it could to support it. For example, in the field of medicine, men and women from Hopkins staffed "two five-hundred-bed military hospital units in the Pacific during World War II" (Warren, 2000, p. 262). Hospital Unit 18, stationed for 2 years on Fiji, displaced to the India-Burma Theater as the war progressed. The other Hopkins unit, General Hospital Unit 118, treated more than 40,000 patients while advancing from Australia to New Guinea and eventually to the Philippines (Warren, 2000, p. 262).[7]

Following World War II, Hopkins' Business Administration programs, including the bachelor's degree in business, swelled to record levels. In fact, Johns Hopkins University led the State of Maryland in the number of accounting students who successfully completed Certified Public Accounting (CPA) exams administrated by the State of Maryland. For some, the approach after WWII was to complete these degree programs on a part-time basis. Such was the case when, in 1945, Robert Lindsay rationalized that "following every great war there is a great depression, so he decided to get a job first and then concurrently work part-time towards a bachelor's degree" (Petersen, personal interview, November 2004). Consequently, the Hopkins part-time program suited his needs.[8]

By 1953, most of Hopkins' business majors were part-time students who worked in business and industry during the day and attended classes at night. As a result, the business programs were transferred from the School of Arts and Sciences to McCoy College, which had been established in 1947 to consolidate all of the evening

---

7 Overall esprit de corps and individual morale were fostered by this Hopkins connection, and by the fact that many of these individuals were closely connected at Hopkins prior to their service during WWII.

8 Joining Noxima as an accountant after WWII, Robert Lindsay advanced through the fiscal channels of the business, eventually becoming comptroller and then senior vice president. Concurrent with his advancement, the profitable Noxima expanded, reconfigured as Noxcell, and today has been absorbed by Procter & Gamble.

offerings of the university. Then, during the 1950s and 1960s, interest increased in graduate management programs, so in 1961 a Master of Science in Management Science program (see Appendix G for details), focusing on the application of new findings in quantitative analysis and general systems theory, became the first graduate-level business degree at Hopkins. During the ensuing decade, a committee consisting of faculty from throughout the university debated the merits of establishing an MBA program. Then after considering the presence of other MBA programs in Baltimore this committee, led by Hopkins' president, Milton S. Eisenhower, decided instead to offer a Master of Administrative Science degree, which would be strong in both management science and economics.

Building on Gantt's pioneering work, Dr. Charles D. Flagle, a major contributor to the Hopkins MSM and the MAS degrees, had earlier developed the concept of Program Evaluation and Review Technique (PERT). Flagle's innovation provided a new tool that still is used throughout the world by project managers. Drs. Flagle and John Young added a strong quantitative emphasis to the program, and Robert Roy, dean of the School of Engineering, provided courses that focused on a practical management approach drawn from his engineering background.

In 1973 arrangements were made to rent classrooms for evening classes at Goucher College. Concurrently, the Evening College opened an off-campus center in Columbia, Maryland, in Joseph's Square, at 5485 Harpers Ferry Road. This new center offered 11 sections of courses—two sections for the Division of Administration and Business, four sections for the Division of Education, and five sections for the Division of Arts and Sciences. A total of about 300 students enrolled. The next year, during the May 1974 commencement, a cohort of 15 graduates received the first MAS degrees. Increased enrollments at the Columbia Center enabled it to move in 1984 from Joseph's Square to the Overlook Building on Twin Knolls Road in Columbia. Facilities included six classrooms, two computer labs, and a conference room. The move also included the need to guide and retain students. The goal was successful; 495 students enrolled. Then, during Academic Year

1984–1985, the Evening College and Summer Session became the School of Continuing Studies.

During the 1980s, enrollments in the MAS program soared as concentrations in quantitative and public administration shifted to information systems, finance, and human resources management. By 1988, the MAS degree program was receiving special national recognition, rated the third-best regionally accredited business school in the Eastern United States by *US News & World Report*. Hopkins' president, Steve Muller, noted that although "the MAS program is not a business school in any ordinary sense … it was gratifying to have the excellence of the work that is done every semester in this program recognized by other business deans." Enrollment in the program expanded exponentially; 89 students completed the MAS program in 1979; in 1990, 400 MAS degrees were awarded. Because of this trend, the Columbia Center acquired additional space in the Overlook Building during Academic Year 1986–1987 and expanded capacity to 10 classrooms, two computer labs, and one conference room. Students enrolled increased to 690.

In January 1987, at the start of the spring semester, the School of Continuing Studies opened its Downtown Center, near the corner of Charles and Saratoga Streets in downtown Baltimore. This center had eight classrooms, two computer labs, an executive conference room, and a 222-seat auditorium, as well as an on-site library.

In 1991 substantial changes continued when the MAS degree became the Master of Science in Business (MSB). The overall focus on economics and management science shifted further to practical management and applied behavioral subjects relevant to the workplace of the 1990s. Concurrent with launching the new MSB, other new degrees appeared—Master of Science in Real Estate, Master of Science in Organizational Development and Human Resources, Master of Science in Information and Telecommunication Systems for Business, Master of Science in Marketing, Master of Science in Finance, a wide range of graduate certificate programs and post-master's certificate programs. Each of these programs focused on specific industries or fields commensurate with the professional needs of students.

In providing for ever-increasing enrollments, the Columbia Center moved during 1992 within Columbia from Twin Knolls to Gateway Corporate Park. This much larger site accommodated rapidly expanding enrollments and provided room for future expansion. Also in 1992, the Washington DC Center opened. Located near DuPont Circle in the Airline Pilot's Association Building, at 1625 Massachusetts Avenue, NW, this center attracted sizable numbers of well-qualified students. Like the Downtown Center in Baltimore, the Washington DC Center offered courses almost exclusively to students in the Business Division.

In September 1994, a team consisting of three members of the Leadership Development Program for Minority Managers won the National Black MBA Case Competition. This three-person team consisted of Jerome Alston, Helen Holton, and Blair Johnson.

The major change for the 1990s occurred during the summer of 1999, with the offering of a Master of Business Administration (MBA) degree. This rigorous practical degree enabled the Business Division in the 2000s to collaborate with other Hopkins schools to offer dual Master's/MBA degree programs in the areas of Medical Services Management, Biotechnology, Nursing, and Public Health. Also in September 1999, Ralph Fessler replaced Stanley C. Gabor as dean of the School of Professional Studies in Business and Education.

During January 2001, at the start of the spring semester, the Baltimore Downtown Center moved to the southwest corner of Charles and Fayette Streets, at 10 North Charles Street. A few months later, space was further consolidated by moving some of the faculty and staff from the seventh floor of 100 North Charles to the third floor of the new Downtown Center.

On December 5, 2006, a gift of $50 million from trustee emeritus William P. Carey enabled Johns Hopkins University to split the business and education components of the School of Professional Studies in Business and Education. January 1, 2007, saw the establishment of the new Carey Business School and the Graduate School of Education. As the teaching of business advances to a higher level with the Carey Business School, the Hopkins tradition of developing innovative business programs for the ever-changing workplace continues.

A Few Colorful Characters

If time and space were available, it would be good to write a story about everyone who was a member of the Business Division during the 90 years reported in this book. Unfortunately, this is not the case, so this section will have only a few stories about extra-special people who contributed substantially to the work of the Business Division. The individuals selected here not only made a substantial difference but are also people who, for the most part, departed some time ago and have been long forgotten or remain unheard of by many. In the future, perhaps, the next generation can write about the present champions at work and those who back them up and accomplish much of the teaching and unglamorous day-to-day administrative work (see Appendix H for an annotated bibliography).

Howard E. Cooper, Jr. (born 1898—died October 9, 1985)

Howard E. Cooper, Jr., came to Johns Hopkins University in 1928, sold his car, and invested the money in IBM stock. As he hung on to this stock until the 1970s, legend has it that his stock split a few times and appreciated somewhat. He taught accounting starting in 1928, while working on his PhD, and in 1932 received a PhD in Political Economics from the Johns Hopkins University Political Science Department. He lived nearby and enjoyed walking, but he became so popular and was loved by so many that traffic would stop on Charles Street because of all the well-wishers offering him a ride. After spending 41 years at Hopkins, he spent most of his remaining 16 years nearby, the major event of his day visiting friends during lunch at the Hopkins Club.

Cooper paid his dues by helping others for 41 years, even giving advice when asked after he retired. When the business programs moved from Gilman Hall to the basement of Shriver in 1953 and the morale of faculty, staff, and students fell, he held the group together and acted as a buffer for those in the Business Division by shielding them from the outside forces. Furthermore, in heading the residual Business Division element, he presented a positive approach to the new environment, helping his colleagues get back to normal. Significant during his stay at Hopkins was that his field of accounting became increasingly popular by rising above bookkeeping to become the valuable management tool it is today. Generations of accountants, comptrollers, and financial vice presidents owe their expertise to the earlier teaching they received from Dr. Cooper.

Gerald F. Dunaway, DBA

Starting in the 1970s, Gerald F. Dunaway made significant contributions over two decades to the Business Division. As the Business Division's leading marketing professor, he provided academic direction for other part-time faculty who were teaching undergraduate and graduate marketing courses. Although skilled in the academic side of marketing, Dr. Dunaway also had a full measure of experience in the real world of marketing, acquired during his 34-year career in marketing and research with the Procter & Gamble Company. Concurrent with his career at Procter & Gamble, he earned an MBA and a doctorate in business administration (DBA) at George Washington University. After he received his doctorate and joined the part-time faculty at Hopkins, it was a real pleasure for colleagues and students alike to see him merge practice and theory in the classroom and actively participate in informal gatherings of faculty. Indeed, he applied new theories and approaches to currently needed challenges in the workplace. In fact, marketing at Procter & Gamble, a mature, conservative company operating worldwide but having a corporate headquarters in Cincinnati, served as a contrast to slick, fast-moving marketing efforts from a few New York companies. When former employees (faculty or students) of these New York firms differed with Gerry Dunaway, a lively discussion would ensue, yielding many lessons learned but in some cases unresolved differences. But, nevertheless, significant learning did take place, and it was fun to be part of it.

Acheson J. Duncan, PhD (born 1904—died 1995)

> [Acheson J. Duncan,] an authority in the field of industrial statistics and quality control, spent 13 years on the faculty at Princeton University and three years in the Army before coming to Hopkins in 1946 as an Associate Professor of Statistics in the School of Business (*The Gazette*, January 16, 1995).

When the business program moved to McCoy College in Academic Year 1952–1953, Dr. Duncan became a member of the faculty in the Department of Mechanical Engineering's program on industrial engineering. In the early 1950s, concurrent with his teaching, he joined forces with W. Edwards Deming in a consulting effort for the United States Department of Agriculture to establish and apply a statistical sampling procedure for the testing of chemical fertilizers being given to American farmers. The task sought to determine the quality of massive amounts of fertilizer using a minimum amount of sampling. Furthermore, the results had to stand up in court, where the two of them would present expert witness testimony. In essence, they proved in court that suppliers were furnishing a lower-quality product to the government for a higher-quality price. The expert statistical sampling procedures developed by these two giants in the field of statistics saved the day for the government. Years later, in the late 1980s, when Deming made a presentation to the Business Division, Dr. Duncan (then retired) was invited. When Deming spotted him in the audience, he called out "Ache!", and they both smiled and laughed with delight.

> Throughout his career, Dr. Duncan wrote extensively on his research in the field, having co-authored two statistical texts. He was the author of a third book, *Quality Control and Industrial Statistics*, first published in 1952 [when he was in the Business Division] that has had five editions and [that has] also [been] printed in Indian and Japanese translations (*The Gazette*, January 16, 1995).

Quiet and unassuming in appearance, he was a touch of academic class in the Business Division from 1946 to 1953.

Charles D. Flagle, Dr. Eng. (born 1919)

Charles D. Flagle is Professor Emeritus, Department of Health Policy and Management, Bloomberg School of Public Health, with a joint appointment in Mathematical Science in the Krieger School of Arts and Sciences.

Dr. Charles D. Flagle has been actively involved with Johns Hopkins University since he graduated with his bachelor's degree in 1940. Eventually appointed a full professor of the Department of Health Policy and Management, he also taught Management Science courses in the Division of Administration and Business in the Evening College and Summer Session, the successor organization to McCoy College. Flagle was actively involved in the development of the Business Division's Master of Science in Management Science degree and its successor, the Master of Administrative Science degree that started in the fall semester of 1971. Particularly talented in mathematics and operations research, he helped bring practical approaches to the use of statistics and management science to everyday activities in business and industry.

In addition to Dr. Flagle's many accomplishments in research, writing, publishing, and administration, he blazed the trail in terms of Health Policy and Management, being a key participant in the School of Hygiene and Public Health's ascent as the major school of public health in the nation (now known as the Bloomberg School of Public Health). He was also a key participant in the evolution of the Business Division during the 1960s and 1970s. In addition to all of these accomplishments, he is the unsung creator of a major theoretical concept that continues to be used in business and industry today: Program Evaluation and Review Technique (PERT), which is a planning method for managing large projects.

"During the 1950's the US Navy faced the immense task of coordinating the efforts of [about] 11,000 contractors involved in developing the Polaris, the first submarine that could remain submerged while launching a long-range ballistic missile" (Bartol and Martin, 1991, p. 306). Charles Flagle's paper, written for a Seminar in Operations Research while he was a graduate student at Hopkins during 1954, described how use of the Gantt Chart could be extended by adding the dimension of probability. Subsequently, Gantt's (Hopkins class of 1880) original work in 1917 and Flagle's concept of adding probability (1954) became the foundation of Program Evaluation and Review Technique (PERT), "which was a computerized, more intricate scheme but nevertheless founded upon the principles of planning and controlling times and costs" (Wren, 1987, p. 137).

> According to Robert Roy (former dean of the School of Engineering), we had a master's and then doctoral candidate by the name of Charles D. Flagle. He is a man of great distinction. Charlie Flagle wrote his master's thesis on a probabilistic Gantt Chart (Petersen, 1984, p. 35).

In addition, years later, a *Journal of Industrial Engineering* article clearly shows Flagle's contribution to the development of the PERT concept. More specifically, Don Malcolm, who worked on PERT for Booz Allen Hamilton, commented, "Dr. Charles Flagle has been quite perceptive in his recognition of the need for and utility of including variability in the scheduling process. [His] notions have proved especially useful in connection with manning large-scale research and development programs" (Flagle, May 1961, p. SR-19).

Mary Levin

Miss Mary Levin began 48 years with the Evening College and its prior organizations in 1923. Starting with the unit titled College Courses for Teachers, she remained as it evolved into the College for Teachers in 1925, McCoy College in 1947, and the Evening College and Summer Session in 1965. She retired in 1971 from her position as executive secretary to Dean Roman Verhaalen. Following a short illness, she died on February 11, 1978. The Mary Levin Scholarship Fund honors her hard work and dedication.

> Established in 1978 for post-master's degree students by the late Cecelia L. Bass, '41, and Leon P. Bass in honor of her sister, the late Mary Levin, former executive secretary to the deans of McCoy College and the Evening College. Now known as the School of Professional Studies in Business and Education (SPSBE Academic Catalog 2005–2006, p. 35).

Robert D. McTeer, PhD

Robert D. McTeer retired in 2006 as chancellor of the Texas A&M University System, but back in the 1980s, he was an unheralded part-time professor in the Business Division. During the day, he headed the Baltimore branch of the Richmond Federal Reserve Region, where in addition to check-clearing operations, he was charged (among other things) with understanding the current business conditions and overall economic conditions in the area. His economic assessments contributed to the periodic publication of the *Beige Book*, a Federal Reserve publication attempting to understand the nation's economy and then prescribe actions to be taken. With his day-to-day experience, he added a real-world perspective to classes about the dismal science in the Master of Administrative Science (MAS) program. At the time, core courses required of all MAS students included two graduate-level economics courses: The Economic Environment and Economic Theory of the Organization. Students gave Dr. McTeer rave reviews for a decade and now, as alumni, continue to comment favorably about his classes of the 1980s.

> Leaving Baltimore in the early 1990s he became President of the Federal Reserve Bank of Dallas and a member of the Federal Open Market Committee. In Dallas he continued to tell it like it is and gained the reputation as an independent voice, or maverick, dissenting from the Alan Greenspan majority twice in 1999 and once in 2002. [Furthermore,] he was frequently mentioned as a possible successor to Greenspan. Bob's free-market views in general, and his vigorous support of free trade in particular gave the Dallas Fed its reputation as "The Free Enterprise Fed" (A&M System's Web site, accessed Oct. 30, 2006).

In Baltimore, as he advanced in the early years of his 36-year career with the Federal Reserve, he always found time for students and Business Division activities. For example, in July 1980, when the Business Division conducted the annual Hopkins-wide Alumni College, he found time to teach an all-day class in contemporary economic thought and the state of the nation's economy. Consequently, Bob McTeer drove to the site of the one-week gathering in St. Mary's County the night before his class to interact with alumni who would be attending the next day. He got to know them, and they related favorably the next day in class. Another example is a presentation he made to Delta Sigma Pi (the business fraternity) on a weekday night after teaching classes two other nights that same week. Speaking about inflation, he presented solutions appropriate for the national level and then described wise investing strategies for the individual investor. They loved it. Bob McTeer represents the ideal attributes of a professor in a graduate business program. Indeed, he contributed substantially to the Business Division.

Francis E. Rourke, PhD (born 1922—died 2005)

Beyond his own busy schedule as a longtime political science professor and chair of the Department of Political Science in the

School of Arts and Sciences, Francis E. Rourke contributed his own time and energy to the Evening College and Summer Session and its successor organization, the School of Continuing Studies. In 1970 he chaired a committee that bore his name to accomplish the task of examining the Evening College and Summer Session and in August 1970 submitted recommendations for future directions of the college. The following is a brief summary of eight recommendations to be implemented by the college (including the Business Division) (see Appendix I for details).

1. Public relations by the college had to be improved. Rather than being an embarrassment, they needed to bring credit on the college and the university.

2. The university and college (as well as the Business Division) had an obligation and an opportunity to help stop social decay in the inner city.

3. Emphasis must be placed on quality in the classroom.

4. As full-time faculty were added, some internal reorganization would be needed.

5. Consider using facilities in addition to institutions of higher learning.

6. Appoint a small core of full-time faculty that is "offered rank, tenure and other privileges equivalent to those offered to faculty of the other schools of the University" (*Rourke Report*, 1970, p. 3).

7. Consider use of facilities on the East Baltimore campus.

8. With the appointment of a full-time faculty, a high-quality graduate-level program for executive development could be created.

As a political science professor, he had a special interest in the field of public administration, with a focus on how to educate leaders and managers who serve the public. He firmly believed that a smarter and more dedicated bureaucrat can be developed by concurrently blending job experience with education; a master of public administration, for example, would be ideal for a young but experienced public servant. He also helped develop the Master of Administrative Science degree, launched in 1971, and later developed the MAS Public Administration option, introduced during Academic Year 1977–1978.

Francis Rourke, 82, died after a long illness in 2005. His obituary indicated that he taught with Hopkins for almost 40 years and provided a real insight on what he was like.[9]

> "I never saw him get angry the whole time I knew him," said Matt Crenson, a political science professor who met Rourke in the early 1960s, when Crenson was a 17-year-old sophomore at Johns Hopkins. "Never shouted, never raised his voice. But when the department needed a leader, Frank was who we turned to."

---

9 When I arrived at Hopkins and became director of the Business Division in 1979, I had a general idea what had to be done, but I didn't have a clue about how to do it. Frank Rourke, as a professor in the School of Arts and Sciences and a senior man in his field, knew how to get things done. He had a pleasant way about him but nevertheless was clear about what had to be accomplished. As chair of the Rourke Committee nine years prior to my arrival, he knew what recommendations concerning our college had been followed and what actions were lacking. But rather than hit me with a list of what he thought I should do, he asked me how I thought things should go. Indeed, he was the kind of person who brought out the best in people. He developed an excellent curriculum for the Public Administration option in the Master of Administrative Science (MAS) program, but unfortunately there were few enrollments. It seemed that employees in the public sector wanted an MBA that could help them in government and again in the private sector when they retired. I later discovered that this was the case in many schools of business that offered a Master of Public Administration (MPA), where the preponderance of students flocked to the MBA program rather than the MPA. Although enrollment in the MAS would grow and then wane over the years, Frank Rourke's contributions and service to the school remained steady.

Rourke, who earned his bachelor's and master's degrees from Yale and his doctorate from the University of Minnesota, studied and taught courses on the presidency, bureaucracy, and public administration. He published numerous books and articles and, over the years, was frequently quoted and interviewed by the news media.

Crenson, who met Rourke on the No. 3 bus and would talk politics with him on the way to campus, said Rourke had a way of diffusing tense situations with his often self-deprecating sense of humor and that he took special pride in nurturing young scholars, including Crenson, who said Rourke was the reason he went into political science (Small, 2005).

Robert H. Roy (born November 21, 1906—died October 8, 2000)

Robert H. Roy is a most unforgettable character. Having spent decades of his career first in business and then in academia, he had a clear understanding of both environments. He contributed substantially to the Business Division, particularly during the 1950s, 1960s, and 1970s. A key figure in the field of Engineering at Hopkins, Robert Roy concluded his academic career as a professor emeritus of industrial engineering and as dean emeritus of the School of Engineering. In addition to teaching Operations Research and Management Science, subjects in the Business Division, his other contributions to the Business Division included the development of new degree programs, including the first graduate-level degree in the Business Division, the Master of Science in Management Science.

As a graduate of the Baltimore Polytechnic Institute, he enrolled at the Johns Hopkins University School of Engineering at the sophomore level in 1925. When he graduated in 1928, he continued playing in the national champion Hopkins lacrosse team as they represented the United States in the ninth Olympic Games, held in Amsterdam during the summer of 1928.

Returning from Europe, he immediately started an engineering career at Williams and Wilkins, Waverly Press. While employed by this company for almost 20 years (1928–1947), he advanced to the position of Chief Engineer and eventually to the position of Vice President of Engineering. In 1947, he received an appointment as Associate Professor of Industrial Engineering in the Department of Mechanical Engineering at the Johns Hopkins University School of Engineering. As a full-time member of the faculty, he advanced to professor and was eventually selected as dean of the School of Engineering. In addition to contributing 25 years (1947–1972) to the study of engineering at Hopkins, he spent considerable time with the Business Division before and after he became dean emeritus. What he added to the Business Division was a pragmatic look at the graduate level of the field of business administration at a time when the division was in a transition from only undergraduate business and accounting programs to prospects at the graduate level as well. As a result, the division successfully moved its focus to a higher level of quality instruction and more appropriate specific content in both undergraduate and graduate degree programs.

John P. Young, Dr. Eng (born 1923—died 1988)

John P. Young was a strong supporter of the Business Division for decades. In addition to teaching Quantitative Analysis III, he taught a wide range of quantitative courses, including Management Science. As a professor of Health Policy and Management in the (then) School of Hygiene and Public Health, he had a full load of teaching and grant proposals to contend with, but he always had time for the Business Division. He was a major contributor in the development of the Master of Administrative Science degree, and years before that, his interest in Operations Research was evident in his work in developing the Master of Science in Management Science degree.

In 1988, the Master of Administrative Science degree had a requirement for a three-credit course in quantitative analysis. This course, titled Quantitative Analysis III, had as prerequisites (you guessed it) Quantitative Analysis I and Quantitative Analysis II. For those who were fearful of math, this course and its prerequisites were often the last courses that they enrolled in prior to graduation. As a result, more than a few prospective students had concern about this course and which instructor would be the best for them. The response from students to each other was always "take Dr. Young's class." As a result, John Young's classes were always full, yielding lots of papers to grade and lots of students to put at ease and then teach. John loved teaching and even taught during the second Summer Session. Such was the case in August 1988, when, after a busy and stressful day, he met with his students for their final exam at night at the Hopkins Downtown Center in Baltimore. He distributed the exams, wished them good luck, and then passed away while students were completing their exams. Students, faculty, and staff will remember Dr. John Young for many years to come and are thankful for his help.

The Courageous Pioneer

Those outside academia who think the life of a professor is soft and without stress should reflect on the actions of Dr. Edward Franklin Buchner (1868–1929) during his 21 years at Johns Hopkins University from 1908 to 1929, when he died two weeks before his 61st birthday. Although any profession could be easy for some, Dr. Buchner gave his all as he fought for what he believed to be in the best interests of both his academic field and the university.

Years before Dr. Buchner arrived in Baltimore, President Daniel Coit Gilman, during his Inaugural Address in 1876, laid the philosophical framework for Buchner's crusade when he stated his hope that arrangements would be "made for the unfolding of philosophy, principles, and methods of education in a way which will be of service to those who mean to devote their lives to the highest departments of instruction" (Buchner, 1929, p. 96b).

Buchner was interviewed by President Remsen and given his first task when he arrived at Hopkins from his teaching post at the University of Alabama. This task was to organize College Courses for Teachers. First presented in Academic Year 1909–1910, the offerings of College Courses for Teachers were described in the university circular as

> courses of instruction [for] teachers whose vocation prevents their attendance at the usual hours.... These courses are to be similar in character, so far as

24

quality and extent of instruction are concerned, to the corresponding courses given in college classes. [Furthermore,] satisfactory work accomplished in these courses will be credited, and under suitable regulations, toward the degree of Bachelor of Arts (Buchner, 1929, p. 75).

An overall explanation of the extent of Dr. Buchner's accomplishments within the context of the field of Education at Hopkins may be helpful in understanding the trials and tribulations he faced as he addressed these challenges. A two-page Hopkins brochure included in his wife's biography of Dr. Buchner provides the following insight about the field of Education at Hopkins.

1908–1909   Arriving in 1908, Dr. Edward F. Buchner is appointed Professor of Education and Philosophy; he organizes the earlier uncoordinated lectures for teachers into a unit titled College Courses for Teachers.

1909–1910   The launching of College Courses for Teachers, with Buchner as director. Under suitable regulations, these courses can be credited toward the Bachelor of Arts degree (AB).

1911–1912   Dr. Buchner also establishes and directs Summer Session, starting in summer 1911.

1915–1916   The Department of Education established, with Dr. Buchner as director. Courses from College Courses for Teachers are now credited toward a Bachelor of Science degree (SB). Thanks to the efforts of Dr. Buchner, the first two women (other than nurses) receive undergraduate degree at Hopkins.

1924–1925   The College for Teachers is established in 1924, with Dr. Buchner as director.

1928–1929   Early in 1929, the School of Higher Studies in Education is authorized to conduct programs leading to the degrees of Master of Education and Doctor of Education, and to become a department of the university on par with the School of Higher Studies in Philosophy.

Enrollment data and the growth in the number of degrees awarded reflect Dr. Buchner's strong efforts and successes.

Growth in Enrollments in the College for Teachers

1909	69
1914	189
1919	345
1924	1206
1926	1532

Growth in Enrollments in Summer Session

1911	335
1916	428
1921	949
1925	918

Number of Degrees Awarded during the Period 1916–1925 in the Department of Education of the Graduate School

AM	25
PhD	5

Number of Degrees Awarded in the College for Teachers

SB 136 (69% of the SB degree holders continue in advanced work in 75% of the departments of the university)

Now for the Real-World Challenges

The story about Dr. Buchner (father of the field of Education at Hopkins) does not end with this listing of his achievements. In fact, the real story behind the scenes emerges from a recently available memoir written by his widow for her children after her husband died in 1929. She pulls no punches in her description of the real world of political intrigue in an academic setting during 1908–1929.

Dr. Buchner's widow, in commenting about the start of her husband's appointment, declares

> His path was thick with obstacles from the very first, and the years were filled with struggle against a lack of any real understanding or sympathy on the part of the authorities, open hostility to the work by the faculty, lack of money, there being no appropriation for anything but his salary of $3,500.00, and barely half-hearted cooperation on the part of the State school officials, who probably had a different candidate for this newly-established chair at the University (Buchner, 1929, p. 74).

In dealing with this troublesome situation, Dr. Buchner used an approach that could work in many situations today. "Father studied the problem, ignored the lions in his path, kept his temper, was patient and magnanimous always toward those who maliciously or ignorantly worked against him, and he toiled unceasingly" (Buchner, 1929, pp. 74–75).

Although women taught many of the classes in the public schools in Baltimore, their education at Hopkins was not equal to that available to their male counterparts. Dr. Edward F. Buchner struggled to gain equality for women at Johns Hopkins University. Initially, it was arranged that the Women's College of Baltimore (now Goucher College) "should bestow the AB degree when earned, upon the women students; the men were to be given credits toward an AB from Hopkins" (Buchner, 1929, p. 76). Commenting on this discrimination further, Mrs. Buchner related that there was no question, in those early days, of a bachelors *[sic]* degree from Hopkins for women. From the beginning there was opposition, overt and covert, to the whole plan—[F]ather was said to be lowering the standards in allowing "old maid school teachers, who couldn't study anyway," on the campus—and [F]ather was content to have the courses of strictly collegiate grade, record proper credits, and leave the question of an undergraduate degree for women to the logic of events (Buchner, 1929, p. 76).

Then Buchner's widow illustrated her husband's winning approach in correcting this terrible injustice. "It would certainly have been a tactical error to conjure up the bug-a-boo of coeducation. He bided his time, letting situations develop which carried their solutions in their hands" (Buchner, 1929, p. 76). Buchner realized that it was more than letting a few women receive a Hopkins degree. In fact, many of his opponents saw his approach as forcing Hopkins to become coeducational. An earlier reference that women would be unable to study revealed that the library and other places where students could study were off-limits to women, so the impact of his approach would have been felt throughout the university. And, after all, the field of Education and Buchner (that fairly new arrival) were far from the central core of interest at Johns Hopkins University.

An opportunity presented itself at the opening assembly, when it was characteristic of President Remsen to focus on enrollments. After discussing the general plan, President Remsen usually asked, "[']But where are the teachers?['] They did seem very few ... [and President Remsen's] tactlessness [in putting Dr. Buchner on the spot publicly] did not help much" (Buchner, 1929, p. 77). If enrollments were to be a measure, Buchner would meet the challenge. So, rather than fight directly for Hopkins to award degrees to women in his education program, he tried a different approach. In his winning strategy, Edward Buchner worked on building his enrollments from 69 students and the offering of 11 courses during the first year of College Courses for Teachers in Academic Year 1909–1910 to what became 343 students and 22 courses in Academic Year 1915–1916.

> At this point, [F]ather took his stand for a degree for which women might be eligible, pointing out that in giving instruction but not a degree, which (women) students were forced to take elsewhere, alumnae were being created for other institutions rather than for Hopkins. When, therefore, the degree of SB (still tactful avoidance of an AB–coeducational quarrel) was established, there were two women all ready to receive it (Buchner, 1929, p. 77).

So, thanks to the wise strategy of Dr. Buchner, M. Theresa Dallam and Martha B. Stephens were the first women other than nurses to receive a baccalaureate-level degree from Johns Hopkins University.[10] This occurred during the Academic Year 1915–1916 commencement exercise, and Dr. Bucher was also proud that in addition to this event Ms. Dallam was admitted to the graduate school, eventually earning an MA degree in English.

Until 1915, Buchner's power to make decisions was rather limited, for he only held the role of chairman of the committee in charge of College Courses for Teachers. His widow describes the composition of this committee as

> made up of people in some cases friendly, in some indifferent, and in some hostile to the whole idea. [Dr. Buchner] knew the work was necessary and important, that it was in accord with the expressed ideas of President Gilman (Buchner, 1929, p. 78).

Describing Buchner's major challenge Mrs. Buchner relates that

---

10 Although Edward Buchner's actions in 1916 were helpful in the crusade for gender equality at Johns Hopkins University, the first Hopkins nurses received their diplomas in June 1891 (Schmidt, 1986, p. 242). Furthermore, in 1892, the "Trustees accept the conditions of a gift [from Mary Garrett] that women be admitted to the Johns Hopkins Medical School [now known since 1924 as the School of Medicine] on the same terms as men" (Schmidt, 1986, p. 242). Then, in "1897 the first physicians graduate in June; 14 men and one woman" (Schmidt, 1986, p. 242). Unfortunately, it will not be until September 1970 that the first female undergraduates arrive on the Homewood Campus for the School of Arts and Sciences. At the start, admission of these full-time undergraduate women is limited to "transfer students and freshmen who can commute from home" (Warren, 2000, p. 267).

[what] made it unnecessarily hard for him from the first was due, in no small measure, to Professor Arthur O. Lovejoy, who was untiring in his hostility, both personal, and professional [and] who even after [F]ather's death, did everything in his power to destroy the structure [Buchner] had raised. He was not the only enemy, but he was the worst. There was professional jealousy, there was failure to understand the legitimacy of the work in the University's program. During the first uncertain year after [F]ather's death, when Professor Lovejoy exerted his strength to overthrow the School of Higher Studies in Education, which had been [F]ather's crowning achievement, President Ames stood firmly with Dr. David E. Weglein, who led the defense; and at the Commemoration Day Exercise in 1931, he made special reference to [F]ather's work as the development of projects in President Gilman's mind since 1887, adding that probably many of the faculty are not aware of this (Buchner, 1929, p. 79).

In 1915 Dr. Buchner's role was changed from chairman of the committee to Director of College Courses for Teachers. Then, by 1924, the name of his organization was changed to the College for Teachers. "This name was not of [F]ather's choice. He wished to [have] it called a School of Education. It was Professor Lovejoy and a docile Academic Council who decided upon the name" (Buchner, 1929, p. 80). A major concern of Dr. Buchner's was the role and composition of the Academic Council. Buchner's department was not represented and

Professor Lovejoy was a member of the council, a self-perpetuating body, and he could and did block [F]ather's path whenever he could. President Ames had caused the Council to be reorganized, and the members [we]re automatically retired at certain periods. One of the first to disappear thus was Professor Lovejoy (Buchner, 1929, p. 79).

Edward F. Buchner's life as a leader in academia certainly illustrates that life in that environment can be full of excitement as well as trials and tribulations. For Buchner, it was anything but dull, and it had its victories as well as its bittersweet moments. Mrs. Buchner explains,

> I remember so well [F]ather coming home late one afternoon, many years ago, while he was still strong and vigorous, and without having stopped to remove his overcoat, saying, with a laugh, and a note of eagerness in his voice: "Well the fight is on!" And I remember equally well hearing him say, years later, with no eagerness and no laugh: "This thing may kill me, but the principle is right and it will live" (Buchner, 1929, p. 80).

Indeed, it did live on, as illustrated by his achievements, which remain today. His widow writes about what he considered to be his pinnacle of achievement:

> Early in 1929, the School of Higher Studies in Education, was authorized to give the degrees of Master of Education and Doctor of Education, and became a department of the University on an exact par with the School of Higher Studies in Philosophy. He was so happy over this that the memory of it softens for me some of the history of its development (Buchner, 1929, p. 81).

Heartfelt thanks go out to Dr. Edward Franklin Buchner, pioneer and father of the field of Education at Johns Hopkins University.

The Human Side of Academia—A Few Anecdotes

A Touch of Splash Turns into a Touch of Class

The establishment of the Downtown Center in Baltimore was an important step forward for the school and the Business Division. This new location downtown, near the heart of Baltimore's business community, offered a good opportunity for us to interact with our constituents on their home turf. Dean Stanley Gabor spent a considerable amount of time and energy on this major initiative, reflecting from time to time on his own observations at New York University, where the opening of a Downtown Center in New York City proved to be successful. More than a year prior to this celebration, members of the faculty and staff joined him on numerous visits to potential sites. There was abundant participation and involvement by all concerned in the eventual selection of the site, near the southwest corner of Charles and Saratoga Streets. During the moments prior to one of our periodic meetings, a tape played the then popular song "Downtown," projecting that everything was happening downtown and that was the place to go.

The Downtown Center dedication on April 22, 1987, was a significant occasion for the school and the Business Division. Although the center had actually opened for classes in January at the start of the spring semester, the idea was to get the "bugs" out of the system and patch up whatever needed a cosmetic touch-up before the actual dedication. And besides, weather warmer than January wouldn't hurt any. Ms. Judi Broida, as the dean's project manager for the new site and a perfectionist in her own right, had everything under control before the president of the university, Steve Muller, arrived. Because of the scheduled appearance of the president, many members of his extended staff decided to attend, and many were looking forward to hearing his remarks.

The room for the ceremony, next to the only entrance to the building, became the largest room in the center when an accordion wall that joined two classrooms slid back, forming a single hall. A greater-than-expected crowd formed, adding to the heat in the room. In addition, weather for this mid-afternoon event in April was warmer than normal, and the air-conditioning unit compensated for this each time the door opened and admitted additional warm, humid air into the building. However, the air-conditioning system had a reservoir located on the ceiling for collecting condensation and could accommodate a volume of water equivalent to about the capacity of a medium-size suitcase. Sitting up front, I noticed that water seemed to overflow the reservoir, spilling in small slurps near where President Muller was standing as he gave his remarks. Ever quick on his feet, he seemed to dodge each overflowing slurp, and all appeared safe for the moment. Then the inevitable happened as the reservoir burst open, dumping the equivalent of a suitcase's worth of water on the president's head. Sitting up front, my initial reaction was to say to myself, "Holy ———, thank God I am not responsible for this ceremony." But President Muller, possessing a sharp wit and confidence in himself, laughed and cautioned the crowd that life is full of surprises, reminding them that no matter how much you plan and check, things beyond your control can happen. Steve Muller, always an elegant individual, expressed his friendship to all of us, making us feel relieved rather than embarrassed by our mistake and his misfortune. Indeed, he turned a touch of splash into a touch of class and revisited the Downtown Center in Baltimore on many occasions, always a dear friend and supporter of the school.

"Now They Are Serving Wine!"

In 1983, an energetic but unflappable student assistant who delivered audiovisual equipment met his match. Accustomed to delivering preplanned loads of equipment prior to class, he was then able to enjoy tapes of Mozart while classes were underway. An equally unflappable person was the leader of a humanistic and somewhat avant-garde program, who conducted his rather large class every Monday night at the Great Hall in Levering.

The traditionally focused student assistant was somewhat annoyed by these Monday-night encounters. In fact, the frequent and spontaneous requests for audiovisual equipment were disrupting what had been a placid Student Services Office filled with his favorite music.

One Monday evening, when bombarded with repeated and impromptu requests for equipment, our student assistant muttered the following comments while dashing between Shaffer and Levering Halls:

"They're moving the furniture."

"By God, they are trying to sit in a circle." (This was untraditional for some at the time.)

"There are so many people they can't fit all of the chairs in a circle."

"Guess what? Now they are sitting on the floor in one big circle."

"They just took their shoes off."

"Now they are serving wine!"

Sometimes the route from the old, traditional ways of doing things to the new can be difficult. In any event, this was the beginning of many changes from the old to the new. Some of the changes were short-lived (such as this one), but other, more durable changes seemed at the time to be just as traumatic.

The Nude Professor

In the early days of personal computers, one helpful professor transported Apple computers to and from Homewood and

Columbia. On each occasion, he set up a personal computer lab, conducted a class, and then prepared to move the computers to the other location.

On one hot June afternoon he removed his shirt while transporting a load of computers in his non-air-conditioned car. Subsequently, he removed his undershirt. In the normal course of events, members of the Homewood staff on the way to Columbia for an in-person registration noticed a car streak by with what appeared to be a nude driver. Later, when both cars were stopped for a traffic light, it was obvious that the driver was our good friend and colleague. However, upon closer inspection, it was also obvious that he was clothed from the waist down. Indeed, this was a memorable occasion that became part of our folklore.

Working in the Office during the 1970s

It is obvious that tremendous improvements were made since the 1970s in the way our students were served. Furthermore, other major improvements, such as those in the area of information systems, curriculum development, faculty selection, and faculty evaluation, have been reported by others. But something that has not been reported is what it was like to work in those "good old days" prior to the development of our current organization. What follows is a brief discussion of operating conditions in the office. As might be expected, conditions in the office have changed substantially since the late 1970s. From day-to-day, it was difficult to notice these changes, but if conditions then are compared with operations today, the differences are startling.

Office Space

Although the Education Division was located in Whitehead Hall, Betty Vaughn recalls when it was once located on the second floor of Shaffer Hall. The balance of the school was located in two large reconverted classrooms (or suites) in Shaffer Hall. More specifically, one former classroom on the second floor of Shaffer (Room 203) housed four divisions: Administration and Business, Arts and Sciences, Engineering, and Continuing Education. A fifth division, Nursing, joined these four other divisions on the second floor a year later. The administrative functions for the school were conducted in Shaffer 103. In fact, during the late 1970s, the dean's office had a rather unusual layout in Shaffer 103. Without a counter in Shaffer 103 (or a wall separating the dean's office), students were served by the first individual who looked up from their desk. The dean's secretary or a person working on catalog copy might stop work to help a student with a drop slip. In the evening, the office was manned by a division director and a student assistant. With five divisions, each director was on duty in Shaffer 103 one weeknight each week and one Saturday morning each month. People who were new in the office often heard stories about what it was like when the school was located in the basement of Shriver Hall. Further back in the organization's history, the Business Division was located in Gilman Hall (as part of the School of Arts and Sciences) prior to joining McCoy College.

Phone System

The rotary dial system obviously had its limitations. In Shaffer 203, where four of the five division directors had their offices, there were four outside lines to accommodate all incoming and outgoing calls. Unfortunately, there were usually more calls than these four lines could accommodate. Sometimes, if you wanted to make a call, you had to use a phone on the first floor. On many occasions students and faculty who were attempting to call the school were greeted by a busy signal.

Duplication

Shaffer Hall and Whitehead Hall each had a Xerox machine. Consequently, anytime something needed to be duplicated for the four divisions located in Shaffer Hall, someone had to take it from the second floor of Shaffer Hall to the first. If that machine was tied up or out of action, the next step was to go to Whitehead Hall. Also, at the time, the Columbia Center, located at Joseph's Square, did not have a Xerox machine, so on some occasions the center director would duplicate material for classes when attending meetings in Shaffer Hall on the Homewood campus. Furthermore, these machines had a limited capacity and were not as speedy or as accommodating as the ones currently in use.

Word Processing

Imagine preparing catalog copy with an IBM electric typewriter. In addition, correspondence was retyped frequently to obtain a flawless copy. All of the benefits we have from personal computers today (including e-mail) did not exist then.

Enrollment Tallies

The head count for each class section was tallied in pencil on a clipboard located in Shaffer 103. It provided accurate information on a "real-time" basis; however, it was the only copy for the entire school. Then, following each registration session, division directors and other staff would gather in the registrar's office and count class cards to determine a tally of the completed registrations. Today, detailed manipulations of enrollment and financial data are completed and available instantly throughout the system, including off-campus sites. Furthermore, data can now be entered throughout the system.

Coffee

One 30-cup percolator coffeepot served all of Shaffer Hall. It took 15–20 minutes to brew, and coffee drinkers usually preferred to buy their coffee at Levering. A collection was taken for coffee, and once every other week or so, someone in the office purchased a can of coffee, a jar of dairy creamer, and a small bag of sugar on the way to the office.

Off-Campus Locations

Columbia Center: The Columbia Center was located at Joseph's Square next to a small restaurant called the Caboose. The owner of this restaurant objected to students parking in spaces he considered critical for his business. In his mind, that amounted to any of the spaces convenient to the Hopkins Center. At times, the dispute over parking spaces created some strained tenant relations. Although four classrooms were located on the first floor of the center, two classrooms shared the second floor with another tenant. Unfortunately, the second floor could only be reached by an outside door located on the far side of the building. Consequently, during inclement weather, raincoats and umbrellas might be required to move from one floor to the other. In addition, the door to the second floor seemed to be locked when one wanted it to be open and open when one wanted it to be locked.

Goucher College Center: In 1979 another off-campus site was located in rented space (for the evening) at Goucher College. Although parking was not a problem, the main difficulty was that the building was often locked in the evening. By the time someone was available (and authorized) to unlock the door, many of our students lost interest. As Goucher is located somewhat near the Homewood campus anyway, students preferred the Homewood location. In a few years, this off-campus site faded from view.

Principal Administrative Officers and Directors in 1979

Dr. Roman J. Verhaalen, Dean

Dr. Richard D. Robbins, Associate Dean

Dr. Margaret L. Courtney, Director of Nursing Program, leading to a bachelor's degree with a Nursing major[11]

Dr. Elaine C. Davis, Director, Division of Education

Dr. Keith E. Glancy, Director, Division of Special Programs

Dr. Nicholas E. Kolb, Assistant Dean and Director of Off-Campus Activities

Dr. Peter B. Petersen, Director, Division of Administration and Business, and Acting Director, Division of Arts and Sciences

Dr. Gerard H. Schlimm, Director, Division of Engineering and Physical Sciences

---

11 Although the program launched in fall 1980, preparation started a year earlier. It was required that applicants be registered nurses and hold either an associate's degree or a diploma in nursing. Dr. Courtney was assisted by Ms. Martha N. Hill, who later earned her doctorate at Johns Hopkins University and for many years continued to serve as the dean of the School of Nursing.

Other Individuals Who Had a Major Role

Dr. Donald C. Klein, part-time position as Coordinator of Behavioral Science programs (at the time located in the Division of Arts and Sciences)

Dr. Margaret M. Murphy, Coordinator, Economic Education[12]

Dr. Barry Weller, Coordinator of Humanities and Life Sciences (part-time position within the Division of Arts and Sciences), mainly hired part-time faculty for the Master of Liberal Arts program

Ms. Danette Baker, secretary for Dr. Peter B. Petersen

Ms. Carolyn Barnes, Administrator, Applied Behavioral Science Program

Mr. Michael Broom, part-time position as Coordinator of Extended Program in the Humanities for Educators, then assistant to Don Klein and an instructor in the Applied Behavioral Science program for several decades

Ms. Peggy Flynn (then Ms. Peggy Swagger), secretary for Dr. Nicholas Kolb

Ms. Marlene T. Higginbotham, Director, Columbia Center

---

12 Dr. Murphy arrived from Loyola College in 1977 with a grant from Black and Decker to teach economics to schoolteachers at a level of detail sufficient for them to then teach effective economics classes at the high school level. This generous grant provided tuition for the students as well as meeting other expenses connected with this program. Dr. Murphy was appointed assistant professor in 1981 and associate professor in 1984. Also in 1984, Dr. Murphy was appointed director of the Columbia Center, just in time to successfully move the center from Joseph's Square, in Columbia, to Twin Knolls, also in Columbia. Later, she departed Hopkins in 1991, becoming vice president of the Baltimore Branch of the Federal Reserve. Returning to the School of Professional Studies in 2005, she taught courses in the Division of Public Safety Leadership but has since relocated to the Boston area.

Ms. Claire Hooper, executive assistant to Dean Roman Verhaalen

Ms. Sharon Lampkin, secretary for Dr. Gerard Schlimm

Mr. Kirk C. McAlexander, Director, Development and Special Services (including Public Relations, Advertising, Catalogs, and Brochures)

Mr. Denny F. Mullins, Business Manager (including Budget and Personnel Management)

Ms. Janice Reiley, secretary for Dr. Richard Robbins

Ms. Betty R. Sattler, administrative assistant for Academic Services

Ms. Teresa N. Schwartz, academic counselor and financial aid officer

Ms. Lynn Wilkinson, Coordinator of Continuing Education (assisted Dr. Glancy in administrating noncredit programs)

Directors of the Business Division, 1953–2006

1. **Dean Edward Hawkins**, professor of Marketing, chaired the Department of Business Economics within what is now the Krieger School of Arts and Sciences. His office was located in Gilman Hall, Room 318. The Department of Business Economics was disestablished in 1953, and remaining students moved to McCoy College, which had been previously established for part-time students in 1947. Full- and part-time business economics programs become part-time programs. Dean of McCoy College—**Francis H. Horn.**

2. **Dr. Howard Cooper**, professor of Accounting and a former member of the Department of Business Economics, led the relocated Business Economics effort in 1953 and prior to his retirement was also appointed associate dean of the Evening College and Summer Session. He taught accounting and was with Hopkins full-time (1928–1969).

3. **Dr. Frederic H. Glade** (no academic rank) was appointed director of the Division of Administration and Business (1969–1979).

4. **Dr. Peter B. Petersen** was appointed an associate professor in 1979—the first academic appointment in the Business Division since before 1953. In 1986 he was promoted to professor. He acted as director of the Division of Administration and Business (August 31, 1979–September 30, 1989).

5. **Mr. Sydney Stern** (no academic appointment) was appointed director of the Division of Administration and Business during the four-month period (October 1, 1989–January 31, 1990).

6. **Dr. Judith K. Broida** (appointed an assistant professor) was appointed assistant dean and director of the Division of Business and Management (February 1, 1990–1994). After 1994, the position was vacant until 1996.

7. **Dr. Elmore Alexander** (appointed a professor) was appointed associate dean and director of the Division of Business and Management (April 15, 1996–January 1998).

8. **Dr. Jon P. Heggan** (no academic appointment), in addition to being associate dean of the school, was appointed acting associate dean and director of the Division of Business and Management (1998–August 31, 1999).

9. **Dr. Sheldon F. Greenberg** was an associate professor when he was appointed acting associate dean and director of the Graduate Division of Business and Management (September 1, 1999–February 2001).

10. **Dr. Peter B. Petersen** was appointed at the start of the last seven months of a long search for an associate dean and director of the division and was acting associate dean and director of the Graduate Division of Business and Management (February 1–August 31, 2001).

11. **Dr. Lynda de la Viña** was appointed a professor as well as associate dean and director of the Graduate Division of

Business and Management (September 1, 2001–January 7, 2004).[13]

12. **Mr. Erik M. Gordon**, an assistant professor, was appointed acting associate dean and director of the Graduate Division of Business and Management (January 8, 2004–October 4, 2004).

13. **Dr. Peter B. Petersen** was appointed acting associate dean and director of the Graduate Division of Business and Management (October 5, 2004–February 13, 2006).

14. **Dr. Toni S. Ungaretti and Dr. William Agresti** were appointed acting co-associate deans and directors, Graduate Division of Business and Management (February 14, 2006–December 3, 2006).

15. **Dr. Pamela G. Cranston**, the university's Vice Provost for Academic Affairs and International Programs, was selected as interim dean of Carey Business School (December 4, 2006–December 31, 2007).

---

13 During Academic Year 2003–2004, the Police Executive Leadership Program and related law enforcement activities depart from the Graduate Division of Business and Management and form their own division, titled the Division of Public Safety Leadership. Dr. Sheldon Greenberg is first appointed assistant dean and director and then associate dean and director of the Division of Public Safety Leadership (2003–2007). With the establishment of the School of Education on January 1, 2008, Dr. Greenberg and his division transfer to the School of Education.

Faculty Appointments to the Graduate Division of Business and Management (1979–2006)

* William W. Agresti, professor

Elmore Alexander, professor

* Michael A. Anikeeff, professor

Wadiah Atiyah, assistant professor

Judith K. Broida, assistant professor

* Celso A. Brunetti, assistant professor

* James R. Calvin, associate professor

* Kwang Soo Cheong, associate professor

Lynda de la Viña, professor

* G. Reza Djavanshir, assistant professor

* Members of the faculty in the Graduate Division of Business and Management during 2006.

William Engelmeyer, assistant professor

Robert Everett, assistant professor

* Erik M. Gordon, assistant professor

Jo Ellen Gray, assistant professor

Sheldon F. Greenberg, associate professor

* Douglas E. Hough, associate professor

* Jay Liebowitz, professor

* Michael G. McMillan, instructor

* Isaac F. Megbolugbe, associate professor

* Richard Milter, associate professor[14]

Glenn Mueller, professor

Margaret M. Murphy, associate professor

* James E. Novitzki, associate professor

Robert Pernick, assistant professor

* Peter B. Petersen, professor[15]

Michael J. Prietula, associate professor

* Members of the faculty in the Graduate Division of Business and Management during 2006.

14 Promoted to professor in the Carey Business School on September 1, 2007.

15 Appointed professor emeritus in the Department of Management by the Johns Hopkins University board of trustees, effective July 1, 2006. After a sabbatical, retired from the Carey Business School on June 30, 2007.

Linda M. Randall, associate professor

Carlos Rodriguez, assistant professor

Susan T. Sadowski, assistant professor

* Beverly A. Sauer, professor

Karen Spencer, assistant professor

Gene Swanson, assistant professor

* Lindsay J. Thompson, assistant professor

* Toni S. Ungaretti, assistant professor

Paul R. Willging, assistant professor

* Elaine M. Worzala, professor

* Ken Yook, associate professor

* Members of the faculty in the Graduate Division of Business and Management during 2006.

Faculty Appointments in the Business Division Prior to Academic Year 1947–1948

Academic Year 1917–1918 Directed by Committee in Charge (unit named "Courses in Business Economics")*

Jacob H. Hollander, PhD	Professor of Political Economy
John B. Watson, PhD	Professor of Experimental and Comparative Psychology
George E. Barnett, PhD	Professor of Statistics
Knight Dunlap, PhD	Professor of Experimental Psychology
Henry Slonimsky, PhD	Associate in Philosophy
Leo Wolman, PhD	Associate in Insurance
Walter F. Shenton, PhD	Instructor in Mathematics
Clare E. Griffin, AB	Instructor in Transportation
Arthur C. Millspaugh, PhD	Instructor in Political Science

* Appreciation is expressed to Dean Ralph Fessler for the use of academic year bulletins 1917–1947, and to Ms. Jeanne Stinchcomb for information, old news clippings, and correspondence from Delta Sigma Pi records and files.

Academic Year 1918–1919 Directed by Committee in Charge

Hollander	Professor of Political Economy
Barnett	Professor of Statistics
Slonimsky	Associate in Philosophy
Millspaugh	Instructor in Political Science

Academic Year 1919–1920 Directed by Committee in Charge (unit name changes to "Courses in Business and Social Economics")

Hollander	Professor of Political Economy
Barnett	Professor of Statistics
Slonimsky	Associate in Philosophy
William O. Weyforth, PhD	Associate in Political Economy*
Broadus Mitchell, PhD	Instructor in Political Economy

Academic Year 1920–1921 Directed by Committee in Charge (unit name changes to "Courses in Business Economics")

Hollander	Professor of Political Economy
Watson	Professor of Experimental and Comparative Psychology
Barnett	Professor of Statistics
Weyforth	Associate in Political Economy
Mitchell	Instructor in Political Economy

Academic Year 1921–1922   Directed by Committee in Charge

Hollander	Professor of Political Economy
Barnett	Professor of Statistics
Weyforth	Associate in Political Economy
Mitchell	Instructor in Political Economy
Schachne Isaacs	Instructor in Psychology

* Full name and highest degree at the time shown when individual is initially appointed and when promoted.

Academic Year 1922–1923 Directed by Committee in Charge

Hollander	Professor of Political Economy
Barnett	Professor of Statistics
William O. Weyforth, PhD	Promoted to Associate Professor of Political Economy
Broadus Mitchell, PhD	Promoted to Associate in Political Economy
Schachne Isaacs, AM	Instructor in Psychology
Robert C. Gillies, AB	Instructor in Political Economy

Academic Year 1923–1924 Directed by Committee in Charge (unit name changes to "Evening Courses in Business Economics")

Hollander	Professor of Political Economy
Barnett	Professor of Statistics
Weyforth	Associate Professor of Political Economy
Mitchell	Associate in Political Economy
George H. Newlove, PhD	Associate in Accounting
Isaacs	Instructor in Psychology
Gillies	Instructor in Political Economy

Academic Year 1924–1925 Directed by Committee in Charge

Hollander	Professor of Political Economy
Barnett	Professor of Statistics
Weyforth	Associate Professor of Political Economy
Mitchell	Associate in Political Economy
Newlove	Associate in Accounting
John Rogers Musselman, PhD	Associate in Mathematics
Schachne Isaacs, AM	Promoted to Associate in Psychology

Academic Year 1925–1926 Directed by Committee in Charge

Hollander	Professor of Political Economy
Barnett	Professor of Statistics
Weyforth	Associate Professor of Political Economy
Mitchell	Associate in Political Economy
Newlove	Promoted to Associate Professor of Accounting
Isaacs	Associate in Psychology
G. Heberton Evans, Jr., PhD	Instructor in Political Economy
J. Earle Uhler, AM	Instructor in English

Academic Year 1926–1927 Directed by Committee in Charge

Jacob H. Hollander, PhD	Appointed Abraham G. Hutzler Professor of Political Economy
Barnett	Professor of Statistics
Weyforth	Associate Professor of Political Economy
Newlove	Associate Professor of Accounting
Mitchell	Associate in Political Economy
Isaacs	Associate in Psychology
Evans	Instructor in Political Economy
Uhler	Instructor in English

Academic Year 1927–1928 Directed by Committee in Charge

Hollander	Abraham G. Hutzler Professor of Political Economy
Barnett	Professor of Statistics
Weyforth	Associate Professor of Political Economy
Newlove	Associate Professor of Accounting

Broadus Mitchell, PhD	Promoted to Associate Professor of Political Economy
John Rogers Musselman, PhD	Promoted to Associate Professor of Mathematics
Isaacs	Associate in Psychology
G. Heberton Evans, Jr., PhD	Promoted to Associate in Political Economy
Uhler	Instructor in English

Academic Year 1928–1929 Directed by Committee in Charge

Hollander	Abraham G. Hutzler Professor of Political Economy
Barnett	Professor of Statistics
Weyforth	Associate Professor of Political Economy
Mitchell	Associate Professor of Political Economy
Evans	Associate in Political Economy
Roy M. Dorcus, PhD	Associate in Psychology
Howard E. Cooper	Instructor in Accounting
Bullock	Instructor in Marketing

Academic Year 1929–1930 Directed by Committee in Charge

Hollander	Abraham G. Hutzler Professor of Political Economy
Barnett	Professor of Statistics
Weyforth	Associate Professor of Political Economy
Mitchell	Associate Professor of Political Economy
Evans	Associate in Political Economy
Cooper	Instructor in Accounting
Bullock	Instructor in Marketing

Academic Year 1930–1931 Directed by Committee in Charge

Hollander	Abraham G. Hutzler Professor of Political Economy
Barnett	Professor of Statistics
Weyforth	Associate Professor of Political Economy
Mitchell	Associate Professor of Political Economy
Evans	Associate in Political Economy
Cooper	Instructor in Accounting
Bullock	Instructor in Marketing

Academic Year 1931–1932 Directed by Committee in Charge

Hollander	Abraham G. Hutzler Professor of Political Economy
Barnett	Professor of Statistics
Weyforth	Associate Professor of Political Economy
Mitchell	Associate Professor of Political Economy
Evans	Associate in Political Economy
Cooper	Instructor in Accounting
Bullock	Instructor in Marketing

Academic Year 1932–1933 Directed by Committee in Charge

Hollander	Abraham G. Hutzler Professor of Political Economy
Barnett	Professor of Statistics
Weyforth	Associate Professor of Political Economy
Mitchell	Associate Professor of Political Economy
Evans	Associate in Political Economy
Cooper	Instructor in Accounting
Bullock	Instructor in Marketing

Academic Year 1933–1934 Directed by Committee in Charge

Hollander	Abraham G. Hutzler Professor of Political Economy
Barnett	Professor of Statistics
Weyforth	Associate Professor of Political Economy
Mitchell	Associate Professor of Political Economy
Evans	Associate in Political Economy
Cooper	Instructor in Accounting
Bullock	Instructor in Marketing

Academic Year 1934–1935 Directed by Committee in Charge

Hollander	Abraham G. Hutzler Professor of Political Economy
Barnett	Professor of Statistics
Weyforth	Associate Professor of Political Economy
Mitchell	Associate Professor of Political Economy
Evans	Associate in Political Economy
Howard E. Cooper, PhD	Promoted to Associate in Political Economy
Roy J. Bullock, PhD	Promoted to Associate in Political Economy

Academic Year 1935–1936 Directed by Committee in Charge

Hollander	Abraham G. Hutzler Professor of Political Economy
Barnett	Professor of Statistics
Weyforth	Associate Professor of Political Economy
Mitchell	Associate Professor of Political Economy
G. Heberton Evans, Jr., PhD	Promoted to Associate Professor of Political Economy
Cooper	Associate in Political Economy
Bullock	Associate in Political Economy

Academic Year 1936–1937 Directed by Committee in Charge

Hollander	Abraham G. Hutzler Professor of Political Economy
Barnett	Professor of Statistics
Weyforth	Associate Professor of Political Economy
Mitchell	Associate Professor of Political Economy
Evans	Associate Professor of Political Economy
Cooper	Associate in Political Economy
Bullock	Associate in Political Economy

Academic Year 1937–1938 Directed by William O. Weyforth, PhD, director of the Evening Courses in Business Economics

Hollander	Abraham G. Hutzler Professor of Political Economy
Weyforth	Associate Professor of Political Economy
Mitchell	Associate Professor of Political Economy

Evans	Associate Professor of Political Economy
Cooper	Associate in Political Economy
Bullock	Associate in Political Economy
Robert G. Deupree, PhD	Instructor in Political Economy

Academic Year 1938–1939 William O. Weyforth, PhD, Director

Hollander	Abraham G. Hutzler Professor of Political Economy
Weyforth	Associate Professor of Political Economy
Mitchell	Associate Professor of Political Economy
Evans	Associate Professor of Political Economy
Cooper	Associate in Political Economy
Bullock	Associate in Political Economy
Deupree	Instructor in Political Economy

Academic Year 1939–1940 William O. Weyforth, PhD, Director

Hollander	Abraham G. Hutzler Professor of Political Economy
Weyforth	Associate Professor of Political Economy
Evans	Associate Professor of Political Economy
Cooper	Associate in Political Economy
Bullock	Associate in Political Economy
Harold H. Hutcheson, PhD	Associate in Political Economy
Lloyd G. Reynolds	Associate in Political Economy

Academic Year 1940–1941 William O. Weyforth, PhD, Director

| Weyforth | Associate Professor of Political Economy |
| Cooper | Associate in Political Economy |

Bullock	Associate in Political Economy
Hutcheson	Associate in Political Economy
Reynolds	Associate in Political Economy

Academic Year 1941–1942 Howard E. Cooper, PhD, Director

Weyforth	Associate Professor of Political Economy
Cooper	Associate in Political Economy
Bullock	Associate in Political Economy
Reynolds	Associate in Political Economy
James D. Scott, D.C.S.	Associate (elect) in Marketing
Reynold E. Carlson, MA	Instructor in Political Economy

Academic Year 1942–1943 Howard E. Cooper, PhD, Director

Weyforth	Associate Professor of Political Economy
Howard E. Cooper, PhD	Promoted to Associate Professor of Political Economy
James D. Scott, D.C.S.	Associate in Business Economics
Carlson	Instructor in Political Economy
Charles C. Killingsworth, MA	Instructor in Political Economy

Academic Year 1943–1944 Howard E. Cooper, PhD, Director
James D. Scott, D.C.S., Acting Director

G. Heberton Evans, Jr., PhD	Promoted to Professor of Political Economy
Weyforth	Associate Professor of Political Economy
Scott	Associate in Business Economics

Carl T. Devine, PhD	Associate in Business Economics
Killingsworth	Instructor in Political Economy

Academic Year 1944–1945 Howard E. Cooper, PhD, Director

Evans	Professor of Political Economy
Weyforth	Associate Professor of Political Economy
Cooper	Associate Professor of Political Economy
Lloyd G. Reynolds, PhD	Promoted to Associate Professor of Political Economy
Carl T. Devine, PhD	Promoted to Associate Professor of Accounting
Killingsworth	Instructor in Political Economy

Academic Year 1945–1946 Howard E. Cooper, PhD, Director

Evans	Professor of Political Economy
Weyforth	Associate Professor of Political Economy
Cooper	Associate Professor of Political Economy
Killingsworth	Instructor in Political Economy

Academic Year 1946–1947 Howard E. Cooper, PhD, Director

Evans	Professor of Political Economy
Howard E. Cooper, PhD	Promoted to Professor of Accounting
Edward R. Hawkins, PhD	Professor of Marketing
Weyforth	Associate Professor of Political Economy
Clarence D. Long, PhD	Associate Professor of Political Economy

Reynold E. Carlson, PhD	Assistant Professor of Political Economy
William H. Slaton, MS	Assistant Professor of Accounting

Chronology of Teaching Business Administration at Johns Hopkins University

1874   During October 1874 "University trustees write to Daniel Coit Gilman, president of the University of California in Berkeley, requesting that he consider the presidency of Johns Hopkins. Gilman travels to Baltimore and meets with the trustees on December 29. He tells them that he would create a major university devoted to research and scholarship. Trustees elect him president the following day" (Warren, 2000, p. 252).

1875   University trustees purchase land downtown for the first campus (see Appendix J for details).

                 The first president of Johns Hopkins University starts his term.

1876   "On February 22, 1876, Daniel Coit Gilman is inaugurated as first President of Johns Hopkins" (Warren 2000, p. 252). [He] "cast the new institution in the mold of the European research-oriented university. Johns Hopkins thus became the first American institution to stress advanced study— the first true university in the modern sense in the United States" (Schmidt, 1986, p. 6).

1876–1877   President Daniel Coit Gilman encourages lectures available to the public, given by renowned professors. "During the first year, at least ten lecturers gave approximately twenty lectures each in Hopkins Hall, an auditorium which had been built on to the back of the Howard Street Building" (Hawkins, 1960, pp. 72–73).

1880   Long before today's numerous business schools, engineers lead the way for improving productivity, quality, and economical approaches for manufacturing and doing business. Henry L. Gantt graduates from Johns Hopkins University in 1880 and, following the advice of President Daniel C. Gilman, attends Stevens Institute of Technology, where he earns a second bachelor's degree in mechanical engineering. In 1887, he will meet and begin a 28-year relationship as a major follower of Frederick W. Taylor, the father of the scientific management movement, who will gain worldwide fame as efficiency experts become popular in business and industry. Gantt will become famous for his work with Taylor as well as in his own right.

1890–1891   First Johns Hopkins nurses receive diplomas, June 1891.

1895   "In addition to the instruction given in the lecture rooms and classrooms, several courses of lectures are given during the winter months, usually at five o'clock in the afternoon, to which the public is invited" (*Manufacturer's Record*, December 6, 1895, Atlantic Edition).

1898–1899   Certificates of proficiency are first awarded to teachers who successfully complete the objectives of the lecture series.

1899–1900   In 1900, the Johns Hopkins Club opens at 706 St. Paul Street.

1909–1910   The first year of College Courses for Teachers. The earlier uncoordinated lectures for teachers are organized into a unit titled College Courses for Teachers (the first identifiable predecessor of the School of Professional Studies in Business and Education). Dr. Edward F. Buchner administers these courses, which lead toward the Bachelor of Arts degree.

1911–1912   The start of Summer Sessions.

1912–1913   The first students are admitted to the School of Engineering, October 1912.

1914–1915   Responding to a request made the previous year by the Central Social Agencies of the city of Baltimore, College Courses for Teachers offers a program of courses for social workers. Significant to the evolution of business programs at Hopkins, one of these courses was titled Political Economy.

                Gilman Hall (on the new Homewood campus) is completed and dedicated, May 1915. Maryland Hall is also completed.

1915–1916   College Courses for Teachers, responding to a request from the Baltimore Life Underwriters Association, presents a special course of 22 lectures about life insurance from January 4, 1916, until the end of the academic year.

An evening lecture about industrial efficiency is given by Henry L. Gantt (Hopkins class of 1880) on Friday evening, April 14, 1916. Gantt, who becomes famous a year later for the Gantt Chart, is a frequent speaker at evening sessions at Hopkins, open to the general public. Gantt's views, often controversial, focus on the workplace and express his dislike of financial manipulation for personal gain, something that he feels could negatively influence both the manufacturing process and outcomes of productivity (see Appendix A for details).

Because of the efforts of Edward F. Buchner, M. Theresa Dallam and Martha B. Stephens are the first women to receive baccalaureate-level degrees at Johns Hopkins University.[16] After their degrees are bestowed upon them at the commencement exercise in 1916, Miss Dallam is admitted to the graduate school and later earns an MA degree in English.

1916–1917 Evening Courses in Business Economics begin, although no degree in this field is offered until later. Although courses in Business Economics were the most limited, they had the highest and most consistent rates of attendance. Life insurance courses transferred from Education to Business. The unit providing courses in Business Economics is the first identifiable predecessor of the Business Division (see Appendix O for a detailed chronology of the years 1916–1947).

---

16 First Hopkins nurses receive diplomas in June 1891; first woman physician graduates in 1897.

Professor Carl C. Thomas, of the Department of Mechanical Engineering, is appointed to direct Night Courses for Technical Workers. The Consolidated Gas, Electric Light and Power Company, along with 10 other leading companies in Baltimore, underwrite this program. At the time, engineers lead the effort for efficiency in the workplace and the education of technical workers. At the time, mechanical engineers lead this effort, now considered the domain of business schools. (Today technical workers, depending on their field, are taught by both engineering and business schools.)

1917–1918   The technical courses are revised to fit the evolving program for Night Courses for Technical Workers. For example, mathematics courses are added to provide the needed foundation for later courses.

Professor Alexander Graham Christie replaces Professor Thomas in the fall of 1917 as the person in charge of Night Courses for Technical Workers and becomes for many years the focal point for the subject of efficiency and effectiveness in business and industry. Echoing the efforts of F. W. Taylor (father of the scientific management movement) at the national level, Christie, also a mechanical engineer, champions the cause of teaching efficiency and effectiveness in the workplace.

Enrollments decrease because of World War I.

1919–1920   "Theo Jacobs named Associate in Political Economy and had charge of the course in case work" (Verhaalen, 1984, p. 77).

1922–1923   Ms. Mary Levin begins 48 years with Hopkins in 1923 as a member of College Courses for Teachers, later to retire in 1971 as executive secretary to the dean of the Evening College.

1924–1925   The College for Teachers is established in 1924.

1925–1926   Members of the University of Maryland's Chi Chapter of Delta Sigma Pi (the business fraternity) gather at their new fraternity house on 923 St. Paul Street to greet the new year, 1926. This rented house "consists of three floors that are able to accommodate about 16 men and currently 10 are living in the house" (*The Chi Crier*, spring 1926).

In February 1926, the Baltimore *Evening Sun* reports that "[t]he Johns Hopkins University will take over the School of Business Administration of the University of Maryland ... beginning next October [1926]." Those students who have completed two years (or more) of work will finish their program at Johns Hopkins University but will receive their Bachelor of Science degree at the University of Maryland. Conversely, students who have completed less than two years at the University of Maryland will complete their program at Johns Hopkins University and also receive their Bachelor of Science degree from Hopkins. The agreement was reached by Dr. Albert F. Woods, President, University of Maryland, and Dr. F. J. Goodnow, President, Johns Hopkins University.

Also in February 1926, the *Baltimore American* reports that "effective with the Academic Year 1926–1927, the University of Maryland will discontinue academic and business courses and the work will be taken over by Johns Hopkins University through its College for Teachers and Evening Courses in Business Economics." In addition, the *Baltimore American* reports that "instruction in accounting by the Johns Hopkins Evening Courses in Business Economics will be broadened to make it the equivalent to the courses now offered by the University of Maryland School of Business Administration." It is not now known to what extent this overall agreement with the University of Maryland was implemented.

1926–1927   Chi Chapter of Delta Sigma Pi (a business fraternity) moves to Hopkins during the fall semester of 1926 from the University of Maryland, where it had been installed in 1922—clear evidence that an undergraduate business program existed at the time at Hopkins.

Chi Chapter's publication (*The Chi Crier*) reveals the brothers' concern about recruiting as they move from the University of Maryland to Hopkins.

"The University of Maryland, like the majority of state universities, is quite cosmopolitan and has such a student body. The Johns Hopkins University, as a privately endowed university, attracts an entirely different type of student, inclined to be aristocratic and harder to meet on equal ground" (*The Chi Crier*, fall 1926).

Within a few months, however, Delta Sigma Pi brothers are fully integrated into activities at Hopkins, and this concern disappears. In fact, their recruiting drive for new members is quite successful.

1928–1929   Howard E. Cooper, Jr., teacher of accounting, begins 41 years as a full-time member of Johns Hopkins University. He teaches accounting in both day and evening programs starting in 1928 (while working on his PhD at Hopkins), becoming associate professor in 1942 and full professor in 1946.

1929–1930   Although Night Courses for Technical Workers has previously existed as a separate corporation, in 1929 they are taken over by Hopkins and become part of the university. Throughout the nation, continuing corporate sponsorship of academic efforts recedes after the stock market crash in 1929 and the start of the Great Depression (which lasts from 1929 to 1940).

1930–1931   On January 15, 1931, Chi Chapter, Delta Sigma Pi (the business fraternity) conducts their first smoker for the spring semester in Levering Hall (constructed by the YMCA) with faculty adviser Dr. Leslie W. Baker (Professor of Accounting).

1931–1932   On October 23, 1931, the first smoker of the fall semester of 1931 is conducted in Levering Hall. Guest speakers are

* Dr. William O. Weyforth, Associate Professor of Political Economics
* Dr. Leslie W. Baker, Chi Chapter Adviser and Professor of Accounting
* Mr. John L. McKewen, President, Delta Sigma Pi Baltimore Alumni Club

Howard Cooper receives a PhD in Political Economics from the Johns Hopkins University Political Science Department in May 1932.

1936–1937   Dr. William O. Weyforth is appointed Director "for Evening Courses in Business Economics. First year report not included with the Department of Political

Economy. First mention of statement of completion" (Verhaalen, 1984, p. 80).[17]

The name of the "Night Courses for Technical Workers" program is changed to "Night Courses in Technology." Dr. Christie (engineering) continues as director.

Construction on the Homewood campus for Johns Hopkins Club, a gift of the Marburg family, is completed in 1937.

1939–1940   Mr. Glen L. Martin of the Glen Martin Company is initiated as an honorary member of Chi Chapter, Delta Sigma Pi (the business fraternity) on May 18, 1940. (The Glen Martin Company later becomes Martin Marietta, and then Lockheed Martin.)

1941–1942   Dr. Howard E. Cooper is appointed Director of Evening Courses in Business Economics, replacing Dr. William O. Weyforth.

1942–1943   Dr. Howard Cooper is promoted to associate professor.

The major drop in enrollment caused by World War II continues until Academic Year 1945–1946 as current and potential students, faculty, and staff are drawn into military service.

1943–1944   Dr. Howard E. Cooper is director; Dr. James D. Scott is appointed acting director.

---

17 One approach for finding the historical relocation of subordinate organizations is to follow the flow of the budget. This is the case in Academic Year 1936–1937, when evening courses are not included in the budget for the Department of Political Economy.

1945–1946   "The conclusion of World War II and passage of the GI Bill of Rights creates a huge influx of veterans into the student body. Russell Baker recollects, 'My Hopkins career was split by the war and it was quite a different place when I came back. Suddenly there were a lot of people there, and most of them were wearing fragments of old military uniforms. Many of them had been in combat. It was a very mature group of people and so much more fun than it had been before. These were people who weren't impressed by the professors. They were constantly challenging and arguing, and the professors loved it. They hadn't had such a good time since they were in college'" (Warren, 2000, p. 263).

1946–1947   "In May, 1947 the Trustees established McCoy College to include all evening classes [meaning part-time classes for adult learners] previously administered in separate units of the University" (Verhaalen, 1984, p. 22).

Dr. Howard Cooper is promoted to full professor.

1947–1948   In 1947 Dr. Francis H. Horn is appointed dean of McCoy College. College named after "John W. McCoy, a Hopkins benefactor and Baltimore business and civic leader" (Warren, 2000, p. 263). The program begins, and attempts are made to consolidate the evening classes remaining throughout Hopkins.

In 1947 part-time undergraduate programs in College for Teachers transfer from the College for Teachers to McCoy College.

1948–1949   Overall enrollment in McCoy College declines during the second year.

During 1949, Chi Chapter initiates Dean Francis H. Horn of McCoy College. Brother Horn came to Hopkins in 1947 as dean of McCoy College, an associate professor of education, and the director of the university Summer Session.

1950–1951   During 1951 Mr. John Motz, Chi Chapter alumnus, is selected as director of the Hecht Company.

1951–1952   Enrollments drop because of the decrease in the number of participating World War II veterans.

Dr. Richard A. Mumma is appointed dean.

1952–1953   The program leading to the Master of Education is transferred from the Faculty of Philosophy (now the Krieger School of Arts and Sciences) to McCoy College, becoming the first graduate-level program in McCoy College.

The administration of the MSE in Electrical Engineering is transferred from the advisory board of the School of Engineering to the advisory board of McCoy College.

Dr. Christie retires June 30, 1953.

1953–1954   The BS with a major in Industrial Supervision and Management is established.

In 1953 the Department of Business Economics is disestablished, transferring its students from the Faculty of Philosophy (now the Krieger School of Arts and Sciences) to McCoy College and relocating their offices from Gilman Hall to the basement of Shriver Hall. Full- and part-time offerings continue only as part-time classes. Dr. Howard Cooper, who continues to head Evening Courses in Business, replaces Dr. Edward Hawkins, who has chaired the Department of Business Economics. Dr. Cooper's longtime secretary, Ms. Angela Lavarello, also moves to Shriver Hall. Hawkins' office has been located in Gilman Hall, Room 318. At the time of its disestablishment, the Department of Business Economics has the largest bachelor's-degree accounting program in Maryland, educating more CPAs than any other accounting program. Dr. Hawkins, also a professor of marketing, departs from Hopkins, and Dr. Acheson J. Duncan, an associate professor of statistics, transfers to the School of Engineering. Other faculty members transfer to other parts of the university or depart from Hopkins altogether.

1954–1955   On March 4, 1955, Governor Theodore McKeldin addresses Delta Sigs, their wives, and guests.

1956–1957   On July 23, 1956, one of the most illustrious Delta Sigma Pi (the business fraternity) brothers—Milton S. Eisenhower, brother of the current sitting U.S. President—is elected the eighth president of Johns Hopkins University.

1957–1958   Tuition increases from $15 to $20 a credit.

President Milton S. Eisenhower is selected nationwide as Delta Sig of the Year.

1959–1960   Almost 7,000 students are enrolled in McCoy College, more than twice the combined enrollment of the other divisions of the university.

1961–1962   Enrollments substantially drop; an oversupply of undergraduate college offerings exists in Maryland,

and community colleges are expanding their offerings as well.

A new degree with a focus on operations research is introduced—the Master of Science in Management Science—starting in the fall semester. The program is offered in McCoy College by the Industrial Engineering Department of the School of Engineering (see Appendix G for details).

1962–1963   The new managerial economics program is inaugurated.

The Milton S. Eisenhower Library opens in 1964 on the Homewood campus.

1964–1965   McCoy College is renamed the Evening College and Summer Session. The college is organized into five divisions: Administration and Business, Arts and Sciences, Education, Engineering and Physical Sciences, and Special Programs.

"Need for a graduate degree in Business Administration is first recognized" (Verhaalen, 1984, p. 86).

1968–1969   Associate Dean Howard Cooper retires. He has been a full-time member of Hopkins for 41 years (1928–1969), and during this time he has taught accounting and headed the residual Business and Economics element that moved from the Faculty of Philosophy to McCoy College in 1953. He held this group of faculty, staff, and students together as they changed from a combined full-time and part-time program to strictly a part-time program. Cooper's optimistic attitude and pleasant demeanor were helpful during this transition. Later, when appointed associate dean of McCoy College (renamed Evening College and Summer Session in AY 1964–1965), he continued to look after the Division of Administration and Business until his retirement.

1969–1970   In October 1969, the Academic Council votes to admit female undergraduates in the School of Arts and Sciences, starting in Academic Year 1970–1971.

Dr. Frederic H. Glade is appointed director of the Division of Administration and Business.

"More graduate than undergraduate degrees awarded.

Dean Mumma retires on June 30, 1970.

Rourke Committee appointed to recommend changes in future direction of Evening College and Summer Session" (Verhaalen, 1984, p. 88).

1970–1971   Dr. Roman J. Verhaalen is appointed the dean of the Evening College and Summer Session.

"Rourke Report stresses [the need for] full-time faculty, graduate business administration, emphasis on graduate degrees, implementation of applied doctorate, and other areas of cooperation" (Verhaalen, 1984, p. 88) (see Appendix I for details).

The Maryland State Board of Higher Education approves the offering of a Master of Administrative Science degree (see Appendix B for details).

1971–1972   Ms. Mary Levin, Executive Secretary (1923–1971), retires after 48 years with the Evening

College and Summer Session and its predecessor organizations.

Students enroll in new Master of Administrative Science degree during the fall semester of 1971.

1972–1973   During March 1973 arrangements are made to rent several classrooms for evening classes at Goucher College.

During 1973 the Evening College opens an off-campus center in Columbia, Maryland, in Joseph's Square, at 5485 Harpers Farm Road. The center occupies the first floor, with four classrooms that were formerly a dance studio with springy floors. The second floor, shared with a small accounting firm, holds two smaller, makeshift classrooms. Prior to using this building, the Division of Education has held classes in Swansfield Elementary School, and Master of Liberal Arts (MLA) classes have been conducted in a rented conference room one night each week at Howard County General Hospital. The new center offers 11 sections of courses—two sections for the Division of Administration and Business, four sections for the Division of Education, and five sections for the Division of Arts and Sciences. Overall, about 300 students enroll. The reason for the high number of Arts and Sciences offerings is that at the time, the MLA program and the Applied Behavioral Science program are part of the Division of Arts and Sciences.

1973–1974   The The Maryland State Board of Higher Education approves offering an MS in Urban Planning.

During May 1974 commencement, a cohort of 15 graduates receives the first MAS degrees.

1974–1975   The MS in Urban Planning is initiated in fall 1974.

1975–1976   "Full implementation of [Evening College] off-campus centers at APL [engineering part-time students], Columbia, and Goucher College" (Verhaalen, 1984, p. 90).

The Chi Chapter of Delta Sigma Pi becomes coed, with Ms. B. Joanne Lowy inducted as first woman member on May 8, 1976. With the demise of several Hopkins' fraternities during the 1960s, this business fraternity becomes the second-oldest fraternity at Hopkins, second only to engineering.

1976–1977   During 1976 about 5,000 students are enrolled in the Evening College, slightly more than half of whom are pursuing graduate degrees.

The MS in Applied Behavioral Science is approved by the Academic Council.

The MAS offers three options—Managerial, Behavioral, and Quantitative.

1977–1978   Public Administration added to the MAS degree as a fourth option.

The MS in Applied Behavioral Science starts in the spring semester of 1978.

During the 1970s the undergraduate–graduate student ratio in the Evening College and Summer Session has shifted from 70:30 to 30:70, increasingly resembling the remainder of Johns Hopkins University and becoming a graduate and professional school in its own right.

Tuition for both graduate and undergraduate courses is $60.00 per credit.

The combined bachelor's/master's program starts. A Bachelor of Science with a major in Management can be combined with a Master of Administrative Science or a Master of Science in Applied Behavioral Science for those students who complete their baccalaureate degree with a grade point average of 3.0 or higher. Rather than needing (for example) 45 credits to complete a Master of Administrative Science degree, these students are required to successfully complete only 30 specified credits.

At commencement on May 26, 1978, the largest number (at that time) of degrees and certificates in the history of the Evening College and Summer Session is conferred—a total of 1,016.

1978–1979   The Master of Science in Management Science is discontinued.

The Associate of Science degree has three business programs: Accounting, General Business, and Management.

The Bachelor of Science degree has three Business majors: Accounting, General Business, and Management.

During the spring semester of 1979, 10 sections of courses are offered during the evening in rented classrooms at Goucher College:

Division of Administration and Business: five sections

Division of Education: two sections

Division of Arts and Sciences: three sections

In time, arrangements at Goucher College will become unsatisfactory. Classroom buildings locked by mistake during the early evening hours cause students to wait out of doors on the Goucher campus during cold January and February evenings while various administrators consume much of each week's class time trying to remedy the situation. Additionally, many of the Evening College students prefer to enroll in classes at the relatively nearby Homewood campus.

During the May 1979 commencement, the Master of Science in Applied Behavioral Science, barely a year old, has its first six graduates.

1979–1980   On August 31, 1979, Dr. Peter B. Petersen follows Dr. Frederic H. Glade as director of the Division of Administration and Business. Petersen is appointed Associate Professor of Management and Organization Theory—the first academic appointment in the Division of Administration and Business and its predecessor organizations since before 1953.

The GWC Whiting School of Engineering opens in September 1979.

The Division of Nursing is established.

Tuition for both graduate and undergraduate courses increased to $70.00 per credit.

During the spring semester of 1980, the first minicourses are offered in the Business Division. Although minicourses of one

76

credit each are being offered in other divisions, the Business Division tests their value by presenting two subjects requested by students. A disadvantage of one-credit courses is that students must complete three of these one-credit courses in order for them to count as a three-credit elective but, more importantly, that a course conducted on two Saturdays from 9:00 AM to 4:00 p.m. has the difficulty of requiring examinations or term papers the second time the class meets. Nevertheless, corporate ethics and a review of math are offered. Both classes have superb instructors.

* Corporate Ethics: Long before its popularity two decades later, Dr. Michael Hooker (then associate dean of the School of Arts and Sciences and later president of the University of Maryland, Baltimore County) teaches an excellent ethics course that commands rave reviews by business students. Later, this course will be offered in a conventional format for three credits.

* Review of Math: Most of the students are looking for a two-Saturday "math boot camp," but others who are more comfortable with math are expecting a fast-moving review and then, perhaps, an extension of what they already know. Unfortunately, the students fall into a bimodal group; the less experienced students are spooked by the experienced students, who think they are wasting their time with "these novices." To complicate the situation, further examinations are conducted at the end of the second day. As might have been expected, all-day classes are not the best approach for teaching math.

Other minicourses will be offered later, such as The Federal Reserve System, by Dr. Robert McTeer, then-president of the Baltimore Branch of the Federal Reserve Bank. It seems that students wanted to learn about the "Fed"—but only one credit's worth rather than a three-credit course. Dr. Gerald F. Dunaway, then an executive with Procter & Gamble, will present an excellent course on marketing, and Mr. Wayne J. Ebrite, then with Merck, will receive superb reviews for his course on consumer behavior. In time, however, minicourses will be discontinued because of the disadvantages already mentioned.

1980–1981   A job fair is conducted on August 27, 1980, in Shaffer and Maryland Halls. Empty classrooms during the summer in the mid-afternoon, suitable for initial discussions with groups of students, enable each company to have its own classroom. The more popular organizations represented by recruiters include Hewlett Packard, C&P Telephone, Baltimore Gas & Electric, Exxon Corporation, BDM Corporation, and the Goddard Space Flight Center.

During 1980, Ms. Marie K. Karpinski is elected the first woman president of Chi Chapter (the Hopkins student chapter), Delta Sigma Pi. She serves in this capacity from 1980 to 1982.

On November 21, 1980, Provost Longaker appoints a committee chaired by Dr. Orest Ranum to "review all aspects of the Evening College programs, to offer critical analysis of its continued existence, and to recommend a course appropriate for the next ten to twenty years" (Ranum, 1982, p. 7).

The college now has 14 full-time faculty—13 in the Education Division and one in the Business Division.

Required annual Business Division–wide faculty meetings begin. Conducted at night between the fall and spring semesters on the Homewood campus, they draw about 85% of the faculty, filling Shaffer Hall, Room 3 (a good-sized auditorium). Book displays by several vendors fill the hallways and two adjacent classrooms in the basement of Shaffer Hall; these vendors also furnish and pay for refreshments. Part-time instructors are particularly drawn to these gatherings by the opportunity to meet, during the breakout sessions, with other instructors who teach courses that they teach; they are also drawn by the venders, who provide the latest books free in their particular field. Meetings at the academic discipline levels (Marketing, Management, Economics, etc.) occur throughout the year as needed.

On February 2, 1981, students from the Business Division assemble in Shriver Hall on the Homewood campus for a lecture sponsored by alumnus Mr. Melvin (Mel) Brown. Mr. William Ginder attends and continues to sponsor subsequent lectures. Students from Homewood, as well as those bussed in from the Columbia Center, fill every seat in the hall to hear speaker Mr. Barber Conable (R-NY), a notable figure in the new Reagan administration.

February 16, 1981, marks the inauguration of the biannual New Student Orientation for Business Students, conducted on this occasion on the Homewood campus.

The first three-credit intersession class (18.433 Business and Morality: Ethics in Context, taught by Drs. Mark Pastin and Michael Hooker) is conducted, on May 29, 30, and 31 and June 5, 6, 7, and 13, 1981 (called May intersession classes).

1981–1982   Dr. Roman J. Verhaalen retires from Deanship on June 30, 1982.

"Board appoints Stanley Gabor as Dean effective 9/1/82 and Roman J. Verhaalen as Dean Emeritus. Some additional administrative changes are being made; gradual transition of the [part-time] engineering program to G.W.C. Whiting School of Engineering is underway" (Verhaalen, 1984, p. 92). The ill effects of this major loss of enrollment income are overcome by the skillful actions of the new dean, Stanley C. Gabor.

The *Ranum Report on the Future Directions of the Evening College and Summer Session* is submitted and presented to the provost (see Appendix K for details).

The first three-credit January intersession classes are conducted during intersession between fall and spring semesters, January 16, 17, 23, 24, and 30, 1982.

The first three-credit spring break intersession classes are conducted. This two-and-a-half-week session is superimposed over the 10-day spring break (March 13, 14, 20, 21, and 27, 1982); it is the least popular intersession format and is subsequently dropped. Years later, the 10-day spring break will also be discontinued.

1982–1983   The first job fair is conducted at Columbia Center for Master of Administrative Science (MAS) students, July 16, 1982.

A job fair is conducted in the Glass Pavilion on the Homewood campus, for MAS students, October 4 and 5.

1983–1984   During the fall semester of 1983, Dr. John Hook starts his 10-year effort in teaching the one-credit course Managerial Self-Assessment Skills. The course, presented on two Saturdays, is offered 12 times each year. Students initially focus on understanding their own skills and then learn how to use these skills to motivate and influence others. He eventually writes a popular book on this subject.

In 1984 the Columbia Center moves from Joseph's Square to the Overlook Building, on Twin Knolls road in Columbia. The project manager for necessary internal remodeling of new site and the move itself is Dr. Margaret M. Murphy, who also becomes director of the center. Facilities include six classrooms and two computer labs (one for IBM personal computers and the other for Apple computers) and a conference room. The move also includes the need to guide and retain students. The goal is judged successful when 495 students enroll.

1984–1985   At the beginning of the fall semester of 1984, an additional approach for attempting to attract high-quality potential students focuses on explaining the academic preparation needed to help them in their current and future careers. Titled "Career Night," it consists of a panel of five practitioner faculty, all accomplished in their own very different careers. The session, conducted in the evening in Shaffer Hall's auditorium on the Homewood campus, starts with a short presentation by each panelist that describes his or her career. Then, the entire panel interacts with each other and the audience, discussing careers generally. The audience subsequently forms into five groups so that each panelist can interact with students interested in the panelist's particular career field. Near the conclusion of these discussions, relevant information about courses and academic programs is made available. This approach continues twice a year (September and January) for six years and is successful in attracting additional high-quality students. As the Office of Career and Life Planning evolves and has much more to offer, the Career Night approach fades from view. All of the panelists volunteer their time: Linda Mistler covers the field of banking, Wayne Ebrite discusses marketing, Donald Kobler focuses on information technology, James Holechek covers the fields of advertising and public relations, and Alfred Johnson discusses careers in accounting and finance. The division director fields questions in other areas and moderates the session.

The Master of Science in Applied Behavioral Science transfers from the Division of Arts and Sciences to the Division of Administration and Business. When this degree was established during Academic Year 1976–1977, it was championed by Dr. Richard J. Allen, then-director of the Division of Arts and Sciences, who had a passion for the subject. Several years later, Dr. David B. House,[18] the new director of the Division of Arts and Sciences, who had an emphasis on the Master of Liberal Arts program, agreed with the Division of Administration and Business that this degree belonged to their division.

The Evening College and Summer Session becomes the School of Continuing Studies.

The Master of Administrative Science (MAS) degree now has four options (now called concentrations):

---

18 After Dr. House departed from the School of Continuing Studies, he became vice president of Bellarmine College in Louisville, Kentucky; on May 15, 2007, he retired as president of Saint Joseph's College of Maine after occupying that post for 12 years.

- Management
- Human Resource Development (formerly the Behavioral option)
- Information Technology (formerly the Quantitative option)
- Public Administration

The Associate of Science degree now has two programs:

- General Business
- Management

At the associate and baccalaureate levels, the Accounting program and major are discontinued because of a lack of enrollments beyond the initial courses.

1985–1986   At the Milton S. Eisenhower Library on the Homewood campus, business books and journals are upgraded after a five-year effort that has involved purchasing significant books and subscribing to key journals. The drawn out process has included determining what to purchase, getting the necessary funds in the library budget year after year, and then making the purchases. The overall quality of holdings in the field of business has now improved from poor to fair. Although new acquisitions will appear to cease after 1947, when the Business Division will move from what is now the Kreiger School of Arts and Sciences to McCoy College, the collection of books in the field of business for the period 1917–1947 is superb, thanks to Professor Alexander Graham Christie, in the School of Engineering during the first half of the 20th century.

The Bachelor of Science degree includes majors in

- General Business
- Management
- Information Technology (replacing the discontinued Accounting major)
- Management/Leadership (a BS degree that is part of the combined bachelor's/master's program)

In 1985 an opportunity was missed to interview Ms. Angela Lavarello—a longtime Hopkins employee who was Dr. Howard Cooper's secretary in Gilman Hall, Room 318—before Business Economics is disestablished and the residual moved to McCoy College. She accompanies Dr. Cooper during 1953 on this move to the basement of Shriver Hall. Although she will retire years before 1985, the phone number of her residence, which will be found in 1985, is 825-0750.

On April 7, 1986, Ms. Judy Bowersox and Ms. Pam Frankhouser join the Business Division and help advise students.

Ms. Judi Broida is appointed director of the expanding Human Resource Management option within the MAS program and the program leading to an MS in Applied Behavioral Science. Soon after her arrival, she receives the concurrent task of being director of the yet-to-be-constructed Downtown Center in Baltimore, near the southwest corner of Charles and Saratoga Streets. Broida develops the new center, essentially acting as project manager for this undertaking, which opened in January 1987. She is assisted in running the behavioral programs by Pam Frankhouser, who advises students and handles day-to-day operations.

During May 1986, Dr. Peter Petersen becomes the first person promoted to professor in the Business Division since Dr. Howard Cooper was promoted to Professor of Accounting during Academic Year 1946–1947.

1986–1987   Columbia Center acquires additional space in the Overlook Building and expands its capacity to 10 classrooms, two computer labs, and one conference room. The number of students enrolled increases to 690.

The MS in Urban Planning and Policy Management is discontinued because of a lack of enrollments.

During January, at the start of the spring semester of 1987, the School of Continuing Studies opens its Downtown Center near the corner of Charles and Saratoga Streets to accommodate the growing number of professionals in downtown Baltimore seeking advanced degrees and enhancement of their skills and education. The center has eight classrooms, two computer labs, an executive conference room, and a 222-seat auditorium, as well as an on-site library and bookstore and academic advising services. Judi Broida is designated director of the Downtown Center. The grand opening ceremony, with an address by President Steve Muller, takes place on April 22, 1987.

1987–1988   Mr. John Baker, who has been teaching with the division since the fall semester of 1983 as a part-time instructor, is selected to lead the rapidly expanding Information Technology option within the MAS degree. Soon after his appointment during the fall semester of 1987, he is given the concurrent task of being the project manager for the development of the school's portion of the Hopkins Montgomery County Campus. Unlike the Downtown Center in Baltimore, the Montgomery County Campus includes other Hopkins Schools, and the overall effort is led by the provost's designated representative, Dr. Edgar E. Roulhac. Noteworthy here is that John Baker, in accomplishing these two tasks, spends a substantial amount of time commuting among the Homewood campus, Downtown Baltimore Center, Columbia Center, and Montgomery County Campus. Mr. John Baker is designated the director of the school's portion of the Montgomery County Campus.

The Division of Administration and Business is rated the third-best regionally accredited business school in the eastern United States out of 110 competitors from Massachusetts to Virginia (*US News & World Report*, 1987, p. 83). A comment about this rating by Hopkins' president, Steve Muller, in his spring 1988 newsletter makes everyone proud:

"Although I do not usually attach too much importance to the various academic rankings published in the popular press, it is worth taking note of one delightfully unexpected bit of recognition. The Master of Administrative Science program in the School of Continuing Studies was rated the third best regionally accredited business school in the Eastern United States by *US News & World Report*. Of course, the MAS program is not itself a business school in any ordinary sense, but it was gratifying to have the excellence of the work that is done every semester in this program recognized by other business deans" (Muller, 1988, p. 4).

During 1987 Pamela Cranston arrives and becomes responsible for academic services, including admissions, financial aid, records and registration, advising, and orientation for the school's degree-seeking and noncredit students at five locations.

The Associate of Science program is no longer available to new students; undergraduate emphasis is placed on potential students who as juniors and seniors will work on completing their bachelor's degrees.

The four options of the Master of Administrative Science degree are further revised:

- Management
- Human Resource Management (formerly Human Resource Development)
- Information Technology
- Public Administration

Business Division students are surveyed at all campuses February 29–March 5, 1988.

The Financial Management option for the MAS degree is being developed.

1988–1989   The Columbia Center further expands the use of the Overlook Building to 12 classrooms, two labs, and one conference room. Enrollments increase to 872.

On July 8, 1988, Dr. W. Edwards Deming, the major figure in the quality movement, lectures an overflow audience of business students at the Downtown Center in Baltimore.

In 1989 a generous gift from the family of Allan L. Berman makes possible the development of a graduate degree in real estate. Before this most welcome gift, a 40–contact hour noncredit program leading to an executive certificate in real estate had proved to be both successful and welcome in the field of real estate.[19]

The Master of Administrative Science degree is revised further by dropping the sparsely populated Public Administration option. MAS now has three options:

- Management
- Human Resource/Behavioral Management (formerly Human Resource Management)
- Information Technology Management (formerly Information Technology)

1989–1990   During July, August, and September of 1989, the advising effort for the rapidly expanding MAS program is brought under control when Dr. Peggy Murphy, director of the Columbia Center, and her assistant, Ms. Betsy Mayotte, in addition to their regular functions, begin advising Management students while Ms. Pam Frankhouser advises Human Resource/Behavioral Management students and Ms. Julie Hughes advises Information Technology students within the MAS program.

Dr. Peter Petersen steps down as director of the Division of Administration and Business after 10 years of running the division (August 31, 1979–September 30, 1989) and then teaches full-time.

Mr. Sydney Stern is appointed director of the Division of Administration and Business and assumes this post on October 1, 1989, departing four months later,

19 A real estate advisory board, active since 1986, continues to assist in the development of the department; as this board matures and grows, it plays an ever-increasing role in shaping the quality and direction of the Real Estate program.

on January 31, 1990. Before coming to Hopkins, he has been vice president of Crown Petroleum and, more recently, dean of the University of Baltimore Business School.

During October 1989, Master of Administrative Science students assemble in Shriver Hall on the Homewood campus for a lecture by Frank Cappiello, a key panelist on the weekly television show *Wall $treet Week with Louis Rukeyser*. Cappiello, also a part-time investment management instructor in the Business Division, starts his presentation with an overview of the economy and then, assuming this overview to be correct, develops a strategy for investing in the equities market. MAS students bused in from outlying campus centers join Homewood MAS students in filling the hall. In addition to a stimulating lecture, the occasion serves as a gathering to bring together MAS students.

Dr. Judith Broida is appointed director of the Division of Administration and Business. She assumes this post on February 1, 1990, having previously been appointed assistant professor when she led the behavioral programs and managed the establishment of the Downtown Center.

1990–1991   During the fall semester of 1990, a Master of Science in Real Estate Development is added to the offerings of the Business Division. Mr. Donald R. Clark, JD, directs the program.

During the fall semester of 1990, the Business Division is redesignated the Division of Business and Management.

During 1991 Mr. Jeremy P. Moyes is selected to direct the new Financial Management option of the MAS degree. As courses are developed, overall function evolves into the Financial Management and International Business element.

A free lecture series, open to the public, begins and is titled "Downtown at Noon." This one-hour lecture series attracts a noontime crowd of mostly corporate employees who work nearby. Audience members are encouraged to bring "brown bag" lunches.

The Columbia Center establishes the first advisory board for off-campus centers. In addition to covering conventional advisory board functions, where members furnish meaningful recommendations, this board also involves members in worthwhile activities and a great deal of work. For example, members conduct periodic gatherings open to the public, titled "Community Dialogs," to discuss items of interest to Howard County and the immediate surrounding communities. Topics include Minority Student Achievement in Public Schools where discussion focuses on successes, challenges, and what the community can do to help. Another topic focuses on suburban sprawl, generating a lot of interest and illustrating how demands by citizens themselves can add to the problem. Meetings are videotaped and then presented by cable television on the local public access channel. The publicity generated by these TV presentations helps generate additional interest in attending Community Dialogs. These efforts bring the Columbia Center and the community together and illustrate one of many successful outreach activities conducted by the Columbia Center.

1991–1992   Beginning in the fall semester of 1991, an MS in business (MSB) replaces the MAS degree (see Appendix L for details). This MSB degree has four concentrations:

- Management
- Financial Management
- Human Resource/Behavioral Management
- Information Technology Management

The name of the degree Master of Science in Real Estate Development is changed to Master of Science in Real Estate. In November 1991, Dr. Michael Anikeeff is selected during a nationwide search and appointed director of the Real Estate program.

The Leadership Development Program (LDP) for Minority Managers is established during the fall semester of 1991. This 15-credit program, when successfully completed, can be used as part of a subsequent Business Division graduate degree program. Ms. Carol Lyles (now Lyles-Shaw) is appointed director.

The Washington DC Center opens. Located near DuPont Circle in the Airline Pilot's Association Building at 1625 Massachusetts Avenue, NW, this center attracts sizable numbers of well-qualified students. Like the Downtown Center in Baltimore, the Washington DC Center offers courses almost exclusively to students in the Business Division.

The Leadership Development Program for Minority Managers wins two national awards for quality and innovation—National University Continuing Education Association (NUCEA).

At the conclusion of the new Master of Science in Business (MSB) program, students participate in the new Capstone course, which requires each student to apply skills developed throughout the MSB program. This course represents an intense, 15-week semester of work and thought that requires each student to act as a team member; rather than presenting individual solutions, students interact with others and develop a team response. For some who are experienced in operating by themselves, a team effort may be a difficult approach as they interact with the same team members over a period of 15 weeks. In fact, the occasional high-achieving solo operator may find this new experience one of the most challenging academic experiences. In this year's Capstone case, students recommended solutions to problems facing Giant Foods, who made key members of their staff available over a 15-week period to interact with teams of students. Then the course concluded with a Capstone case competition in which key executives from Giant Foods selected the winning team from each class and the best team from the overall graduating class.

A distinguishing feature of the Capstone course is that students work on a current real-world business case. The facts are not prepackaged as they might appear in the typical case-driven graduate-level course. As in the real world, students determine which facts might be important, which facts were unlikely to be useful, and how to ascertain the needed facts. This will prepare them for conditions they will face as they take on greater responsibility as their careers progress. (Capstone brochure, fall 2006, p. 2).

1992–1993   During the summer 1992 semester, two new degrees are added:
- MS in Information and Telecommunications Systems for Business

- MS in Marketing

The Master of Science in Business has five concentrations:
- Management
- Financial Management
- Human Resource Management
- Information Technology Management
- Marketing

During August 1992, the Columbia Center moves from Twin Knolls to a more suitable building in Gateway Park, also in Columbia. This much larger site accommodates rapidly expanding enrollments and provides room for future expansion. The key challenge for Betsy Mayotte, director of the center, was not to disturb or interrupt academic activities during the move. Excellent teamwork among faculty, staff, and students enables the second Summer Session of 1992 to conclude at Twin Knolls and the first day of the fall semester of 1992 to begin on schedule at the new center in Gateway Park.

In September 1992, Mr. Matt Will joins the Finance and International Business element as a member of the part-time faculty.

On September 23, 1992, Dr. W. Edwards Deming (the father of the quality movement) returns to Hopkins and lecturers Hopkins trustees, faculty, and students during a packed session at the Berman Auditorium located in the Baltimore Downtown Center.

The Master of Science in Marketing degree program is launched. Ms. Cathy A. Trower is director of the MS in Marketing as well as of the Marketing concentration in the MSB degree. Trower also serves as director of the Business undergraduate program.

Middle States Accreditation praises the School of Continuing Studies.

At the May 1993 commencement exercise, the first Master of Science in Real Estate degrees at Johns Hopkins University are conferred. Hopkins becomes one of five universities nationwide to award a Master of Science in Real Estate.

During Academic Years 1992–1993 and 1993–1994, advisory boards are established at the Downtown Baltimore Center, the Montgomery County Campus, and the Washington DC Center. Members of these boards are committed to expanding business education at Johns Hopkins throughout the Baltimore/Washington region. A member of the Washington DC Center's advisory board from a major corporation in the private sector gained an appreciation of what the Washington DC Center and the school had to offer; as a result of this relationship, Hopkins classes leaning toward graduate business degrees have been conducted in this large company for many years. Thus, in this particular case, a working relationship developed by working on an advisory board is beneficial to both Hopkins and the company.

1993–1994   The Master of Science in Information and Telecommunications Systems for Business (MS/ITS) is first offered. Two concentrations in this 45-credit graduate degree are Information Systems and Telecommunication Systems. Unique in this program, a Capstone course requires teams of students, along with a member of the faculty, to work with an actual company to produce and deliver a needed Information Technology project during the semester.

The Bachelor of Science in Business has five majors:
- Computer Information Systems
- Finance
- General Business
- Human Resources
- Marketing

The Master of Science in Business has seven concentrations:
- Advanced Business Studies
- Financial Management
- Human Resource Management
- Information Technology Management
- International Business
- Management
- Marketing Management

On August 16, 1993, four months before his death on December 20, Dr. W. Edwards Deming (at age 93) returns to Hopkins for a third time and lectures an overflowing gathering of students and alumni at the Columbia Center. Although at the time Deming charges corporations $60,000 for a full day of lectures and meetings, his three one-day visits with the Business Division are free.

Ms. Pam Williams arrives January 1994 and serves as an academic adviser supporting the newly created advising center headed by Ms. Patricia DeLorenzo (at this time Ms. Patricia Wafer). Concurrent with other organizational changes, the advising center is replaced and Ms. Pam Williams (in her role as academic adviser) moves to the Finance and International Business element, headed by Mr. Jeremy Moyes.

1994–1995 In August 1994, Mr. John Baker steps down as director of the information technology element and is replaced by Dr. William Engelmeyer.

The fall semester of 1994 sees the beginning of the accelerated Master of Science in Business (for business professionals). This MSB degree program enables students who have completed the Hopkins undergraduate degree in business with a grade point average of 3.0 or higher to continue with their education and earn this master's degree by taking only 11 specified courses (33 credits).

The Police Executive Leadership Program (PELP) begins during the fall semester of 1994. This graduate-level program for police executives recommended by their chiefs becomes a pioneer program in the field of law enforcement. Unlike the standard graduate degree in criminology, this unique Hopkins degree has a curriculum that focuses on police executive leadership. Dr. Sheldon Greenberg directs this effort from the start.

During the fall semester of 1994, a significant certificate program is launched. It is the Johns Hopkins University Business of Medicine certificate program with the School of Medicine, with a cohort of 41 senior-level Hopkins physicians.

During 1994, Dr. Judith Broida departs. The division director position remains open until 1996.

Mr. Jeremy Moyes departs and is replaced temporarily by Dr. Michael Anikeeff (also director of the Real Estate element), who is subsequently replaced when Dr. Sarah Bryant is appointed chair of the Finance and International Business element.

The Hopkins LDP team wins the National Black MBA Case Competition in September 1994, the first year of Hopkins' participation. Jo Ellen Gray is the LDP director, and the team is coached by Christina Rodriguez. The case involves a Procter & Gamble product as case study. This national-level competition, sponsored by Procter & Gamble and the National Black MBA Association, is conducted in San Francisco. The three-person Hopkins team consisted of Jerome Alston, Helen Holton, and Blair Johnson.

With the increase in off-campus centers and the substantial increase in enrollments at each location, a major concern is how library resources can be provided for hundreds of graduate students at each of four off-campus sites. At first, a spare room at each site is used to develop an ad hoc library; unfortunately, these pathetic collections of books can in no way measure up to the needs of hundreds of graduate students. Fortunately, the World Wide Web and access to library resources via the Internet come to the rescue.

The Leadership Development Program (LDP) for Minority Managers expands to the Washington DC Center during the spring semester of 1995.

Ms. Cathy Trower departs during February 1995. In her absence, the Marketing and undergraduate degree programs become part of the Real Estate

Department, under the direction of Dr. Michael Anikeeff.

1995–1996   Two additional concentrations are added to the MS/ITS degree—Management and Advanced Technology. Enrollments are substantially in excess of expectations, with over 300 students enrolled in this new program and almost 100 students enrolled concurrently in the Information Technology concentration within the Master of Science in Business.

The Hopkins Leadership Development Program for Minority Managers team places second at the National Black MBA Case Competition during September 1995 in Boston.

In the fall semester of 1995, physicians from outside Hopkins are admitted to the Hopkins Business of Medicine certificate program.

The MSB with a concentration in Medical Services Management is launched in the fall semester of 1995.

During November 1995, Dr. James E. Novitzki arrives and teaches in the Information Technology element.

Betsy Mayotte helps establish the Hopkins-wide committee for collaboration around technology. Titled the "Sub Committee on Electronic and Distance Education (SEDE)," it brings together representatives from every Hopkins school for the purpose of sharing ideas and making the most of new resources. As interest in this activity grows, an annual symposium is conducted and efficient use is made of new resources.

Dr. Elizabeth Cooper-Martin is selected as director of MS in Marketing in January 1996 but departs in June 1996.

During the spring semester of 1996, the MSN/MSB dual-degree program with the School of Nursing is launched.

During April 1996, Dr. Elmore Alexander is appointed associate dean and director of the Division of Business and Management; he is also appointed professor.

Dr. James R. Calvin is appointed director of the Leadership Development Program and assistant professor in the Department of Management.

In June 1996, Marketing becomes part of the Management element, renamed the Department of Marketing and Management, directed by Dr. Jo Ellen Gray. The Marketing element is staffed by Mr. Christopher Tucker and Ms. Kristen Swick.

The finance element moves from Baltimore Downtown Center to Columbia Center during the fall semester of 1995. In addition, Ms. Pam Williams becomes program director. Dr. Bryant and Ms. Williams solidify curriculum and choice of part-time faculty.

1996–1997   Senior-level health care administrators and other clinicians, such as nurses and physician assistants, are admitted to the Hopkins Business of Medicine certificate program during the fall semester of 1996.

Dr. William Engelmeyer steps down as chair of the Department of Information Technology in mid-1996 and is replaced by Dr. Sheldon F. Greenberg, who is also director of Police Executive Leadership Program.

Mr. Wadiah Atiyah is selected as a member of the Department of Finance during the middle of 1996 for the purposes of adding an accounting concentration and certificate to the Master of Science in Business and preparing for a potential 150-credit hour CPA program. Atiyah completes the PhD program at American University during May 1997 and is appointed assistant professor.

The Hopkins LDP team places second at the National Black MBA Case Competition, conducted in September 1996 in New Orleans.

During December 1996, Page Barnes becomes a member of the Department of the Business of Health.

Dr. Sarah Bryant, chair of the Finance element, departs near the end of 1996.

The Graduate Certificate in Investments (GCI) is first offered.

Almost 500 students are enrolled in the MS/ITS degree program.

1997–1998   On July 1, 1997, Dr. Toni S. Ungaretti is appointed assistant dean and Director of Undergraduate

Studies when undergraduate programs spin off from the Division of Business and Management. Dr. Ungaretti leads this effort from the start. The initial program includes a Bachelor of Science in Business and Management and a Bachelor of Science in Interdisciplinary Studies.

During mid-1997, Dr. Sheldon F. Greenberg steps down as acting chair of the Department of Information Technology and is replaced by Dr. Michael J. Prietula (appointed associate professor), who heads both the Information Technology element and the Finance element. The name of department is changed to the Department of Commerce and Technology.

Dr. Carlos Rodriguez is appointed director of the Marketing element within the Department of Marketing and Management during the summer of 1997, and Ms. Katherine Wilson is selected as senior business adviser and executive program associate in October 1997. Wilson assists Rodriguez in day-to-day operations.

Dr. Pamela Cranston, the school's Associate Dean for Academic Services, departs. Under her direction (1987–1997), student services have improved substantially and, in some cases, have become models for other schools to follow.

During fall 1997, the Finance element becomes the Department of Finance and moves from the Columbia Center to 201 North Charles Street in Baltimore. Dr. Michael Prietula departs, and Dr. Robert Everett (who is appointed assistant professor) chairs the newly designated Department of Finance.

Ms. Pam Williams becomes senior program director for Department of Finance.

Dr. Wadiah Atiyah departs during the spring semester of 1998.

During the spring semester of 1998, the Hopkins Business of Nursing certificate program with the School of Nursing begins.

The Hopkins Business of Medicine certificate program is offered during the spring semester of 1998 in a distance learning format in 19 cities across the country.

During June 1998, the Marketing element splits off from what is now the Department of Management and Marketing and becomes the Department of Marketing; Management becomes the Department of Management and Organization Development. Dr. Carlos Rodriguez directs Marketing, and Dr. Gray directs Management and Organization Development.

During 1998, Dr. Elmore Alexander departs and Dr. Jon P. Heggan, in addition to his regular duties as associate dean of the school, is appointed acting associate dean and director of the Division of Business and Management.

A graduate certificate in Information and Telecommunications Systems, consisting of five courses, is introduced.

1998–1999   The Hopkins LDP team places second at the National Black MBA Case Competition during September 1998 in Detroit.

During fall 1998, Ms. Pam Williams becomes administrative director of the Department of Finance and also conducts the department's day-to-day operations.

During September 1998, the first external review in recent memory is conducted of an element in the Business Division. In this particular case, the Real Estate Department seeks evaluation of its curriculum, overall operating systems, faculty, staff, and students. The key question to be answered by this evaluation is *How does the School of Continuing Studies graduate real estate model compare with similar full-time graduate programs at major universities in the United States?* An independent evaluation team consisting of professors of real estate from leading universities finds the Hopkins Department of Real Estate to be comparable with the best graduate-level Real Estate programs in the United States.

During December 1998, Deborah Carson Boyd is selected as program coordinator to assist Katherine Wilson.

Dr. Susan Sadowski arrives during 1999 and is appointed assistant professor in the Department of Finance.

The Office of Electronic and Distance Education is formed. Betsy Mayotte is appointed Assistant Dean, Electronic and Distance Education and manages the infrastructure that enables the partnership for the Business of Medicine to provide distance education to 35–40 cities in 22 states. One of the many tasks involved is understanding and then complying with the laws and regulations of 22 states concerning distance education.

Enrollments in the MS/ITS degree increase substantially as almost 40% of students from Telecom industry and almost 30% career changers attempt to move into Information Technology. Furthermore, two Post Master's certificates are added—one in Advanced Technology and the other in Electronic Commerce. Enrollment in Information Technology courses during the spring semester of 1999 reaches 1,324.

1999–2000   Dr. Ken Yook arrives in June 1999 and is appointed assistant professor in the Department of Finance.

On July 1, 1999, the School of Continuing Studies is renamed the School of Professional Studies in Business and Education (SPSBE), and the Business Division is redesignated the Graduate Division of Business.

During the summer 1999 semester, the MBA degree replaces the MSB (see Appendix M for details):

Foundation	16 credits
Core	22 credits
Electives (concentration)	13 credits
Capstone	3 credits
Total	54 credits

During mid-1999, Dr. Michael J. Prietula steps down as chair of the Department of Information

Technology and is replaced by Dr. James E. Novitzki.

During September 1999, Ralph Fessler is appointed acting dean of SPSBE, replacing the retiring Stanley C. Gabor.

On September 1, 1999, Dr. Sheldon Greenberg is appointed acting associate dean and director of the Graduate Division of Business and Management.

During the fall semester of 1999, Dr. Paul Willging begins leading a program in the Department of Real Estate having to do with senior housing and care. Eventually the subject becomes a track in the Master of Science in Real Estate program, as well as a certificate program. Dr. Willging also presents the subject of senior living and health care in the Geriatric Department of the Bloomberg School of Public Health.

Wilson continues to conduct day-to-day operations for the Marketing Department and, with the earlier departure of various directors, responds (starting in November 1999) in a wider fashion to questions concerning the Marketing Department, also completing various requirements concerning the department.

During the fall semester of 1999, the MSB program in Medical Services management is replaced by the MBA in Medical Services Management. In a similar fashion, the MSN/MSB is replaced by the MSN/MBA.

During the same semester, the Division of Undergraduate Studies adds a Bachelor of Science in Information Systems.

During 1999, the Division of Undergraduate Studies initiates a certificate program in nonprofit business management that wins national awards and becomes the basis for partnerships at the graduate level with the Institute for Policy Studies (IPS).

The on-site graduate certificate program in MS/ITS for the Department of Defense is started at Fort Meade, MD. In addition, a new concentration in electronic business added to the MBA program.

2000–2001   Although Ms. Patricia DeLorenzo (then Ms. Patricia Wafer) has accomplished much of the early coordination for developing joint programs with the Hopkins medical community, the establishment of the Business of Health Department and the selection of Dr. Douglas Hough to chair this department in October 2000 set the joint ventures in motion. In fact, the rapidly expanding certificate and degree programs continue to flourish under his direction. Furthermore, this spirited and successful example of joint ventures helps establish similar arrangements between the Business Division and other Hopkins Schools.

Dr. Ralph Fessler is appointed dean of the School of Professional Studies in Business and Education.

The Master of Science in Finance (MSF) is launched during the fall semester of 2000.

Ms. Pam Williams departs during fall 2000.

Dr. Robert Everett departs during the spring semester of 2001.

The offices for the Department of Finance move from Baltimore Downtown Center to Washington DC Center, where most of MSF students attend class. Dr. Yook conducts day-to-day operations.

Members of the advisory board for the Department of Real Estate vote to tax themselves $2,500–$10,000 annually to generate funds to help further develop the department's programs. Members consist of prominent individuals in the real estate and urban development community, representing many different areas of interest in the field of real estate. Members' advisory efforts focus on

1. Curriculum development

2. Research

3. Job placement for students

4. Fundraising to support the department's programs

As a result of their favorable financial position, the advisory board underwrites the department's newly created Capital Markets program, including the salary necessary to hire a full-time professor for this activity.

During January 2001, the Baltimore Downtown Center, located near Charles and Saratoga Streets, moves to the Southwest corner of Charles and Fayette Streets (10 North Charles). Concurrently, the Business Division moves from the second floor of 201 North Charles to the third floor of the new Downtown Center and later further consolidates its space by moving some of the faculty and staff from the seventh floor of 100 North Charles to the third floor of the Baltimore Downtown Center.

On February 1, 2001 (at the start of the last seven months of a long search), Dr. Peter Petersen is appointed acting associate dean and director of the Graduate Division of Business and Management.

On September 1, 2001, Lynda de la Viña is appointed associate dean and director of the Graduate Division of Business and Management.

MS/ITS is revised commensurate with suggestions from companies employing graduates of this program. Furthermore, two new MS/ITS graduate certificates are added: Information Systems and Telecommunication Systems. In addition, the Department of Defense provides a five-year grant to offer the MS/ITS graduate certificate at Fort Meade, MD.

2001–2002   Arrangements are concluded to begin an on-site MS/ITS graduate degree program at Booz Allen Hamilton. Through the end of 2006, 10 cohorts with over 250 students are enrolled in this program at Booz Allen Hamilton. Also during this academic year, a graduate certificate in Instructional Technology for Web-Based Professional Development and Training is added.

Dr. Kwang Soo Cheong arrives in August 2001 and is appointed assistant professor in the Department of Finance.

A gala reception is held on September 7, 2001, for the opening of the Passano Gallery and to mark the inaugural exhibit about the historic Baltimore company, Waverly Press (previously called Williams & Wilkins Company, begun in 1893). This gallery is named in honor of the work, time, and resources given by School of Professional Studies alumni E. Magruder (Mac) Passano, Jr., and Helen M. Passano; their daughters Catherine (alumna), Tammy, and Sarah; Mac Passano's late father, Edward M. (Ned) Passano, a 1927 Hopkins graduate; and Mac's grandfather, Edward Boetler Passano. Additions to the family include Catherine's husband Seth McDonnell (alumnus); their children, Emma, Abby, and Cate; Tammy's husband, Justin Wiggs; and Sarah's husband, Michael Meech. Construction of the gallery on the first floor of the Downtown Center is accomplished through the continued generosity of the Passano family. It highlights the use of this building for business programs by featuring Baltimore's business history.

Dr. Susan Sadowski departs during the fall semester of 2001.

2002–2003   During the fall semester of 2002, the Hopkins Business of Medicine Certificate program is first offered at the Washington DC Center.

A concentration in Information Security is added to the MS/ITS degree. Additionally, the MBA degree adds a concentration on Information Technology for students who want a greater technology focus in their degree.

Dr. Michael McMillan arrives in January 2003 and is appointed an instructor in the Department of Finance.

Dr. Ken Yook is appointed acting director of the Department of Finance.

The second exhibit at the Passano Gallery at the Downtown Center is opened. Titled the "History and Evolution of Baltimore's Charles Center," it features the work of the late Baltimore photographer Marion E. Warren. This compelling story relates key portions of Baltimore's renaissance, starting with the creation of the Charles Center. Indeed, the Hopkins Downtown Center facing the towering One Charles Center is located at the site of another Baltimore business history site, the old Hamburger Building. In portraying this story, Mame Warren, Director of Hopkins History Enterprises, conducts and documents oral history interviews and writes the narrative for the exhibit.

2003–2004   LDP for Minority Managers graduate (2002) Jerry Dawson is promoted to vice president of Jones Lang LaSalle, July 14, 2003.

Dr. Celso Brunetti arrives August 2003 and is appointed assistant professor in the Department of Finance.

The graduate certificate in Financial Management (GCFM) is launched.

The Police Executive Leadership Program and related law enforcement activities depart from the Graduate Division of Business and Management and form their own division, titled the Division of

Public Safety Leadership. The location shifts from 201 North Charles Street in Baltimore to a building at 6716 Alexander Bell Drive, adjacent to Columbia Center. Dr. Greenberg, who led this effort from the start, is appointed assistant dean and director and then associate dean and director.

During the fall semester of 2003, the MBA in Medical Services Management program is first offered at the Washington DC Center.

In the fall semester of 2003, the MPH/MBA program starts with the Bloomberg School of Public Health.

During the fall semester of 2003, the MS/MBA Biotechnology program begins with the Krieger School of Arts and Sciences.

On January 7, 2004, Dr. Lynda de la Viña departs.

On January 8, 2004, Mr. Erik Gordon is appointed acting associate dean and director of the Graduate Division of Business and Management.

On March 1, 2004, LDP for Minority Managers graduate (1996) Anthony A. Lewis is promoted to president of Verizon, Washington DC.

The Information Technology Department receives a five-year grant from GEICO Insurance to fund two students each year to conduct data mining and to research topics of concern to the insurance industry.

2004–2005   In July 2004, Mr. Edward St. John donates the largest gift ever received by the Business Division—$5.9

million to establish the Edward St. John Department of Real Estate.

In October 2004, Dr. Peter Petersen is appointed acting associate dean and director of the Graduate Division of Business and Management.

During November 2004, Dr. Ken Yook (acting director of the Department of Finance) directs the Business Division's effort in the World MBA Asia Pacific Tour. Assisted by MBA academic adviser Ms. Margaret Fallon, he attempts to recruit qualified MBA and MSF students in nine cities: Tokyo, Seoul, Taipei, Hong Kong, Shanghai, Beijing, Singapore, Kuala Lumpur, and Bangkok. In addition to having face-to-face discussions with over 600 potential students, Dr. Yook and Ms. Fallon learn that China will undoubtedly be the largest overseas MBA market in the future—and, furthermore, that Chinese universities are seeking partnerships with foreign universities. As a result of this trip, increasing numbers of applications from qualified students from Asia are being received.

In November 2004, LDP for Minority Managers graduate (1994) Helen Holton is reelected to the Baltimore City Council.

The MS/ITS undergoes major revision to provide more flexibility for students and to be more competitive with other similar programs in the area.

Emphasis is placed on the renewal of what had been good recruiting and outreach to the community. A previous drop in enrollments causes a sustained decrease in enrollments as a small cohort of graduate students moves through the system semester after semester from their first course to graduation. One approach for compensating for this continuing gap in enrollments is to increase the enrollment of high-quality graduate students to begin their programs. Unfortunately, other schools in the Baltimore–Washington area also experience a similar situation, so emphasis is placed on improving initial contacts with high-quality students and improving the division's outreach activities with the community. Next, the entire orientation process is studied and reformed. Work that started in AY 2004–2005 takes time to mature and take hold, but comparing 2006 to 2005 indicates an overall 17% increase in admissions and a 21% increase in inquiries.

2005–2006 Course fees for Academic Year 2005–2006

Graduate Division of Business and Management

$505 per credit for graduate-level courses (Homewood/Downtown Baltimore/Columbia)

$575 per credit for graduate-level courses (Montgomery)

$650 per credit for graduate-level courses (Washington DC)

$520 per credit for Business Transitions program (Homewood)

Division of Undergraduate Studies

$400 per credit for .100–.400-level business and information systems courses, except those offered in Washington DC

$400 per credit for .100–.400-level liberal arts courses, except those offered in Washington DC

$410 per credit for all undergraduate courses offered in Washington DC

During September 2005, the Hopkins LDP team is among the top six finalists at the National Black MBA Case Competition, conducted in San Diego.

Mr. Edward St. John's generous gift also leads to the establishment of the first full-time program at Hopkins in graduate Real Estate. This full-time Master of Science in Real Estate program, launched in September 2005, differs from the current program by focusing on younger students having little or no experience in the field of real estate. Consequently, a rigorous selection process focuses on bright young men and women having exceptionally high potential. The initial pilot program consists of four students.[20] After a nationwide search, professor Elaine Worzala is selected to direct the program.

Dr. Ken Yook is appointed director of the Department of Finance.

Ms. Julia Nussdorfer, program coordinator in the Department of Finance, arrives in November 2005.

As international students enroll in the Business Division's graduate-degree programs (the majority of them in the MS in Finance program), there is a need to help these students better understand English. Consequently, two courses for English Speakers of Other Languages (ESOL) are offered.

---

20 The fall 2006 full-time program expanded further.

Professional Writing for Non-Native Speakers of English

Professional Speaking/Pronunciation for Non-Native Speakers of English

The alumni survey of those who completed Master of Science in Finance indicates a high level of satisfaction.

The Leadership and Management in the Life Sciences graduate certificate program begins.

In January 2006, LDP for Minority Managers graduate (2002) Jessica P. Montoya is promoted to executive assistant to Senior Vice President of External Affairs and Public Policy, DaimlerChrysler Corporation.

During February 2006, Dr. Peter Petersen steps down for a third time as director of the Graduate Division of Business and Management and is replaced by co-directors Dr. Toni Ungaretti and Dr. William Agresti. Petersen is appointed professor emeritus in the Department of Management by the Johns Hopkins board of trustees, effective July 1, 2006, and departs Baltimore after 26½ years full-time with the Business Division for a one-year sabbatical (July 1, 2006–June 30, 2007).

An informative video produced about LDP for Minority Managers appears on the Business Division Web site and is successfully used for recruiting and development.

A dual MBA/MSITS degree program is launched, and two additional graduate certificates are added—

Information Security Management and Competitive Intelligence.

A Flurry of Activity

From 1994 to 2006, during the closing six years of the Gabor administration and the opening six years of the Fessler administration, there is a particular flurry of activity in the School of Professional Studies in Business and Education (SPSBE). Overall, the major efforts seem to focus on

- Quality: Increasing quality in all aspects of the school, ranging from initial contacts in recruiting students, what happens in the classroom, and interactions with alumni.
- Partnerships: Establishing effective partnerships with business and industry; various organizations in the public, private, and nonprofit sectors; and sister schools within Johns Hopkins University. The Graduate Division of Business and Management attempts (with a wide range of success) to establish partnerships with every school within Johns Hopkins University. The Division of Undergraduate Studies is particularly active in these efforts and in some cases leads the way. Also noteworthy are the Information Technology Department's work with the federal government and Booz Allen Hamilton and the Management Department's training programs for minority managers in the health care insurance industry. Although the volume required to describe these efforts would surpass the space that outlines the entire history of the Business Division up to 2006, the following list of credit programs

offered illustrates these collaborations.

Current degree programs in the Graduate Division of Business and Management:

- Master of Business Administration
- Master of Business Administration in Medical Services Management
- Master of Science in Finance
- Master of Science in Information and Telecommunication Systems for Business
- Master of Science in Marketing
- Master of Science in Organization Development and Strategic Human Resources
- Master of Science in Real Estate
- Master of Business Administration/ Master of Science Information and Telecommunication Systems (MBA/ MSITS)
- Master of Public Health/Master of Business Administration
- Master of Science—Master of Business Administration Biotechnology
- Master of Science in Nursing in Health Systems Management/Master of Business Administration

Current graduate certificate programs offered in the Graduate Division of Business and Management:

- Hopkins Business of Medicine® Graduate Certificate Program
- Hopkins Business of Nursing® Graduate Certificate Program
- Graduate Certificate in Competitive Intelligence

- Graduate Certificate in Financial Management
- Graduate Certificate in Information and Telecommunications Systems
- Graduate Certificate in Information Security Management
- Graduate Certificate in Investments
- Graduate Certificate in Risk Communication in Organizations
- Graduate Certificate in Technical Innovation and New Ventures
- Graduate Certificate in Leadership and Management in the Life Sciences
- Leadership Development Program for Minority Managers
- Graduate Certificate in Senior Living and Health Care Real Estate
- Skilled Facilitator Certificate
- Post-Master's Certificate in Electronic Business
- Post-Master's Certificate in Information and Telecommunication Systems

Current degrees offered in the Division of Undergraduate Studies:
- Bachelor of Science in Interdisciplinary Studies
- Accelerated Master of Arts in Teaching
- Bachelor of Science in Business and Management
- Advancing Business Professionals Program (Accelerated)
- Bachelor of Science in Information Systems

- Graduate Certificate in Adult Learning
- Business Transitions (Graduate Certificate in Business and Management)

2006–2007   During September 2006, the Hopkins LDP team finishes in the top six finalists at the National Black MBA Case Competition, held in Atlanta.

In October 2006, LDP for Minority Managers graduate (1998) Oral Muir is promoted to Senior Director of eCommerce, Marriott International.

Enrollments throughout the entire Business Division increase (see Appendix N for further details).

Johns Hopkins University receives "a $50 million gift from trustee emeritus William Polk Carey to launch its first graduate school of business" (Beatty, December 5, 2006, p. A8). The gift establishes separate business and education schools by "splitting in two its existing School of Professional Studies in Business and Education, creating the new Carey Business School as well as a separate graduate school of education" (Beatty, December 5, 2006, p. A8). Both schools will begin operating on January 1, 2007. The Carey Business School "will be launched with a $100 million funding plan, with the additional money to be raised from other donors" (Fuller, December 5, 2006).

The Last Hurrah—One month before retirement the author addressed the school's graduates. Indeed, it was his proudest moment in 26½ years at Hopkins. Visible on the left side of podium are William Agresti, associate professor (three months later promoted to professor) and co-director of Johns Hopkins Business Programs; Gloria M. Lane, associate professor and chair of the Department of Special Education. Visible on the right side of the podium are Michael A. Anikeeff, professor and chair of the Edward St. John Department of Real Estate; William J. Neugebauer, faculty associate and assistant principal, Howard County Public Schools; Amy M. Yerkes-Schmaljohn, associate dean for academic affairs, School of Professional Studies in Business and Education; and Mariale Hardiman, chair of the Department of Interdisciplinary Studies and Assistant Dean for Urban School Partnerships.

Epilogue

In studying the 90-year history of the Business Division, there are significant lessons to be learned about leadership and personal conduct. Some of the more important ones are provided here.

Lessons Learned about Leadership

Edward F. Buchner (1868–1929): As reported by his wife after Dean Buchner's death in 1929,

> [h]is path was thick with obstacles from the very first, and the years were filled with struggle against a lack of any real understanding or sympathy on the part of the authorities, open hostility to the work by the faculty, lack of money, there being no appropriation for anything but his salary of $3,500.00 (Buchner, 1929, p. 74).

His response to all this was that he "studied the problem, ignored the lions in his path, kept his temper, was patient and magnanimous always toward those who maliciously or ignorantly worked against him, and ... toiled unceasingly" (Buchner, 1929, pp. 74–75).

Howard E. Cooper, Jr. (?–1985): After the 1953 disestablishment of the Department of Business Economics, the residual element moved from the Faculty of Philosophy, located in Gilman Hall,

Room 318, to offices in McCoy College, located in the basement of Shriver Hall. Furthermore, their full-time and part-time programs became strictly part-time; consequently, the morale of the faculty, staff, and students plummeted.

His response to this was magnificent. During this transition, Dr. Cooper, the leader of this residual element, held this group of faculty, staff, and students together by his optimistic attitude and pleasant demeanor. Howard Cooper, an unselfish leader, sheltered his colleagues and subordinates from external forces and represented them well for many years. When appointed associate dean years later, he continued to look out for their interests until he retired in 1969 (Petersen, 1980s, discussions with Wilson Shaffer and alumni).

Peter B. Petersen (1932–): A succession of 13 directors led the Business Division from 1979 to 2006; the Education Division had only two. The turnover of directors for the Business Division was often initiated by changes in personal circumstances or by the lure of a new challenge outside the division. However, some of these Business Division directors had expectations that did not fit the situation. Others tried (with little success) to change processes and procedures to reflect those in their prior organizations. Still others became lobbyists, bypassing the chain of command in service of two major objectives—establishing an MBA program and creating a business school.

His response was to do his job, not crusading for goals above his level of discretion—such as the establishment of an MBA program and the creation of a business school. These tasks, properly addressed by others much higher in the chain of command, are initiatives that will come about when the time is right. And that is exactly what happened in the case of both. Lobbying efforts at the division level did more harm than good, unlike concentrating on doing one's job and doing it well—something that needs no permission, but only a willingness to get on with it, and advancing efforts by working smarter, not harder.

Lessons Learned About Personal Conduct

There is a popular belief that life and careers flow like a roller coaster. The idea is that if things are going exceptionally well, you had better enjoy it, because sooner or later the roller coaster will zoom down to difficult times. Conversely, if you are in a slump, good days lie ahead. **But the real message is how to deal with the ups and downs in life.** You can stay on the sunny side of life during both occasions. During a downturn, think positively and help others. In good times, give credit to your subordinates. Essentially, it is not the condition of how things are, but rather how one handles them.

In our culture, it seems important to win, but in reality **it is not whether you win or lose but how you play the game.** Your colleagues and bosses will remember how you operated long after the actual win or loss has come and gone. So, as you fight the good fight in your career, take your pursuits to a higher, more professional level and stay on the sunny side of life. A good reputation can even be strengthened during a highly competitive situation.

We know the ethical way, but the difficult task is trying to stick entirely with an ethical approach in a fast-moving, demanding situation. So, rather than testing the limits of what one can ethically get away with, **just do what you know is right and get on with your work.**

Take particular care not to cast about disparaging remarks concerning people or organizations. Additionally, do not vent your frustrations by gossiping about others, and do not tolerate subordinates who gossip and say nasty things about others. Instead, **get above it all, work at a professional level, and strive to bring out the best in everyone you interact with.**

In reviewing these lessons learned, it seems **so much easier to write about all of these good things than to do them. Perhaps in the future—say, 20 or 30 years from now—people interacting with people will continue to be the most difficult task. If that is the case, we should learn these lessons now.**

Appendix A
Henry L. Gantt's Presentation at
Johns Hopkins University
on April 14, 1916

Henry L. Gantt (1861–1919) made frequent presentations in the evening at Hopkins. Open to the public as well as to faculty, staff, and students, his sessions particularly attracted those who were interested in efficiency and effectiveness in the workplace. In manufacturing, the label today used by some for such a discussion would be "production management." As Gantt advanced in his career, he gained fame at the national level and is remembered today for the Gantt Chart, now used in a software package (that bears his name) used for temporal comparisons. Gantt had a passion for what he was doing and put all of his energy into his presentations.

Gantt's Background and Career[21]

Henry Lawrence Gantt was born on May 20, 1861, a few days after the start of the Civil War, on a family plantation located along the Patuxent River in Calvert County, Maryland. When their 69 slaves, the most owned by a family in that part of Maryland, were lured to work as servants and

21 Extracted from Petersen, P. (1986). Correspondence from Henry L. Gantt to an old friend reveals new information about Gantt. *Journal of Management*, 12(3), pp. 339–350.

laborers at a nearby Union Army installation, a series of financial mishaps began that left the Gantt family destitute. These reverses eventually forced the family to depart from their 200-year-old home and relocate in Baltimore.

The 12-year-old Gantt's fortune changed with his acceptance as a student at McDonogh, a newly established free school for academically bright boys from poor farm families. At McDonogh he received his academic base and the benefit of a positive influence from several dedicated educators. After four and a half years, Gantt graduated from McDonogh and was then successful in obtaining a tuition scholarship from Johns Hopkins University, while McDonogh continued to provide him room and board. Records in the archives at Hopkins show that Gantt completed their baccalaureate program, which was then normally three years, in only two years, and that he received the Bachelor of Arts (AB) degree on June 9, 1880. After graduation, Gantt returned to McDonogh as a teacher of natural science and mechanics.

In 1883, following the advice of Johns Hopkins president Daniel C. Gilman, Gantt attended Stevens Institute of Technology, where he earned a degree in mechanical engineering within a year. His first professional position was as a draftsman at Poole and Hunt, an iron foundry and machine shop, then located on the edge of Baltimore. After returning once again to teach at McDonogh for a year, he was employed in November 1887 by Midvale Steel Works in Philadelphia. At Midvale he met and began his lengthy association with Frederick W. Taylor, the father of scientific management. Gantt at this time saw his role as being that of determining the most economical methods of operating machine tools in the Midvale shop. Gantt benefited professionally from his association with Taylor, and, over the years, developed into one of the primary pioneers in the field of scientific management.

What Gantt Discussed during His Lecture

Although the Great War had started in 1914, the United States had not entered the conflict in Europe at the time of Gantt's presentation at Hopkins on April 14, 1916. Nevertheless, Gantt was very much involved in a personal crusade during the month of April 1916 for motivating people to get the nation prepared industrially in the event it had to participate later in the war. In an industrial setting during those days, Gantt's overall theme was that "preparedness is the ability to get things done." The gist of it all was that good planning along with efficiency and effectiveness in the industrial workplace would enable America's military forces to have the logistical support needed to win. On April 27, 1916, a few days after his lecture at Hopkins, his views were published in *The Iron Trade Review*.[22]

> In considering the subject of preparedness, either for peace or for war, it is imperative that we learn, as quickly as possible the lessons which are being made clear to us by the developments in Europe. In order to do this, we must ask ourselves why it is that Germany has shown so much greater efficiency, both from a military and an industrial standpoint, than the allies. It is becoming perfectly clear that the principles underlying industrial and military efficiency are the same and that a nation to be efficient in a military sense, must first be efficient industrially.

A Lesson to be Learned

We have talked efficiency in this country for several years, and many books have been written on the

22 Gantt, H. L. (1916, April 27). Preparedness is ability to do things. *The Iron Trade Review*, 936.

subject, but many of us feel that the actual results so far have been lamentably small. It is believed we would be much more nearly in the class with England than with Germany if we were suddenly confronted with her problem. It would seem, therefore, that we should find the fundamental reasons why England presented such a strong contrast to Germany, and see if we cannot learn something there from.

It is only a short time since England led the world in arts, but recently Germany has demonstrated her superiority to both England and France.

We must ask ourselves how this happened. It would seem to be something on this manner. The financiers of England, feeling that wealth could purchase whatever was needed for themselves and their national life, have devoted their energies for a number of years to securing wealth which was produced by others rather than making strenuous efforts to produce it themselves. In this attempt they sent abroad millions of dollars to develop industries in foreign lands, which brought them great returns. The leaders of Germany, on the other hand, not being able to exploit foreign peoples to the extent which was possible in England, turned their attention to developing their own resources, and the ability of their own people. When the supreme test came, Germany was found to be a nation of people who, in general, knew what to do and how to do it; while the industries of England, were, in too many cases, controlled by people who understood only their commercial side.

As an engineer, Gantt appealed to other engineers as well as to manufacturers and entrepreneurs. At the time of his lecture in April 1916, Production Management, along with Shop Management, was taught at Hopkins by the School of Engineering, which was then only four years in existence. But, nevertheless, in the fall of

1916, both Engineering and Business professors taught different forms of business administration and effective management. In fact, the teaching of business administration did find a home of its own in the fall semester of 1916 when evening courses in business economics were first taught at Johns Hopkins University. Indeed, the unit providing these courses in business economics is the first identifiable predecessor of the Business Division.

Appendix B
Master of Administrative Science (MAS) 1971–1991

With the departure of Dean Richard A. Mumma on June 30, 1970, and the arrival of the new dean, Roman Verhaalen, there was an opportunity for the college to reflect and to attempt to move the academic programs in the Evening College and Summer Session to a higher level. With this in mind, the Rourke Committee was appointed to recommend changes in the future directions of the Evening College and Summer Session. One of the recommendations by the Rourke Committee was to consider the establishment of a master's program in Executive Development. This recommendation, favorably received by the Evening College, was comparable to similar recommendations going back to Academic Year 1964–1965, when the need for a master's degree in business became apparent. The idea of a graduate degree in Executive Development particularly took hold when Milton S. Eisenhower took an interest in the matter. The idea, with Milton Eisenhower's encouragement, evolved further into a proposal he signed and dispatched to the Maryland State Board of Higher Education requesting that the Evening College offer a Master of Business Administration (MBA) degree. When the proposal was circulated for comment, Loyola College of Maryland strongly objected. Consequently, Milton Eisenhower, Loyola's Father Joseph A. Sellinger, Jr., and Roman Verhaalen met to discuss the matter. Loyola removed their objection after the three men agreed that the title Master of Business Administration (MBA) would not be used by Hopkins until all three of them had left office. Subsequently students enrolled in the new Master of Administrative Science (MAS) degree during the fall semester of 1971, five months after Milton Eisenhower began his second term as president, following Lincoln Gordon. Then a cohort group of 15 graduate students received the first MAS degrees during the May 1974 commencement. Many years later, during the summer 1999 session, long after all three of the members of the meeting had retired from office, Hopkins finally offered the MBA degree.

There were modifications to the original MAS, but by Academic Year 1977–1978, the curriculum had, for the most part, settled down for the long haul. This version presented in the Academic Year 1977–1978 bulletin is shown below.

Master of Administrative Science Degree

The primary objective of the degree of Master of Administrative Science is to develop managerial generalists rather than functional staff specialists. It is intended primarily for persons who aspire to or already have management responsibility, but who wish to increase their potential. The program emphasizes the concepts, methodology, theories, and tools of modern management. The approach is interdisciplinary through economics, behavioral sciences, management, and quantitative methods in order to achieve a breadth of view for general management responsibility. Three options are available: managerial, behavioral, and quantitative.

Admission. To be admitted to the program, the applicant must meet the general requirements for admission to a graduate program. While there are no specific requirements concerning the subjects included in the applicant's undergraduate studies, courses in college mathematics, statistics, economics, psychology, sociology, and political science are considered desirable.

Program Requirements. The required 45 credits, fifteen courses of three credits each, may be completed in as little as two years, but must be completed within five years. All courses must be taken in the Evening College and Summer Session. The curriculum for the Master of Administrative Science degree is outlined below.

Required Core (18 credits)

18.402 Quantitative Analysis III
18.491 Accounting and Data Information Systems and Analysis
18.701 Economic Theory of the Organization
18.703 Organization Theory and Design
18.706 The Economic Environment
55.747 Foundations of Management Science I

Options (27 credits) Select One of the Following Options

Managerial Option

Requirements (15 credits or more from following courses)

18.401 Management Decisions and the Total Environment
18.403 The Evolution of Management
18.408 Money and Banking
18.409 Investment Management
18.411 Seminar in Operations Management
18.412 Management of the Multi-National Firm
18.413 Financing Public Organizations
18.485 Budgeting, Planning, and Control
18.486 Accounting for Administrative Science
18.705 Seminar in Marketing Management
18.707 Seminar in Manpower Management
18.708 Seminar in Financial Management
18.709 Policy and the Legal Environment
18.710 Seminar in Policy Formulation and Management

Electives (12 credits or less of appropriate courses numbered 400 and above)*

Behavioral Option

Requirements (15 credits or more from following courses)

18.401 Management Decisions and the Total Environment

18.414 Management Control in Public Organizations
18.427 Advertising
18.436 Labor Relations
18.704 Human and Group Behavior Environment
18.705 Seminar in Marketing Management
18.707 Seminar in Manpower Management
20.423–424 Theories of Personalities
23.409 Group Development
23.410 Organization Development
23.416 Personal Planning Workshop

Electives (12 credits or less of appropriate courses numbered 400 and above)*

Quantitative Option

Requirements (15 credits or more from following courses)

18.411 Seminar in Operations Management
18.486 Accounting for Administrative Science
18.708 Seminar in Financial Management
55.409–410 Stochastic Systems
55.721–722 Probability and Stochastic Processes
55.748 Foundations of Management Science II
55.755–756 Introduction to Probability and Statistics

Electives (12 credits or less of appropriate courses numbered 400 and above)*

* To be selected from advanced courses offered in administrative science, applied social science, business, education, engineering—environmental, geography, management science, political science, psychology, sociology, and urban planning.

Essentially what this amounts to is a requirement to complete
- 6 core courses
- 5 courses from one of the three options

- 4 graduate-level electives offered from a wide selection through the Evening College

_____

- Totaling 15 graduate-level three-credit courses

It should be pointed out however, that one of the required core courses has two undergraduate prerequisites: Quantitative Analysis I (four credits) and Quantitative Analysis II (three credits). Consequently, those who don't have a prior business or engineering degree take seven additional credits.

Results Were Positive

The number of students completing the MAS degree increased from 15 in 1974 to 400 in 1990. As a result of these substantial increases in enrollment, the Business Division expanded, hiring additional faculty and staff who in turn developed degree programs in their own fields or specialties. Then, as other degrees became available, many potential MAS students were attracted to the newer graduate degrees that were more to their liking, such as financial management and information technology. Consequently, although there was a substantial rise in enrollments in the MAS degree during the 1980s, there was a leveling off—and some decline—in the years to come.

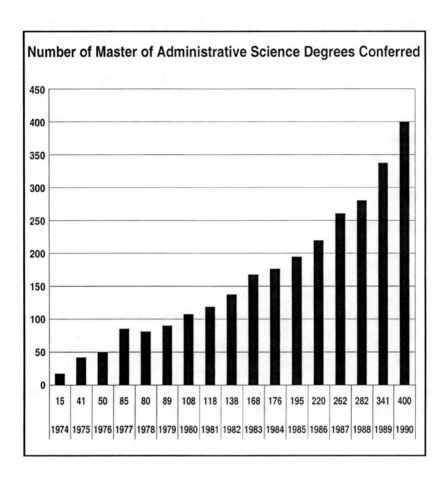

Number of Master of Administrative Science Degrees Conferred

	15	41	50	85	80	89	108	118	138	168	176	195	220	262	282	341	400
	1974	1975	1976	1977	1978	1979	1980	1981	1982	1983	1984	1985	1986	1987	1988	1989	1990

Appendix C
Carey Business School
Announcements

1. Major Announcement from the Dean: E-mail message from Dean Fessler to SPSBE full-time faculty and staff, December 5, 2006.

2. JHU Launches Schools of Business, Education: E-mail message from President William R. Brody to Hopkins faculty, staff, and students, December 5, 2006.

3. Major Announcement from the Dean: E-mail message from Dean Fessler to SPSBE alumni, December 5, 2006.

4. Article in Baltimore *Sun*: Johns Hopkins Receives $50 Million Donation: Gift designated for creation of business, education schools, December 5, 2006.

Subject: Major Announcement from the Dean
From: Ralph Fessler <fess@jhu.edu>
Date: Tue, 05 Dec 2006 06:02:52-0500
To: SPSBE-Fulltime@listproc.hcf.jhu.edu

Dear colleagues,

As President Brody shared in his message earlier today, the university's board of trustees has approved the separation of our business and education programs to create two separate schools—The Johns Hopkins University Carey Business School and The Johns Hopkins University School of Education.

This historic decision, which will take effect on January 1, 2007, is based on a number of significant and evolutionary factors. SPSBE has a long history of serving part-time students in a variety of fields (education, business, engineering, nursing and liberal arts). Through natural evolution, other schools at Johns Hopkins have incorporated many of what were once SPSBE offerings into their own programs, thus focusing SPSBE's portfolio on business, education and public safety leadership. Over the years, SPSBE has grown enrollments, expanded programs and research activities, and increased financial support. Now, poised for even greater growth, SPSBE's faculty, students and alumni will benefit further by the creation of two separate schools, which will provide greater flexibility and allow each field of study to focus more specifically on its mission, programing, research, and development activities. SPSBE's Division of Undergraduate Studies will operate under the Carey Business School; the Division of Public Safety Leadership will operate under the School of Education.

The Carey Business School will benefit from a $50 million gift from the W.P. Carey Foundation, which was given on behalf of the Foundation by Wm. Polk Carey, chairman of W.P. Carey & Co.—a New York City-based investment firm—and trustee emeritus of The Johns Hopkins University. The gift honors his great-great-great grandfather, James Carey of Loudon, a Baltimore shipper, member of Baltimore's first City Council, chairman of the Bank of Maryland, relative to Johns Hopkins and ancestor to a number of initial trustees of The Johns Hopkins University and Hospital. Consistent with the university's practice in the case of its named schools, the School will bear the official name "The Johns Hopkins University Carey Business School"; however, it will be referred to as the Carey Business School of Johns Hopkins University for all external marketing purposes.

We know that you have many questions, and we will try to answer as many as we can at this early stage. For now, we have prepared a faculty/staff Q&A (http://atwork.spsbe.jhu.edu/QandA). Additional press release information for the Carey Business School can be found at http://www.jhu.edu/news/univ06/dec06/schools.html, and for the School of Education at http://www.jhu.edu/news/univ06/dec06/schools-soe.html.

The plan is for the two schools to share an administrative infrastructure, the Professional Schools Administration (PSA), which will provide continuity of daily business operations. Betsy Mayotte, associate dean for SPSBE administrative services, will head this new unit. I will serve as dean of the School of Education, and a national search will begin immediately for a dean of the Carey Business School. Until a new dean is selected, Pamela Cranston, the university's vice provost for academic affairs and international programs, will serve as interim dean. Many of you know Pam and remember her prior role as associate dean for academic services in the School of Continuing Studies, where she was responsible for admissions, financial aid, records and registration, advising and orientation for the school's degree-seeking and noncredit students at five locations.

As the two schools move forward in the year ahead, we anticipate leadership and infrastructure adjustments as opportunities arise and resources grow. You will be notified as developments occur. In the meantime, Dr. Cranston, Betsy Mayotte, and I, working as a transition team, will be making campus visits this week to meet with faculty/staff and answer questions. The schedule is as follows:

Tuesday, December 5
Education Building (for all Homewood SPSBE employees)
2:00 p.m.–3:00 p.m.
2nd floor, Room 219–The Hall

Wednesday, December 6
Washington, D.C. Center
10:30 AM–11:30 AM

Room 1C2
Montgomery County Campus
1:30 p.m.–2:30 p.m.
Gilchrist Hall (new name of center building at MCC), Room 215

Thursday, December 7
Downtown Baltimore Center
10:30 AM–11:30 AM
Room LL3

Columbia Center
1:30 p.m.–2:30 p.m. Education and PSL
2:30 p.m.–3:30 p.m. Center staff, student and alumni relations, enrollment management, undergraduate business
Rooms 211/212

I am confident that our rich history and core values will serve as a strong foundation for both schools as they move into the future. Your role as faculty and staff will be key to their success, and I thank you in advance for your continued support and involvement during this exciting time. I look forward to seeing you at our campus visits.

Sincerely,
Ralph Fessler
Dean

JOHNS HOPKINS
U N I V E R S I T Y
SCHOOL OF PROFESSIONAL STUDIES
201 Shaffer Hall, 3400 N Charles Street

Subject: JHU launches schools of business, education
From: JHBroadcast <JHBroadcast@jhu.edu>
Date: Tue, 05 Dec 2006 05:05:39-0500
To: recipients@listproc.hcf.jhu.edu
December 5, 2006

Dear Faculty, Staff and Students:

I have outstanding news to report from yesterday's meeting of the board of trustees.

The board, acting in part in response to the largest gift for business education in the history of Johns Hopkins, has voted to establish two new schools within the university: the Carey Business School and the School of Education.

The two schools are being formed, of course, on the foundations of very successful programs in our School of Professional Studies in Business and Education. They will build those programs in new and innovative ways, creating important new opportunities for our students and for the companies and schools that employ them.

The Carey Business School will be launched with a $100 million funding package that includes a magnificent $50 million gift from trustee emeritus William Polk Carey. The school will have a distinctive focus: It will seek to graduate business leaders equipped with both finely honed management skills and broad-based, interdisciplinary knowledge from other Johns Hopkins divisions. Among the approaches it will take will be a new five-year bachelor's/MBA option for liberal arts and engineering undergraduates in the Krieger School of Arts and Sciences and the Whiting School of Engineering.

The focus of the School of Education is equally important: to address, through its academic and research programs, the most pressing problems facing America's pre-K-12 public school systems, problems like school leadership, alternative sources of teachers and curricular reform.

Ralph Fessler, now dean of SPSBE, will be dean of the School of Education. We are launching a national search for the dean of the Carey School. Pamela Cranston, vice provost for academic affairs and international programs, will serve as interim dean.

I want to thank Bill Carey for his most generous naming gift for the Carey Business School. By honoring a distinguished ancestor, he also is making possible an exciting leap forward for business education at Johns Hopkins, the university that he and generations of his family have so ardently supported.

I also want to thank in advance everyone—trustees, faculty, leadership, staff, and students and alumni—whose hard work and commitment will help these two newest Johns Hopkins schools fulfill their vast potential.

This is a great day for Johns Hopkins. Next week's Gazette stories about the two new schools are available online in advance at http:www.jhu.edu/~gazette/2006/11dec06/11schools.html   and http:www.jhu.edu/~gazette/2006/11dec06/11schools qa.html

Sincerely,
William R Brody

Subject: Major Announcement from the Dean
From: "Johns Hopkins University" <RalphFessler@jhu.edu>
Date: Tue, 5 Dec 2006 08:59:50-0500
To: <jeannestinchcomb@yahoo.com>

Dear SPSBE alumni,

I am pleased to share with you a momentous and exciting event in the history of our school. Yesterday, the board of trustees of the university approved the separation of our business and education programs to create two separate schools—The Johns Hopkins University Carey Business School and The Johns Hopkins University School of Education.

This historic decision, which will take effect on January 1, 2007, is based on a number of significant and evolutionary factors. SPSBE has a long history of serving part-time students in a variety of fields (education, business, engineering, nursing and liberal arts). Through natural evolution, other schools at Johns Hopkins have incorporated many of what were once SPSBE offerings into their own programs, thus focusing SPSBE's portfolio on business, education, and public safety leadership. Over the years, SPSBE has grown enrollments, expanded programs and research activities, and increased financial support. Now, poised for even greater growth, SPSBE's faculty, students, and alumni will benefit further by the creation of two separate schools, which will provide greater flexibility and allow each field of study to focus more specifically on its mission, programing, research, and development activities. SPSBE's Division of Undergraduate Studies will operate under the Carey Business School; the Division of Public Safety Leadership will operate under the School of Education.

The Carey Business School will benefit from a $50 million gift from the W.P. Carey Foundation, which was given on behalf of the Foundation by Wm. Polk Carey, chairman of W.P. Carey & Co.—a New York City-based investment firm—and trustee emeritus of The Johns Hopkins University. The gift honors his great-great-

great grandfather, James Carey of Loudon, a Baltimore shipper, member of Baltimore's first City Council, chairman of the Bank of Maryland, relative to Johns Hopkins and ancestor to a number of initial trustees of The Johns Hopkins University and Hospital. Consistent with the university's practice in the case of its named schools, the School will bear the official name "The Johns Hopkins University Carey Business School"; however, it will be referred to as the Carey Business School of Johns Hopkins University for all external marketing purposes.

We know that you have many questions, and we will try to answer as many as we can at this early stage. For now, we have prepared an alumni Q&A sheet that can be found on www.spsbe.jhu.edu/alumni/QandA/. Additional press release information for the Carey Business School can be found at http://www.jhu.edu/news/univ06/dec06/schools.html, and for the School of Education at http://www.jhu.edu/news/univ06/dec06/schools-soe.html.

The plan is for the two schools to share an administrative infrastructure, the Professional Schools Administration, which will provide continuity for daily business operations. Betsy Mayotte, associate dean for SPSBE administrative services, will lead this unit. I will serve as dean of the School of Education, and a national search will begin immediately for a dean of the Carey Business School. Until a new dean is selected, Pam Cranston, the university's vice provost for academic affairs and international programs, will serve as interim dean. From 1987–1997, Dr. Cranston was the associate dean for academic services for the School of Continuing Studies (now SPSBE), where she was responsible for services such as admissions, financial aid, records and registration, advising and orientation for the school's degree-seeking and noncredit students at five locations.

As the two schools move forward in the year ahead, you will be updated as developments occur. **In the meantime, if you have any questions, you can email them to <u>studentalumniQA@jhu.edu</u>.**

I am confident that our rich history and core values will serve as a strong foundation for both schools as they move into the future. Your role as alumni will be key to their success, and we thank you in advance for your continued support and involvement during this exciting time.

Sincerely,

Ralph Fessler
Dean

SCHOOL OF PROFESSIONAL STUDIES

201 Shaffer Hall, 3400 N Charles Street
Baltimore, MD 21218

Johns Hopkins receives $50 million donation

Gift designated for creation of business, education schools

BY NICOLE FULLER
SUN REPORTER
ORIGINALLY PUBLISHED DECEMBER 5, 2006

The **Johns Hopkins University** has received a $50 million gift that will establish separate business and education schools, university officials announced late yesterday.

William Polk Carey, a trustee emeritus at Hopkins, is donating the money through his W.P. Carey Foundation. The gift is the largest to Hopkins in support of business education, the university said in a statement.

The Carey Business School and the School of Education will begin operating Jan. 1, replacing the university's School of Professional Studies in Business and Education. The business school will be launched with a $100 million funding plan, with the additional money to be raised from other donors, university officials said.

"More than a century ago, **Johns Hopkins University** forever broke the mold in American medical and graduate education, establishing revolutionary new approaches that remain central even today to the preparation of physicians and scholars," William R. Brody, president of Hopkins, said in a statement. "Bill Carey's generosity makes it possible for Johns Hopkins to break the mold again, this time in the education of our nation's leaders in finance, industry and entrepreneurship."

The university is launching a national search for a dean to head the business school, Brody said. Ralph Fessler, a Johns Hopkins faculty member since 1983 who has served as dean of the existing school of business and education since 2000, will head the School of Education, university officials said.

Under his leadership, Brody said in the Hopkins announcement, the School of Education will bring research-based approaches to the top-priority needs of the nation's public schools, ranging from teacher training to ensuring a safe environment.

The Carey Business School will concentrate on teaching students specialized business skills and providing cross-disciplinary knowledge from other Hopkins programs, the announcement said.

"The key to future economic growth is quality business education, and this school will be dedicated to producing our country's next generation of business leaders," Carey said.

The gift, one of the largest in Hopkins' history, is Carey's second $50 million donation in support of business education. In 2003, the foundation's donation to Arizona State University established the school's W.P. Carey School of Business.

The Hopkins business school will be named after William Carey's great-great-great-grandfather, James Carey, an 18th- and 19th-century Baltimore shipper, banker, member of Baltimore's first City Council and a relative of university founder Johns Hopkins.

W.P. Carey (AP photo) Dec 5, 2006

Retrieved online on December 5, 2006, from:
http://www.baltimoresun.com/news/education/bal-md.
hopkins05dec05,0,6175539.story

Appendix D
A Short Version of the Business Division's History[23]

Almost since its inception 130 years ago, Johns Hopkins University has been offering innovative business courses, led by a dynamic faculty whose impact often spreads far beyond Baltimore. In 1876, the year Johns Hopkins enrolled its first students, Daniel Coit Gilman, Hopkins' first president, established the tradition of opening some classes and lectures to the general public. Henry L. Gantt, from the class of 1880, became a frequent speaker at the Hopkins lecture series, presenting his new and sometimes controversial ideas about management to members of Baltimore's business community. Gantt, who would become a major figure in the scientific management movement, created management and manufacturing procedures that led to greater efficiencies and profits. Fascinated by graphs, he invented the temporal comparison still known as the Gantt Chart. Even today, some of the latest project management software packages bear his name.

In 1916, Hopkins added evening courses in Business Economics for part-time students. Energetic individuals such as Gantt fostered the growth of the new field of business administration. The concept

---

23 Occasionally, writers of proposals and reports need a short summary of the history of teaching Business Administration at Hopkins. From personal experience, I found that they need it both quickly and briefly. Although a short 90-year history could be difficult to produce, three versions are attempted. The longest version is in the body of the text, and a short version and an even shorter version are included in Appendixes D and E, respectively.

of "working smarter" to enhance profits became the rage, promoted by efficiency experts who considered Gantt a pioneer. At Hopkins, Howard Cooper led the way in teaching best accounting practices from 1928 to 1969. Following World War II, the Hopkins program in accounting became the most popular in Maryland, producing more CPAs than any other school in the state.

A Master of Science in Management Science program, focusing on the application of new findings in quantitative analysis and general systems theory, became the first graduate-level business degree at Hopkins in 1961. A few years later, a faculty committee from throughout the university debated the merits of establishing an MBA program. Led by Hopkins' president, Milton S. Eisenhower, the committee decided instead to offer a Master of Administrative Science degree, which would be strong in both management science and economics. This degree was awarded to its first 15 graduates in 1974.

By 1988, the MAS degree program was receiving special national recognition, rated the third-best regionally accredited business school in the Eastern United States by *US News & World Report.* Hopkins' president, Steve Muller, noted that although "the MAS program is not a business school in any ordinary sense ... it was gratifying to have the excellence of the work that is done every semester in this program recognized by other business deans." Enrollment in the program expanded exponentially; 89 students completed the MAS program in 1979; during 1990, 400 MAS degrees were awarded. In 1991 substantial changes continued when the MAS degree changed to the Master of Science in Business (MSB). Concurrent with launching the new MSB other new degrees appeared—Master of Science in Real Estate, Master of Science in Organizational Development and Human Resources, Master of Science in Information and Telecommunication Systems for Business, Master of Science in Marketing, Master of Science in Finance—as well as a wide range of graduate certificate programs and three post-master's certificate programs. Each of these programs focused on specific industries or fields commensurate with the professional needs of students.

The major change for the 1990s occurred in 1999 with the offering of a Master of Business Administration (MBA) degree. This rigorous practical degree enabled the Business Division in the 2000s to collaborate with other Hopkins schools to offer dual Master's/MBA degree programs in Medical Services Management, Biotechnology, Nursing, and Public Health.

On January 1, 2007, a gift of $50 million from trustee emeritus William P. Carey enabled Johns Hopkins University to split the business and education components of the School of Professional Studies in Business and Education and to establish the new Carey Business School and Graduate School of Education. As the teaching of business advances to a higher level with the Carey Business School, the Hopkins tradition of developing innovative business programs for the ever-changing workplace continues.

Appendix E
An Even Shorter Version of the
Business Division's History[24]

In 1876, when Johns Hopkins University enrolled its first students, Daniel Coit Gilman, Hopkins' first president, established the tradition of opening some lectures in the evening to the public. Although most of these evening lectures pertained to the arts rather than the sciences, a considerable number of businesspeople attended. On occasion, members of the business community requested specific lectures, such as a special course of 22 lecturers about life insurance that was conducted from January 4, 1916, until the end of the academic year. In addition to Hopkins faculty, experts from the business community spoke on their particular areas of interest. Such was the case when Henry L. Gantt (class of 1880) spoke about industrial efficiency on April 14, 1916.

The start of evening courses in Business Economics in 1916, however, was the first identifiable predecessor of the Business Division. Eventually, a sound business program emerged and grew under the auspices of the Faculty of Philosophy, now known as the Krieger School of Arts and Sciences. Immediately following WWII, an active accounting program became the most popular in Maryland,

24 Occasionally, writers of proposals and reports need a short summary of the history of teaching Business Administration at Hopkins. From personal experience, I found that they need it both quickly and briefly. Although a short 90-year history could be difficult to produce, three versions are attempted. The longest version is in the body of the text, and a short version and an even shorter version are included in Appendixes D and E, respectively.

producing more CPAs than any other school in the state. Then, in 1953, the Department of Business Economics was disestablished, transferring its students to McCoy College, earlier established in 1947 for part-time programs. In the fall semester of 1961, a major event in the teaching of business at Hopkins occurred when the Business Division launched its first graduate-level degree, the Master of Science in Management Science. This degree, followed by the Master of Administrative Science degree, offered in the fall semester of 1971, started a trend in the Business Division in which more graduate than undergraduate degrees would be awarded. Enrollments in the program expanded exponentially; 15 students completed the MAS program in 1974, and 400 degrees were awarded in 1990.

In 1991, substantial changes continued when the MAS degree changed to the Master of Science in Business (MSB). The overall focus on economics and management science shifted further to practical management and applied behavioral subjects relevant to the workplace of the 1990s. Concurrent with appointments of additional full-time faculty, new degrees appeared—Master of Science in Real Estate, Master of Science in Organizational Development and Human Resources, Master of Science in Information and Telecommunication Systems for Business, Master of Science in Marketing, Master of Science in Finance—as well as a wide range of graduate certificate programs and post-master's certificate programs. Each of these programs focused on specific industries or fields commensurate with the professional needs of students. The major change for the 1990s occurred in 1999 with the offering of a Master of Business Administration (MBA) degree. This rigorous, practical degree enabled the Business Division in the 2000s to collaborate with other Hopkins schools to offer dual Master's/MBA degree programs in Medical Services Management, Biotechnology, Nursing, and Public Health.

On January 1, 2007, a gift of $50 million from trustee emeritus William P. Carey enabled Johns Hopkins University to split the business and education components of the School of Professional Studies in Business and Education and establish the new Carey Business School and Graduate School of Education. As the teaching of business advances to a higher level with the Carey Business School, the Hopkins tradition of developing innovative business programs for the ever-changing workplace continues.

Appendix F
Newly Discovered Correspondence Reveals Glimpse of the Organizational Structure for Teaching Business Administration at Johns Hopkins University in 1926

Information is sparse about the organizational structure for teaching Business Administration at Hopkins prior to 1953. Four major histories about Johns Hopkins University and one history of the Evening College and Summer Session are void, as far as business administration is concerned, prior to the 1953 move of Business Administration from the Faculty of Philosophy to McCoy College. Although there is a detailed description of the Education Division and its prior units going all the way back to Academic Year 1909–1910, historical records for Business Administration other than annual catalogs seem to have vanished. As some proof that history is never totally eradicated, correspondence discovered in December 2006 reveals a glimpse into this void (this correspondence is attached).

HOPKINS TO TAKE OVER MARYLAND BUSINESS SCHOOL

Students Are To Make Transfer Next October.

CITY NEEDS ONLY ONE SUCH COURSE, IS VIEW

Some To Get Degrees From State, Others From New Alma Mater.

The Johns Hopkins University will take over the School of Business Administration of the University of Maryland, it was learned today.

Some of the courses involved are evening courses. Beginning next October, the students who are now studying at the University of Maryland will study under the direction of the Hopkins teachers.

Negotiations Closed.

This was decided a few days ago at a meeting of representatives of the two schools. It ended negotiations which had been conducted for several months.

Those students who have completed two years of work in the University of Maryland will take such courses at the Hopkins as will give them sufficient credits to complete the qualifications needed for the degree of bachelor of science. They will then be given their degrees by the University of Maryland.

Some To Get Hopkins Degrees.

Those students who have completed less than two years at the University of Maryland when the arrangement becomes effective next October will be given credit for advanced work in the Hopkins School. They will get their degrees from the Johns Hopkins.

The Hopkins degrees will be conferred only on those students who, through day classes as well as night classes, get sufficient credits to qualify them for the degree of bachelor of science in business.

Students to the number of 315 are involved. Some are part-time students. Some are full time.

It is said that the consolidation was made because it was felt by both schools that there was not sufficient demand in Baltimore for such training as to support the two schools. One school of the sort, it was thought, could be more effective and more prosperous than two.

Last August Dr. H. N. Diamond of New York University was brought to Baltimore to become the dean of the School of Administration of the University of Maryland.

Not Indefinitely Committed.

It is said that taking over the classes in business administration does not commit the Johns Hopkins University to the policy of conducting such classes indefinitely in the future. There is some feeling that such classes should be eliminated from the Hopkins work when it organizes its new plan to make a graduate school of itself.

Hopkins would not under any circumstances abandon the evening classes in business administration while there was evidence of need for them in Baltimore, it is said. But it is said that it is conceivable that it might ten years hence transfer them to some other school.

"Does the consolidation mean closer relations between the University of Maryland and the Hopkins than have existed in the past?" Provost C. K. Edmunds, of the Hopkins, was asked. Dr. F. J. Goodnow, the president of the Hopkins, is out of town.

"It means simply that students in the classes of business administration who have formerly studied in the University of Maryland will now study in the Hopkins," he said.

Consolidation Idea Dropped.

About ten years ago a plan for the consolidation of the University of Maryland with the Johns Hopkins University was discussed. That involved the possibility that the Hopkins would take over the law school, the schools of medicine, dentistry and pharmacy of the University of Maryland. After it had been considered for some time, it was abandoned.

It is said that the present consolidation does not involve renewal of that plan. The Hopkins does plan, it is said, to add a graduate school of law to its organization. But this would be to furnish opportunity for study of the higher aspects of law, and a degree would be necessary to qualify those wishing to enter it. The Hopkins, it is said, has no plan to establish a school to train men to become practicing attorneys.

The merger has no bearing on the University of Maryland's schools of law, medicine or pharmacy or on the work it is doing at College Park, it is said.

Dr. Woods' Statement.

Dr. Albert F. Woods, president of the University of Maryland, said:

"The agreement was made after Dr. F. J. Goodnow and myself had discussed the matter. It means closer relations with the Hopkins to the extent that work formerly done here will be done at the Hopkins in the future.

"When the Hopkins realizes its plan to drop the first two years of undergraduate department the University of Maryland, with other Maryland schools, probably will be required to do more of that work."

Both officers of the University of Maryland and officers of the Hopkins explain that there can be no arrangement between the Hopkins and the University of Maryland whereby the latter takes over all the work of the first two years when the Hopkins quits that. That will be distributed among all the higher schools of Maryland.

Baltimore Sun, February 1926

Hopkins and U. of M.

COLLEGE HEADS WELCOME PLAN TO DIVIDE WORK

Compromise Predicted By the Baltimore American Cuts Competition In Universities

A close working agreement between the Johns Hopkins University and the University of Maryland, with resultant elimination of competing courses, was agreed upon at a conference yesterday of authorities of the two institutions.

Under the plan adopted, effective with the college year of 1926–27, the University of Maryland will discontinue academic and business courses, and the work will be taken over by the Johns Hopkins, through its college for teachers and evening courses in business economics.

Instruction in accounting by the Johns Hopkins evening courses in business economics will be broadened to make it equivalent to the courses now offered in the school of business administration of the University of Maryland.

BOTH WELCOME MOVE.

Authorities of the two institutions have for some time been working on the plan ratified yesterday. That such a compromise was under consideration was told exclusively in the Baltimore American some days ago.

According to a statement issued at the conclusion of the conferences yesterday, the new plan of co-operation meets the needs of the University of Maryland as well as of Johns Hopkins, and is enthusiastically received by both institutions.

The following detailed description of the new arrangement is given:

Beginning with the academic year 1926–27 the University of Maryland will discontinue offering instruction in the city of Baltimore in all academic and business subjects except in so far as certain academic courses may be offered as an integral part of the curricula of instruction in the schools of pharmacy, dentistry, medicine and law of that university.

Thereafter the University of Maryland will not offer such academic and business courses in the city of Baltimore so long as the Johns Hopkins University continues to make available instruction in such courses in the afternoon and evening through its college for teachers and its evening courses in business economics.

ACCOUNTING SHIFTED.

The courses in accounting in the evening courses in business economics of the Johns Hopkins University will be extended, beginning with the academic year 1926–27, so as to make available instruction in accounting equivalent in range to that now being offered in the school of business administration of the University of Maryland.

After the discontinuance of the above-mentioned courses of the University of Maryland, instruction in academic and business subjects will be available in the college for teachers and evening courses in business economics of the Johns

Hopkins University for students who are at present registered in the school of business administration of the University of Maryland.

Matriculated students in the school of business administration who by the end of the present academic year will have completed at least two years college work at that school may by offering the requisite number of points, obtain the degree of bachelor of science in business from the University of Maryland.

Baltimore American, February 3, 1926

Universities Use Economic Wisdom

ACCORD between the University of Maryland and Johns Hopkins University brings a welcome warmth to the somewhat chilly atmosphere of the higher learning.

Men in authority in both institutions got together and talked business. They found a way for both universities to gain advantage by eliminating certain competing courses and by broadening the scope of work elsewhere.

It happens that the field in which the agreement is reached related mainly to business. The practical manner in which economic laws were applied to the spots in which competition interfered with efficiency is surpassing proof that both sides understand what's what.

Baltimore American editorial, February 3, 1926

University of Maryland
SCHOOL OF BUSINESS ADMINISTRATION
Office of the Dean
34 South Paca Street
Telephone: Plaza 1100

(circa February 1926)   Baltimore, Maryland

To Students of the School of Business Administration:

Newspaper publicity has recently been given to a plan for continuing the work of the students in this school in conjunction with the Evening courses in Business Economics at the Johns Hopkins University. It was our intent to notify our students individually of this plan prior to outside publication of the facts.

There is enclosed a statement of the arrangements which have been made to meet the needs of our students. The Johns Hopkins courses have been extended to cover the scope of our accounting curriculum, and in general to offer as wide a range of business instruction as is offered by the University of Maryland. In addition through the College for Teachers a Bachelor of Science degree will be available to students, the greater part of whose work may be in business subjects.

The College of Arts and Sciences of the University of Maryland at College Park will accept upon transfer credits obtained in the School of Business Administration. Students of the School of Business Administration matriculated for the B. S. degree who wish full-time day instruction are advised to communicate with Dean F. E. Lee to arrange to transfer to the College of Arts and Sciences.

The following relates to students anticipating taking advantage of the arrangement with the Johns Hopkins University.

There are four classes of students now working for completion of their courses at this school.

First: B. C. S. candidates. This degree will not be conferred after June, 1926.

Second: B. B. A. candidates. Those with less than 62 points of work completed may matriculate at the Johns Hopkins University for the B. S. degree. The requirements are practically identical. Those with 62 points credit or more may either complete their work for a Johns Hopkins' B. S. degree, or upon presentation of

158

certification of completion of the requisite points may obtain their degree at the University of Maryland.

Third: Candidates for the Bachelor of Science in Business. The same conditions will apply as in the case of B. B. A. students.

Note: The University of Maryland will not confer degrees of B. B. A. or B. S. in Business after June, 1930. Hence, students expecting to complete the requirements in Johns Hopkins' classes and to apply credits toward a Maryland degree must do so prior to that date.

Fourth: Certificate of Business Proficiency candidates. This certificate is at present granted upon the completion of 62 points in business subjects. Students who have completed 31 credits toward this may complete the required work in the Johns Hopkins classes and apply for a certificate at the University of Maryland. No such certificates will be awarded by The University of Maryland after June, 1928.

Students expecting to registers *[sic]* in the Johns Hopkins classes with the intention of working for a degree will present to the Director of the College for Teachers a transcript of their credits at the University of Maryland (and those obtained in any other college or university). Each such case will be passed upon individually by the Director of the College for Teachers and appropriate advanced credit awarded.

The matriculation requirements of each such students will also be passed upon individually.

All students working for certificates or degrees are requested to take up the matter of completing their work with the Dean or his Assistants. We will require that every student whose intent it is to work for a degree at the University of Maryland shall register such intention prior to May 1, 1926, in order that records may be made of the work to be completed in Johns Hopkins University to be applied towards a Maryland degree.

Herbert w. Diamond, Dean
School of Business Administration

HMD/ECL

ANNOUNCEMENTS OF ARRANGEMENTS 1926–27
(circa February 1926)

Students in the School of Business Administration have doubtless noticed recent newspaper announcements concerning the discontinuance of courses in the School of Business Administration of the University of Maryland at the end of the present academic year and the carrying on of such instruction by the Johns Hopkins University. In order to avoid any misapprehension on the part of the students concerning the proposed changes it has seemed desirable to bring to their attention the nature and extent of instruction that will be available to them at the Johns Hopkins University and the arrangements that have been made for the continuance and completion of their studies. It is impossible to state, as yet, in its entirety the exact curriculum of courses that will be offered next year at Johns Hopkins. When the curriculum is completely arranged copies of the catalogue describing the instruction will be mailed to all students. In the meantime, however, it is hoped that the following preliminary statement will serve to dissolve the uncertainties of some students concerning the opportunities that will be open to them.

COURSES TO BE OFFERED

Students in the School of Business Administration are primarily interested in the instruction in business subjects that will be available in the evening. In the past the Johns Hopkins University has been offering through its Evening Courses in Business Economics, courses in the following subjects:

Principles of Political Economy
Current Economic Problems
Money and Banking
Corporation Finance
Investments
Business Statistics
Labor Problems
Personal Administration
Business Psychology
Credits and Business Barometrics
Principles of Advertising

Principles of Suretyship
Casualty Insurance
Commercial Law
Advanced Commercial Law
English Grammar and Composition
Business English
Public Speaking
Elementary Accounting
Corporation and Cost Accounting
Advanced Accounting and Auditing

It is expected that substantially this same list of courses will be continued in the future. In addition, however, there will be a considerable extension of the instruction in accounting. Four or five new courses in that subject will be added to the schedule so that the work will cover the same range as that which has been given at the School of Business Administration. Mr. Leslie W. Baker will be added to the staff of instructors in Accounting in the Evening Courses in Business Economics. It should be understood, therefore, that thorough instruction will be provided to prepare students for the examination for certified public accountants as well as for training in the practice of accounting. It is probably that certain other courses of a business nature will also be added to the Evening Courses in Business Economics.

ACADEMIC COURSES
In addition to these courses, instruction is offered in the College for Teachers of the Johns Hopkins University in the afternoon (4 to 6 p.m.) and evening in a wide range of academic subjects. Circulars are available at the office indicating the complete list of such courses offered in 1925–26. Through this college, moreover, opportunity will be open to students in the evening classes to obtain the Bachelor of Science degree. The detailed requirements for matriculation and graduation are likewise set forth in the circular.

ENTRANCE REQUIREMENTS AND DEGREES
In general it may be said that a high school education is required for matriculation in the College for Teachers. For graduation it is

required that at least 120 points of credit be obtained including the completion of certain prescribed academic courses. A student, however, may offer courses in business economics and accounting as a "major" in the College for Teachers and for such students it will be possible for a preponderance of their work to be done in those fields.

TRANSFERS

Arrangements have been made whereby matriculated students in the School of Business Administration of the University of Maryland, who, by the end of the present academic year will have completed at least two years college work, may, by offering the requisite number of points, obtain the degree of Bachelor of Science in Business from the U of M. The additional points required for this purpose may be obtained through the satisfactory completion of courses in the College for Teachers or the Evening Courses in Business Economics of the Johns Hopkins University and certification to the Registrar of the University of Maryland to that effect.

The U of M does not expect, however, to award degrees to any students at present registered in its School of Business Administration who by the end of this academic year will have completed less than two years of college work. For such students the opportunity of obtaining the degree of Bachelor of Science will be available through the College for Teachers of the Johns Hopkins University by meeting the usual requirements of that College for matriculation and completion of courses. It is understood that the preponderance of work will probably be in business subjects. Students in the School of Business Administration who wish to obtain their degree in this way should present individually their applications for matriculation and advanced standing at the College for Teachers.

The opportunity of obtaining the degree of Bachelor of Science from the Johns Hopkins University through the College for Teachers will likewise be open, upon the same conditioned [sic] as mentioned in the preceding paragraph, to students who have completed two years work or more at the University of Maryland.

It is expected, however, that such students will do at least their last year's work at the Johns Hopkins University.

NON MATRICULATED STUDENTS

For students who have a high school education or its equivalent and who wish to pursue a connected group of courses, such as those in accountancy, but who do not wish to work for a degree, provision is expected to be made at the Johns Hopkins University for the award of some form of certificate in recognition of the completion of the prescribed group of courses. Details in regard to this will be announced in the circular of the Evening Courses in Business Economics for the year 1926–27.

SPECIAL STUDENTS

It should be particularly noted that although a high school education or its equivalent will be required at the Johns Hopkins University for the degree of Bachelor of Science or for the above mentioned group certificate, no special academic training is required for admission to individual courses. An instructor, however, may refuse admission to his course of an applicant who in his opinion is not capable of profiting from the course.

DAY STUDENTS

Students who are in a position to pursue a full-time morning course of study are also advised of the opportunities for business instruction at Johns Hopkins in the School of Business Economics in which the degree of Bachelor of Science in Economics is awarded. Admission to this school is based upon the usual requirements for college entrance.

It is expected that the circular describing the 1926–27 Evening Courses in Business Economics and the catalogue of the School of Business Economics will be completed within about two months so that copies can be placed in the hands of students in time to enable them to plan their courses for next year before the close of the present term.

International Fraternity of Delta Sigma Pi

May 18, 1926

TO: Board of Directors

SUBJECT: Transfer of Chi Chapter to Johns Hopkins University

For your information, the School of Business Administration of the University of Maryland has been absorbed by Johns Hopkins University, effective at the opening of the college courses next fall.

Johns Hopkins has not absorbed the entire University of Maryland but just the School of Business Administration. Both Johns Hopkins and Maryland have offered courses in Commerce and both have had fairly large registration, but it has been felt by the uniting of both departments far greater service could be rendered to the prospective students.

This means, therefore, after the close of the present college year, our Chi Chapter will go out of business as far as the University of Maryland is concerned. However, practically all of the students now attending the School of Business Administration of the University of Maryland will transfer to Johns Hopkins in the fall and at a regular meeting of Chi Chapter held February 5th, a motion was unanimously passed that Chi Chapter petition the Board of

Directors to transfer their charter from the University of Maryland to Johns Hopkins University as of October 1st, 1926.

There is nothing contained in our laws to cover such an emergency and in discussing the matter, Brother Fackler and myself feel if the Board can grant chapters, they certainly have the power to change their location or revoke charters for good cause. This is rather an unusual situation and while it may happen again, we can provide for it in the future by adding a section to our constitution and by-laws at the Madison Convention that will cover such emergencies. In the meantime, however, action should be taken regarding this particular situation as Chi Chapter must give notice to their present landlord on July 1st as to whether or not they will remain in their chapter house. In fact, they propose purchasing their chapter house, but, of course, if there would be any legal difficulty in regard to transferring the chapter to Johns Hopkins, they would like to know of it this spring.

Johns Hopkins is a university of very high standing and the location of our Chi Chapter at Johns Hopkins instead of Maryland would in no way detract from the prestige of Delta Sigma Pi. In fact, it would probably add to their prestige. Chi Chapter is extremely active and will carry on in the new location equally as well as they have at Maryland.

We request, therefore, your vote on the approval of the transfer of our Chi Chapter from the University of Maryland to Johns Hopkins University effective October 1st, 1926.

This letter is being sent [to] you in duplicate. Please indicate your vote on one copy, returning to the Central Office at once, retaining the other copy for your files.

Fraternally,

Jim

James H. Fry
Secretary-Treasurer

HGW: A

June 15, 1949
Mr. James H. Fry
1625 E. North Avenue
Baltimore, Maryland

Dear Jim:

Your letter of June 7 regarding the possibility of a separate Delta Sigma Pi Chapter in the day school at Johns Hopkins University has been referred to me for attention. While I met with Dean Hawkins briefly at Madison, Wisconsin, in April, during the meeting of the American Association of Collegiate Schools of Business, and I have known him since his undergraduate days at Penn State, we did not discuss in detail the various angles of two chapters of Delta Sigma Pi on the Johns Hopkins campus.

It would seem to me that this matter is something that Chi Chapter and our local alumni should investigate at length and make a report to The Central Office for their consideration. There are advantages and disadvantages to two chapters on the same campus and the Grand Council would want to be absolutely certain that the local situation, the physical facilities and the registration would be ample to justify the dual chapter operation. I have exchanged considerable correspondence with John McKewen in this connection and the next move is for us to receive a report on the local situation. It is particularly desirable that this be available in its final form by the time of our Grand Council meeting in Baltimore, preceding the 17th Grand Chapter Congress, and if the committee desired to have an appointment to appear before our Grand Council and explain the local situation in greater detail, that could be easily arranged providing I have sufficient advance notice.

Fraternally yours,

SCW:as
CC: Allen L. Fowler
CC: John L. McKewen

Grand Secretary-Treasurer

DITCH REALTY COMPANY, INC.

Realtors . Insurance

11 EAST TWENTY-FIRST STREET - BALTIMORE 18, MD.

BELMONT 9063-4810

June 7, 1949

Mr. James D. Thompson
Central Office
Delta Sigma Pi
222 W. Adams Street
Chicago, Illinois

Dear Jim:

I have talked with John McKewen and Dean Hawkins and have made an effort to find out what has developed on the question of a new chapter in the Day School at Hopkins since your last visit to Baltimore. Apparently, Dean Hawkins and Gig Wright have worked together on the subject and, at this time, efforts have been made to form a Club, to begin operations next fall.

John McKewen seems to feel that the biggest question is still whether to combine the Day and Night School in Chi Chapter, or to have an entirely new Chapter.

The Active Chapter is ready and anxious with time and personnel to assist on either of the two plans, but, at the moment, the new idea seems to be awaiting the direction of Brothers Wright and Hawkins.

Fraternally,

Jim

James H. Fry
Secretary-Treasurer
JHF:G

Appendix G
Master of Science in Management
Science (MSM) 1961–1978

Starting in the fall semester of 1961, the Master of Science in Management Science (MSM) was offered in McCoy College by the Industrial Engineering Department in the School of Engineering. This new degree focused on Operations Research and was developed by the collaborative effort of dean of the Engineering School Robert H. Roy, Dr. Charles D. Flagle, and other professors who had an interest in Operations Research and Management Science. Robert Roy had been interested in Operations Research for many years. In fact, when Johns Hopkins University was involved with the U.S. Army in the area of Operations Research during the 1950s, he had the opportunity to integrate and apply his experience in industry and his scholarly work.[25] Dean Roy's interests are also shown in his many books and scholarly articles. In his 1958 book *The Administrative Process*, he discusses Operations Analysis and explains the value of Operations Research. Furthermore, his 1986 book *Operations Technology: Systems and Evolution* presents a

---

25 During an interview in 1984, Dean Roy explained the relationship between Hopkins and the U.S. Army, stating that the Johns Hopkins University Operations Research Office was "under exclusive contract with the Department of the Army, like APL [Applied Physics Laboratory] is to the Department of the Navy" (Petersen, 1984, p. 24). Dean Roy added, "They asked me to be on their advisory board and I served on it for a number of years" (Petersen, 1984, p. 23).

considerable discussion on Operations Research and all sorts of systems, including Intelligent Systems.

A 1961 brochure presented the original MSM degree

The Johns Hopkins University announces a program leading to the degree of Master of Science with a major in Management Science. This program will be offered in McCoy College, the evening college of the University, by the Industrial Engineering Department of the School of Engineering.

The program is open to properly qualified graduates of four-year colleges and universities who have majored in Arts and Sciences, Business, or Engineering.

A college graduate who is not interested in obtaining the degree may enroll in any course in the program as a *special student*, provided he can meet the qualitative standards for admission and has completed the specific prerequisites, if any, for the course he wishes to take.

ADMISSION

The applicant must submit to McCoy College a formal application and official transcripts of all previous college or university study before beginning the program.

The applicant must hold a bachelor's degree from an approved college or university with an average of B (3.0) or better in the latter half of his undergraduate program. The undergraduate program must have included mathematics through differential equations and a one-year course in each of the following: economics, accounting, and statistics. (A knowledge of physics is desirable but not required.)

Applicants whose undergraduate program did not include one or more of the subjects listed above may take such courses in McCoy College. A student may enroll in a graduate course for which he has the prerequisites and concurrently take an undergraduate prerequisite which he is lacking.

RESIDENCE

The equivalent of one full year of study, which is taken on a part-time basis during the evening hours, must be completed within five years. The time limit begins when a student first enrolls in a graduate course.

COURSE REQUIREMENTS

The degree is earned by the successful completion of the three required courses listed below plus 27 credits in elective courses, all of which must be taken in McCoy College.

A grade of B or above is required for graduate credit, but one term-grade below B may be counted towards the degree.

Normally Principles of Administration 55.401–402 should be taken during the first year of graduate study. The other required and elective courses may be taken in any order, provided the prerequisites are met.

Each course meets once weekly for two hours and carries three credits per term. The courses are described below.

Neither an essay nor a foreign language is required.

REQUIRED COURSES
　　Principles of Administration 55.401–402 (6 credits)
　　Mathematical Methods of Operations Research 55.403–404
　　　　(6 credits)
　　Cost Analysis 55.405–406 (6 credits)

ELECTIVE COURSES
　　Introduction to Statistical Theory 55.407 (3 credits)
　　Theory of Analysis of Variance and Regression 55.408 (3
　　　　credits)
　　Probability and Stochastic Processes 55.409–410 (6 credits)
　　Advanced Principles of Engineering Psychology 55.411–412 (6
　　　　credits)
　　Elementary Inventory Systems 55.413 (3 credits)
　　Advanced Inventory Systems 55.702 (3 credits)
　　Design of Experiments 55.703 (3 credits)
　　Analysis of Response Surfaces 55.704 (3 credits)
　　Stochastic Systems 55.705–706 (6 credits)
　　Linear Programing 55.707 (3 credits)
　　Theory of Games 55.708 (3 credits)
　　Economic Theory (6 credits)
　　Mathematical Economics (6 credits)

Advanced Symbolic Logic (6 credits)
Computer Theory and Programing (6 credits)

The Final Version

Although the original version had 45 credits of solid material pertaining to management science, there was a demand for a wider array of courses directly related to either operations research or statistics. As a result the MSM degree was revised into two options.

Required courses	15 credits
Quantitative electives consisting of an Operations Research option or a Statistics option	18 credits
General electives	12 credits
TOTAL	45 credits

A subsequent bulletin had this description:

The Degree of Master of Science with a Major in Management Science (MSM)

Operations research is the application of the scientific method to the solution of problems in business, government, and eleemosynary organizations. It embodies the important concepts of multidiscipline teams who seek to supply quantitative information and recommendations in order that optimal decisions may be made by executives. The program emphasizes both theoretical and applied work in methodologies such as mathematical programing, computer science, and stochastic systems. The applications may have their basis in problem areas such as inventory and production systems, managerial economics, health services, and transportation or communications networks.

Admission. In addition to the general requirements for admission to a graduate program outlined in the section on admission, the applicant's undergraduate program must have included three semesters of calculus and a course in matrix theory or linear algebra. Those who wish to meet the requirement in matrix theory should take Matrix Theory 11.409.

Course Requirements. The degree may be earned by the successful completion within five years of the required courses listed below plus sufficient electives to bring the total to 45 credits. The course requirements are:

Required courses (five terms)
Introduction to Probability and Statistics 55.755–756
Foundations of Management Science II 55.748
Two of the following:
Foundations of Management Science I 55.747
Analysis for Applications 55.757
Matrix Analysis for Applications 55.758

Quantitative electives (six term courses)
Operations Research Option. At least three term courses
      selected from:
Introduction to Mathematical Programing 55.401–402
Probability and Stochastic Processes 55.407–408
Linear Programing 55.707
Inventory Systems 55.413
Theory of Games
Computer Modeling of Social Systems 55.421

Statistics Option. At least three term courses selected from:
Stochastic Systems 55.409–410
Regression 55.759
Design of Experiments 55.703
Statistical Methods
Statistical Computing
Statistical Inference

Three additional term courses are to be selected from Management Science graduate offerings.

General electives

Electives may be selected from courses listed under Management Science, Computer Science, Mathematics, Numerical Science and Administrative Science.

Neither an essay nor a knowledge of a foreign language is required in the program. Minimum quality standards for graduate programs will be required.*

With the disestablishment of the School of Engineering, the stewardship of this graduate degree program passed to McCoy College. Dean Roy, the last dean of the School of Engineering, relates, "The faculty of Philosophy was converted into the Faculty of Arts and Sciences and Engineering was merged into it. That was about 1965, give or take" (Petersen, 1984, p. 31). Then, as information technology became more popular in terms of a career field and the needs of industry, more students were drawn to a Master of Science in Computer Science. In fact, by 1982 the majority of courses in the Evening College were in engineering, and the most popular graduate program was a Master of Science in Computer Science. But there were complications as well—a master's degree in management science that seemed to be a cross between management and math did not attract many students. The management students wanted an MBA or something comparable; the mathematically inclined drifted toward graduate math degrees. With inadequate enrollments and an ongoing Master of Administrative Science degree, the Master of Science in Management Science was discontinued in Academic Year 1978–1979.

* Characteristics and contents of the Master of Science in Management Science (MSM) degree program extracted and summarized from annual catalogs and brochures published during 1961–1978.

Appendix H
Annotated Bibliography:
History of the Business Division

- *A brief history of Johns Hopkins University.*
  - * 51 pages taken from the Hopkins Web site: http://webapps.jhu.edu/jhuniverse/information_about_hopkins/about_jhu/a_brief_history_of_jhu/
  - * First page and a half provides a brief history of JHU
  - * About 20 other presented events are milestones for SPSBE

- *Alumni Directory, 1988, The Johns Hopkins University School of Continuing Studies, Evening College and Summer Sessions, McCoy College.* Compiled and published by Carleton Graphics, South Bend, IN.
  - * Short history of the school and the division (p. VIII)

- *75th Anniversary of Chi Chapter, Delta Sigma Pi, November 23, 1997.*
  - * Spiral book published on the occasion of the anniversary
  - * History of the Hopkins' student chapter and alumni chapter
  - * Written by Jeanne Stinchcomb, president of alumni chapter

- *Annual Report, 1980–1981.* The Johns Hopkins University Evening College and Summer Session. Published September 1981.
  - * A treasure trove of information giving statistics of programs throughout the school at the start of the 1980s
  - * Chronology of degree approvals, fall 1952–May 1981 (there were no graduate programs in the Evening College 1951–1952) (pp. 21–22)
  - * Lists MS with a major in Management Science and master of administrative science (p. 21)
  - * Progress in Division of Administration and Business (p. 3)
  - * Mel Brown lecture (p. 3)

- Combined bachelor's and master's program brochure 1978–1979.

- Bartol, K. M., & Martin, D. C. (1991). *Management.* New York: McGraw Hill.

- Beatty, S. (2006, December 5). Johns Hopkins Receives $50 Million Donation. *The Wall Street Journal*, p. A8.

- Buchner, H. Louis C. (1929). *Edward Franklin Buchner: A memoir written for his children by their mother.*
  - * Memoir loaned by Dean Fessler, who received it from one of Ed Buchner's grandsons
  - * 54 pages of Buchner's experiences as a child and young man
  - * Graduated from Western College and Yale in 1893
  - * Chair of Philosophy & Education, University of Alabama (1903–1908)
  - * Professor of Education, with a salary of $3,500 per academic year
  - * Organized college courses for teachers (first offered 1909–1910) with classes held Tuesday, Wednesday,

Thursday, Friday, and Saturday, 4:10–6:00 p.m. and 9:00 AM–1:00 p.m. Saturdays (p. 78)
* Although until 1915 Buchner ran it all but only had the status of chairman of a committee in charge of the college courses for teachers
* By 1924 number of students increased to 1,206 and courses to 78; name was changed to College for Teachers—"This was not [Buchner's] choice. He wished to [have] it called a School of Education" (p. 80)
* "In the year of father's death (1928–1929) attendance was 1,526 and number of courses offered was 89" (p. 80)
* In 1911 established a Summer Session (p. 80)
* Early in 1929 established the School of Higher Studies in Education, authorized to award degrees of master of education and doctor of education
* Died August 1929—spent 21 years at Hopkins (p. 81)
* Salary never rose beyond $4,500 (p. 81)
* Listing of a half-century of progress in the field of Education at Hopkins (1876–1926); good outline to quote (p. 96)
* Balance of book reverts to earlier family events involving Ed Buchner

• Circular for Evening College May 1974
    * The 1974–1975 academic year catalog

• Circular for Evening College May 1976
    * The 1976–1977 academic year catalog

• Circular for Evening College May 1977
    * The 1977–1978 fall and spring catalog, referred to as the year catalog

• Circular for Evening College May 1978
    * The 1978–1979 year catalog

- Circular for Evening College May 1980
  * The 1980–1981 year catalog

- Circular for SPSBE, May 2005, for Academic Year 2005–2006.
  * May be the last printed catalog
  * History of JHU (p. 2)
  * Coverage of Business Division (pp. 69–173)
  * Good outline of programs and the participants; nothing about history of the school

- *Evening College Newsletter*, Spring 1978, *VII*(2). Baltimore: JHU.
  * Combined BS/MS program—good description (p. 3)

- *Evening College Newsletter*, Fall 1979, *IX*(1). Baltimore: JHU.
  * Comments about evening college by Provost Longaker (p. 1)
  * Petersen appointed Director of Business Division (p. 2)
  * Klein and Weller appointed coordinators (p. 12)

- *Evening College Newsletter*, Summer 1982, *XI*(3). Baltimore: JHU.
  * Gabor appointed Evening College dean (p. 1)
  * Farewell remarks by Roman Verhaalen, departing dean (p. 1)
  * New courses and approaches in Business Division (p. 2)
  * Delta Sigma Pi sponsors job forum (p. 3)
  * Scholarship key awarded at May 1982 commencement to Marie Karpinski (p. 2)

- Flagle, C. D. (1961, May). Probability based tolerances in forecasting and planning. *The Journal of Industrial Engineering*, pp. SR 19–SR 23.

- Flagle, C. D. Paper for Seminar in Operations Research. (1954, February 23). "Probability based tolerances in forecasting and planning." Seminar Paper No. 16.

- Fuller, N. (2006, December 5). Johns Hopkins Receives $50 Million Donation. *Baltimore Sun.*

- Hawkins, H. (1960). *Pioneer: A history of the Johns Hopkins University, 1874–1889.* Ithaca, NY: Cornell University Press.

- Haywood, Mary Ellen & Shivers, Frank R., Jr. (2004). *The architecture of Baltimore.* Baltimore: Johns Hopkins University Press.

- *The Johns Hopkins University Gazette.* (1987, November 3), p. 12.

    - "Survey [by *US News & World Report*] found that Hopkins has the third-best regional business school in the eastern U.S.—third out of 110 competitors from Massachusetts to Virginia."

- Macksey, Richard. (1976). *A brief academic history of The Johns Hopkins University: The pioneer century 1876–1976.* Published by Johns Hopkins University.

- *Manufacturer's record.* (1895, December 6). Atlantic Edition.

- MAS brochure (mid-1980s) outlining program

- Master of Science in Management Science brochure
    * Good description of new program in McCoy College, 1961

- Muller, S. (1988, January 15). President Steve Muller's letter to alumni, parents, and friends (p. 4)

- *New Evening College Degree* brochure
  - * Master of Administrative Science, beginning 1971—initial arrangement of courses will change

- *Report on the future directions of the Evening College and Summer Session.* Published in September 1981.
  - * Rourke Report, 1970; major change 1970–1980; undergrad to grad enrollments (p. 4) and good chart (p. 8)
  - * Good coverage of trends (Business Division) (pp. 20–21)
  - * Good comparison of applications Business Division, undergraduate and graduate 1974–1980 (p. 39)
  - * Decline in graduate programs in Education Division (p. 18)
    - · 1000 students 1974–1975
    - · 500 students 1979–1980

- Odds and Ends: papers from Petersen's files adding to or clarifying the history of the Business Division
  - * Folder Number One (Business Division)
    - · September registrations, 1953–1978, including number of students in each class and name of each class
    - · February registrations, 1954–1981
    - · Summer registrations, 1965–1978
    - · Telephone roster of School of Continuing Studies faculty and staff, 1989
  - * Folder Number Two (Business Division)
    - · Article in the *Gazette* (October 10, 1989) reports Sydney Stern selected as new Director of Business Division and also provides information about activities in October 1989
    - · Draft of anecdotes developed for history of Business Division

- Minutes of September 24, 1980: Academic Council of the Homewood facilities critical of the Evening College
- Photographs
  - Two photographs of presentation by Barber Connible
  - Two photographs of Jim Getty
  - Two photographs of information systems three-day noncredit course
* Folder Number Three (Business Division)
  - Names of the 15 members of the initial MAS graduating class of 1974
  - Same list, but copied from the graduation circular—one MD but all men; now over half are women
* Folder Number Four (Business Division)
  - Full-time faculty needs in the Business Division (memo to the dean)
  - Meeting of Division Advisory Committee
    - May 7, 1976
    - April 2, 1980
    - December 10, 1982
    - May 26, 1983
* Folder Number Five (Business Division)
  - Proposed course offerings, 1979/1980
  - MAS classes scheduled at Evening College Center at Goucher College, fall 1977–spring 1980
  - 1979 Summer Session classes
* Folder Number Six (Business Division)
  - 1978–1979 course offerings
  - Memo to all Evening College directors of the need to reduce offerings for 1978/1979: cancel 17 courses currently planned from spring 1979 offerings; enrollment level should average over 20 students per section—three locations were Homewood, Columbia, and Goucher College
  - In fall 1977, four full master's degree programs in Columbia

- Very good and detailed report on the Columbia Center fall 1977
- Folder Number Seven (Business Division)
- Bar chart on number of MAS degrees conferred
- Eight-page chronological file
- Degree statistics for the fall term of 1977 for the Columbia Center, which lists number of class enrollments for each course of study
- Improved enrollment statistics for fall term 1977—MAS 168 enrollments for 7 sections

- Petersen, P. B. (2004). *The great Baltimore fire.* Baltimore: The Maryland Historical Society.
  * Provides the role of Gilman following the fire and quotes from Gilman's personal correspondence about the fire; also lists the university's losses due to the fire

- Petersen, Peter B. *Chronological overview (long version) of the history of the Business Division,* pp. 1–9.

- Petersen, P. B. (1984, November 16). A further insight into the life of Henry L. Gantt: The papers of Duncan C. Lyle. *Southern Management Association 1984 Annual Meeting Proceedings,* 198–200. New Orleans, LA. Paper and essence of findings cited in text: Wren, D. (1987). *The evolution of management thought* (3rd ed.). New York: John Wiley & Sons.
  * Excellent material about Gantt's Hopkins connection

- Petersen, P. B. (1986, August 15). Henry Gantt and the new machine (1916–1919). *Academy of Management Best Paper Proceedings 1986,* 128–132.
  * Provides a good insight into Gantt's political ideas and the role of engineers in running industry

- Petersen, Peter B. (1984, February 28). *Reflections of Dean Emeritus Robert H. Roy.* Baltimore, Johns Hopkins University, pp. 1–35.

* Reflections about Christie (p. 16)
* Departmental libraries, then MSE

• Photo album with yellow cover
  * Photos
    · Two photos of Joseph's Square, Evening College Columbia Center, 1979 (p. 7)
    · Two photos of Twin Knolls, Evening College Columbia Center, mid-1980s (p. 6)
    · Two photos of 203 Shaffer Hall, Business Division Office, early 1980s (p. 19)
    · Photo of 203 Shaffer Hall, Business Division Office, remodeled and three people added, mid-1980s (p. 18)
    · Photo of Ginney Kively (p. 14)
    · Photo of Nancy Fulton (p. 14)
    · Photo of Richard Robbins (p. 14)
    · Photo of Peggy Swagger (p. 15)
    · Photo of Lennie Carter (p. 15)
    · Photo of Barbara Plummer (p. 16)
    · Photo of Ralph Fessler (p. 35)
    · Photo of Judy Bowersox (p. 35)
    · Photo of Stanley Gabor (p. 35)
    · Photo of Nancy Norris (p. 36)
    · Photo of Richard Allen (p. 36)
    · Photo of Ralph Fessler (p. 36)
    · Photo of Harry Lejda's going away party (pp. 37, 39)

• Photos in box
  * Construction of current Columbia Center
  * Good photo of Betsy Mayotte
  * Good photo of Stanley Gabor

• Roy, R. H. (1958). *The administrative process.* Baltimore: Johns Hopkins University Press.

- Roy, R. H. (1986). *Operations technology: Systems and evolution.* Baltimore: Johns Hopkins University Press.

- *Ranum Report on the Future Directions of the Evening College and Summer Session.* (1982). Hamburger Archives, MSEL, p. 7.

- School of Continuing Studies Academic Year 1987–1988 course schedule
  - * This is for fall 1987 and spring 1988

- Schmidt, John. (1986). *Johns Hopkins: Portrait of a university.* Baltimore: Johns Hopkins University.
  - * Part-time engineering programs go to the Whiting School of Engineering, 1983 (pp. 137–138)
  - * History of the school and Gabor's role (pp. 145–151)
  - * Hopkins chronology (pp. 241–250)
  - * Good list of references
    - John C. French. (1979). *A history of the University founded by Johns Hopkins.* Arno Press, 492 pages.
    - Hugh Hawkins. (2002). *Pioneer: A history of the Johns Hopkins University.* Baltimore: JHU Press, 384 pages.
    - Alan M. Chesney. (1943). *The Johns Hopkins Hospital and the Johns Hopkins School of Medicine: A chronicle: Early years, 1867–1893.* Baltimore: JHU Press, 412 pages.
    - Thomas Bourne Turner. (1974). *Heritage of excellence: The Johns Hopkins Medical Institutions 1914–1947.* Baltimore: JHU Press, 656 pages.
    - Augusta Tucker. *(1973). It happened at Hopkins: A teaching hospital. Balti*more: Johns Hopkins Hospital, 283 pages.
    - Francesco Cordasco. (1960). *Daniel Coit Gilman and the other protean PhD*

- *A*braham Flexner. (1946). *Daniel Coit Gilman: Creator of the American type of university. Harcourt Brace & Co.*
- Fabian Franklin. (1910). *The life of Daniel Coit Gilman.* Dodd Mead & Co.
- Helen Hopkins Thom. (1984). *Johns Hopkins: A silhouette.* University Microfilms International, 125 pages.
- A. McGehee Harvey. (1976). *Adventures in medical research: A century of discovery at Johns Hopkins.* Baltimore: JHU Press, 480 pages.
- Richard Macksey. (1976). *A brief academic history of the Johns Hopkins University: The pioneer century.*

- Sharkey, Robert P. (1975). *Johns Hopkins: Portrait of a university.*
  - Photo Biology Building, 1900, downtown (p. 31)
  - Caption to photo (p. 32) tells of dates when three major buildings built on Homewood campus
  - 1947, many of the evening offerings of the university are consolidated into a new division called McCoy College
  - 1963, Master of Liberal Arts initiated in McCoy College
  - 1966, McCoy's title changed to Evening College
  - 1971, Evening College offers two new degrees
    - Master of Science in Computer and Environmental Engineering
    - Master of Administrative Science
  - March 1973, Evening College opens a center in Columbia, MD, and one at Goucher College

- *US News & World Report.* (1987, November 2), p. 83.
  - MAS program selected as third-best in the eastern United States

- Verhaalen, Roman J. (dean emeritus of Evening College and Summer Sessions). (1984, November). *75 years of pioneering part-time student education.* Baltimore.
  - * One of the best sources of details about the school (first half of book)
  - * Second half of book has an outstanding chronological listing, 1909–1982
  - * Gabor appointed dean, September 1, 1982

- Warren, Mame. (2000). *Johns Hopkins: Knowledge for the world 1876–2001.* Baltimore: Johns Hopkins University (not JHU Press).
  - * Interesting organization; covers JHU as a whole rather than by school; covers major themes chronologically—not much about SPSBE and its prior organizations

- Wren, D. (1987). *The evolution of management thought* (3rd ed.). New York: John Wiley & Sons.

- Wren, Daniel A. (2002). *Collegiate education for business administration at the University of Oklahoma: A history.* Price College of Business.
  - * Excellent table of contents
  - * Good title for his first chapter
  - * Good approach to the history of a business school

Appendix I
The Rourke Report on Future Directions of the Evening College and Summer Session (Submitted August 1970)

Prior to Dean Richard Mumma's retirement on June 30, 1970, an ad hoc committee appointed by the president of Johns Hopkins University reviewed the operation of the Evening College and Summer Session. This committee, chaired by Francis E. Rourke, a political science professor in the School of Arts and Sciences, consisted of a distinguished group of professors from throughout the university. In addition to their review they presented eight clear recommendations about the future directions that the school should consider.

The advisory board of the Evening College and Summer Session received this report in August 1970 as Roman Verhaalen assumed his new role as dean. The eight recommendations of the Rourke Report on Future Directions are particularly significant in terms of services to disadvantaged groups in the inner city, full-time faculty appointments, tenure for full-time faculty, the need for a graduate business program, the importance of having a greater emphasis on quality of instruction, and the possible need for some internal reorganization.[26]

Recommendations of the Rourke Report on Future Directions

Recommendation 1: The Committee feels that in recent years it has been very unfortunate that news stories released to the press have failed to reflect an adequate appreciation of the activities of the Evening College in a number of key areas. As a result the University has often suffered public relations setbacks in situations in which it could have much improved its public image by presenting full information on Evening College programs.

The Public Relations Office of the University should make a special effort to take Evening College programs into account in making public announcements about changes in University programs and policies.

Recommendation 2: The Committee believes that it is urgent for the Evening College to provide maximum services to disadvantaged groups in the inner city. Located as it is on the border of slum neighborhoods, the University has an obligation and an opportunity to help arrest physical and social decay in its own backyard.

We recommend that a committee be established to evaluate the activities the Evening College is presently carrying on in the inner city, and to propose additional programs that match the University's assets with inner city needs.

Recommendation 3: (A) Quality of Instruction—All students registered in the Evening College Center at the Applied Physics

---

26 These recommendations, copied here in their entirety, can be found in the Johns Hopkins Archives under Francis Rourke, Ad Hoc Committee Report on Future Directions of the Evening College and Summer Session, 1 October 1975, pp. 12–13. JHU Archives, Record Group 05.001, Dean, Evening College and Summer Session, "Annual Reports." Further information containing Dean Roman Verhaalen's response to each of these recommendations can be located in Verhaalen, 1984, pp. 33–38.

Laboratory are routinely given a questionnaire covering (a) quality of each course, (b) evaluation of students' impressions of the instructor, and (c) physical facilities. Results are made available to the individual instructor, and the effect seems to have been favorable leading to higher ratings for instructors in areas where they were previously reported to be weak, and to improvement in selection of texts and in other aspects of given courses.

We suggest here that an alternative procedure be considered which seems likely to lead to essentially the same positive results. The instructor himself should be encouraged to give the APL questionnaire to the students taking his course or courses. The results would enable the instructor to discover and hopefully improve, where needed, areas of technique or course material without the dangers that are perceived when such material is routinely made available to the administration.

(B) Programs and Majors—Some kind of formal procedure for monitoring course offerings, requirements, and prerequisites for majors or programs of study in the Evening College seems necessary. Of particular concern here are the relatively large and important programs in business and education. For such programs we recommend use of visiting committees of professors from other universities. Such committees should be made up of active professors in the field, and where appropriate, could include members of the Johns Hopkins staff. Their sole function would be to evaluate strengths and weaknesses of the program concerned.

Recommendation 4: Although the Evening College has been effectively and efficiently administered over the past years some internal reorganization may be desirable in the future in order to meet the demands of a general shift in the enrollment pattern more efficiently. This may be the case when full-time faculty are engaged for the Evening College program. We feel that it is desirable to have the current relationship between the Evening College and Summer Session maintained because of the close interrelationship between the programs, faculty, and students of the two operations.

Recommendation 5: At the present time, all but a relatively small number of specialized courses are given on the Homewood Campus; the only other sites being at other branches of the University. Suggestions have been made from time to time that use be made of facilities other than institutions of higher education for credit courses, e.g., public school facilities, governmental facilities, or industrial sites.

It is important to distinguish between the location of a course offering, i.e., its headquarters or home base, and locations where specific class periods within the course might be held. For portions of some courses, student activity or instruction at off-campus sites may be desirable or necessary, just as the use of guest lecturers who are not members of the Evening College instructional staff may be advantageous. It is not our intent to discourage practices such as these. Rather, we limit ourselves to the recommendation that, whenever possible, the credit course itself be based at one of the branches of the University.

Recommendation 6: Dean Richard A. Mumma, in his recent report to the President of the University for the academic year 1969–70 states that, "The Evening College would be greatly strengthened by the appointment of a small core of full-time faculty" [Evening College *Newsletter*, Fall 1971, inside last page].

This committee arrived at much the same conclusion. Particularly relevant to our deliberations was the proposal for the introduction of a Master's program in Executive Development and the recent decision of the University to dissolve the Department of Education in the Division of Arts and Sciences. We, therefore, recommend that a small core of full-time faculty be recruited where necessary for the Evening College, and that they be offered rank, tenure, and other privileges equivalent to those offered to faculty of the other schools of the University.

Recommendation 7: It has been suggested to the Committee that steps should be taken for the Evening College to make use of the educational facilities available on the East Baltimore campus.

The Committee has considered (various) proposals, but it does not feel that it can make specific recommendations for Evening College participation at the East Baltimore campus at this time.

Recommendation 8: The Evening Division has long had a large undergraduate program in the management area. This Committee believes that steps should now be taken to establish a more advanced program at the Master's level in Executive Development.

The lack of an advanced program in management was the most frequently mentioned educational criticism both in the formal survey of opinions of present Evening College students and in volunteered responses to a letter sent by this Committee to all members of the Evening College faculty.

The Committee believes that its recommendation concerning appointment of full-time Evening College faculty and procedures for monitoring quality of instructional programs provide *[sic]* assurance that the Executive Development program can be maintained at the high level of quality characteristic of this University.

Appendix J
Maps

1. Initial Location of Johns Hopkins University at West Monument and North Howard Streets (circa 1905)

2. Johns Hopkins Hospital and Medical School (circa 1905)

3. Johns Hopkins University, Johns Hopkins Club, and Peabody Institute (circa 1907)

4. Johns Hopkins University Grounds: New Location Now Developing (circa 1907)*

5. Homewood Campus (circa 1915)*

6. Homewood Campus (1946)

7. Homewood Campus (1979)

8. Homewood Campus (1987)

9. Initial Downtown Baltimore Center when located at Charles and Saratoga Streets (1987)

10. Columbia Center when at Twin Knolls (1987)

11. Homewood Campus (2005)

12. Columbia Center when at Gateway Park (2005) and Downtown Baltimore Center when at Charles and Fayette Streets (2005)

13. Montgomery County Campus (2005) and Washington DC Center (2005)

* Courtesy of Government Publications/Maps/Law Library, Sheridan Libraries, Johns Hopkins University.

JOHNS HOPKINS UNIVERSITY
PLAN OF BUILDINGS

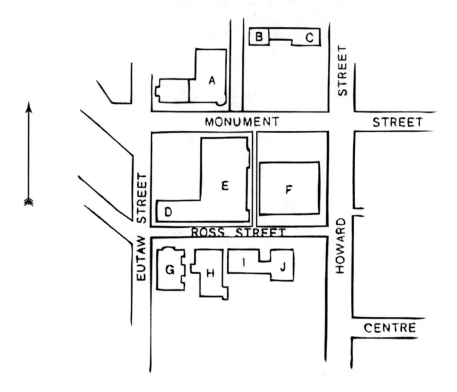

A. Physical Laboratory

B. Power House

C. Treasurer's Office

D. Levering Hall

E. McCoy Half, Administration Bldg.

F. Gymnasium and Cage

G. Biological Laboratory

H. Chemical Laboratory

I. Geological Laboratory

J. State Scientific Bureaus:
   Md. Geological Survey
   Md. State Weather Service
   Md. State Bd. of Forestry
   Md. State Roads Corn.

(circa 1905)

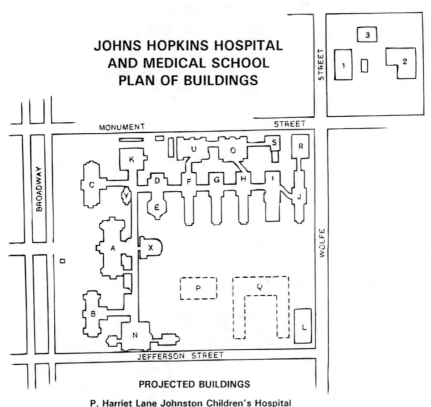

**JOHNS HOPKINS HOSPITAL
AND MEDICAL SCHOOL
PLAN OF BUILDINGS**

PROJECTED BUILDINGS

P. Harriet Lane Johnston Children's Hospital
Q. Phipps Psychiatric Clinic

HOSPITAL
A, Administration
B-C. Pay Wards
D-H. Wards
I. Isolating Ward
J. Colored Ward
K. Kitchen
L. Laundry
N. Nurses' Home
O. Dispensary
R. Pathological

S. Phipps Dispensary
U. Amphitheatre
X. Apothecary
Y. Diet School

MEDICAL SCHOOL
1. Woman's Memorial Building
2. Physiological Laboratory
3. Hunterian Laboratory

(circa 1905)

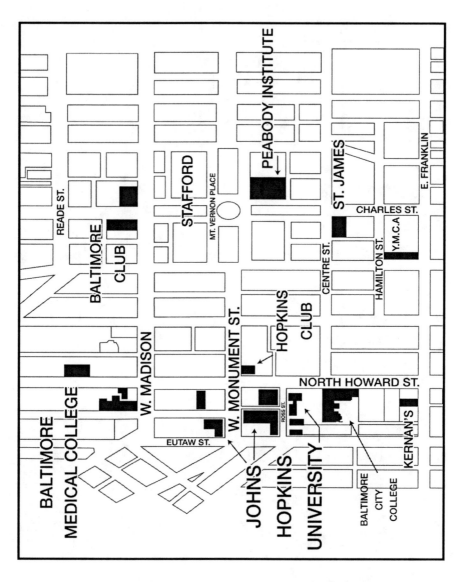

Johns Hopkins University, Johns Hopkins Club and
Peabody Institute (circa 1907)

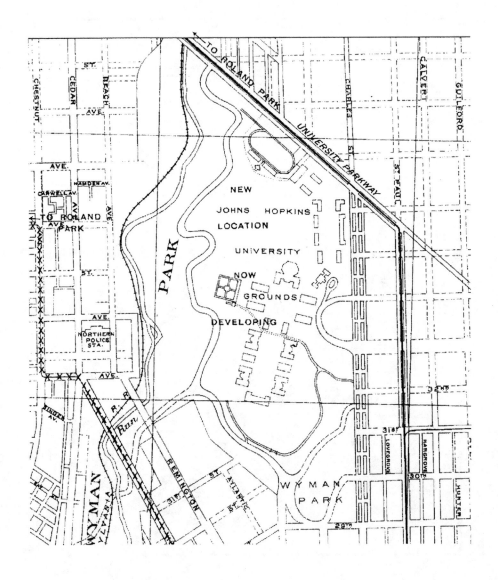

(circa 1907)

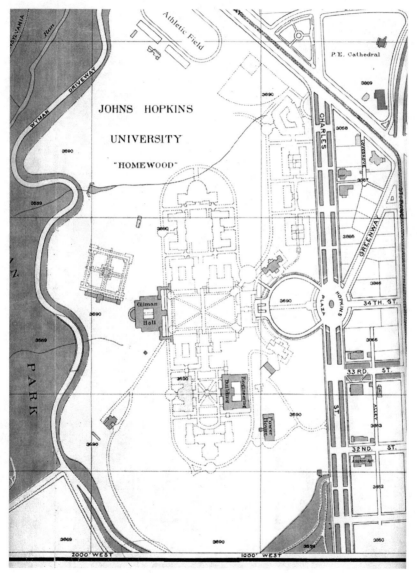

JOHNS HOPKINS

UNIVERSITY

"HOMEWOOD"

(circa 1915)

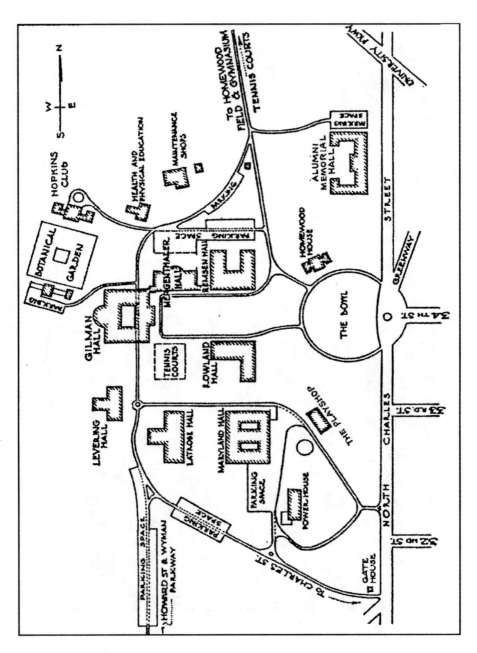

Homewood Campus 1946

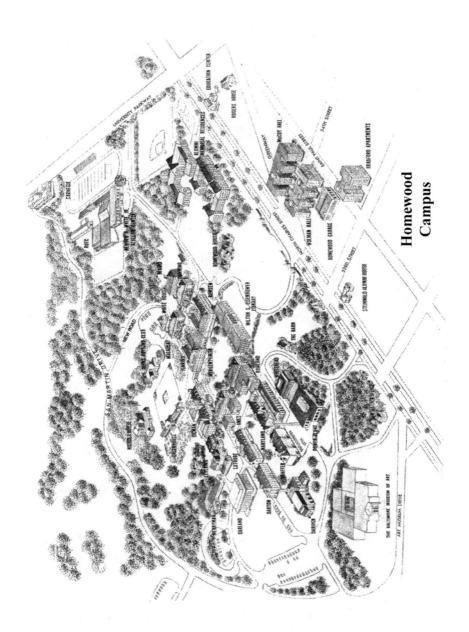

Homewood Campus

Evening College Circular 1979-1980

HOMEWOOD CAMPUS OF THE JOHNS HOPKINS UNIVERSITY

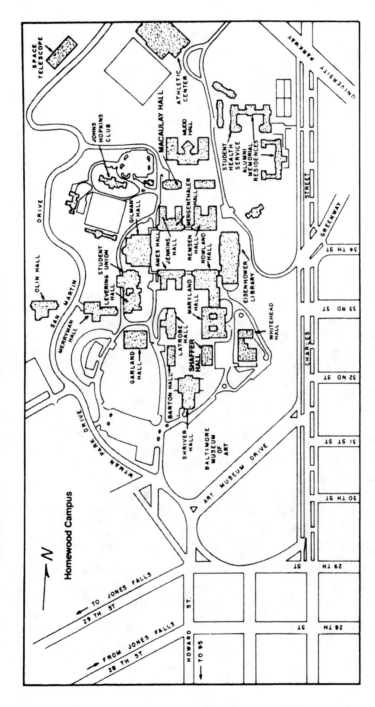

Homewood Campus

School of Continuing Studies Course Schedule 1987-1988

SCHOOL OF CONTINUING STUDIES CENTER
IN DOWNTOWN BALTIMORE

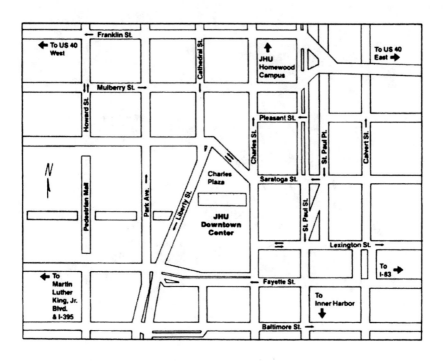

Initial Downtown Center site when located near the corner of Charles and Saratoga Streets

School of Continuing Studies Course Schedule 1987-1988

SCHOOL OF CONTINUING STUDIES CENTER
AT COLUMBIA

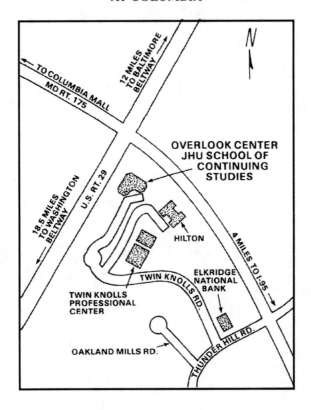

Columbia Center When Located at Twin Knolls

School of Continuing Studies Course Schedule 1987-1988

HOMEWOOD CAMPUS

Eva Lane, Director
Baltimore Regional Centers

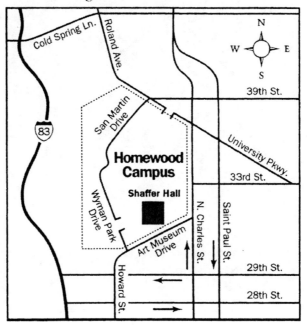

COLUMBIA CENTER
Jackie Deyo, Director

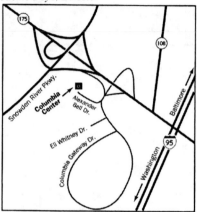

DOWNTOWN CENTER
IN BALTIMORE
Eva Lane, Director
Baltimore Regional Centers

SPSBE Academic Year Catalog 2005-2006

204

MONTGOMERY COUNTY CAMPUS

Blanca Poteat, Director
Washington Regional Centers

WASHINGTON DC CENTER
Blanca Poteat, Director
Washington Regional Centers

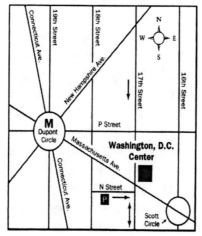

SPSBE Academic Year Catalog 2005-2006

Appendix K
The Ranum Report on Future Directions of the Evening College and Summer Session (Findings Presented during Academic Year 1981–1982)

On November 21, 1980, slightly more than 1½ years before Dean Verhaalen's retirement, Provost Longaker appointed a committee of distinguished professors from throughout the university to review the operations of the college and to consider future directions. More specifically, they were charged to "review all aspects of the Evening College programs, to offer critical analysis of its continued existence, and to recommend a course appropriate for the next ten to twenty years" (Ranum, 1982, p. 7).

Chaired by Dr. Orest Ranum, this committee submitted their report and presented their findings during Academic Year 1981–1982. The committee related that since the Rourke Report in 1970, the college had changed from focusing predominantly on undergraduate students to focusing on graduate students. Although undergraduate programs continued, approximately 70% of the students were enrolled in graduate programs.

> The [Ranum Report] makes a variety of recommendations: (1) a renewed emphasis on

the liberal education of undergraduates, (2) the appointment of discipline oriented Advisory Boards for arts and sciences, for engineering, for the noncredit continuing education function, (3) the transfer of all part-time student engineering programs and degrees to the G.W.C. Whiting School of Engineering; the recommendation was similar to those in the 1981 report of the Westgate Committee and that of the 1980 visiting committee to assess the need for Evening College degree programs accredited by the Accrediting Board for Engineering and Technology (ABET). The Committee's recommendation to transfer engineering programs was additionally based on the Hopkins precedent of having all professional degree programs, full- and part-time, under one jurisdiction as in medicine, nursing, and public health. The Committee also recommended (4) that the Master of Administrative Science degree be retained rather than implementing the MBA and that further full-time faculty in Business not be employed,[27] (5) that the possibility of establishing a Learning Skills Laboratory be explored and (6) that noncredit continuing education should be

---

27 After reading this comment one might think that the future did not have much in store for the college's Business Division. Nevertheless, student enrollments soared, and subsequently the number of Master of Administrative Science (MAS) degrees awarded annually rose from 108 in 1980 to over 400 a decade later. In 1987 (during this same decade) *US News & World Report* rated the Hopkins Business Division as the "third best regionally accredited business school in the eastern United States—third out of 110 competitors from Massachusetts to Virginia" (*US News & World Report*, 1987, p. 83). President Steve Muller wrote, "It was gratifying to have the excellence of the work that is done every semester in this [MAS] program recognized by other business deans" (Muller, 1988, p. 4). Two decades later, the number of full-time professors expanded, from 1 in 1980 to 21 in 2000. Indeed, the Business Division gained a faculty comparable, in terms of size and composition, to that of many conventional business schools. Furthermore, a Master of Business Administration degree (MBA) was offered starting in the summer semester of 1999.

directly related to the primary academic areas of the University and that its mission and scope be reduced, a position that contrasted with that of the Freedman/McMahon Consultant's Report and the Allen Committee's Report.

The Ranum Committee noted that the Education Division with its full-time faculty functioned as do other academic departments at Hopkins; that the College attracted increasing amounts of funds through grants and program support gifts; that the College had a faculty and staff that was enthusiastic, efficient, dedicated, loyal and of high morale; and that the operation of the Evening College continues to provide a net financial benefit to the University (Verhaalen, 1984, p. 52).

In a section of the [Ranum] report entitled *Planning for the Future* the Committee concludes its deliberations with these statements:

As we end our discussions it is apparent that the following working principles are supported by what we have learned.

1. The degree programs and course offerings of the Evening College as they are now constituted meet the needs of well qualified part-time students in the Baltimore–Washington area.

2. The morale of the faculty and staff of the Evening College is high. The dedication to teaching and eagerness to share findings of research carried out in disciplines as they are applied to the inummerable *[sic]* technical questions of our society make the Evening College a powerfully effective complement to other divisions in the University and a service to society.

3. Pre-professional and professional training are the principal functions of the Evening College. On the strength of these

programs rests the reputation of the University in its immediate environs.... Advisory boards of qualified faculty should
review faculty appointments in every part of the Evening
College. The pressure on keeping enrollments at 10 or above
in some courses must be monitored for possible effects on
course requirements and grading. The established procedures
for evaluating teaching ought to be continued....

4. Whenever possible the Evening College should draw upon
faculty and staff from other divisions of the University....

5. The Evening College's strength should be primarily in
graduate education.... At the same time a small, but coherent
undergraduate program must be continued in the Evening
College since the University does not offer undergraduate
part-time education in other divisions....

6. The Evening College's fiscal accountability should rest with the
dean of the Evening College.... The fiscal priorities currently established for the Evening College seem to be consistent
with its mission, and ought to be continued. The "Contribution" that the Evening College makes to the University and its
services to other divisions of the University seem consistent
with its role as primarily a teaching rather than as a research
division of the University.

7. The dependence of the University upon endowed resources
and research funds requires that it make more than the usual
effort to coordinate its efforts in degree programs and faculty
hiring.

8. Whenever possible the Evening College should avail itself of
the support services already available at Homewood and the
Applied Physics Laboratory, to avoid duplicating services for
students and administration.

9. The part-time character of the Evening College faculty, while an asset for Hopkins in many ways, is a liability on matters of curricular and program leadership. Part-time faculty may not be able to serve on committees to review programs and faculty appointments, for example, or to develop the *esprit de corps* of departments, yet their ideas on curricular matters remain indispensable (*Ranum Report*, pp. 35–36).

Appendix L
Master of Science in Business (MSB)
1991–1999

A graduate-level business degree was first offered in 1961, halfway through these 90 reported years of teaching Business Administration at Hopkins (1916–2006). Then, a decade later, in 1971, a second version was introduced, becoming the major degree of the division. A third approach in the evolution of graduate business degrees at Hopkins was introduced in 1991, representing a substantially different approach from the earlier two. In fact, this third approach is better understood by first reviewing the earlier two approaches.

First approach—The Master of Science in Management Science (MSM) (1961–1979). This degree tended to focus on mathematical subjects suitable for careers in engineering. For example, one of its prerequisites required an undergraduate mathematics program through differential equations, including three semesters of calculus and a course in matrix theory or linear algebra, and a one-year course in statistics. Courses in the program included Operations Research, Theory and Analysis of Variance and Regression, and Stochastic Systems. Essentially, this degree was a graduate business degree written by engineers.

Second approach—The Master of Administrative Science (MAS) (1971–1991). This degree at the time was considered a theoretically focused graduate business degree. It required 10 credits of Quantitative Analysis for those who did not have prior courses in this field; other courses, for example, included Management Science, two graduate-level economics courses, and a wide array of equally theoretical courses.

Third approach—The Master of Science in Business (MSB) (1991–1999). This approach represents the thoughtful work of Dr. Judith Broida, Mr. John Baker, Ms. Pam Frankhouser, Ms. Carol Lyles (now Lyles-Shaw), Mr. Jeremy Moyes, and Ms. Cathy A. Trower. The overall idea was to offer a version of the MBA that would help develop potential leaders that employers would want on their team. Surveys and interviews of a wide range of employers yielded valuable information that clearly indicated that employers wanted to hire potential leaders who had people skills and who would be willing the give unselfishly of themselves to help their subordinates and peers. Unwanted was the aggressive backstabber who would sacrifice all for personal career gains. Employers mentioned very little about technical skills, sometimes remarking, "we can teach them the technical skills on the job and what we really need are people who can get along and hopefully inspire subordinates rather than bully them."[28]

Dr. Broida, who led the effort in developing this degree, had just assumed the position of director of the Business Division, having

---

28 It seems that every few years, the general theme in curriculum development for graduate-level business administration returns to the idea of providing employers with the type of graduates they want. Surveys are taken, interviews are conducted, and focus groups are held. It seems to be no surprise that employers are consistent in what they are looking for. Consequently, future attempts are well served by reviewing the curriculum of this MSB degree as they develop their own programs. Critics of behavioral approaches call them "touchy-feely," abstract wastes of time; detractors of practical, nontheoretical approaches claim that the program has moved to a lower level, such as that of the community college, for graduate students. But this is what employers want: potential employers want subordinate leaders who can get the work accomplished without bullying their subordinates. Conversely, in academia, a high value seems to be placed in teaching unusable theory. In contrast, the MSB degree dared to present a practical approach.

worked years earlier in leadership positions in the real world of business, and concurrently completed the MAS degree in 1979. Years later, starting in 1986, she headed the behavioral programs in the Business Division. Consequently, she had clearly formed ideas about the focus of this new degree—that many of the quantitative and theoretical courses should be replaced by leadership courses with a behavioral science approach and, above all, practical courses that filled the needs of potential employers.

Some of the details within the Master of Science in Business program expanded further as the degree was offered for 8½ years (1991–1999). The latest version presented in the Academic Year 1997–1998 catalog describes the extent of the alternatives that students could select from within the MSB degree. In some respects, this particular form seemed to attempt to be all things for all people. In time, however, many of these alternatives would become graduate degree programs in their own right. Then, in 1999, the Master of Science in Business was replaced by a fairly standard MBA as the last of four graduate business degrees, covering a period of 45 years (1961–2006). Portions of the Academic Year 1997–1998 catalog, describing the many alternatives within the MSB degree, are extracted and copied below.

MASTER OF SCIENCE IN BUSINESS

The Master of Science in Business degree focuses on contemporary business themes from a cross-disciplinary viewpoint. The program emphasizes the latest concepts, practices, and skills necessary for effective leadership for professionals from a broad range of backgrounds. The curriculum balances the practical with the theoretical, and includes special emphases on international business, advanced technology, management, business ethics, and workforce diversity.

Course Requirements

Students must complete the required 48 credits in the Division of Business and Management within six years. With approval, a student may transfer a maximum of six graduate credits of prior study from a regionally accredited college or university.

Students begin the program with eight foundation courses that provide the basic building blocks for more advanced study. The curriculum for these courses is based on the common body of knowledge recommended for graduate business education by the American Assembly of Collegiate Schools of Business (AACSB).

Candidates for the MS in Business must complete the following eight courses before registering for any concentration courses. Because the curriculum is flexible, the foundation courses need not be taken in sequence; however, 790.601 Accounting for Decision Making must be completed before 790.603 Managerial Finance.

Outline of the curriculum for the Master of Science in Business degree

	Courses	Credits
Foundation	8	24
Concentration	5	15
General Electives	2	6
Capstone	1	3
Total	16	48

790.601	Accounting for Decision Making
790.602	Business Economics
790.603	Managerial Finance
790.604	Leadership and Organizational Behavior
790.605	Marketing Management
790.607	Information Systems Management
790.608	Management of Human Resources
790.611	Statistics for Business

Concentration Courses (15 credits)

With the assistance of an adviser, students declare a concentration upon completion of their foundation courses. Students then select five courses at the 700 level from the approved concentration list. The program offers six concentration areas:

1. Advanced Business Studies
2. Finance

3. International Business
4. Management
5. Management of Technology
6. Marketing Management

I. Advanced Business Studies

The Advanced Business Studies concentration is designed for students interested in obtaining a broad business background. This option offers depth of knowledge in the primary functional areas of business, including finance, management, marketing, information technology, and leadership. After taking the eight foundation courses, students progress to the following advanced concentration courses:

756.701	Corporate Financial Theory
761.726	Managerial Strategy and Policy
761.736	Advanced Leadership Studies
762.712	Marketing Strategy I
771.730	Seminar in Technology Developments

II. Finance

Financial management is vitally important to the economic health of all companies and individual investors. As we enter the 21st century, the change in the economic structure of the world and its transformation into an information-based economy will continue to have a major impact on the financial systems and markets.

Financial management has become vitally important to understanding, evaluating, and analyzing the technological effects on global financial transactions and its impact on the domestic and international movement of capital. The two tracks in the finance concentration provide an understanding of financial theory and practice as it applies to capital management, valuation, and control.

The two tracks in the finance concentration are the Corporate Finance Track and the Financial Analysis Track.

The Financial Analysis Track is specifically designed to qualify students to sit for the CPA examination while simultaneously obtaining a Master of Science in Business with a Finance concentration. Students interested in this track must consult individually with the Director of Accounting Programs to design a program that meets the requirements for the CPA exam.

1. Corporate Finance Requirements

756.701   Corporate Financial Theory (first concentration course)
(3) Three Concentration Electives
756.710   Advanced Corporate Finance: A Case Study Approach (final concentration course)

Concentration Electives

756.702	Capital Markets
756.724	International Financial Management
756.726	Financial Statement Analysis
756.735	Investment Banking
756.750	Financial Management of the Small Business
756.752	Financial Analysis of Mergers and Acquisitions
756.760	Investment Analysis and Portfolio Management
756.761	Derivative Securities
751.705	Intermediate Financial Accounting
751.709	US Federal Income Tax
751.715	Advanced Financial Accounting
751.722	Cost Accounting
751.731	Auditing

2. Financial Analysis Requirements

Depending on previous academic coursework, students may be required to take the following courses to fulfill the requirements for this track.

756.701	Corporate Financial Theory
751.705	Intermediate Financial Accounting
751.709	US Federal Income Tax
751.715	Advanced Financial Accounting

756.710   Advanced Corporate Finance: A Case Study
           Approach

General Electives

751.722   Cost Accounting
751.731   Auditing

III. International Business

The growth of international business has been a major stimulus for economic change. Capital markets are expanding, major trade alliances are forming throughout the world, and companies are developing partnerships and other relationships through mergers and acquisitions.

Students concentrating in international business explore corporate reaction to this globalization. Major areas of focus include international finance, regional analyses, marketing, management and technology.

International Business Requirements

753.700   International Trade and Monetary Theory (first concentration course)
753.761   Case Studies in International Business

Note: Students concentrating in International business must take three of the concentration electives listed below.

Concentration Electives

756.719   Latin America: A Regional Analysis
756.720   Europe in the '90s: Economic and Political Restructuring
756.722   The Pacific Rim: A Study in International Trade
756.724   International Finance Management
756.762   Emerging Markets
761.721   Global Strategic Management
761.737   Cross-cultural Management
771.715   Technology in International Business
762.719   International Marketing

IV. Management

The role of managers and leaders today is constantly changing. Contemporary managers must engage in new and innovative problem solving strategies, lead a diverse and global workforce, develop partnerships with customers and competitors, manage horizontally and across teams, and utilize technology as a competitive advantage. These new demands affect all organizations—public, nonprofit, corporate, education, and the small business owner. The management concentration is designed to prepare students for the leadership challenges of the next century.

Students may choose any five 700 level management course selections to fulfill the concentration requirement, or they may take all five courses from one of the three management concentration areas: Strategic Management, Entrepreneurial Management, and Change Management.

Note: All students are required to complete 761.726, Managerial Strategy and Policy, as part of the Management concentration.

Concentration Areas:

1. Strategic Management

761.721	Global Strategic Management
761.722	Managerial Integrity and Ethics
761.724	Project and Team Management
761.725	Management Decisions: Judgment and Tools
761.736	Advanced Leadership Studies
761.744	Health Care Management and Policy
771.750	Seminar in Technology Developments
756.752	Financial Analysis of Mergers and Acquisitions

2. Entrepreneurial Management

761.725	Business Law
761.730	Management: A New Paradigm
761.735	Business Planning: Start-Up
761.736	Advanced Leadership Studies
771.750	Seminar in Technology Developments

756.750　　Financial Management of the Small Business

3. Change Management

761.707　　The Management of Quality
761.728　　Managerial Assessment and Organizational Culture
761.737　　Cross-cultural Management
761.738　　The Minority Manager
761.743　　Leading the Changing Organization
782.713　　Diversity and Conflict in Organizations
782.741　　The Art and Practice of Becoming a Learning Organization

V. Management of Technology

The rapid advances in technology today require all managers to fully understand the current developments in information technology and their application to the work environment. The curriculum provides managers with the knowledge and skills necessary to plan for and to manage technology to develop and implement effective information and telecommunication systems that solve problems and achieve organization goals and objectives.

Select five courses (at least three must be 700 level courses) to fulfill the concentration requirement:

772.611　　Information System Architecture
772.612　　Telecommunication System Architecture
772.614　　Systems Analysis and Design
771.710　　Organizational and Legal Issues in Technology
771.713　　Re-engineering Through Technology
771.715　　Technology in International Business
771.719　　Technology Transfer
771.750　　Seminar in Technology Developments
773.750　　Advanced Topics in Information Technology
775.701　　Strategic Planning for Information Systems
775.704　　Information Systems Economics
775.715　　Facility Management
775.730　　Project Management for Information Systems

VI. Marketing Management

Marketing expertise has emerged as the key factor in determining the success of many organizations. Corporations, nonprofit organizations, and entrepreneurial businesses are intensifying their marketing efforts and perfecting strategic marketing plans as they grow and change. The marketing concentration prepares students to lead organizations through complex challenges in the global marketplace. State-of-the-art marketing practices, theories, and trends are combined in results-oriented courses that equip students with the skills and knowledge necessary to make sound marketing decisions in an increasingly market-driven, competitive economy.

Select five 700-level courses to fulfill the concentration requirement:

762.701	Marketing Ethics
762.702	Consumer Behavior
762.703	Customer Service: Strategy and Tactics
762.704	Professional Selling
762.705	Managing the Sales Force
762.706	Negotiation for Effective Selling
762.707	Advertising Campaigns
762.708	Creative Concept Development
762.711	Promotional Strategy and Management
762.712	Marketing Strategy I
762.713	Marketing Law
762.716	New Product Development
762.717	Marketing Research I
762.718	Marketing Research II
762.719	International Marketing
762.720	Marketing Strategy II (prerequisite: Marketing Strategy)
762.721	Marketing and High Technology
762.722	Business-to-Business Marketing

* General Elective Courses (6 credits)

In addition to the foundation curriculum, the concentration requirement, and the Capstone course, students select two additional courses (six credits) from the list of approved 500-level general business courses. Alternatively, after students declare a concentration, they may choose electives from among 700-level MS in Business concentration courses.

1. Finance and International Business

756.555	Personal Investing
790.505	Analytical Tools for Business

2. Management

761.330	Business Presentations for Managers
761.555	Management for Productivity
790.501	Business Communications

3. Management of Technology

771.570	Information and Telecommunications Concepts
790.505	Analytical Tools for Business

4. Applied Behavioral Science

782.578	Building Teams and Developing Teamwork
782.598	Effective Negotiation and Conflict Management

5. Marketing Management

762.551	Public Relations and Publicity
762.552	The Practice of Advertising
762.553	Marketing of Services

* Capstone Courses (3 credits)

Students complete the Capstone requirement (790.801 The Application of Business Policy) as the final course in the MS in Business program. The Capstone, which is interdisciplinary and case based, provides an opportunity to synthesize and apply all previous graduate coursework through the evaluation of business policy decisions. Cases used in the course are based on regional organizations.

ACCELERATED MASTER OF SCIENCE IN BUSINESS

The Accelerated Master of Science in Business Program is intended for individuals with an undergraduate degree in business and progressive professional experience. The program builds upon business knowledge acquired as an undergraduate, and professional experience gained in the workplace. This program requires 33 credit hours rather than the 48 credit hours required for the traditional Master of Science in Business.

Admission

Admission to the program is highly selective and is based on an evaluation of the candidate's academic achievements, professional experience, and accomplishments that indicate the potential for significant management and leadership roles.

Applicants are expected to meet the general requirements for admission to a School of Continuing Studies graduate program. In addition, applicants for the accelerated program must hold a bachelor's degree in a business discipline, generally earned within the past eight years, from a regionally accredited college or university. Candidates must have a strong academic record; most admitted have a cumulated grade point average of 3.2 or better. Applicants also must have completed the undergraduate equivalent of the MS in Business foundation course requirements. In addition, they must demonstrate management ability and leadership potential. Three or more years of experience in a business or professional environment is preferred.

Program Requirements

Students must complete the required 33 credits for the Accelerated MS in Business degree within four years.

	Courses	Credits
Core	5	15
Concentration	5	15
Capstone	1	3
Total	11	33

* **Core Courses (15 credits)**

Candidates for the Accelerated MS in Business are required to complete these core courses before registering for the Capstone. The core courses may be taken in any sequence:

753.700   International Trade and Monetary Theory
756.701   Corporate Financial Theory
761.726   Managerial Strategy and Policy
762.712   Marketing Strategy I
771.750   Seminar in Technology Developments

* **Concentration Courses (15 credits)**

With the assistance of an adviser, students declare a concentration and then select a minimum of five concentration courses at the 700 level from the approved list. The program offers five concentration areas.

I. Finance
II. International Business
III. Management
IV. Management of Technology
V. Marketing Management

* **Capstone Courses (3 credits)**

Students complete the Capstone requirements (790.801 The Application of Business Policy) as the final course in the program. The Capstone, which is interdisciplinary and case based, provides an opportunity to synthesize and apply all previous graduate course work through the evaluation of business policy decisions. Cases used in the course are based on regional organizations (SCS AY Catalog, 1997–1998, pp. 60–64).

Appendix M
Master of Business Administration
(MBA) 1999–Present

During September 1979, I had the privilege of accompanying Dean Roman Verhaalen (then-dean of the Evening College and Summer Session) when he met with President Steve Muller in his office in Garland Hall. After discussing business programs, President Muller asked for my thoughts about the Master of Administrative Science (MAS) degree, then the division's graduate business degree. I responded that the name of the degree was unknown and that what we needed instead was a Master of Business Administration (MBA) degree. President Muller explained why Hopkins did not offer an MBA degree. Almost a decade earlier, when President Milton Eisenhower submitted a proposal for an MBA to the State Board of Higher Education, the proposal was subsequently submitted to local colleges for comments. Father Sellinger, then-director of Loyola's business programs, objected because it would reduce enrollments in Loyola's MBA. Consequently, President Muller, Dean Verhaalen, and Father Sellinger met to resolve the matter and agreed that Hopkins would offer an alternative degree; however, Hopkins would also have the right to have an MBA degree when all three of them departed from their current positions. By the summer semester of 1999, Hopkins was long overdue for an MBA, since two of these men had died and the third had been retired for several years.

In 1998, Dr. Gene Swanson, a former accounting professor at Loyola and a knowledgeable person about MBA programs, was selected to develop and launch the long-awaited Hopkins MBA program. Although there was a substantial involvement of the Hopkins business faculty, the final draft of the MBA curriculum consisted of a rather standard MBA program offered at many business schools. Indeed, that is what the faculty and staff wanted—something that would generally fit the AACSB mold and in time be part of an overall effort to gain AACSB accreditation. Launched during the summer semester of 1999, the new and very popular MBA program consisted of a 54-credit program. Although changes were made from 1999 to 2006, the final version before the start of the Carey Business School on January 1, 2007, is presented here as a verbatim extract from the Academic Catalog for 2005–2006.

PROGRAM REQUIREMENTS

The MBA program of 54 credits consists of required foundation and core courses, five concentration or elective courses, and an innovative Capstone course. After completing the required courses, students should contact their advisers to declare concentrations or electives they intend to pursue. Students are expected to be proficient in the latest MS Office software. Students must complete the programs of study within six years.

In electing courses, students must adhere to the following requirements:
* Register for a course only when its prerequisite courses or additional stated requirements are completed.
* Complete all foundation courses prior to taking any core or elective courses.
* Register for the Capstone course in the final semester and after completion of all required courses; only one elective course may be taken during the same semester as the Capstone course.

The MBA program offers an innovative Executive Leadership Ethics course sequence that is required for all students admitted to the MBA program beginning with the fall semester 2003. These three one-credit courses are designed to prepare Hopkins

MBA graduates to meet the ethical challenges of business and managerial leadership in a complex global economy. Conducted in an intensive, interactive pass/fail workshop format, the three courses are taken sequentially in the required and elective phases of the MBA curriculum.

Students are encouraged to complete the foundation ethics requirement, 761.624 Foundations of Moral Leadership, in their first semester of enrollment. This requirement must be completed within the first two semesters of enrollment. The core ethics requirement, 761.728 Moral Leadership and the Global Economy, must be completed prior to enrolling in any elective courses. The third ethics requirement, 761.729 Moral Leadership and Business Practice, is designed to be taken with the MBA elective courses and should be completed before enrolling in the MBA Capstone.

CURRICULUM

An outline of the curriculum for the Master of Business Administration degree follows:

	Courses	Credits
Required Courses (Foundation & Core Courses)	14	38
Concentration or Elective Courses	5	13
Capstone	1	3
Total	20	54

* **Foundation Courses (16 credits)**

761.624	Foundations of Moral Leadership (1 credit)
790.609	Financial Management
790.611	Financial Accounting
790.614	Business, Government and the World Economy
790.615	Marketing Management
790.616	Statistics for Business

* **Core Courses** (22 credits)

| 753.701 | Managerial Economics |

756.701	Corporate Finance
761.700	Managerial Communication
761.728	Moral Leadership and the Global Economy (1 credit)
761.731	Management and Organizational Behavior
762.703	Marketing Strategy
771.732	Quantitative Decision Making for Business
771.750	Information Technology Integration for Business

Concentration or Elective Courses (13 credits)

After they complete their required courses and with assistance of their advisers, students choose the electives they intend to pursue or declare a concentration. The courses, 761.729 Moral Leadership and Business Practice, should be taken with the MBA concentration courses or electives.

MBA Concentrations

Students interested in more focused study may choose from one of the 11 concentrations, following the requirements listed below.

I. Accounting
II. Competitive Intelligence
III. Finance
IV. Human Resources
V. Information Security Management
VI. Information Technology
VII. International Business
VIII. Management
IX. Marketing Management
X. Nonprofit Management
XI. Senior Living and Health Care

I. Accounting

The Accounting concentration is designed for the student who wants to pursue a career in accounting and/or as a financial manager. The curriculum provides students with the accounting and financial courses and knowledge base that are needed to qualify for professional credentials such as Certified Public Accounting (CPA), Certified Management Accounting (CMA), Certified Financial Manager (CFM), and Chartered Financial Analyst (CFA).

Accounting Requirements

1. 751.705 Intermediate Financial Accounting (required)
2. 761.729 Moral Leadership and Business Practice (required)
3. Two or three Accounting electives selected from the following:

751.604	Managerial Accounting
751.709	U.S. Federal Income Tax
751.715	Advanced Financial Accounting
751.722	Cost Accounting
751.731	Auditing
756.726	Financial Statement Analysis

4. Optional: One finance elective selected from the following:

756.710	Advanced Corporate Finance: A Case Study Approach
756.724	International Financial Management
756.732	Econometrics in Finance
756.752	Mergers, Acquisitions, and Valuation
756.760	Investment Analysis and Portfolio

II. Competitive Intelligence

Competitive intelligence (CI), as defined by the Society of Competitive Intelligence Professionals (SCIP), is a "systematic and ethical program for gathering, analyzing, and managing external information that can affect your organization's plans, decisions, and operations."

Competitive intelligence should be part of everyone's job description—from president to analysts. Areas where CI professionals work include competitive intelligence or analysis; marketing planning, research, or analysis; strategic planning; information center or services; business development/product planning/R&D; financial planning/counterintelligence; and others.

Through the Competitive Intelligence concentration, students can apply leading-edge decision-making, analytical, and knowledge management techniques, strategies, tools, and methodologies to enhance organizational intelligence. The "professional of tomorrow" will need to possess these knowledge areas and skill sets to be competitive in the marketplace.

Competitive Intelligence Requirements

1. 761.729 Moral Leadership and Business Practice (required)
2. Students take the following four courses to fulfill the concentration requirements.

771.710   Organizational and Legal Issues in Technology
773.721   Competitive Intelligence
773.701   Data Mining and Discovery Informatics
776.716   Knowledge Management Systems

III. Finance

The Finance concentration provides a comprehensive understanding of corporate finance, securities analysis, portfolio management, and financial institutions and markets. Students who elect to pursue an MBA concentration in Finance typically work as financial or investment analysts in corporations, investment firms, or financial institutions.

A grade of B or better must be earned in 756.701 Corporate Finance to declare a concentration in Finance.

Finance Requirements

1. 756.710   Advanced Corporate Finance: A Case Study Approach (required)
2. 761.729   Moral Leadership and Business Practice (required)
3. Three Finance electives selected from the following:
   751.705   Intermediate Financial Accounting
   753.724   Global Entrepreneurship: A Case Study Seminar
   756.711   Applied Corporate Finance
   756.715   Financial Risk Management
   756.720   Fixed Income Securities
   756.724   International Financial Management

756.726	Financial Statement Analysis
756.730	Financial Modeling
756.731	Financial Institutions Management
756.732	Econometrics in Finance
756.752	Mergers, Acquisitions, and Valuation
756.760	Investment Analysis and Portfolio Management
756.761	Derivative Securities
756.780	Advanced Portfolio Management

IV. Human Resources

Students learn about the development and management of the workforce and how individuals, through their performance, enhance the value of organizations.

Human Resources Requirements

1. 782.720 Critical Issues in the Development and Management of Human Resources

   Note: This must be the first course taken for the Human Resources concentration.
2. 761.729 Moral Leadership and Business Practice
3. 782.714 Human Resources, Labor Relations and Employment Law
4. 782.723 Performance Analysis and Improvement Strategies
5. Choose one concentration course from the following:

782.706	Career Management
782.712	Staffing, Recruitment, and Selection
782.715	Compensation and Benefits
782.724	Principles of Training and Development

V. Information Security Analysis

Organizations are increasingly aware of the devastating effects of security breaches—viruses and worms infecting computer networks. This sense of urgency has spurred the creation of a wide range of new technologies, but they must be thoughtfully integrated with well-designed policies, practices, processes, and training. The information security management concentration will complement the broader MBA courses with knowledge of the issues, techniques, and best practices for managing the information security function in an organization.

Information Security Management Requirements

1. 773.719 Information Security Foundations
2. 761.729 Moral Leadership and Business Practice
3. Choose any three of the following courses:

774.715 Financial Issues in Managing a Security Operation
774.716 Security Architecture
774.717 Implementing Effective Information Security Programs
776.754 E-Business Security

VI. Information Technology

Rapid changes in information technology provide enormous challenges and opportunities for modern business. The Information Technology concentration is designed for students who have entered the MBA with strong technical backgrounds and want to increase or broaden their technical knowledge as part of their MBA or for those students who want a more general technology concentration.

Information Technology Requirements

1. 761.729 Moral Leadership and Business Practice (required)
2. Students choose four courses from the list below to fulfill the concentration requirements.

770.515 Database Management Systems: Structure and Design
770.517 Information and Telecommunication Systems Architecture
770.610 Business Telecommunications
770.618 Project Management for Information Systems
770.627 IT Strategic and Change Management
771.710 Organizational and Legal Issues in Technology
771.713 Business Processes and Change Management

771.751	The Internet and Electronic Commerce
771.760	Electronic Business Strategies
773.700	Database Development and Programing
773.701	Data Mining and Discovery Informatics
773.719	Information Security Foundations
773.721	Competitive Intelligence
773.750	Advanced Topic in Information Technology
773.752	Basic Web Site Development and Information Architecture
774.701	Telecommunication Systems and Network Design Analysis
774.702	Enterprise Network Systems
774.715	Financial Issues in Managing a Secure Operation
774.716	Security Architecture
774.717	Implementing Effective Information Security Programs
774.760	Wireless and Broadband Communications
776.716	Knowledge Management Systems
776.736	IT Enterprise Architecture
776.754	E-Business Security

VII. International Business

The growth of international business has been a major stimulus for worldwide economic change. Capital markets are expanding, major trade alliances are forming throughout the world, and companies are developing international, global alliances, partnerships, and other relationships through mergers and acquisitions.

Students concentrating in international business explore corporate reaction to and participation in this globalization. Major areas of focus include international economics, international finance, emerging markets and entrepreneurship, marketing, management, and technology.

International Business Requirements

1. 753.761 Case Studies in International Business (required)
2. 761.729 Moral Leadership and Business Practice (required)

3. Three concentration electives selected from the following:

753.700	International Trade and Monetary Theory
753.724	Global Entrepreneurship: A Case Study Seminar
753.762	Emerging Markets: Developing & Transitional Economies
756.724	International Financial Management
761.721	Global Strategic Management
761.737	Cross-Cultural Management
762.719	International Marketing
771.715	International Business and the Electronic Marketplace

VIII. Management

Today's managers must engage in new and innovative problem-solving strategies, lead a diverse and global workforce, develop partnerships with customers and competitors, manage horizontally and across teams, and utilize technology for competitive advantage.

These new demands affect all organizations—public, nonprofit, corporate, education, and small business. The management concentration is designed to prepare students for leadership challenges, problem solving, and decision making in organizations.

Management Requirements

1. 761.729 Moral Leadership and Business Practice
2. 761.726 Managerial Strategy and Policy (required concentration course for all students declared in management)
3. Choose three concentration courses from the following:

753.724	Global Entrepreneurship: A Case Study Seminar
761.721	Global Strategic Management
761.723	Business Law
761.724	Project and Team Management
761.725	Management Decisions: Judgment and Tools
761.XXX	Cross-Cultural Communication
761.XXX	Risk Communication

761.730	Business and Management Case Studies in Leadership Ethics
761.735	Business and Fiscal Planning: Start-Up
761.740	Entrepreneurship
782.705	Conflict Resolution and Mediation Process
782.718	Facilitating Strategic Planning, Problem-Solving, and Decision-Making
782.736	Advanced Topics in Organizational Learning and Change
782.743	Advanced Leadership Theory & Practice
782.747	Leading Organizations: Strategy, Structure, and Roles
782.749	Managing for Competitive Advantage: Diversity and the Global Workforce

IX. Marketing Management

Marketing and social marketing expertise have emerged as key factors in determining the success of many organizations. Corporations, nonprofit organizations, governmental and public sector organizations, and entrepreneurial businesses increasingly recognize the key roles marketing plays in achieving their goals, whether those goals involve growing a business or influencing social conduct. The Marketing Management concentration prepares students to lead organizations through complex challenges in the global marketplace. State-of-the-art marketing practices, theories, and trends are combined in results-oriented courses that equip students with the skills and knowledge necessary to make sound marketing decisions.

Marketing Management Requirements

1. 761.729 Moral Leadership and Business Practice
2. 762.702 Consumer Behavior Analysis
3. 762.717 Marketing Research I
4. Students elect two courses from the following list:

762.706	Marketing Negotiations and Bargaining
762.711	Promotional Strategy, Management and Design
762.719	International Marketing

762.722	Business-to-Business Marketing
762.732	Brand Management (formerly Brand Management and Pricing Strategies)
762.755	Marketing of Services
762.756	Special Topics in Marketing

All other courses offered through the marketing department are open to Master of Science in Marketing students only.

X. Nonprofit Management

The MBA concentration in Nonprofit Management, offered in partnership with the Johns Hopkins Institute for Policy Studies (IPS), addresses the managerial philanthropic/volunteer needs of the large and rapidly expanding nonprofit and public service sectors of the U.S. and global economy. Leadership in nonprofit and public service sectors requires a unique set of knowledge, skills, and judgment capabilities not emphasized in the traditional profit-oriented MBA program. The MBA concentration in Nonprofit Management prepares midlevel managers and professionals for executive leadership roles in nonprofit and public sector organizations. The Nonprofit Management concentration is also useful for management consultants whose practice includes nonprofit and public sector clients.

Nonprofit Management Requirements

1. 786.701 The Nonprofit Sector: Scope, Structure, and Dynamics
2. 786.702 Managing the Nonprofit Organization: A Strategic Framework
3. 786.703 Partnering for Results
4. 786.704 Financial Management for Nonprofits (1.5 credits)
5. 761.729 Moral Leadership and Business Practice (required)
6. Choose at least one elective from the following courses (1.5 credits each):

786.705	Ethics and Accountability
786.706	Resource Development (Fundraising)
786.707	Advocacy I
786.708	Advocacy II

786.709   Marketing
786.710   Leadership
786.711   Program Development
786.712   Conflict Resolution
786.713   Evaluation and Monitoring for Nonprofits
7. Capstone: 786.801 Competitive Strategy for Nonprofits (required for students concentrating in

Nonprofit Management in place of 790.801 Competitive Strategy)

XI. Senior Living and Health Care

Senior housing and long-term care impacts not only the real estate industry, but also the healthcare industry. Demographics and the changing capital markets provide opportunities for innovative development, investment, and management in the senior housing and long-term care industry. Financial institutions and real estate and health care firms can be expanded or restructured to take advantage of this opportunity if they understand the risks and uncertainties. Public and private real estate or health care specialists, management consultants and industry analysts, lawmakers and policymakers, trade association executives and professionals, and investors will find this track valuable.

Senior Living Requirements

1. 767.610 The Senior Living and Health Care Enterprise
2. 767.620 Seniors Housing and Health Care Development
3. 767.630 Marketing Issues for the Senior Living and Health Care Marketplace
4. 767.640 Senior Living and Health Care Business Operations and Management
5. 761.729 Moral Leadership and Business Practice

General MBA Electives

Students pursuing 12 credits of electives in lieu of a specific concentration can choose from several 600- or 700-level courses in a variety of discipline areas. However, students must meet all course prerequisite(s) prior to course registration. The following is a list of criteria for general elective course selection as specified by each department.

Ethics

All courses above the three required courses are acceptable.

Marketing

All courses under the MBA/Marketing Management concentration are acceptable. All other courses offered through the marketing department are limited to concentration majors only.

Management

All courses under the MBA/Management concentration are acceptable, provided prerequisite requirements listed have been fulfilled.

Nonprofit Management

All courses under the MBA/Nonprofit Management concentration are acceptable, provided prerequisite requirements have been fulfilled.

Real Estate

The following selected courses from the Master of Science in Real Estate program may be taken for a general concentration with department approval and provided that prerequisites have been met. All other courses in this area are limited to concentration majors only.

767.691	Foreign Real Estate Development
767.699	International Real Estate Markets
767.700	Real Estate Enterprise
767.710	Real Estate Analysis
767.776	Real Estate Finance
767.777	Real Estate Investments
767.786	Quantitative Real Estate Portfolio Analysis
767.796	Real Estate Portfolio Management
767.797	Real Estate Capital Markets

Organization Development and Strategic Human Resources

All courses under the MBA/Human Resources concentration are acceptable, provided that any prerequisites have been met. Courses in the ODSHR program are restricted unless approved by the department's program adviser.

Accounting

All courses under the Accounting concentration are acceptable, provided prerequisite requirements have been fulfilled.

Finance

All courses under the Finance concentration are acceptable, provided prerequisite requirements have been fulfilled.

International Business

All courses under the International Business concentration are acceptable, provided prerequisite requirements have been fulfilled.

Information Technology

All 77X.XXX courses can be taken, provided prerequisite requirements have been fulfilled, with the exception of 770.600 IT Budget and Financial Management and 770.601 Technical Writing.

MBA Capstone Course (3 credits)

All MBA students must complete the Capstone requirement as their final course in the MBA program. The Capstone course, 790.801 Competitive Strategy, is interdisciplinary and provides an opportunity to synthesize and apply knowledge and skills from graduate course work through the evaluation of business policy decisions. The Capstone course may be offered in different formats. Cases are based on real organizations. In some semesters, the program may offer the experience in two or more of the following options: a case involving a traditional business organization, one involving a nonprofit or public sector organization, one involving an entrepreneurial or start-up organization, or an individual or group project.

The Capstone course is open only to MBA students. All required courses and the Level III ethics seminar (761.729 Moral Leadership and Business Practice) must be completed prior to enrolling for the Capstone.

Weekend MBA

The Hopkins Weekend MBA Program is designed for individuals unable to attend classes during the week. Weekend MBA classes meet on Saturdays. The MBA degree can be earned in two years. Admissions decisions are made on a rolling basis, but space is limited. Students in the Weekend Program take a pre-set array of courses determined by the MBA program. All students take all of the courses as a cohort and may not waive courses, substitute courses, or transfer credit for courses taken elsewhere. Students who wish to pick electives or waive courses should enroll in Johns Hopkins regular, flexible MBA program. Students who are interested in the cohort locations and schedule should visit business.jhu.edu/mba/weekendmba.cfm, or contact the MBA program office (SPSBE Academic Year Catalog 2005–2006, pp. 74–80).

Appendix N
Statistics: School of Professional Studies in Business and Education[29]

1. School of Professional Studies in Business and Education, two-page handout (circa 2006)

2. School of Professional Studies in Business and Education, three-page fact sheet (circa 2006)

---

29 Although these two handouts accurately reflect the history of the Graduate Division of Education, the portion of the school's history pertaining to the Division of Undergraduate Studies and the Graduate Division of Business and Management are shown below.

Fall 1916–spring 1919	Courses in Business Economics
Fall 1919–spring 1920	Courses in Business and Social Economics
Fall 1920–spring 1923	Courses in Business Economics
Fall 1923–spring 1947	Evening Courses in Business Economics
Fall 1947–spring 1953	Evening Courses in Business Economics

(known as the Business School)

Fall 1953-In 1953, the Department of Business Economics is disestablished, transferring its students from the Faculty of Philosophy (now the Krieger School of Arts and Sciences) to McCoy College and relocating their offices from Gilman Hall, Room 318, to the basement of Shriver Hall. Full- and part-time offerings continue only as part-time classes.

The school's history after the start of the fall semester of 1953 is identical for both Business and Education.

JOHNS HOPKINS
UNIVERSITY

SCHOOL OF PROFESSIONAL STUDIES
IN BUSINESS AND EDUCATION

The School of Professional Studies in Business and Education (SPSBE) has a long history of educating leaders who, in turn, improve the quality of life in their communities and beyond.

With a commitment to developing and applying best practices to meet societal and workforce needs, the School focuses on creating innovative programs, often in partnership with regional corporations, school systems, nonprofit organizations, and government agencies.

Through these partnerships, the School's faculty, students, and alumni attend to some of the most challenging issues that face urban communities: improving educational outcomes for children, creating safe neighborhoods, cultivating minority leadership, developing better housing for seniors, and fostering economic stability and growth. Many of these university-community partnerships have been recognized and adopted as national models.

Enrollment*

Undergraduate —900
Graduate —4,000
Noncredit —2,500

Living Alumni —28,000

Student Profile

Male —39%
Female —61%
Average Age —32

Student/
Faculty Ratio—15:1

The **Graduate Division of Business and Management** is home to the MBA as well as nationally recognized programs such as Hopkins Business of Medicine and the Leadership Development Program for Minority Managers. The Division's Edward St. John Department of Real Estate features the only program of its kind focused on the field of Senior Living.

The **Graduate Division of Education** is the leading provider of master's degrees in education

across Maryland. In partnership with Baltimore City and other regional school districts, the division has developed innovative programs to support the recruitment, preparation, and retention of teachers, principals, and other educational leaders.

SPSBE AT A GLANCE

Founded in 1909, the School was the first to:

• Offer Johns Hopkins degrees for working professionals enrolled on a part-time basis

• Enroll women as undergraduates on the Homewood campus

• Extend Johns Hopkins' reach across the region through off-campus centers

Academic Programs

SPSBE's four academic divisions offer an array of bachelor's and master's degree programs, undergraduate and graduate certificates, and the degree of doctor of education. Flexible formats meet the needs of working professionals.

*Rounded numbers

The **Division of Public Safety Leadership** features bachelor's and master's degrees in law enforcement, fire and EMS leadership, homeland security leadership, and intelligence analysis. The Police Executive Leadership Program, the first of its kind, counts more than 30 chiefs of police among its alumni.

SPSBE's **Division of Undergraduate Studies** sustains a vibrant learning community for adult students who are pursuing bachelor's degrees while managing the demands of family and work life.

The school also offers two noncredit programs: the Odyssey program, which features liberal arts courses and lecture series for adults; and the Evergreen program, which provides educational and social opportunities for semi-retired and retired individuals.

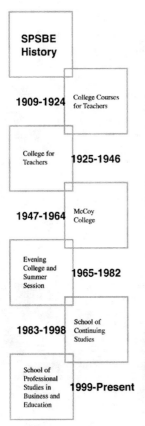

SPSBE History

1909-1924 College Courses for Teachers

College for Teachers **1925-1946**

1947-1964 McCoy College

Evening College and Summer Session **1965-1982**

1983-1998 School of Continuing Studies

School of Professional Studies in Business and Education **1999-Present**

Academic Programs

Graduate Division of Business and Management
410-516-0755
busspsbe@jhu.edu

Graduate Division of Education
410-516-8273
edspsbe@jhu.edu

Division of Public Safety Leadership
410-312-4400
pelp@jhu.edu

Division of Undergraduate Studies
410-516-0775
ugspsbe@jhu.edu

Centers for Applied Research

Center for Research and Reform in Education
410-616-2310
rslavin@cddre.org

Center for Technology in Education
410-312-3800
cte@jhu.edu

Noncredit Programs

Odyssey
410-516-4842
odyssey@jhu.edu

Evergreen
410-309-9531
evergreen@jhu.edu

SPSBE Campus Locations

Columbia Center
From Baltimore:
410-290-1777
From Washington, DC:
301-621-3377
colspsbe@jhu.edu

Downtown Center in Baltimore
410-516-0700
dtcspsbe@jhu.edu

Homewood Campus
410-516-7185
hwdspsbe@jhu.edu

Montgomery County Campus
301-294-7040
mccspsbe@jhu.edu

Washington, DC Center
202-588-0597
wdcspsbe@jhu.edu

Administrative Offices

Office of the Dean
410-516-7820

Office of Academic Affairs
410-516-7820

Admissions
410-872-1234
spsbe.admissions@jhu.edu

Career Services
410-290-1934
From Washington, DC:
301-621-3377
careerservices@jhu.edu

Center for Teaching and Learning
410-312-2899
ctl@jhu.edu

Development
410-516-7567
spsbedevelopment@jhu.edu

External Affairs
410-516-7188
spsbe.external.affairs@jhu.edu

Financial Operations
410-516-8593

Marketing and Communications
410-516-6680
SPSBE Magazine:
spsmag@jhu.edu

Student and Alumni Services
410-309-1270
studentalumni@jhu.edu

JOHNS HOPKINS
UNIVERSITY

SCHOOL OF PROFESSIONAL STUDIES
IN BUSINESS AND EDUCATION

Shaffer Hall • 3400 N. Charles Street
Baltimore, MD 21218-2680

WWW.SPSBE.JHU.EDU

SCHOOL OF PROFESSIONAL STUDIES IN BUSINESS AND EDUCATION

HISTORY AND OVERVIEW

Many factors contribute to the quality of life in communities—economic vitality, quality schools, an atmosphere of safety and security, and opportunities for personal and professional development. The School of Professional Studies in Business and Education has a long history of educating leaders who, in turn, improve the quality of life in their communities and beyond.

Founded in 1909 as College Courses for Teachers, the school has borne several names that reflect its dynamic evolution. Today, it offers flexible format programs designed to meet the diverse needs of working professionals. The School offers graduate and undergraduate programs in its four academic divisions: Business, Education, Public Safety Leadership, and Undergraduate Studies. In addition, the School furthers its applied research activities through the Real Estate Institute, the Center for Technology in Education, and the Center for Reading Excellence.

With a commitment to developing and applying best practices to meet societal and workforce needs, the School focuses on creating innovative programs, often in partnership with regional corporations, nonprofit organizations, and government agencies. Through these partnerships, the School's faculty, students, and alumni attend to some of the most challenging issues that face urban communities: improving educational outcomes for children, creating safe neighborhoods, cultivating minority and professional leadership, developing better housing for seniors, and fostering economic stability and growth. Many of these university-community partnerships have been recognized and adopted as national models.

In addition, the School offers lifelong learning programs in its noncredit Odyssey program and Evergreen program, which provide educational and social opportunities for semi-retired and retired individuals.

More than 4,500 students enroll in flexible degree programs on the University's Homewood campus and in convenient locations in downtown Baltimore, Washington DC, and Maryland's Howard and Montgomery counties.

HIGHLIGHTS

- The School was the first on the Homewood campus to enroll women as undergraduates.

- The School was the first to offer Johns Hopkins degrees for working professionals enrolled on a part-time basis.

- The School was the first to extend Johns Hopkins' reach across the region by opening off-campus centers.

- The Real Estate Institute in the Graduate Division of Business and Management features the only program of its kind focused specifically on the field of Senior Housing Care.

- The Graduate Division of Education in partnership with the Baltimore City Public School System and other regional school systems has developed innovation programs to support the recruitment, preparation, and retention of teachers for the region's neediest schools.

- The Division of Public Safety Leadership features the Police Executive Leadership Program, the first program of its kind, and lists 30 Chiefs of Police as its graduates nationwide.

FACTS
Undergraduate/post-baccalaureate student enrollment............895
Graduate student enrollment...3,896
Noncredit student enrollment...2,571
Student-faculty ratio...15:1
Living alumni...25,124

ADMINISTRATION

Ralph Fessler
Dean

Sheldon Greenberg
Director
Division of Public Safety Leadership

Ed Pajak
Interim Associate Dean
Graduate Division of Education

Pete Petersen
Interim Associate Dean
Graduate Division of Business

Debbie Rice
Assistant Dean
Financial Operations

Toni Ungaretti
Assistant Dean
Division of Undergraduate Studies

Amy Yerkes
Associate Dean
Academic Affairs

ADVISORY COUNCIL

Donald J. Shepard, chair
Chair, Executive Board
Aegon N.V.
Chair, Aegon USA, Inc.

James T. Brady
Consultant

J. Joseph Casey
Senior Vice President
Trammell Crow Company

Kenneth W. DeFontes, Jr.
Vice President
Electric Transmission and Distribution
BGE

ADVISORY COUNCIL (con't)

Donna Easton
President
Easton Communications Group

Lisa Egbuonu-Davis
Vice President, Global Outcomes
Pfizer, Inc.

Nancy S. Grasmick
State Superintendent of Schools
Maryland State Department of Education

Grady Hopper
Vice President
United Parcel Service

John A. Hunter
Senior Vice President
Customer Services
QVC, Inc.

Thomas E. Katana
Baltimore, MD

Teresa Knott
Maryland State Department of Education

John P. Kyle
Julien J. Studley, Inc.

Donald Manekin
Partner
Manekin LLC

E. Magruder Passano, Jr.
President and CEO
One Waverly LLC

Gene A. Spencer
Vice President
Investor Relations
Fannie Mae

June E. Streckfus
Executive Director
Maryland Business
Roundtable for Education

ALUMNI COUNCIL MEMBERS

Linda S. Adamson SPSBE '91
Rizwan Ahmed SPSBE '00, '02
William E. Buchanan SPSBE '50, A&S '51, SPSBE '78
J. Joseph Casey SPSBE '74, '97
Effie Dolan SPSBE '00
Clarence Edwards SPSBE '96
Valerie A. Farmer SPSBE '00
Joel Fedder SPSBE '64
Miriam Davis Green SPSBE '62
Paul A. Matlin PEAB '70, PEAB '72,
SPSBE '81, ENGR '84
Joseph McGowan SPSBE '04
Bryan M. McMillan SPSBE '00, '02
G. Paul Neitzel SPSBE '74, ENGR '79
Ellen L. Oppenheimer SPSBE '79
Joanne Pipkin SPSBE '84
Kenneth K. Seidl SPSBE '95, '97
Regina G. Turner SPSBE '94
Edward S. Tuvin SPSBE '93

SPSBE REGIONAL CHAPTER PRESIDENTS

Boston, Massachusetts
Joanne Pipkin '84
13 Hardin Road
Portsmouth, NH 03801

St. Louis, Missouri
Fran Levy '73
1574 Beacon Woods
Ballwin, MO 63021-6918

West Virginia
Bertie R. Cohen '35
311 McKinley Avenue
Fort Hill
Charleston, WV 25314

STUDENT REPRESENTATIVE

Cynthia Rogers, Division of
Undergraduate Studies

STAFF CONTACT INFORMATION

Chris Atkins Godack
Director, External Affairs and Alumni Relations
School of Professional Studies in Business and Education
103 Shaffer Hall
3400 N. Charles Street
Baltimore, MD 21218
Tel: (410) 516-8590
Fax: (410) 516-3323
cgodack@jhu.edu
www.spsbe.jhu.edu

Appendix O
The Early Years (1916–1947)

Academic Year 1916–1917

During Academic Year 1916–1917, Johns Hopkins University moves to formalize its earlier efforts of providing lectures to members of the business community who are unable to attend day classes on a regular basis. For years, these individuals have shown ever-increasing interest in attending what have been heretofore uncoordinated lectures of topics that chanced to be available. In fact, these lectures for businesspeople are heavily subscribed to and then fully attended session after session by numbers of students that surpass those of conventional classes. Furthermore, members of the business community request specific classes relevant to their profession. For example, during 1915 the Education and Conservation Committee of the Baltimore Life Underwriters Association requested a special course of lectures on life insurance. As a result, the unit College Courses for Teachers (organized in Academic Year 1909–1910) responded by presenting a special course of 22 lectures about life insurance lasting from January 4, 1916, until the end of Academic Year 1915–1916. This changes during Academic Year 1916—1917, when the offering of life insurance sessions transfers from College Courses for Teachers to the newly created Courses in Business Economics.

Academic Year 1917–1918

In the following Academic Year 1917–1918, a 12-page bulletin (dated 1917) becomes the first bulletin (often referred to as a catalog) of the Business Division. Its rather long title, "Courses in Business Economics offered by The Johns Hopkins University 1917–1918" clearly announces the intentions of the Business Division. The names of the four committee members in charge of the Courses in Business Economics are listed: "Frank J. Goodnow, President of The Johns Hopkins University; Jacob H. Hollander, Professor of Political Economy; Edward F. Buchner, Professor of Education [and Director of College Courses for Teachers]; and George E. Barnett, Professor of Statistics" (Bulletin, 1917, p. 2).

Faculty for these classes include a number of key members of the then-current Hopkins faculty, as well as individuals who appear to have been part-time faculty. The list for Academic Year 1917–1918 includes

Jacob H. Hollander, PhD, Professor of Political Economy, teaching Money and Banking

John B. Watson, PhD, Professor of Experimental and Comparative Psychology, teaching Psychology of Advertising

George W. Barnett, PhD, Professor of Statistics, teaching Investments

Knight Dunlap, PhD, Professor of Experimental Psychology, teaching Social Psychology

Henry Slonimsky, PhD, Associate in Philosophy, teaching Social Ethics

Leo Walman, PhD, Associate in Insurance, teaching Casualty Insurance; Life Insurance

Walter F. Shenton, PhD, Associate in Mathematics, teaching Statistics

Clare E. Griffin, AB, Instructor in Transportation, teaching Transportation; Political Economy

Arthur C. Millspaugh, PhD, Instructor in Political Science, teaching Comparative Government; Municipal Government and Political Politics

Hugo P. Wise, AB, teaching Business English

Broadus Mitchell, AB, teaching Social Problems

J. Wallace Bryan, PhD, teaching Commercial Law

Bernard S. Gomprecht, AB, teaching Principles of Salesmanship

Elmer S. Hatter, CPA, teaching Cost Accounting

Frank J. O'Brien, AB, teaching Industrial Management

Karl Sinonwald, PhD, teaching Business Expression

Ernest E. Wooden, CPA, teaching Theory of Accounts (Bulletin, 1917, p. 3)

Significant is the sophistication of the courses (described further in the bulletin) that are being taught in what was essentially a business administration program in 1917.

Other information of interest reveals that the university opens this academic year on Tuesday, October 2, 1917, and that following a general assembly on Friday, October 12, courses in Business Economics begin on Monday, October 15, 1917. Furthermore, one day of classes is suspended for Thanksgiving Day, and the Christmas recess lasts from Saturday, December 22, 1917, until Thursday afternoon, January 3, 1918. In addition, all classes are suspended for Commemoration Day (no longer observed in 2006), and courses in Business Economics are closed on May 24, 1918.

Following a short discussion of the overall program for Courses in Business Economics, the bulletin addresses selection of courses, admissions and attendance, location of classes, tuition, course descriptions, and the schedule of classes.

Courses in Business Economics

The Johns Hopkins University will offer during Academic Year 1917–18 the following series of afternoon and evening courses of instruction in subjects of direct interest and value to young men and women actually engaged in or contemplating entrance into business, industry and commerce. Such instruction is made available at hours and under conditions designed to meet the convenience of those likely to make use thereof.

SELECTION OF COURSES

Students are advised not to limit their choice of courses to those subjects that are directly related to the particular business or activity in which they are engaged. All students, employed in business or in social service, will find the course in the Elements of Political Economy and in Statistics of particular value, as supplying a sound foundation for the more intelligent pursuit of the specialized courses. Such general courses should, indeed, whenever possible, precede or accompany special courses. The courses in the Theory of Accounts and in Cost Accounting will be found profitable not only by those who wish to become professional accountants, but by all classes of business men interested in and concerned with the details of the financial organization of modern industry. Similarly, employers of labor, as well as social workers, will find of value the courses in Social and Labor Problems, Social Psychology, Social Ethics, and Industrial Management.

While the courses are designed in the main to offer instruction to those engaged in various fields of business and social activity, the instruction will be designed to meet the needs also of those who have a more general interest in the subject. The courses, for example, in Life Insurance and in Casualty Insurance are designed primarily for those engaged in the life and casualty insurance business. The instruction will, however, conform to the needs of business men who are large carriers of personal and business insurance, and to social workers who are interested in the recent developments in the fields of industrial and social insurance.

Instruction in modern languages and in a wide range of subjects ordinarily included in a college curriculum, as well as in engineering subjects, is available in the "Teachers' Courses" and in the "Engineering Courses," offered by this University. Detailed announcements in reference to these courses can be had upon application to the Registrar of the University.

ADMISSION AND ATTENDANCE

There are no formal examinations for admission. Students, both men and women, will be admitted to such courses as they are found qualified by the respective instructors to pursue with advantage.

The satisfactory completion of any of these courses will be recognized by the award of a certificate of attendance. Credits so received may be used, upon matriculation, toward the degree of Bachelor of Science.

LOCATION

The courses will be given in the Mechanical Engineering Building, Homewood (Charles and Thirty-Second Streets).

TUITION FEES

The tuition fee is $20.00 for each course of two hours weekly extending through the academic year. Fees are payable at the office of the Treasurer of the Johns Hopkins University, Academic Building, Room 121. Before payment of fees can be made, applicants must receive from the Registrar a card stating the course or courses to be taken (Bulletin, 1917, pp. 5–7).

SCHEDULE

Monday
Social Ethics, 8:00–10:00 p.m.
Social and Labor Problems, 8:00–10:00 p.m.
Industrial Management, 8:00–10:00 p.m.
Casualty Insurance, 8:00–10:00 p.m.

Tuesday
Money and Banking, 8:00–10:00 p.m.
Investments, 8:00–10:00 p.m.
Social Psychology, 8:00–10:00 p.m.
Business Expression, 8:00–10:00 p.m.
Life Insurance, 5.10–6.10 p.m.

Wednesday
Principles of Salesmanship, 8:00–10:00 p.m.
Business English, 8:00–10:00 p.m.
Comparative Government, 8:00–10:00 p.m.
Transportation, 8:00–10:00 p.m.

Thursday
Psychology of Advertising, 8:00–10:00 p.m.
Life Insurance, 5.10–6.10 p.m.
Commercial Law, 8:00–10:00 p.m.
Theory of Accounts, 7.30–9.30 p.m.

Friday
Political Economy, 8:00–10:00 p.m.
Statistics, 8:00–10:00 p.m.
Cost Accounting, 8:00–10:00 p.m.
Municipal Government and Political Parties, 8:00–
10:00 p.m. (Bulletin, 1917, p. 12)

Academic Year 1918–1919

The number of business economics courses, and corresponding instructors, decreases substantially from 20 courses offered by 17 instructors in Academic Year 1917–1918 to 10 courses offered by nine instructors in Academic Year 1918–1919. Furthermore, like a few of the academic bulletins during the early years of Business Economics, the one for 1918–1919 contains a full-page photo of a building. In this case, it is a photo of Maryland Hall, labeled the Mechanical and Electrical Engineering Building. In fact, today the building looks almost unchanged since its construction in 1915, with the exception of the subsequently added entrance in the center of the building facing the lower quadrangle, and a healthy lawn replacing the dirt and mud puddles on the lower quadrangle in front of the building. As might be expected, business economics classes are conducted in this building.

Academic Year 1919–1920

During this academic year the number of Business Economics classes offered increases from 10 to 13, with the number of instructors increasing from 9 to 10. The inside of the rear cover of the bulletin is rather informative in that the printer of the bulletin, the Johns Hopkins Press of Baltimore, advertises the sale of some of its publications. Included are academic journals, Johns Hopkins University bulletins and reports, and a 128-page paper by the famous Hopkins professor B. L. Gildersleeve. Also for sale is a publication written in German. The outside of the same rear cover contains a promotional piece relevant to the entire university. Revealing are the gender exclusions listed under some of the school names. The listing of various schools and programs on the outside of the rear cover also shows what would become the Business

Division—but in this case as part of a consolidated listing that includes Business and Engineering "Evening Courses in Business and Social Economics and in Engineering."

THE JOHNS HOPKINS UNIVERSITY
BALTIMORE
Founded 1876

A FACULTY OF 350 PROFESSORS, ASSOCIATES,
INSTRUCTORS AND LECTURERS

SPECIAL LIBRARIES AND WELL-EQUIPPED
LABORATORIES

GRADUATE SCHOOL OF ARTS AND SCIENCES
Degrees AM and PhD
(Open to Men and Women)

GRADUATE SCHOOL OF MEDICINE
Degree M.D.
(Open to Men and Women)

COLLEGE OF ARTS AND SCIENCES
Degree AB
(Open to Men)

DEPARTMENT OF ENGINEERING
Degrees B. Eng. and S.B. in Chem.
(Open to Men)

COLLEGE COURSES FOR TEACHERS
Degree S.B.
(Open to Men and Women)

SCHOOL OF HYGIENE AND PUBLIC HEALTH
Degrees D.P.H., S.D., and S.B. in Hyg.
(Open to Men and Women)

SUMMER COURSES
With AM, AB, and S.B. credits
(Open to Men and Women)

————————————

SUMMER COURSES FOR GRADUATES IN MEDICINE
(Not offered in 1919)

————————————

EVENING COURSES IN BUSINESS AND SOCIAL
ECONOMICS AND IN ENGINEERING
(Open to Men and Women)

————————————

THE JOHNS HOPKINS PRESS PUBLICATIONS

————————————

STATE BUREAUS
Maryland Geological Survey, Maryland Weather Service,
Maryland Forestry Bureau
(Bulletin, AY 1919–1920, back cover)

Academic Year 1920–1921

In this academic year the number of instructors increases from
10 to 12 and the number of courses increases from 13 to 14. In
addition, advice to students about the selection of courses (shown on
pp. 5–6 in the Academic Year 1920–1921 Bulletin) presents logical
groups of courses for subjects such as Finance, Salesmanship and
Advertising, Transportation, Labor, Foreign Trade, and General
Subjects. This array of topics reveals the scope and depth of the
curriculum of the Business Administration program at Johns
Hopkins University in the early 1920s.

The location of classes starting this academic year also shows
the involvement of the American Institute of Banking and the use
of facilities by the Business Division at the School of Hygiene and
Public Health.

SELECTION OF COURSES

Students should feel free to make any selection
of courses that best meets their individual needs.

The following grouping of subjects is suggested, however, as an aid to students:

FINANCE

Money and Banking

Corporate Finance

[Investments]

[Foreign Exchange]

Political Economy

[Business Statistics]

Elementary Accounting

Legal Aspects of Business Practice

SALESMANSHIP AND ADVERTISING

Salesmanship

Advertising

Business Psychology

Political Economy

[Business Statistics]

Legal Aspects of Business Practice

TRANSPORTATION

Railway Accounting

[Merchant Marine Administration and Operation]

Political Economy

[Business Statistics]

Elementary Accounting

LABOR

[Labor Problems]

Industrial Relations

Business Psychology

Political Economy

[Business Statistics]

FOREIGN TRADE

Foreign Trade

[Foreign Exchange]

[Merchant Marine Administration and Operation]

Salesmanship and Advertising Group

GENERAL

Current Economic Problems

Political Economy

[Business Statistics]

Elementary Accounting

Legal Aspects of Business Practice

Business Psychology

Business English

The groups are arranged with the purpose of providing the student specialized instruction in that field in which he is particularly interested, and at the same time with the idea of furnishing certain general courses that will serve as a solid foundation for the more intelligent pursuit of the specialized courses. Political Economy, Elementary

Accounting, and Business Statistics are examples of such general courses.

The group headed "General" contains a list of those subjects that may appeal to those who have no special interest in any one of the other groups. However, some or even all of these courses may well accompany the more specialized studies. The course in Current Economic Problems is designed particularly to meet the needs of those who may be interested in the broader social aspects of our present economic life and its unsettled problems.

The following courses, indicated in the groups above by brackets, will not be given in 1920–1921:

Investments.

Foreign Exchange.

Business Statistics.

Merchant Marine Administration and Operation.

Labor Problems.

Instruction in modern languages and in a wide range of subjects ordinarily included in a college curriculum, as well as in engineering subjects, is available in the "Teachers' Courses" and in the "Engineering Courses" offered by this University.

LOCATION

The courses in Corporation Finance, Money and Banking and Legal Aspects of Business Practice will be given in rooms of the Baltimore Chapter of the American Institute of Banking, 15 South Street; the courses in Current Economic Problems and in Industrial Relations, will be given in the lecture room of the School of Hygiene and Public Health,

Linden Avenue and Monument Street; all other courses in the Mechanical Engineering Building, Charles and Thirty-second Streets.

TUITION FEES

The tuition fee is $20.00 for each of the courses extending through the academic year. Fees are payable at the office of the Treasurer (Gilman Hall, 121) (AY 1920–1921 Bulletin, pp. 5–7).

Two courses quite unlike today's offerings are presented in Academic Year 1920–1921 for the first time at Hopkins. The first, Principles of Suretyship, is a subject pertaining to situations in which one has contracted to be responsible for something occurring or not occurring. Some subjects taught today, such as quality assurance or zero defects, are descendants of the suretyship taught at Hopkins and other universities during the 1920s. Baltimore's role as a 1920s railway hub makes the inclusion of a course in railway accounting quite apropos; in fact, the university's benefactor, Johns Hopkins, made much of his fortune in the railroad industry during the 1800s.

PRINCIPLES OF SURETYSHIP

Instruction will be given by lectures and quizzes on the theory and practice of corporate suretyship, which to a considerable extent, has found its home in Baltimore. The course will include among other things: consideration of the historical beginnings of personal and corporate suretyship, methods by which surety obligations are examined, assumed, supervised and adjusted; analogies with banking, insurance and other forms of business; effect of corporate suretyship upon the administration of estates in probate courts, the custody of public funds, execution of private and public construction contracts and various forms of private employment; statutes, court decisions, copies of bonds and other

261

forms used in the practical workings of the business. Special lecturers will address the class from time to time on various phases of the subject.

The course is designed not only for those who are in the employ of surety companies or who contemplate making such a connection, but also for those who are interested generally in the rapid development of this form of commercial activity.

DR. RADCLIFFE   Wednesday, 8:00–10:00 p.m. (Bulletin, AY 1920–1921, p. 13)

RAILWAY ACCOUNTING

The purpose of this course is to enable those now engaged in the railroad business and others contemplating entering railroad service or the service of the Interstate Commerce Commission to acquire a general knowledge of the principles and practices of railway accounting. A knowledge of the fundamentals of bookkeeping is a necessary requirement for this course.

The following topics will be taken up in the course: income and general accounts; balance sheet and general books; freight, passenger, and miscellaneous revenue accounts; disbursement accounts and statistics; accounting for capital expenditures; accounts of the treasury department; collection of the railroad company's revenues; demurrage; storage; mail and express revenues; auditing of station accounts; loss and damage and overcharge claims; handling of per diem and car mileage accounts. A study will be made of the Interstate Commerce Commission's classifications and accounting instructions. The relation of the various classifications and accounts to each other and to the general balance sheet will be covered.

MR. DEVERELL   Monday,   8:00–10:00   p.m.
(Bulletin, AY 1920–1921, p. 14)

Academic Year 1921–1922

During Academic Year 1921–1922, the number of instructors increases from 12 to 13; the number of courses offered remains 14. These are year-long courses, starting in October at the beginning of the fall semester and ending in May at the end of the spring semester, as illustrated in the course description for Business English.

BUSINESS ENGLISH

> This course devotes the first half-year to the study of grammatical usage and structure, requiring weekly themes on commercial topics of general importance, such as the letter of credit, the clearing house, royalty, patent, bill of lading, income tax, [and] mortgage. During the second half-year, the class studies the composition of such business letters as those of recommendation, introduction and application, and those of buyer, seller and collector, as well as advertisements, reports and office notices. Special attention is given to the style of commercial forms. The reading of selected books is prescribed, among them being Palmer's *Self-Cultivation in English and Trades* and *Professions,* Husband's *America at Work,* and Eliot's *Training for an Effective Life.*

MR. UHLER   Wednesday, 8:00–10:00 p.m.

Academic Year 1922–1923

During Academic Year 1922–1923, the number of instructors increases from 13 to 14, and the number of courses offered increases from 14 to 15. Dr. William O. Weyforth, who had been listed as an

Associate in Political Economy, is listed, beginning this academic year, as Associate Professor in Political Economy.

Academic Year 1923–1924

The title of the unit presenting the course bulletin changes from "Courses in Business Economics" to "Evening Courses in Business Economics." The number of instructors increases from 14 to 15, and the number of courses from 15 to 19. Among the instructors is now one professor of political economy, one professor of statistics, and one associate professor of political economy. A revised accounting program now offers a full program to allow those who complete it to sit for the Certified Public Accountant (CPA) examination administered by the State of Maryland.

ACCOUNTANCY COURSES

The University is now prepared to offer in the Evening Courses in Business Economics instruction preparatory for the profession of Accountancy. For several years a course in Elementary Accounting has been given. This year there is included in the curriculum a course in Corporation and Cost Accounting; and in the year 1924–25 a third course in Advanced Accounting and Auditing will be added. Through these courses and the ones in Commercial Law and Political Economy provision has been made for those who are preparing for the examinations for Certified Public Accountant. Following is the three-year schedule of courses advised for such students:

First Year—Elementary Accounting, Commercial Law.

Second Year—Corporation and Cost Accounting, Advanced Commercial Law.

Third Year—Advanced Accounting and Auditing, Political Economy.

Students interested in the Accountancy courses should apply for the special circular describing them (Bulletin, AY 1923–24, p. 5).

Academic Year 1924–1925

For Academic Year 1924–1925 the number of instructors remains at 15, and the number of courses offered increases from 19 to 20. For the first time since the start of the Business Division, the composition of the governing element changes with the addition of Associate Professor of Political Economy William O. Weyforth as secretary. As a result, the Committee in Charge of the Evening Courses in Business Economics has the following members:

Frank J. Goodnow, President of the Johns Hopkins University
Jacob H. Hollander, Professor of Political Economy
Edward F. Buchner, Professor of Education
George E. Barnett, Professor of Statistics
William O. Weyforth, Associate Professor of Political Economy
(Bulletin, AY 1924–1925, p. 2).

The tuition schedule for 1924–1925 lists courses offered and shows amounts charged.

TUITION FEES

The tuition fees per course are as follows:

Credits and Business Barometrics	...	$ 30.00
Elementary Accounting	...	$ 25.00
Corporation and Cost Accounting	...	$ 25.00
Advanced Accounting and Auditing	...	$ 25.00
Income Tax Accounting	...	$ 25.00
Mathematics of Finance and Accounting	...	$ 25.00
Current Economic Problems	...	$ 20.00
Political Economy	...	$ 20.00
Corporation Finance	...	$ 20.00
Money and Banking	...	$ 20.00
English Grammar and Composition	...	$ 20.00
Business English	...	$ 20.00
Public Speaking	...	$ 20.00
Business Psychology	...	$ 20.00

Principles of Salesmanship	...	$ 20.00
Principles of Advertising	...	$ 20.00
Commercial Law	...	$ 20.00
Advanced Commercial Law	...	$ 20.00
Labor Problems	...	$ 20.00
Casualty Insurance	...	$ 20.00

Fees are payable in advance at the office of the Treasurer in the Chemical Laboratory. Students will not be admitted to classes until they present cards received from the Treasurer showing that tuition fees have been paid (Bulletin, AY 1924–1925, p. 7).

Academic Year 1925–1926

For Academic Year 1925–1926 the number of instructors decreases from 15 to 14 and the number of courses from 20 to 19. The academic rank of George H. Newlove changes from Associate in Accounting to Associate Professor of Accounting.

Academic Year 1926–1927

For Academic Year 1926–1927, the number of instructors increases from 14 to 16, and number of courses offered increases from 19 to 22. Noteworthy here is the new title given to the senior professor of the Business Division, Jacob H. Hollander, who led this effort from the very beginning in 1916; he is now the Abraham G. Hutzler Professor of Political Economy. Apparently a generous gift from Abraham Hutzler, the owner of a large department store of the time in downtown Baltimore, endowed the first chair in the Business Division during Academic Year 1926–1927. Details on how students enrolled in Evening Courses in Business Economics may earn the degree Bachelor of Science are stated for the first time in this year's bulletin. Furthermore, cooperative arrangements with associations and businesses have evolved substantially and are described in detail, revealing that additional classes are conducted in downtown Baltimore.

COOPERATIVE ARRANGEMENTS

American Institute of Banking. The following courses are given by the University in cooperation with the Baltimore Chapter of the American Institute of Banking; Political Economy, Money and Banking, Commercial Law, Advanced Commercial Law, Corporation Finance, Current Economic Problems, Credits and Business Barometrics, English Grammar and Composition, Business English, Real Estate, [and] Elementary Accounting.

Members of the Chapter who take these courses should make arrangements for admission with the officers of the Chapter.

National Institute of Credit. The course in Credits and Business Barometrics is given in cooperation with the Baltimore Association of Credit Men and the Baltimore Chapter of the National Institute of Credit. The Institute is the Educational Department of the National Association of Credit Men. Members of the Association should register through the office of the Baltimore Association of Credit Men, 301 West Redwood Street. Other persons should enroll in the usual way through the University.

Real Estate Board of Baltimore. The course in Real Estate Principles and Practices is given in cooperation with the Educational Committee of the Real Estate Board of Baltimore. Registration for this course may be made through the secretary of that board as well as through the University.

Casualty Insurance. The course in Casualty Insurance is given with the cooperation of the Maryland Casualty Company, the United States Fidelity and Guaranty Company, and the New Amsterdam Casualty Company.

LOCATION

The courses in Commercial Law and in Money and Banking will be given in the rooms of the Baltimore Chapter of the American Institute of Banking, on the fourth floor of the Park Bank Building, Lexington and Liberty Streets. All other courses will be given in the Mechanical Engineering Building, at Homewood, Charles and 32nd Streets (Bulletin, AY 1926–1927, pp. 7–8).

Academic Year 1927–1928

For Academic Year 1927–1928, the number of instructors increases significantly from 16 to 21, and the number of courses offered does the same, from 22 to 28. During this academic year there is a record number of academically ranked instructors, with two professors, four associate professors, two associates, and one instructor. The balance of 28 instructors is made up of part-time appointments. In addition, for some time there has been an installment plan for students who enroll in three or more courses. This plan is shown, along with a refund policy for Evening Courses in Business Economics.

Total fee for course	First installment	Second installment
$25.00	$15.00	$10.00
30.00	20.00	10.00
35.00	20.00	15.00
55.00	35.00	20.00

Fees may be paid at the office of the Treasurer in the Chemistry Laboratory at Homewood, or on the registration evenings, October 6 and 7, in the Mechanical Engineering Building. Payment may also be made by check through the mail. Students will not be admitted to classes until they present cards received from the Treasurer showing that tuition fees have been paid.

The fee for matriculation as a candidate for the degree of Bachelor of Science is $5. The fee for graduation as Bachelor of Science or for the award of a "Statement of Completion" is also $5.

REFUNDS

The budget for the Evening Courses in Business Economics is made up on an annual basis. Fees are fixed and income is calculated on the assumption of payment of fees for the entire year. Consequently no refund for an uncompleted portion of a course can be made after the first three meetings of the class in which a student is registered, except in case of withdrawal on account of prolonged illness or removal from the city. In any case a registration fee of $3 will be charged the withdrawing student (Bulletin, AY 1927–1928, p. 10).

Academic Year 1928–1929

The number of instructors increases from 21 to 24 and number of courses from 28 to 30. Howard Cooper, who arrived in 1928, is listed in this bulletin for the first time and has the academic rank of Instructor in Accounting, with his highest degree at the time recorded as MS. Another individual who will be present with Howard Cooper in the 1960s is Edward J. Stegman, CPA, also an accounting instructor but, unlike Cooper, part-time. All 24 instructors are listed here.

INSTRUCTORS

Jacob H. Hollander, PhD, Abraham G. Hutzler Professor Political Economy, *Current Economic Problems*

George E. Barnett, PhD, Professor of Statistics, *Investments*

William O. Weyforth, PhD, Associate Professor of Political Economy, *Money and Banking*

Broadus Mitchell, PhD, Associate Professor of Political Economy, *Political Economy; American Economic History*

G. Heberton Evans, Jr., PhD, Associate in Political Economy, *Business Statistics; Corporation Finance*

Roy M. Dorcus, PhD, Associate in Psychology, *Business Psychology*

Howard E. Cooper, MS, Instructor in Accounting, *Corporation Accounting*

Roy J. Bullock, M.B.A., Instructor in Marketing, *Marketing*

J. Wallace Bryan, PhD, LL.B., CPA, *Elementary Accounting*

Edwin T. Dickerson, AM, LL.B., *Commercial Law*

W. Curtis Stith, Jr., AB, *Principles of Advertising*

George J. Clautice, Executive Secretary, Baltimore Association of Commerce, *Credits and Business Barometrics*

William H. Vickers, Manager, Employment and Personnel Department, Consolidated Gas and Electric Light and Power Company, *Personnel Administration*

Leslie W. Baker, CPA, *Cost Accounting; Principles of Auditing; Income Tax Accounting; Specialized Accounting*

William H.S. Stevens, PhD, Assistant Chief Economist, Federal Trade Commission, *Business Organization and Management*

William E. Ferguson, *Real Estate Principles and Practices*

R. Dorsey Watkins, PhD, LL.B., *Advanced Commercial Law*

Halsey E. Ramsen, AB, Assistant Manager, Whitaker Paper Co., *Salesmanship and Salesmanagement*

Harry E. Gilbert, AM, LL. B., *Real Estate Appraising*

C. R. Wattenscheidt, LL. B., *Real Estate Law*

Francis E. A. Litz, PhD, Instructor in English, Baltimore City College, *Business English; Public Speaking*

Paul M. Wheeler, AM, Instructor in English, Goucher College, *English Grammar and Composition*

Edward J. Stegman, CPA, *Auditing Practice and Accountant's Working Papers*

Charles H. Schnepfe, CPA, *Advanced Accounting Theory and Problems*

(Bulletin, AY 1928–1929, p. 3)

Academic Year 1929–1930

During Academic Year 1929–1930, the numbers of instructors and courses continue to increase to new highs—instructors from 24 to 27 and courses offered from 30 to 32. The course schedule for 1929–1930 is presented for the first time in a matrix format that is easy to read and that aids students in planning their schedules. Unfortunately, this coincides with the dawn of the Great Depression (1929–1940).

With the departure of President Goodnow and the July 1, 1929, arrival of President Joseph S. Ames (the fourth president of the university), the composition of the Committee in Charge of the Evening Courses in Business Economics changes. In addition to the change in presidents, Hopkins suffers the loss of Edward F. Buchner, a member of this committee from the very beginning, when he dies on August 19, 1929. Now, for the first time, the committee that governs the Evening Courses in Business Economics consists of a new Hopkins president and three members of the unit. Dr. Buchner from the College for Teachers is not replaced on the committee.

SCHEDULE OF COURSES 1929–1930

Hours	Monday	Tuesday	Wednesday	Thursday	Friday
6.30–8.10 p.m.	American Economic History Business Statistics	Marketing	English Grammar & Composition Advanced Accounting Problems	Mathematics of Finance Income Tax Accounting	Advanced Business Psychology Personnel Administration
8.10–9.50 p.m.	Money and Banking Real Estate Principles Advertising Elementary Accounting Advanced Auditing & Accountant's Working Papers	Political Economy (Section A) Investments Business Organization & Management Public Speaking Commercial Law Auditing Principles & Practice	Credits & Business Barometrics (7.20–9.50 p.m.) Business English Corporation Accounting Specialized Accounting Political Economy (Section B)	Current Economic Problems Corporation Finance Salesmanship Elementary Accounting Cost Accounting	Business Psychology Advanced Commercial Law Foreign Trade Real Estate Appraisal & Law

(Bulletin, AY 1929–1930, p. 11)

Academic Year 1930–1931

For Academic Year 1930–1931 the number of instructors remains unchanged at 27, but the number of courses offered increases from 32 to 34. Courses in this bulletin are arranged differently for this academic year, organized in terms of their major subjects so that every individual course falls in one particular category. Major subject categories are Economics, Accounting, Law, Psychology, English, and Mathematics.

Academic Year 1931–1932

The impact of the beginning of the Great Depression, now being felt, may be the reason for the decreases in the number of instructors from 27 to 24 and in the number of courses offered from 34 to 31.

Academic Year 1932–1933

The numbers of instructors and courses both increase by one. Academic Year 1932–1933 lists 25 instructors and offers 32 courses. Although Howard Cooper (who will be at Hopkins for 41 years) continues to hold the academic rank of Instructor in Accounting, the listing of his highest degree changes from MS to PhD.

Academic Year 1933–1934

With a decrease in enrollments because of the Great Depression, the number of instructors drops from 25 to 20, and the number of courses offered drops from 32 to 25. As might be expected, the reduction in instructors is only in part-time instructors; the full-time instructors remain unscathed.

Academic Year 1934–1935

The number of instructors remains the same, but the number of courses offered increases by one; 20 instructors are listed and 26 courses are offered. Dr. Howard Cooper receives a promotion from Instructor in Accounting to Associate in Political Economy. Furthermore, a new format this year lists instructors at the start of each subject grouping of courses, in addition to their regular listing at the start of the bulletin.

ECONOMICS

Professor Hollander
Professor Barnett
Dr. Weyforth
Dr. Mitchell
Mr. Corner

Dr. Evans
Dr. Bullock
Mr. Clautice
Mr. Ramsen

ACCOUNTING

Dr. Cooper	Mr. Stegman
Dr. Bryan	Mr. McCord
Mr. Baker	Mr. Smith

LAW

| Mr. Thomsen | Dr. Watkins |

PSYCHOLOGY

Dr. Bentley

ENGLISH

| Dr. McManaway | Dr. Lyons |

Academic Year 1935–1936

On July 1, 1935, President Ames retires and is succeeded by President Isaiah Bowman. Consequently, the composition of the Committee in Charge of the Evening Courses in Business Economics changes, with President Bowman replacing President Ames; Hollander, Barnett, and Weyforth continue as members. This academic year, the number of instructors listed decreases from 20 to 19, and the number of courses offered decreases from 26 to 25. The Chi Chapter of Delta Sigma Pi (the business fraternity), which had moved from the University of Maryland to Johns Hopkins University in 1926, offers a scholarship key that continues to be awarded in the 21st century. A notice in the 1935–1936 bulletin describes this award.

DELTA SIGMA PI SCHOLARSHIP KEY

The Delta Sigma Pi Scholarship Key is awarded each year to that male student in the Evening Courses in Business Economics who, upon satisfying the requirements for a Statement of Completion, ranks highest in scholarship for the entire course. The winner of the key is determined by a faculty committee on scholarship appointed especially for the purpose.

The key is given by Chi Chapter of Delta Sigma Pi at Johns Hopkins University. This professional fraternity has chapters located in the leading universities throughout the United States and Canada that have schools of business administration.

This award is currently given to the student who ranks highest in scholarship at the undergraduate level.

Academic Year 1936–1937

During Academic Year 1936–1937, the number of instructors increases from 19 to 21, and the number of courses offered decreases from 25 to 24. In addition, this academic year's bulletin continues to offer an unusual list of courses under the overall subject category of Economics. Today, many of these courses presented in a more conventional business curriculum would be listed elsewhere. For example, along with an array of typical economics courses are some unusual bedfellows for an Economics category, such as Principals of Advertising, Salesmanship and Sales Management, Marketing, Business Statistics, Elements of Business Administration, Mercantile Credit, Investments, and Corporation Finance.

Academic Year 1937–1938

During Academic Year 1937–1938, the numbers of instructors and courses offered remain unchanged at 21 and 24, respectively. Although Professor Jacob H. Hollander, PhD, the Abraham G. Hutzler Professor of Political Economy, continues to teach and to be listed as the senior professor, Dr. William O. Weyforth, Associate Professor of Political Economy, is appointed to the newly created position of director of the Evening Courses in Business Economics and continues to teach as well. This academic year also marks the creation of a new committee that attempts to unify most of the part-time programs at Hopkins. This development in 1937 of a higher level committee seems to foreshadow the creation of McCoy College 10 years later in 1947. The staffing of both of these committees is reflected below.

Executive Committee of the Summer, Afternoon and Evening Courses

Isaiah Bowman, PhD, ScD, LL. D., President of the University, Chairman

Alexander G. Christie, M. E., Professor of Mechanical Engineering, Vice-Chairman Director, Night Courses in Technology

Edward W. Berry, Provost of the University, Dean of the College of Arts and Sciences

Florence E. Bamberger, PhD, Director of the College of Teachers

Robert B. Roulston, PhD, Director of the Summer School

William O. Weyforth, PhD, Director of the Evening Courses in Business Economics

Committee in Charge of the Evening Courses in Business Economics
Isaiah Bowman, Chairman, President of the University

Jacob H. Hollander, Abraham G. Hutzler Professor of Political Economy

George E. Barnett, Professor of Statistics

William O. Weyforth, Director, Associate Professor of Political Economy

Also significant for Academic Year 1937–1938 is the addition of Dr. Wilson Shaffer to the list of instructors. Scheduled to teach Business Psychology, he is no stranger to Johns Hopkins University. As a student, many years earlier, he was famous for his accomplishments as a baseball player on the winning Hopkins baseball team and later earned a doctorate and went on to be well-known in his field of psychology. Then, decades later, he became dean of the College of Arts and Sciences and provost of Johns Hopkins University; after his retirement, the building named in his honor housed, in succession, McCoy College, the Evening College, the School of Continuing Studies, and the School of Professional Studies in Business and Education.

Along with the creation of what seems to be a higher-level committee to govern, advise, or perhaps watch over part-time programs, an additional committee is formed to supervise the course of study leading to the degree of Bachelor of Science (SB) given to graduates of part-time baccalaureate programs. In contrast, the AB degree is awarded to graduating members of baccalaureate programs in the College of Arts and Sciences. Note that many of the same representatives from various part-time programs are on this new committee.

Advisory Committee on the Degree of Bachelor of Science

Isaiah Bowman, President of the University (Chairman)

F. E. Bamberger	E. B. Mathewa
E. W. Berry, ex officio	R. B. Roulston
A. G. Christie	W. O. Weyforth
H. C. Lancaster	D. E. Weglein
K. Malone	M. Levin (Sec'y)

This committee was constituted by resolution of the Trustees June 1, 1915, and subsequently enlarged, to supervise the course of study leading to the degree of Bachelor of Science (Bulletin, AY 1937–1938, p. 4).

Academic Year 1938–1939

During Academic Year 1938–1939, the number of instructors listed increases from 21 to 22; the number of classes offered remains the same.

Academic Year 1939–1940

During Academic Year 1939–1940, the number of instructors listed increases from 22 to 28, and the number of courses offered increases from 24 to 26. Cooperative arrangements with the business community continue; their status for Academic Year 1939–1940 is shown below.

Cooperative Arrangements

National Institute of Credit. The course in Mercantile Credit is given in cooperation with the Baltimore Association of Credit Men and the Baltimore Chapter of the National Institute of Credit. The Institute is the Educational Department of the National Association of Credit Men. Members of the Association should register through the office of the Baltimore Association of Credit Men, 301 West Redwood Street. Other persons should enroll in the usual way through the University.

The Johns Hopkins University cooperates with the Baltimore Association of Credit Men and the National Institute of Credit in preparing members and others for the awards of Associate and Fellow of the National Institute of Credit. The following program has been approved by the National Institute of Credit of the National Association of Credit Men. Those who complete this program will qualify for the engrossed diploma awards of Associate and Fellow respectively of the National Institute of Credit.

Associate Certificate
      Political Economy
      Mercantile Credit
      Elementary Accounting
      Business English
Fellow Certificate
      Commercial Law
      Marketing
      Public Speaking
      Money and Banking or
      Corporation Finance

Real Estate Board of Baltimore. The course in Real Estate Fundamentals and Practice is given in cooperation with the Real Estate Board of Baltimore (Bulletin, AY 1939–1940, p. 13).

Academic Year 1940–1941

During Academic Year 1940–1941, the number of instructors decreases from 28 to 27; the number of courses offered remains the same, at 26. Dr. Jacob H. Hollander departs, and Dr. William O. Weyforth, Director of Evening Courses in Business Economics, becomes senior instructor for the unit. It is interesting to find that the title Abraham G. Hutzler Professor of Political Economy disappears when Dr. Hollander departs. Both Hollander and Weyforth have been with the Evening Courses in Business Economics program since its inception. In this academic year, a new committee is established. The Committee on Advanced Standing has representatives from part-time programs and is chaired by William O. Weyworth, director of Evening Courses in Business Economics. Abolished starting with this academic year is the Committee in Charge of the Evening Courses in Business Economics. In addition, the granting of advanced standing is explained in the Academic Year 1940–1941 bulletin.

Advanced Standing

Advanced standing may be granted to applicants who offer approved collegiate or professional courses with a scholarship grade of 70 or C and above, in a college, scientific school, normal school, training school, or technical school in advance of high school graduation.

Correspondence courses and extension courses not conducted on the campus of the institution offering these courses are not accepted for advanced standing.

Advanced standing granted upon examination is subject to the payment of the tuition fees for the courses thus absolved (Bulletin, AY 1940–1941, p. 10).

Academic Year 1941–1942

During the Academic Year 1941–1942, the number of instructors listed decreases from 27 to 24, and the number of courses offered decreases from 26 to 25. Furthermore, in this academic year, none of the full-time instructors in Evening Courses in Business Economics have the academic rank of professor, and only Dr. William O. Weyforth has the rank of associate professor. In fact, this year marks the lowest ebb in ranked professors in the unit. However, this will change. Furthermore, Dr. Cooper, who is an Associate in Political Economy, serves on all three committees (Executive Committee, Advisory Committee on the Degree of Bachelor of Science, and the Committee on Advanced Standing) and concurrently teaches accounting.

Academic Year 1942–1943

During Academic Year 1942–1943, the number of instructors increases from 24 to 26, and the number of courses offered increases from 25 to 28. In addition, the number of associate professors who are full-time in the unit increases when Dr. Cooper is promoted from Associate in Political Economy to Associate Professor of Political Economy.

Academic Year 1943–1944

The impact of World War II on the availability of faculty and enrollment finally hits as the number of instructors listed in the bulletin decreases from 26 to 20 and the number of courses offered decreases from 28 to 22. Dr. G. Wilson Shaffer, who will become dean of the College of Arts and Sciences, teaches Psychology with Courses in Business Economics for the last time. Also, Dr. G. Heberton Evans, Jr., an economist, joins the unit full-time as a professor, becoming the ranking member and the only professor in the unit. Dr. Cooper, an associate professor of political economy, does not teach this year but continues as director of Evening Courses in Business Economics, and a member of the three committees mentioned last year.

Academic Year 1944–1945

During Academic Year 1944–1945, the number of instructors listed increases from 20 to 22, and the number of courses offered increases slightly from 22 to 23. Dr. Cooper directs the unit, serves on the three committees, and teaches accounting. The full-time faculty now includes one professor and four associate professors.

Academic Year 1945–1946

During Academic Year 1945–1946, the number of listed instructors decreases slightly from 22 to 21, and the number of courses offered increases from 23 to 25. Full-time faculty now includes one professor and two associate professors. Dr. Cooper continues as director of the unit and a member of the three committees (the chair of the Committee on Advanced Standing) and concurrently teaches accounting. As the new dean of the College of Arts and Sciences, Dr. Shaffer, who until recently taught psychology in the evening (in addition to his other duties as a professor in the College of Arts and Sciences), is now a member of the Executive Committee of the Summer, Afternoon and Evening Courses. In addition, Mr. Granville F. Atkinson, a part-time instructor who will continue teaching Federal and State Taxation well into the 1980s, begins teaching with Evening Courses in Business Economics. Provisions for returning servicemen are included starting in this bulletin. However, typical of the gender insensitivity of the time, there is no mention of servicewomen, even though the Courses in Business Economics program is coeducational.

Provisions for Returning Service Men

The University is cooperating with the Baltimore office of the U.S. Veterans Administration at 1315 St. Paul Street in the case of men who wish to continue their education under the so-called G. I. Bill of Rights (Servicemen's Readjustment Act) or under the Vocational Rehabilitation Law 16.

Information concerning individual problems may be secured from the Registrar of the University (Bulletin, AY 1945–1946, p. 7).

Academic Year 1946–1947

During the Academic Year 1946–1947 the number of listed instructors increases substantially from 21 to 27, and the number of classes offered also increases, from 25 to 28. Dr. Edward R. Hawkins, Professor of Marketing, who will later become the last director of the Evening Courses in Business Economics, joins the unit. Dr. Cooper is promoted, and his professorial designation changes from Associate Professor of Political Economy to Professor of Accounting. Cooper continues to be director of the Evening Courses in Business Economics and continues as a member of three committees and the chair of one of them, the Committee on Advanced Standing. The list of instructors includes three professors full-time in Evening Courses in Business Economics and three associate professors also in the unit full-time. Along with describing provisions for returning servicemen, this bulletin indicates that men and women honorably discharged from military service will be given priority for attending over subscribed classes.

Registration Directions and Information

It is probable that the demand for certain courses will exceed the University's facilities and therefore priority will be given to students in the following groups:

1. Men and women honorably discharged from military service who meet the matriculation requirements.

2. Other students already matriculated and in good standing if they have been in attendance during the past five years.

3. Students who satisfactorily completed courses during 1945–46.

4. Persons selected by business and industrial firms with whom arrangements have been made by the University (Bulletin, 1946–1947, p. 11).

SCHEDULE OF COURSES 1946–1947

Hours	Monday	Tuesday	Wednesday	Thursday	Friday
6.30–8.10 p.m.	Business English (Section 2) Federal and State Tax Accounting Fire and Casualty Insurance	Advanced Commercial Law Principles of Advertising Money and Banking Accounting Principles (Section 3)	Business Statistics Business English (Section 1) Political Economy (Sec. 1 & 2)	Public Speaking Salesmanship and Salesmanagement Labor Relations	Advanced Accounting Problems Credit Management Accounting Principles (Section 3) Advanced Accounting Principles (Section 2)
8.15–9.55 p.m.	Accounting Principles (Sec. 1 & 2) Auditing Principles and Accountant's Working Papers American Economic History	Commercial Law Marketing Real Estate Principles and Practice Psychology of Industrial Relations	Advanced Accounting Principles (Section 1) Elements of Business Administration Specialized Accounting	Accounting Principles (Sec. 1 & 2) Business Psychology Business English (Section 3)	Investments Cost Accounting Personnel Administration Political Economy (Section 3)

(Bulletin, AY 1946–1947, p. 15)

Appendix P
Designations of the Unit Teaching Business Administration at Hopkins (1916–2006)

Academic Year 1916–1917 to Academic Year 1918–1919

Courses in Business Economics (3 academic years)

Academic Year 1919–1920

Courses in Business and Social Economics (1 academic year)

Academic Year 1920–1921 to Academic Year 1922–1923

Courses in Business Economics (3 academic years)

Academic Year 1923–1924 to Academic Year 1946–1947

Evening Courses in Business Economics (24 academic years)

Academic Year 1947–1948 to Academic Year 1952–1953

Evening Courses in Business Economics; also known as "the Business School" (6 academic years)

Academic Year 1953–1954 to Academic Year 1963–1964

Moves to McCoy College from the Faculty of Philosophy and maintains current program
Evening Courses in Business Economics (11 academic years, including similar names)

Academic Year 1964–1965 to Academic Year 1989–1990

McCoy College renamed the Evening College and Summer Session; division name changes to the Division of Administration and Business (26 academic years)
During Academic Year 1984–1985, Evening College and Summer Session renamed School of Continuing Studies, but division's name unchanged

----

Academic Year 1990–1991 to Academic Year 1998–1999

Division name changes to Division of Business and Management (9 academic years)

Academic Year 1997–1998 to Academic Year 2006–2007

On July 1, 1997, Division of Undergraduate Studies established (10 academic years)

Academic Year 1999–2000 to Academic Year 2006–2007

On July 1, 1999, school name changes to School of Professional Studies in Business and Education; simultaneously, division name changes to Graduate Division of Business and Management; designation of the Division of Undergraduate Studies remains unchanged (8 academic years)

On January 1, 2007, name of unit teaching Business Administration at Hopkins changes to
Carey Business School—a business school at last

Appendix Q
Full-Time Faculty and Staff in the Undergraduate and Graduate Business Divisions and Those at the School Level Who Provided Leadership and Support during 2006

The 90th Year of Teaching Business Administration at Hopkins

Members of the Division of Undergraduate Studies during 2006

Antoinette Sapet (Toni) Ungaretti, PhD, associate dean, director, and assistant professor—For 31 years, Toni Ungaretti was a key member of the School of Continuing Studies (SCS) and School of Professional Studies in Business and Education (SPSBE). In January 1976 she joined the Education Division as a part-time instructor. For many years she taught a course on human growth and development that she had created for the Counseling Department. During this time she held the rank of professor at Dundalk Community College, where she was Director of Education Programs and Coordinator of Academic Advising.[30]

---

30 Many thanks to Thomas Allen Crain for interviewing Dr. Ungaretti and subsequently writing this biographical sketch. His willingness to help out is always appreciated.

Then, in 1988, Toni was asked by JoEllen Roseman to teach a seminar in a new certification program for Maryland math and science teachers. The success of her efforts led to greater involvement with teacher development. In 1991, she was offered a position as assistant professor and coordinator of the Master of Arts in Teaching (MAT) program. She redesigned the program and prepared it for a program approval review and site visit by the Maryland Higher Education Commission in 1993. Her efforts were enormously successful.

In May 1993, Dr. Ungaretti became the first chair of the Department of Teacher Development and Leadership. From a fledgling program with only six students, the MAT program grew to become a cornerstone of the Division of Graduate Education and one of the strongest teacher preparation programs in the state. Among her other notable accomplishments, Toni created the first professional development schools in Maryland, funded by the state (1994); the intensive school immersion (SIMAT) cohort programs for teacher certification; and a master's degree program for math and science educators that sought to remedy the disconnect between science and math as taught in the classroom and as applied in the real world.

In 1997, as the School of Continuing Studies prepared for a change in its name and mission, Toni was offered another challenge: creating and overseeing a new Division of Undergraduate Studies in the School of Professional Studies in Business and Education (SPSBE). Named assistant dean and director of undergraduate studies in the spring of that year, she quickly reorganized two existing degree programs and added a third, producing Bachelor of Science programs in Interdisciplinary Studies, Business and Management, and Information Systems. Her work in rethinking the curriculum around core competencies and outcomes became a model as JHU prepared for a site visit by the Middle States Higher Education Commission in 2004. Toni was asked to serve on the university-wide Commission on Undergraduate Education, and the core competencies and assessment tools that she helped to create proved useful to the other divisions. The Division of Undergraduate Studies was given very high marks on its accreditation review, and at the final hearing one reviewer remarked that the rest of the university could learn a great deal from it. The reviewer (from the University of Pennsylvania) had been particularly impressed by the overwhelmingly positive response to his queries by members of SPSBE's faculty and student body, and by the Undergraduate Division's thorough documentation of its learning outcomes.

During her time at the helm of the Undergraduate Division, some of Toni's other accomplishments included putting the undergraduate division on stable financial footing, strengthening faculty development, partnering with the Humane Society of America and the Office of Patents and Trademarks in Northern Virginia (among others), and creating a post-baccalaureate Business Transitions program, providing a bridge between undergraduate and graduate business.

As SPSBE prepared for yet another change of identity, and as Toni's reputation for strong leadership and expertise in curriculum and faculty development grew, she was asked to play an increasingly important role in the Division of Graduate Business and Management. Between 2005 and the creation of the new Carey Business School in January 2007, she provided leadership to the MS in Organization Development and Strategic Human Resources; led a faculty team to redesign the graduate certificate in Nonprofit Management; assisted in the development of the MBA Fellows program as an integrated, outcomes-based curriculum; developed a partnership and an international consultancy course with a university in Augsburg, Germany; developed an interdisciplinary course in collaboration with the Maryland Institute College of Art; began the process of exploring the possibility of a joint program with Peabody Institute; and was involved in much more, including her ongoing work with faculty at the Medical School and School of Nursing.

When Dr. Pete Petersen stepped down as interim associate dean and director of the Graduate Division of Business and Management in February, 2006, Toni was asked to serve as interim co-director, along with Bill Agresti. In this capacity, she was vital to maintaining faculty morale and direction during a time of great uncertainty and the transition of the school from its continuing studies roots to its reinvention as a business school. Throughout this time, she maintained her primary concern with students and faculty, teaching, and learning.[31]

John R. Baker, Sr.—John Baker, who had been teaching as a part-time instructor with the Business Division since the fall semester of 1983, was selected in November 1987 to lead the rapidly expanding Information Technology option within the Master of Administrative Science (MAS) degree. Indeed, his office would in time become the Department of Information Technology. As part of his appointment, he was given the concurrent task of being the project manager for the development of the school's portion of the (then-under-construction) Johns Hopkins University Montgomery County Campus. Unlike the Downtown Center in Baltimore, the Montgomery County Campus included other Hopkins schools. Baker then became the first director of the school's portion of the Montgomery County Campus. In 1991, he stepped down from his activities at the Montgomery County Campus and concentrated on running the Department of Information Technology. At that time, it included the information technology option of the MAS degree, the undergraduate program in Information Systems, and the school's noncredit offerings in technology training. It was during this time that Baker designed the Master of Science in Information and Telecommunications Systems for Business degree. These were bustling times of expansion and rapid change. Years later, in August 1994, he finally stepped down as director of the department and was replaced by William Engelmeyer. After

---

31 After the creation of the Carey Business School, Toni accepted a position as assistant professor and interim chair of the Management Department; later, in the fall of 2007, she was offered the position of assistant dean and director of the Office of Teaching and Learning within the Carey Business School, a position that she currently holds.

spending the following year teaching and working on various projects in the Department of Information Technology, Baker decided to try his hand in the private sector in the technology field. All during this time, he continued to teach for the department. Two years later, he was invited to return as a senior adjunct faculty member and taught a full load of classes. In addition, for a part of each week he helped by advising students, participating in information sessions, and working with Dr. James Novitzki to design new courses and programs.

In July 1999, Baker joined the Division of Undergraduate Studies to develop and manage the Bachelor of Science in Information Systems. He later also led the way in managing and developing noncredit technology courses in the training program known as Connect. Outgoing, friendly, and caring about people, he disarmed the fears of many adult students about computers and technology and was instrumental to these lifelong learners' quests for second chances at a first-class education. These men and women could be apprehensive about new technology, but Baker's ability to calmly convey this new knowledge reduced their fears and fostered their success. Today, he is again a full-time faculty member of the Information Technology Department and is the director of two undergraduate degree programs: the BS in Business and Management and the BS in Information Systems. Teaching at least one semester each year since 1983, Baker has been part of the evolution of teaching information technology to both undergraduate and graduate students in the School of Professional Studies in Business and Education.

When asked if he had any unforgettable moments, Baker recalled the many presentations he made promoting the center to the public in Montgomery County. They particularly liked seeing a four-by-three-foot model he used to show how the campus would look when completed. The eight-inch-tall model of the campus, complete with buildings and trees, and covered in Plexiglas, was the perfect visual to capture the imagination of the public. One day, while preparing for one of these lectures, he noticed that

Dr. Edgar (Ed) Roulhac had the model permanently attached to the center's wall. Being the considerate person he is, Dr. Roulhac permitted Baker to take the model off the wall, leaving two large holes where it had been attached. As a result, Baker was able to use it as a presentation aid in his talk. In a subsequent "recognition" ceremony, Roulhac had the staff roaring with laughter as he presented a black rubber mallet to John in "commemoration" of his "remodeling" of the center's wall.

Dorothy Becraft—In July 1999, Dottie Becraft became a member of the School of Professional Studies in Business and Education, working in Suite 180 at the Columbia Center with Susan Shaffer, Robin Reed, Kelly Williams, and Theressa Rose in the Business Division's Graduate Admissions Office. During that summer, the launch of the MBA program brought an initial surge in enrollments. Then, in November 2000, after the surge subsided, Dottie Becraft joined Dean Toni Ungaretti as her administrative assistant in the Division of Undergraduate Studies. Initially located in Shaffer Hall, Room 103, the office later relocated to Room 201. As the dean's administrative assistant, Becraft became involved in the division's major offerings and activities, including the Bachelor of Science in Interdisciplinary Studies, the Bachelor of Science in Business and Management, the Advancing Business Professional program, and the Bachelor of Science in Information Systems. In addition, another major effort was the development of noncredit technology courses for the training program known as Connect. Other significant activities included the Odyssey program and the inclusion of the popular Evergreen Society as part of the division. Furthermore, activities within the division also included the Business Transitions program, able to lead to a graduate certificate in Business and Management and the opportunity to include these credits in an MBA program.

A major activity of the division while Becraft was the dean's administrative assistant included a visit by Middle States that focused, at the time, on undergraduate studies. In fact, the visit's excellent results included the comment that the Division of Undergraduate Studies could serve as a model for others to follow. Particularly noteworthy was that students were more involved in the overall process as well as in day-to-day activities. As a member of the team, Becraft played a meaningful part in all of these activities.

About 20 years ago, Becraft started taking college-level courses, completing about 15 credits before she began participating in 1999 in a program in the Division of Undergraduate Studies leading to a Bachelor of Science in Business and Management. In fact, at the conclusion of 2006, she was about halfway through the 120-credit program. After departing from the School of Professional Studies in December 2006, she is now the administrator for a Geriatrics Medical Education program at the Johns Hopkins University School of Medicine. Asked if she recalled any very special occasions, she described how proud and delighted she was when her colleagues Peppi Faulk and Ty Rich received their degrees from Johns Hopkins University.

Stacey J. Brown—During August 2002, Stacey Brown became a member of Johns Hopkins University as an academic program coordinator for information technology and business programs in the Division of Undergraduate Studies in the School of Professional Studies. Located in Suite 180 at the Columbia Center, she advanced to her current role as adviser and Senior Academic Coordinator for Undergraduate Business Programs. Brown is currently located temporarily on the third floor of the Columbia Center while her new office as a member of the Carey Business School is being renovated on the second floor. Asked if she recalled any significant or heartwarming moments, she described an emotional panel presentation by one of their graduates at a new student orientation where he mentioned the importance of taking care of your own health and how important it is to lead a healthy lifestyle. This particular student experienced a serious health problem, but he returned the next year giving a similar presentation that helped motivate that group as well. He later applied and was accepted to the Carey Business School,

Leadership Development Program, and is now pursuing his MBA. Thanks to the support and encouragement, it seems that a good number of undergraduate business students, after finishing their degrees, are motivated to advance further with graduate business degrees from Hopkins.

Thomas A. Crain—On November 15, 1993, Tom Crain became a member of the Division of Arts and Sciences within the School of Continuing Studies, where he was appointed Director of Noncredit Liberal Arts Programs. In that capacity he developed and staffed about 130 noncredit courses each year. Networking with professionals in the field, he was successful in attracting excellent instructors who presented courses that commanded rave reviews. As part of this function, he developed program brochures and other promotional material. Particularly noteworthy was the Odyssey program brochure, with its compelling illustrations and well-written copy, often considered the best brochure in the entire school. Then, on June 1, 1997, he joined the newly established Division of Undergraduate Studies, where he directed the Bachelor of Liberal Arts and the Bachelor of Science in Interdisciplinary Studies programs. In this position, he participated in all aspects of the program, including recruiting and advising students, recruiting and developing faculty, editing of publications, and marketing programs. Beyond his day-to-day activities, Tom Crain is a published poet and has founded and edited two literary magazines. Furthermore, Crain is a PhD candidate at Johns Hopkins University who has completed the doctoral course work and two area exams. His commitment to furthering his own studies contributes to and complements the division's programs with his own efforts.

Katherine Cruit—Katie Cruit was the program coordinator for the Interdisciplinary Studies program from January 2004 until September 2006. In this capacity, she assisted Tom Crain with many of the logistical details connected with running the baccalaureate degree program in Interdisciplinary Studies, such as ordering books for classes and responding to questions from faculty and students. Working also on the database system, she provided input to Prospect Tracker recording the status of prospective students starting with details about their initial inquiries. Tracking the status of these individuals, she took action to respond to their questions and reported their current status every two weeks. Cruit also assisted Irene Edmond-Rosenberg by advising special students and helped Tom Crain further by coordinating the many details connected with the Alpha Sigma Lambda National Honor Society for undergraduates in continuing higher education, including helping to identify those students who could apply for membership.

Cruit was quick to offer that her greatest joy working in the division was when students learned that they had been accepted into the program and actually started the program. She recalls meeting students for the first time, remembering that when she met them for the first time she would indicate that "coming here today was the hardest step"—they had now completed the admissions process and were starting the program.

Deborah A. DeFord—Deborah DeFord became a member of the staff at Johns Hopkins University during February 2001, working in the registrar's office certifying the accomplishments of students and alumni. She responded to potential employers, certifying whether or not applicants had the academic qualifications they claimed when applying for positions. Furthermore, she certified class standings for students who completed programs and verified the status of current students, needed for the issuance of insurance policies. Then, starting in July 2003, DeFord became a member of the Division of Undergraduate Studies in the School of Professional Studies as the noncredit registration coordinator for the Odyssey program. During 2005, as enrollments in Odyssey classes dropped because of limited parking on the Homewood Campus DeFord assisted in processing faculty evaluations, ordering books for classes, obtaining examination copies for instructors, and preparing and assembling faculty packets before each class. In August 2006, DeFord became an administrative coordinator in the Computer Science Department in the GWC Whiting School of Engineering.

Asked about any unusual events while at Hopkins DeFord recalled an embarrassing moment when she worked in the registrar's office in the basement of Garland Hall. On one particular occasion, while speaking to an elderly alumnus, she had to shout to be heard while talking on the telephone during a lengthy conversation. DeFord had the added challenge of maintaining the conversation while her co-workers and students waiting at the office counter chuckled at her plight.

Irene Edmond-Rosenberg—Irene Edmond-Rosenberg started at Johns Hopkins University in July 1996 as a senior academic adviser with the Division of Undergraduate Studies in the School of Continuing Studies, later renamed the School of Professional Studies in Business and Education. Then, in March 2007, she moved to the Carey Business School MBA program.

Paul R. Hutchinson—On October 1, 1999, after May graduation from the University of Maryland with a bachelor's degree in psychology, Paul Hutchinson became a member of the staff in Student Services, located on the first floor of Shaffer Hall. While working at the front desk, he interacted in person and on the telephone with potential students, often as the first person contacted about taking courses or enrolling in a degree program. He quickly learned basic information about the school's programs and learned where to direct potential students for more detailed guidance. Hutchinson also responded to all manner of questions from students who were already enrolled; however, unlike potential students, they often knew more about their programs than he did. In fact, in responding to questions about such things as refunds for dropped courses he would certainly be quoted if he answered with a more generous refund than provided. Consequently, from the start he had to learn how to answer questions in a confident manner about almost anything relevant to the School of Professional Studies.

On April 1, 2002, after 2½ years on the job in Student Services, he joined the Division of Undergraduate Studies. Working with John Baker on Undergraduate Information Systems courses and programs, Hutchinson continued to interact with potential students, recruiting those qualified to take courses and enroll in the Bachelor of Science in Information Systems program. In addition to recruiting and advising students, he got to know the faculty and, if the situation warranted, was able to find a qualified member of the faculty as a needed replacement. Starting in 2003, Hutchinson handled noncredit Information Systems Courses as an additional function, interacting with lifelong learners who wanted to gain an understanding of the subject without needing to earn a grade. Titled "Connect," this program helped many individuals have a second chance at a first-class education, for many of them later moved on to credit courses and degrees.

While a member of the Division of Undergraduate Studies, Paul Hutchinson received a Master of Science in Organizational Counseling from the Graduate Division of Education, a degree that he started and finished as a Hopkins employee. Asked if he recalled any unusual events while working at Hopkins, Hutchinson explained a situation involving a student about to graduate whom he had known for some time. A few days before graduation, he called this hard-working, conscientious student and told him that he would be unable to graduate because an audit just conducted revealed that he lacked three credits. Before his friend and associate could respond with anything more than a gasp, Hutchinson told him that he had actually earned the highest grade point average and would receive the Bachelor of Science in Information System's Award in addition to the degree. Indeed, Hutchinson enjoys a rapport with the students in the program and is quick to help them in their endeavors.[32]

M. Jennifer Moessbauer—Starting in 1995 as academic program coordinator in the Graduate Division of Education,

32 In October 2007, after 8 years in the school (SPSBE/Carey Business School), Paul Hutchinson moved to the Johns Hopkins Bloomberg School of Public Health as Assistant Director of Career Services.

Moessbauer was subsequently promoted in 1996 to marketing communications coordinator. Then, on July 1, 1997, she accompanied Dr. Toni Ungaretti during the establishment of the Division of Undergraduate Studies and until 2007 served as administrative director of the Division of Undergraduate Studies. As the administrative director, she performed financial, marketing, administrative, and personnel functions for the division. She could always be counted on to meet deadlines with accurate responses concerning the budget and catalog copy. Marketing credit programs (within the constraints of a tight budget) included developing brochures and advertising copy for offerings in business, information systems, and interdisciplinary studies as well as noncredit programs such as Odyssey, Evergreen, and Connect (noncredit technology). Moessbauer was also particularly helpful in the human side of the operations, handling personnel matters for the division. But beyond these important functions, her good sense of humor and cooperative spirit added to the well-being of the group.

Janet S. Roberts—Janet Roberts began her long association with Johns Hopkins University in the Student Loan Office on the Homewood campus in 1979, and in the Office of Student Financial Services in 1981. From 1986 to 1992, she left to raise her two daughters and then rejoined Hopkins in July 1993 as an education support services coordinator for the Odyssey program in the School of Continuing Studies, conducted by Carol Bogash and later led by Tom Crain. Roberts speaks fondly of her mentor, Peggy Hemmeter, followed by Susan Mrozowski. From May to October 1997, she was the administrative secretary for the assistant dean and director of the Division of Undergraduate Studies. Beginning in October 1997, Roberts joined the Odyssey program as an Academic Program Coordinator I and was promoted to Academic Program Coordinator II in 2002. With the establishment of the Carey Business School on January 1, 2007, Roberts moved to the Krieger School of Arts and Sciences when it took over the Odyssey program.

Evergreen Society (during 2006)[33]

Kathy Porsella, Director, Evergreen Society—During May 2006, the Evergreen Society celebrated its 20th anniversary. Equally impressive is the fact that this organization has been led by the same person for both decades. Indeed, Kathy Porsella is an example of how some people are motivated at Johns Hopkins University. First as coordinator and then as director of this effort, she became identified with the Evergreen Society and, with the full support of Dean Stanley C. Gabor, developed a passion for the program. Care for this effort and the love of its instructors and students captivated her. In fact, there is considerable evidence that this sort of motivation is successful in many walks of life when individuals are given both the authority and responsibility to accomplish a task and then are left alone to do it.

The focus of the Evergreen Society's programs is on lifelong learning and its mission is to "enhance the leisure time of semi-retired and retired individuals by providing stimulating learning experiences and the opportunity for new friendships" (www. evergreen.jhu.edu, accessed April 3, 2007). Offering 9 courses during the first year, the program now conducts about 80 courses a year. Each 12-week course meets weekly from 10:00 AM to noon or from 1:00 p.m. to 3:00 p.m.; the more popular courses include discussions of a wide range of interests, including comparative religion, international relations, opera, and motion pictures. Classes are presented at three Hopkins locations, but the most popular setting is the Montgomery County Campus, followed

---

33 During the summer of 2007, the Evergreen Society "joined the Master of Liberal Arts program and the noncredit Odyssey program within the Center for Liberal Arts in the Krieger School of Arts and Sciences" (Prime Time News for retirees of Johns Hopkins University, spring 2008, 15(2), p. 4). Then, in 2008, the Evergreen Society changed its name to the Osher Lifelong Learning Institute (OLLI) at Johns Hopkins University. An initial $100,000 grant from the Osher Foundation will be used to engage additional faculty, to provide scholarships, and to enhance outreach to prospective students. The grant may be renewed for two more years, after which OLLI will be eligible for an endowment of at least $1,000,000.

by Grace United Methodist Church in Baltimore and then the Columbia Center.

Porsella has successfully recruited some of the best professors at Hopkins to present the courses; in fact, the Evergreen Society program is so successful that there are waiting lists of potential members. Contributing to this effort was Claire Hooper, Gabor's executive secretary in 1986. Ironically, she was the first person Porsella met while waiting to be interviewed by Dean Gabor two decades ago; Hooper became Porsella's assistant years later after she retired during the mid-1990s. With people like Kathy Porsella and the late Claire Hooper, it is small wonder that the Evergreen society has been so successful.

Susan J. Howard—Susan Howard joined Johns Hopkins University in 1996 and was in the Department of Information technology office, then situated in the Bechtel Building, located several blocks from the Montgomery County Campus. In 1997, Howard became a member of the Evergreen Society as its sole administrator in the Montgomery County Campus, reporting to the director of the Evergreen Society, Kathy Porsella, located at the distant Columbia Center in Howard County. Dealing with students, instructors, and guest speakers, she responds to their questions and makes arrangements for classes, including specific classrooms, books, and handouts. At the moment, there are 22 Evergreen courses being conducted at the Montgomery County Campus. Each course meets weekly for two hours for a total of 12 weeks. One of these courses, titled "The Evergreen Lecture Series," has a different instructor each week. Needless to say, there is a substantial amount of coordination for Howard to accomplish.

Asked if she could recall any unforgettable moments, Howard mentioned her first field trip with the Evergreen Society, attended by a combined group of senior citizens from Baltimore and Montgomery County who met for a presentation at the Applied Physics Lab in Laurel, Maryland. Soon after the lights dimmed and the lecture began, an elderly gentleman who was snoring loudly rested his head on her shoulder. Although surprised at the time, she now knows what to expect and has grown fond of the entire group, including the man who was snoring.

Wafa B. Sturdivant—Before becoming a staff member of the Evergreen Society, Sturdivant interviewed with Director Kathy Porsella, who then asked her to meet with the late Claire Hooper. The meeting with Claire Hooper convinced Sturdivant that she wanted to be part of the Evergreen staff. Interacting on the job with Hooper would be fun and exactly what Sturdivant was looking for; besides, the members of the Evergreen Society were an extremely nice group of people. Her new job entailed working with members at two of their three locations, the Columbia Center and the Grace United Methodist Church, located at the corner of Charles Street and Northern Parkway in Baltimore. Asked to identify her major task, Sturdivant responded that it was "getting to know the members." In fact, a total of about 250 meet at her two locations. Members come from all walks of life and include many interesting people who have had exciting careers and unusual experiences. In addition, members value their connection with Johns Hopkins; in some cases it represents a major focus in their lives. An example of their interest is the situation in which a couple, in an effort to downsize, sold their house and moved to smaller suitable quarters near the Rockville Campus so that they would be closer to activities in the Evergreen Society. Asked if she could recall a memorable occasion, Sturdivant responded that her first day on the job was a rather stimulating one. As the person representing the Evergreen Society at the Grace United Methodist Church that day, she had been told to remind members to wear their name tags. As luck would have it, one distinguished-looking gentleman publicly objected, "I don't need to wear a name tag, because everyone here knows me." Thus challenged on the first day on the job in front of the group, she quickly responded, "But I don't know you." The man laughed as he put on his name tag, and the two become the best of friends.

Members of the Graduate Division of Business and Management during 2006

Office of the Dean (during 2006)

Pamela G. Cranston, interim dean—Long before Dr. Cranston became interim dean of the Carey Business School, she had a lengthy association with one of this unit's predecessors. Two years prior to her arrival in 1987, the School of Continuing Studies had evolved from the Evening College and Summer Session. Dr. Cranston inherited a fragmented, inconsistent student services effort that had suffered the coming and going of various mid-managers. The department needed a unified effort to identify what services should be furnished and who should perform them at the various levels and locations. This was also a busy time, for the year of Cranston's arrival coincided with the opening of the Baltimore Downtown Center near the corner of Charles and Saratoga Streets and the planning and development of the new Montgomery County Campus. As a result, Cranston stepped into her new position during a bustling time of rapid expansion of locations, the arrival of new members of the faculty and staff, and an increase in the various types of student services. After several internal reorganizations and a few further adjustments, the unified function of student services took shape under the leadership of Dr. Cranston and the support of the school's dean, Stanley C. Gabor. Appointed associate dean for academic services in the School of Continuing Studies during 1995, she continued in this role until she departed in 1997 for a position at the Association of American Medical Colleges. In this new role, she had a number of significant positions for almost six years, including being associate vice president of the Division of Medical Schools Services and Studies and deputy executive director of the National Resident Matching program.

Returning to Johns Hopkins University in 2002 as assistant vice provost, she was subsequently appointed a year later associate provost for academic affairs: a post that she held from 2003 to 2006. Then, on July 1, 2006, Cranston became vice provost for academic affairs and international programs. Finally, less than six months later, on December 5, 2006, when the Johns Hopkins University board of trustees approved the creation of the Johns Hopkins University Carey Business School, Dr. Pamela Cranston was selected as the interim dean.

William W. Agresti, acting co-associate dean and co-director, Graduate Division of Business and Management—*See* Department of Information Technology

Margaret A. Fallon—Marnie Fallon became a member of the School of Continuing Studies during February 1994, working part-time at the Columbia Center with Betsy Mayotte and Karen Beaman. In December 1996, she became a full-time member of the Business Division, joining Dr. Jo Ellen Gray in the Department of Management and Marketing at the Baltimore Downtown Center Annex. After about two months, she moved back to the Columbia Center with the department when it displaced to Columbia. Then, with the arrival of Dr. Carlos Rodriguez, the department split into two departments—the Department of Marketing, headed by Rodriguez, and the Department of Management and Organizational Development, headed by Gray. Fallon remained at the Columbia Center, working with the Department of Management and Organizational Development with Cynthia Tucker and Cathy Deyo (now Wilson) until April 2000, when she moved to the Washington DC Center as part of the overall effort of admissions and advising for the Business Division.

In a rapidly expanding organization with four or five different sites, one might expect to relocate from time to time as it suited organizational changes in structure and changes in locations of off-campus sites. Such was the case in the Business Division during the late 1990s. With her various moves, Marnie Fallon recalls an unusual event in 1997 when several people responded to a strange situation. A major portion of the Business Division, located in the original Downtown Center Annex, was plagued by worn-out office space and leaky pipes that tended to seep on Monday. Old coffee cans on the top of file cabinets and desks caught most of the drips, and it was discovered that the culprit was wastewater discharged from an ad-hoc mini-apartment located above the office. So the closing of the mini-apartment, used on weekends, solved the problem—or so they thought. Apparently, one occupant was uninformed, and subsequently the water discharged from the apartment became too much for the decaying pipes, causing a substantial shower of wastewater on desks, rooms, and cubicles in the Business Division.

The person most affected on that wet Monday morning in 1997 was Pete Petersen. Responding to his call for help, Marnie Fallon, Robin Reed, and Cathy Deyo rushed to the rescue. Books, papers, and boxes of research material flew in every direction as the contents of Petersen's room were evacuated. Everyone was soaked, Robin's shoes were ruined, and the area was a mess; luckily, however, much was salvageable. Petersen will always remember the help he received on that occasion.

Marnie's willingness to lend a hand and roll with the punches serves the Business Division well. She is currently supporting a new approach started in 2004 (that continues today) that focuses on returning advising efforts to the academic department level where the same advisers interact with the same students from the time they inquire about admission until they graduate. With this new arrangement, Marnie Fallon is responsible for MBA students located at the Washington DC Center and the Montgomery County Campus, as well as those MBA students in 2006 located in an off-campus site in Southern Maryland. Her dedication and enthusiasm with students, faculty, and staff is much appreciated.[34]

R. M. Erik Gordon—On December 21, 2006, Dr. Lex McCusker, dean of the Howe School of Technology Management announced

---

34 The class of 2005 honored Marnie Fallon by presenting her with a plaque for her service and dedication at their commencement reception during May 2005.

the appointment of R.M. 'Erik' Gordon as the Associate Dean for Management Programs in the Howe School of Technology Management. Erik Gordon is also appointed as the Schulman Family Chair Professor of Technology and Business Management at Stevens Institute of Technology ... Erik comes to us from Johns Hopkins University where he was leading their Graduate Division of Business and Management. Before that, he was at the University of Florida, where he directed their MBA program. (http://howe.stevens-tech.edu, accessed April 2, 2007)

Mary Honeyblue—During August 2002, the Business Division was most fortunate when a temporary service sent Mary Honeyblue to work as a secretary/receptionist. In fact, members of the division were so impressed that three months later, in November, she was hired on a full-time basis. Now, almost five years later, she continues to greet people as they exit the elevator on the third floor of the Downtown Center in Baltimore. But more than merely acting as a greeter (and provider of security), she also knows where the occupants of the third floor are at any given moment and is able to direct guests in the right direction. Always abreast of what is transpiring, she furnishes the latest changes in the schedule and updates passersby on the latest happenings. Serving under six different directors since her arrival, Honeyblue's flexibility and resourcefulness have been unshakeable.

Honeyblue's thoughtful nature goes a long way toward boosting individual morale and maintaining the esprit de corps of the office. She makes arrangements for office birthday parties and always ensures that no one is forgotten. Her latest event, a baked potato bar with all the trimmings, is just a small example of her creativity in these endeavors. So—many thanks to Mary for her happy smile and sunny disposition, particularly during a period of change and uncertainty at the closing months of 2006.

Peter B. Petersen—*See* About the Author

April Stanson—During the 90-year history of teaching Business Administration at Johns Hopkins University, April Stanson may hold the record for being senior administrative assistant to more deans during a four-year period than anyone else. In fact, she worked with six directors of the division (also referred to as associate deans) since her arrival in December 2002. In this role, she kept these deans on schedule, getting them to their meetings on time and maintaining the electronic calendars of the principal members of the division. Behind the scenes, she organized meetings, recommended who should attend, and transcribed the minutes. She also assisted department chairs by keeping them informed on what was going on and kept them abreast of the many changes that became part of the fast-moving routine as the division evolved into the Carey Business School. But, beyond all this, she kept the new deans out of trouble as she helped them navigate their new organizational culture.

Toni S. Ungaretti, acting co-associate dean and co-director, Graduate Division of Business and Management—*See* Division of Undergraduate Studies

Mervyn Warner—Mr. Merv Warner joined the School of Continuing Studies on June 25, 1995, working with Sherri Wood in the Business and Information Services Office on the second floor of Shaffer Hall. Following a reorganization in April 1999, he began working with Dr. James Calvin, director of the Leadership Development Program (LDP) for Minority Managers. Although senior program coordinator of the LDP, Merv advised many students who years later would be more than advisees; indeed, they would become close friends. In 2003, he became Assistant Director of Admissions and Advising, working with Ms. Sabree Akinyele, where he advised both MBA and Information Technology students. As programs and off-campus centers evolved, the advising of MBA students is now conducted by Merv Warner and Marnie Fallon; Warner advises MBA students at the Baltimore Downtown Center and the Columbia Center, and Fallon advises students at the Washington DC Center and the Montgomery County Campus.

Concurrently, the advising of Information Technology students is conducted by the Department of Information Technology. Merv Warner also advises MBA students at Booz Allen Hamilton, located at Tyson's Corner, Virginia, and Marnie Fallon advises MBA students in southern Maryland. Merv has fond memories of meeting students as they start their programs and then working with them until graduation—and, in some cases, beyond graduation. In one example, he recalls working with a student who had been just discharged from the service and worked for Hopkins in East Baltimore. Determined to rapidly complete both the LDP and MBA and move on with his career, he received assistance from Warner with late registration, enrolled in the LDP, and was included as a member of the Hopkins team that participated in the national level Black MBA Case Competition. He later decided to leave his full-time job so that he could concentrate on his studies and, as a result, completed his MBA within two years. With his Hopkins experience and Warner's good advice and mentoring, this graduate has a fantastic job and a promising career; indeed, Merv Warner couldn't be more proud.

Office of Recruiting and Business Outreach (during 2006)

Elizabeth K. Mayotte, Director, Office of Recruiting and Business Outreach—*See* Associate Dean for SPSBE Administrative Systems in 2006

Louise E. Lancaster—Louise Lancaster started at the School of Nursing in 1993 as an administrative assistant to five full-time graduate program faculty. Before going to her next position, she supported a total of 10 faculty. In 1995, she took the position as administrative assistant to Dr. Jackie Campbell, director and chair of the doctoral program at the School of Nursing. Ms. Lancaster completed approximately 30 grants (formatting, proofing, copying, and mailing) while at the School of Nursing and was with Dr. Campbell until April 1998, at which time she left Hopkins because of health issues. Ms. Lancaster returned to Hopkins at the School of Professional Studies in April 2001 as the program assistant of the MBA program. In 2004, when Lynda de la Viña was the associate dean, she created the position of Executive Education Outreach Coordinator, which Ms. Lancaster held until coming to the Undergraduate Department in January 2007. She has always worked closely with students and faculty in every position at Hopkins and has been involved with the Ginder lectures for the last three years, usually coordinating the logistics (catering, invitations, printing, etc.).

Eva Lane—Eva Lane began working at Hopkins as special events director at the Baltimore Downtown Center in October 1990. The Downtown Center, almost four years old at the time, was directed by Jan Moylan. Events at the Berman Auditorium acquainted the public with the Hopkins Downtown Center in Baltimore and the programs presented by the Business Division; indeed, this public exposure proved so beneficial that a special events director was necessary, and subsequently Eva Lane was selected for the position. Lane was then promoted to assistant director of the center and in 1997 was promoted to director of the center, a position she occupied until 2003. As SPSBE Centers evolved and expanded, they seemed to fall into a southern group (DC and the Montgomery County Campus) and a northern group (Homewood, the Downtown Baltimore Center, and the Columbia Center), so a director was appointed for each of these two major elements to facilitate better control and communications. As a result, Lane was appointed director of the Baltimore Regional Centers (Homewood, the Downtown Baltimore Center, and the Columbia Center), a position she held from 2003 to 2005. Particularly skilled in dealing with the public as well as with business, industry, and government, Lane concurrently established an outreach effort during this 15-year period.

Following another realignment in 2005, she spent half of her time with the Business Division on outreach activities and the other half on special projects in the office of the SPSBE dean, acting in this capacity until the establishment of the Carey Business School on January 1, 2007.[35]

Lane was very much involved in one bit of Business Division folklore concerning W. Edwards Deming, who made a presentation in Berman Auditorium on September 23, 1992. Deming, famous for his work as the undisputed leader in the quality movement, was credited for helping the Japanese in their industrial renaissance, starting in 1950. During a presentation in a classroom at the Downtown Center four years earlier (July 8, 1988), Deming required a special type of pen of the highest quality to use with an overhead projector, and a last-minute dash to a nearby art store produced the needed pen. In preparation for this presentation, Ceil Kilian (Deming's secretary) was contacted and the specific type of pen identified. A full set of pens of all colors was purchased and it seemed that all was ready for the master. Unfortunately all were unaware that Deming did not (at age 92) want to climb the seven or eight stairs to the stage in the Berman Auditorium. The high-tech projector and the fixed screen were in position, Hopkins trustees and other prominent guests were waiting to take their seats, and now Deming was ready to cancel the presentation and go home. The door to the auditorium kept opening as VIPs tried to enter and then closing as they were pushed back out. Lane rose to the occasion by dispatching Marcus Jackson (a campus police officer), who brought in an overhead projector from one of the classrooms, along with a screen on a tripod that collapsed from time to time. Finally the low-tech screen stabilized, and Deming was guided to his position next to the low-tech overhead at floor level. Lane and Jackson had saved the day—or so all thought. But Deming, when he saw the pens, seemed to explode as he threw all of the colored pens in Lane's direction. What was not known was that he only used black pens. However, the lecture was a success—it also made the newspapers in Baltimore and Washington the next morning, and the story about Deming and his pens continues as a very private in-house story within the Business Division. Deming

---

35 After the establishment of the Carey Business School, Eva Lane became coordinator of the MBA Fellows program.

returned the following year, this time to the Columbia Center, where at age 93 he gave his last lecture with us.[36]

Christina M. Potter—When she became a member of the Business Division during the fall semester of 2000, Christina Potter arrived at the division's busiest time since the enactment of the GI Bill at the end of World War II. The MBA had finally arrived. Indeed, after years of discussions, the MBA degree had finally been launched during the fall semester of 1999. A year had passed since the "rollout," and current students who were in the prior "flagship" degree of the division (the Master of Science in Business) wanted to know what they would have to do to transfer to the MBA program. Essentially, how many more credits would it take to get the MBA? Although an explanatory letter had been mailed to students and information sheets had been distributed, students wanted to talk to a human being, and that's where Potter fit in, working in the Department of Management. Using her skills in dealing with the public, she put callers' minds at ease on these questions and many more dealing with both management and behavioral science courses. Working with Cynthia Tucker, who had been in the division since the early 1980s, Potter also dealt with an endless number of part-time faculty. Their concerns pertained to what courses they were going to teach as well as the location, day of the week, and specific time of their class. Other challenges she solved along with Cathy Wilson concerned ordering textbooks and reducing the negative impact of the wrong book or edition arriving just prior to the start of class. In addition, she successfully handled students on those rare occasions when an instructor didn't show up for class, and responded to the flood of calls following the sighting of the first snowflake: *Are classes for tonight canceled?* As the workload shifted to recruiting students for other graduate degrees as well as for the MBA degree, she transferred

---

36 On three occasions with the Business Division, we appreciated that he charged nothing, even though his all-day sessions at the time were commanding as much as $60,000.00 a day from business and industry. Unfortunately, four months after his last presentation at Hopkins on August 16, 1993, at the Columbia Center, Dr. Deming passed away at the age of 93 on December 20, 1993.

to the Office of Admissions and dealt with prospective graduate students and with setting up open houses at four locations—Baltimore, Columbia, Montgomery County, and Washington DC. Open houses evolved into information sessions, but both required getting people to attend, having a successful session, and knowing who attended for a follow-up—as well as a follow-up for those who RSVP'd but did not attend, so that they could attend a future session. Then, years later, at the close of 2006, Potter rejoined the Department of Management as new programs in the department expanded and required her assistance. In fact, she is a woman for all seasons who understands the administrative side of teaching Business Administration.[37]

Robin M. Reed—Ms. Robin Reed remembers clearly February 12, 1996, as the date when she became a member of the Business Division. Since then, she has become very much involved in the admissions process for thousands of business students. Indeed, Ms. Reed's experience is the story of the Business Division's admissions process during recent years and a tribute to those who worked with her. Before she arrived, the application process was handled at the school level during the 1970s and early 1980s, and then at a combination of school level and division level from the mid-1980s until the early 1990s. A flood of applications for the new MSB degree during the beginning of the fall semester of 1991 encouraged the evolution of a decentralized approach. So, during the spring semester of 1996, when Robin Reed reported to Susan Marzullo (now Susan Shaffer), applications with their transcripts were handled at division level with close coordination with the respective academic departments within the division. In time, Peggy Kelly and Claudia James handled the

---

37 Concurrent with all these activities, Christina Potter also led a rather active life as a student. In the fall semester of 2001, she enrolled in the SPSBE undergraduate business program Advancing Business Professionals and, by attending on a full-time basis, graduated in May 2004 with a BS in Business and Management. Then, during the fall semester of 2004, she started the MBA program; she expects to graduate from the Carey Business School in May 2009 with an MBA degree with a concentration in Competitive Intelligence.

admissions process for the Montgomery County Campus and the Washington DC Center. Then, during Dr. Elmore Alexander's administration, admissions for the Business Division's programs were consolidated in a first-floor office next to the main door at the Columbia Center in Gateway Park. Returning to Baltimore during Dr. Heggan's administration, the division's Admissions Office (located in an extension of the old Downtown Center) hit its highest peak of activity with the introduction of the new MBA during the summer of 1999. Added to the team were Ms. Cathy D. Wilson and Ms. Marnie Fallon. Activity was so brisk that when members of the admissions team returned to their desks after an absence of 10 or 15 minutes they were greeted with a flurry of telephone messages. To handle the surge in activity, Christina M. Potter, who had been in the Management Department since the fall semester of 2000, also joined the admissions office. Then, when Susan Marzullo departed, Kelly Williams became director, and when she in turn departed to join the Police Executive Leadership program, she was followed by Ms. Sabree Akinyele, who departed in 2003. In 2004, when Ms. Elizabeth Mayotte was appointed Director of Recruiting and Business Outreach, she faced a time of decreasing enrollments and, with a team effort involving Robin Reed, Christina Potter, and Dr. Bill Agresti, reversed declining enrollments, in fact generating substantial increases. During the past three decades, recruiting has been a significant function, with a range of approaches ranging from open houses to information sessions. Ms. Reed has also been a vital part of every variation of these approaches since she arrived in 1996.

Academic Departments (during 2006)

Department of the Business of Health (during 2006)

Douglas E. Hough, chair—Selected as chair of the Department of the Business of Health in October 2000, Dr. Douglas Hough joined an established department that had worked for years on joint programs with other Hopkins schools. As an economist experienced in the field of health care and the first professor to head this department, he helped raise the department's efforts to a new level. In time, this department's joint ventures would involve joint graduate degree programs with almost all of the schools at Johns Hopkins University, including noncredit and graduate certificate programs. Key in the success of these joint efforts with other Hopkins schools was the trust, respect, and rapport between the Department of the Business of Health and its counterpart departments in other Hopkins schools. Doug Hough's hard work and focus on high-quality academic programs continues to strengthen this established relationship. Several examples of new programs include the Hopkins Business of Medicine certificate program, offered started in fall 2002 at the Washington DC Center; the MBA in Medical Services Management, offered starting in fall 2003 at the Washington DC Center; the Master of Public Health/Master of Business Administration joint degree program, offered with the Bloomberg School of Public Health starting in fall 2003; the Master of Science/Master of Business Administration Biotechnology program, begun with the Krieger School of Arts and Sciences in fall 2003; and the graduate certificate program Leadership and Management in the Life Sciences, begun during Academic Year 2005–2006.

Page W. Barnes—Page Barnes started in the School of Continuing Studies in 1996 as a program assistant to Patricia DeLorenzo (formerly Wafer), director of the Department of the Business of Health. At that time, there were only one certificate and two degree programs to support. Since then, the program has expanded rapidly, becoming the only graduate degree program to partner with four schools at Johns Hopkins University (the schools of Medicine, Nursing, Arts and Sciences, and Public Health). Important to the prestige of the School of Continuing Studies was the willingness of its peer schools at Hopkins to join in a joint degree program. This required a well-developed academic program as well as other schools' having the utmost confidence in the caliber and professionalism of SPSBE's faculty and staff. Page Barnes' professionalism earned her a reputation as a dependable person who could handle tasks when the department's director was unavailable. For example, when individuals in the School of Medicine could not reach the director of the department and needed accurate information in a timely fashion, Barnes responded quickly to their questions with dependable information. Although the person to call was the director of the Business of Health Department, callers were confident in calling Page Barnes, for they knew she would be reliable and efficient.

When DeLorenzo departed in March 2000, Barnes ran the department for seven months until Dr. Douglas Hough's arrival in October. Part of the division's folklore at the time was the case of a convincing imposer who claimed to be a physician and wanted to enter the program but was unfortunately mentally imbalanced. Another office legend is the time when Barnes arrived at the office early one morning and responded to the usual volume of voice mail messages from students. One student who called the night before indicated that it was an emergency and that she should call him on his mobile phone immediately. After Page called him and asked whether it was a good time for her to call, he asked several administrative questions about class but then had to terminate the call because he was deeply involved in a surgery. But, stepping back from folklore, it should be noted that the progress of this department is substantial, with eight major programs currently under way. Of course, much of the credit goes to the director, but, as in many other situations in the Business Division, accolades should be given to the backup team—in this case, Page Barnes.[38]

Katherine Clarke—Kathy Clarke started with Johns Hopkins University in 2000 as a member of the SPSBE Education Support Staff, in which position she coordinated room scheduling for SPSBE classes on the Homewood campus. She then became a member of the Business Division in January 2006 as an administrative assistant in the Department of the Business of Health, responding to phone calls and e-mail messages from enrolled and prospective students. Keeping track of perspective students by posting Prospect

---

38 In May 2007, Page Barnes became executive specialist to the interim dean of the Carey Business School.

Tracker, she makes sure that their questions are answered and that they receive packets of information they request. Furthermore, she also prepares and dispatches invitations to the pregraduation ceremony conducted by her department. From a human interest point of view, she jokingly explains about an embarrassing moment when her photo appeared on the first page of the *Hopkins Gazette.* On this occasion, she was a judge at the annual Hopkins Chili Cook-Out Contest, holding a large box of empty jars used by contestants to submit their products. It appeared to her friends and colleagues alike that she "had eaten the whole thing." Kathy Clarke also participates each year as a helper in the annual SPSBE picnic; in fact, in 2006, she kept things lively as the disk jockey.

Sheronda Gordon—In September 1997, she began her association with Johns Hopkins University as a member of the Hopkins Controllers Office and then became a member of the Department of the Business of Health in December 2006. As an academic program coordinator, she focuses on three relatively new and popular programs.

1. MS-MBA in Biotechnology

2. MBA in Life Sciences

3. Graduate certificate in Leadership and Management in the Life Sciences

In this role, she is the key individual and point of contact for the day-to-day operation of these three programs.

The Edward St. John Department of Real Estate (during 2006)

Michael Anikeeff, chair—Arriving in November 1991, Dr. Mike Anikeeff championed the Hopkins graduate Real Estate effort during the next decade and a half, starting with an existing initial program that became an excellent Master of Science in Real Estate. Evaluated by an external review of peer institutions in September

1998, the Hopkins Master of Science in Real Estate program was found to be on a par with the five universities nationwide that offer this degree. In addition, forming an advisory board during the early years paid off in now having a mature board of experts willing to give their time, energy, and, on occasion, financial support. For example, during Academic Year 2000–2001, this board voted to tax themselves $2,500–$10,000 annually to generate funds to help further develop the department's programs. Ever proactive, Mike Anikeeff's efforts created a favorable atmosphere when in July 2004 Mr. Edward St. John donated the largest gift ever received by the Business Division, $5.9 million to establish the Edward St. John Department of Real Estate. Furthermore, St. John's generously and Anikeeff's leadership led to the establishment in September 2005 of the first full-time program at Hopkins in Graduate Real Estate.[39]

Mary Lou Foley—Mary Lou Foley started at the Columbia Center in March 1989, job sharing with Hope Grandel and staffing the front desk two evenings a week and alternate Saturdays. At the time, classrooms were fully committed in a smaller center, then located at Twin Knolls in Columbia; she can recall running overhead projectors from classroom to classroom, including on weekends, when classes conducted next door in the Hilton Hotel required moving overhead projectors up the hotel stairs. Some of her more challenging moments include dealing with audiovisual requests and classroom temperature fluctuations. Inevitably, when thermostats were adjusted with an extreme adjustment, this yielded the opposite effect for the next class that occupied the room. It seems that the center's staff get involved in many tasks indirectly related to the classroom; for example, they strive to get students, faculty, and staff out of the building at the end of their classes and safely into their vehicles. In this regard, she can recall putting cardboard under tires in an icy parking lot as well

---

39 In 2007, Dr. Michael Anikeeff, professor and chair of the Edward St. John Department of Real Estate at Johns Hopkins University Carey Business School, was awarded the Richard T. Ely Distinguished Educator Award by Lambda Alpha International. This award is presented to the person who has achieved excellence within the academic world in the field of land economics.

as melting ice by pouring hot water from a large coffeemaker. But beyond this direct face-to-face assistance, she operated in a series of behind-the-scenes jobs at the center. In the position of evening and weekend coordinator (1993–1996), and later as Columbia Center facilities coordinator (1996–2005), Foley essentially coordinated and solved problems. For example, she made the daytime staff aware of what had transpired the night before and, as appropriate, coordinated with external support elements such as the MSE Library about specific situations that had to be remedied. As a result, students received the best possible support. In 2005, after spending 16 years at the Columbia Center, Mary Lou Foley made a major career change when she transferred to the Edward St. John Department of Real Estate in the Graduate Division of Business and Management. In her current position as academic program administrator, she supports full-time and part-time faculty in the department and also supports the chair of the department.

Isaac F. Megbolugbe—Isaac Megbolugbe became a member of Hopkins in September 2003 when he was appointed an associate professor in the Edward St. John Department of Real Estate within the Graduate Division of Business and Management. He had previously been employed as the Vice President for Research and Development with the Fannie Mae Foundation. In his initial role at Hopkins, he directed the Seniors Housing and Care program and then in 2005 was appointed director of the Master of Science degree program in Urban Planning and Development. In addition to his current teaching and advising role, Megbolugbe coordinates the Community Development and the Senior Living and Healthcare Real Estate tracks within the Master of Science in Real Estate program, including research projects in housing finance and mortgage markets. He is also an avid researcher and a prolific writer, with a substantial number of significant publications in his field. He is also most helpful to students as he applies both the theory of his research and his real-world experience at Fannie Mae to the pragmatic questions facing today's real estate markets.

Indeed, students appreciate his frank classroom discussions about contemporary real estate issues.

Marie C. Moineau—Marie Moineau began her long association with Johns Hopkins University at the School of Medicine in December 1987 and transferred to the Division of Administration and Business within the School of Continuing Studies on September 8, 1998. As a new member of the Real Estate Department, she joined Dr. Mike Anikeeff, who had led the Real Estate program since November 1991. Arriving just in time for the fall semester, she learned quickly that graduate students in the field of Real Estate had a reputation for registering late for class. As real estate professionals already on the job, these students (only aware of their commitments in the real world from day-to-day) were not about to pay in advance for a class they might have to drop. When faced with determining which under-enrolled classes should be canceled, she learned from Mike Anikeeff (who would make the decision) that a certain amount of magic was involved in fighting off the budgeters who wanted sparsely enrolled classes canceled as soon as possible. Consequently, Anikeeff and Moineau held their breath until the last minute, knowing that the classes would fill up. Indeed, this was the case, but it often led to some tense moments at the start of each semester.

Moineau also learned that unlike students in some of the other academic disciplines, a few graduate real estate students (currently practicing in the field) could on occasion be aggressive and sometimes cunning to deal with on the phone. However, Moineau, armed with facts, was able to cope in spirited situations by being fair and acting professionally, quickly defusing the situation and look at the request objectively, such as whether a closed class might handle an additional student. In fact, during the past nine years she has become a legend in the field of Real Estate at Hopkins; everyone dealing with Marie knows they will be taken care of and interacts accordingly. This results in a highly professional organization in which people respect each other, and the Hopkins Real Estate programs are considered among the best in the nation.

Margot Rome—In March 2002, Margot Rome became a member of the Graduate Division of Education within the School of Professional Studies in Business and Education. Then, in July 2005, she transferred to the Edward St. John Department of Real Estate, where she coordinates events and acts as the department's Web site administrator. Before moving to Baltimore five years ago, she worked in the corporate world for 14 years at a mutual fund investment firm in Westchester County in the distant suburbs of New York City. She loves Baltimore and enjoys learning about Charm City, in particular how the real estate industry has evolved over the years. As the coordinator of events, she organizes frequent activities for the advisory board, faculty, staff, students, and alumni. In fact, her work on events blends in with her other role as the department's Web site administrator. For example, in the case of internships and jobs, she networks with members of the advisory board, faculty, and alumni, coming up with fantastic opportunities for their department's graduates. In addition, because of her efforts and the favorable reputation of the department and its graduates, a substantial number of opportunities are also being offered by organizations not otherwise connected with Hopkins. As a mother of three and a grandmother, Margot Rome has found her niche in Baltimore and in Johns Hopkins University.

Elaine M. Worzala—Dr. Elaine M. Worzala was appointed professor when she joined the Business Division's Edward St. John Department of Real Estate in June 2006. A prolific writer with much teaching experience and a highly favorable reputation in her field at the national level, Worzala was selected to direct the Hopkins full-time cohort-based Accelerated Master of Science in Real Estate. Dr. Worzala teaches a wide range of courses in the field of real estate, including real estate finance and investments, introductory real estate, real estate feasibility, real estate valuations, and a real estate investments case course. Before becoming a member of Johns Hopkins University, Worzala was the director of the Master of Science in the Real Estate program and the director of research at the Burnam-Moores Center for Real Estate at the University of San Diego. Furthermore, in the area of university administration at the highest levels, she served as interim assistant provost at the University of San Diego during 2004 and 2005. Before coming to the University of San Diego, she was a member of the faculty at Colorado State University and a visiting professor at the University of Connecticut's Real Estate Center.

The Accelerated Master of Science in Real Estate students who completed their degree requirements and celebrated with a ceremony in October 2006 received quite a surprise. Edward St. John, the benefactor of the department and the keynote speaker, congratulated the class by presenting each of the 10 students with a gift of $1,000.[40]

Department of Finance (during 2006)

Ken Yook, chair—Dr. Ken Yook joined Hopkins in June 1999 when the SPSBE rolled out the MBA program. When the department chair, Dr. Robert Everett, departed in 2002, Dr. Yook assumed the interim chair position. At the same time, the Finance Department moved from the Baltimore Downtown Center to the Washington DC Center to accommodate the majority of students. Also during 2001–2002, the Finance Department experienced a difficult time when Matt Will, a member of the full-time faculty, and three staff members, Pamela Williams, Nicole Washington, and Karla Tassey, departed. Fortunately, Dr. Yook managed the department without lettings things fall between the cracks during this challenging

40 In January 2008, Dr. Worzala accepted a position as the director of the Center for Real Estate Development at Clemson University. She left with very mixed emotions, having been excited about the prospects of building up the Carey Business School. However, the opportunity at Clemson University included a job for her spouse and the ability to trade a 45-minute commute for a five-minute drive. As a professor of real estate, she understands the complexities involved with a relocation decision, and at this point in her life, with two small children, quality of life for her family weighed heavily in her decision.

time. Dr. Yook was finally appointed the department chair in 2004. Under his leadership, the MS in Finance program became one of the most successful programs developed by the SPSBE. Begun in fall 2000 with less than 10 students, it grew to a program with over 150 students in six years and ranked in the top 20 in a 2005 survey of competitive finance program rankings conducted by the company Global Derivatives. In response to the continuous improvement in instructional quality, top-notch part-time faculty recruitment, and the development of new elective courses to meet market demand, student satisfaction with the program has been overwhelming. An alumni survey in 2006 indicated that 90% are either "very satisfied" or "generally satisfied" with the program and say that the program helped them get a new job or promotion. Furthermore, Dr. Yook's participation in the World MBA Asia Pacific Tour with Marnie Fallon in 2005 provided a good opportunity to promote Hopkins business programs in Asian countries. Indeed, Dr. Yook has been an ardent advocate for international students.

Celso Brunetti—Celso Brunetti joined the Department of Finance on August 18, 2003, as an Assistant Professor of Finance, having previously held a position as visiting professor in the Department of Economics at the University of Pennsylvania in Philadelphia. In addition to teaching graduate-level finance classes at Hopkins, Dr. Brunetti was given the task of examining two major finance courses that had grown stale and needed rejuvenation. He completely revised both courses (Financial Management and Corporate Finance), including course objectives, syllabuses, and selection of textbooks. Furthermore, he changed the teaching approach to include a solid quantitative foundation that would help students throughout the overall financial management program. Realizing that in some cases different instructors would be needed, Brunetti set out to recruit and select the very best. Consequently, both courses were substantially improved, and, in turn, the overall financial management portion of the MBA program and the theoretical framework for the Master of Science in Finance were also improved.

Dr. Brunetti also spent considerable time and effort with others in developing the financial management portion for an in-house MBA program for a corporate client. Unfortunately, the client had a change in direction, and although it seemed that this effort was for naught, clear heads prevailed as Brunetti and his colleagues redesigned this program as an MBA Fellows program that is currently evolving into an Executive MBA program. The first class (a cohort of 30 students) started in November 2006. With a background in econometrics, Brunetti is currently focusing his research efforts in three areas:

1. How to measure risk in financial markets

2. How to forecast a currency crisis

3. The impact of hedge funds on overall market prices and risk

Also as a member of the Business Division's Joint Faculty Subcommittee, he helped develop potential directions for the integration of the Graduate and Undergraduate Divisions and participated in the presentation of the Report of the Joint Faculty Subcommittee during spring 2006 to the SPSBE Academic Council.

In addition to these activities, Brunetti spends considerable time helping students with their career decisions and in some cases puts these students in contact with future employers. Moving further in this direction, Brunetti and his fellow professors are developing internship programs in the Department of Finance that will count as a three-credit elective for those who successfully complete the internship. Outgoing and comfortable with students, he adds much to the program.

Kwang Soo Cheong—Dr. Cheong received a PhD in economics from Stanford University in 1994 and while a doctoral candidate taught undergraduate courses in economics and mathematics at Stanford. Following graduation, he taught at the University of Hawaii as an Assistant Professor of Economics and then became a member of SPSBE's Graduate Division of Business and Management as an assistant professor in August 2001. Arriving at Hopkins, he took charge of revising the contents of all economics and international business courses. An outgrowth of his effort was the creation of the two new courses, Business, Government and the World Economy and Managerial Economics, both of which still belong to the required courses for the MBA and other master's programs at Carey Business School. Extending his interest in teaching matters, he worked with colleagues in the Education Division, going through training on effective pedagogical methods, serving as a faculty mentor to adjunct faculty members, and making a joint presentation on outcome-oriented course design at a national conference on teaching and faculty development.

At Hopkins, he has taught a wide range of graduate-level finance and economic courses; according to him, his favorite course to teach is Econometrics in Finance, which is a computer lab course combining theoretical principles and hands-on exercises to the point at which students can conduct empirical studies of their own. His research interests include finance/corporate finance, public finance, industrial organizations, income distribution, and the Korean economy. He has not only published his research work in respected journals but also made numerous presentations at scholarly conferences. His professional activities include being an editor of the *New Economics Papers* and *Applied Economics Research Bulletin* and a contributor to the *World Income Inequality Database,* as well as a member of various professional organizations. He has also served as a reviewer for many journals and textbooks. At the university level, he represented SPSBE as a member of the university-wide Library Advisory Committee, helping to advise the library leadership on potential library policy, services provided, and financial issues. Beyond his work at Hopkins and participation in academic activities at the regional and national level, Cheong is also talented at the international level. He is an active member of the Korea-America Economic Association and the International Council of Korean Studies and during 1999–2001 was a member of the Advisory Council on Democratic and Peaceful Unification of Korea (a constitutional organization chaired by the president of Korea). Furthermore, along with Dr. Ken Yook, he is a supporting faculty member for the Hopkins Korean Graduate Student's Association, which was originally created by a group of Korean students in the SPSBE Business Division.

Promoted to associate professor in July 2006, Dr. Cheong is active at the SPSBE and Business Division levels, including membership in various academic committees and faculty activities. He particularly enjoys working with students in and out of the classroom and as an advisor to graduate students, helping them with career guidance as well as with their academic pursuits. In the normal course of events, he teaches a full load of classes as well as overseeing the adjunct faculty teaching economics courses while concurrently finding time to work on research, writing, and publishing. In his office, piles of books and file folders almost completely cover the floor, except the space for his chair making him feel like a "pilot in a cockpit"; the walls are also covered by many printouts, along with the old poster for the Hopkins MBA featuring his picture—according to him, it was quite a fun experience to pose for this poster. When asked if he recalled another unusual or funny situation, he confided about a certain period of time in 2003 when he was mistaken for the department chair by many people in other departments, for he worked very closely with the then–associate dean of business, getting involved in various administrative matters and participating in numerous school meetings. Indeed, he once served as an interim department chair two years later.

Kelly Haskins—During the time that the department lost all three staff members, Kelly Haskins arrived in October 2001 as an academic program coordinator. Promoted to academic advisor in 2004, Haskins has contributed greatly to building the finance program.

Michael McMillan—Michael McMillan became an instructor in the Department of Finance in January 2003.

> Prior to pursuing an academic career, Dr. McMillan was a securities analyst and portfolio manager, with Sturdivant & Company, Bailard, Biehl, and Kaiser, and Merus Capital Management. Dr. McMillan received his PhD in Accounting and Finance from The George Washington University, his MBA from Stanford University, and his BA in Economics and Sociology from the University of Pennsylvania. He is a member of Beta Gamma Sigma and the CFA Society of Washington DC (http://carey.jhu.edu/faculty/index, accessed April 18, 2007)

McMillan is also a member of the Council of Examiners of the CFA Institute. As an instructor in the Department of Finance, he teaches a wide range of courses that incorporate his experience in both academia and the actual practice of accounting and finance.

As in many colleges and universities, members of the Hopkins faculty differ in their outlooks or approaches to teaching even though they may successfully teach the same courses. Indeed, that is one of the many characteristics of the Hopkins faculty that benefits students. Dr. McMillan is an example of such a person, because, unlike many professors throughout the fields of accounting and finance, McMillan views both disciplines as one. Perhaps this is because his education and professional experience in the real world integrated both accounting and finance in his own mind; thus his approach in teaching in both fields is to realistically demonstrate how they can best support each other. He also noticed during information sessions with potential students that many of them are interested in earning the designations of Certified Public Accountant (CPA) and Charted Financial Analyst (CFA). Consequently, he conducts sessions with students from time to time on how these designations can be earned. Unlike the CPA examination administrated under the auspices of the state, the CFA examination is offered by a recognized professional association. McMillan's active involvement in CFA examinations offers students a realistic understanding of the work involved in achieving this goal as well as the motivation to go for it.

Julia Nussdorfer—Julia Nussdorfer was a high school French teacher before joining the Finance Department as an academic program coordinator in November 2005. She has been a valuable asset to the department.[41]

Department of Information Technology (during 2006)

James E. Novitzki, chair—Arriving in November 1995, Dr. Jim Novitzki taught information technology courses in the relatively new Master of Science in Information and Telecommunications Systems for Business degree as well as in the most popular degree in the Business Division at the time, the Master of Science in Business. During the decade prior, the Information Technology element had expanded from merely supporting the Master of Administrative Science program to having its own degree program, starting in Academic Year 1993–1994. Concurrently, during the 1990s, the Information Technology field expanded rapidly in business and government, along with many variations in the approach for teaching the subject in academic business programs. Countless office workers and their managers crammed not only into degree programs but also into available noncredit courses to learn how to operate personal computers. In this ever-changing environment, Novitzki followed Dr. Michael J. Prietula during mid 1999 as chair of the Department of Information Technology. Since then, Jim Novitzki has been a "man for all seasons" as the field continues to evolve along with a corresponding proliferation of degrees and approaches for teaching the subject. In time, the curriculum, containing an excessive number of courses, settled down into an approach that provided what students needed and their employers wanted. Along with this concentration of necessary material, the curriculum kept abreast with the field by adding relevant courses

41 In October 2007, Julia was promoted to Academic Program Administrator.

such as information security and competitive intelligence. Novitzki was also instrumental in establishing partnerships with business and government so that long-term arrangements and contracts could enable certificate and degree programs to be taught to groups of students at their work sites.

William W. Agresti—Joining the Business Division in September 2001, Dr. William Agresti was appointed an associate professor in the Department of Information Technology, where his experience and knowledge of the application of information technology in the "real world" was most welcome. Formerly a program director at the National Science Foundation, he is well-known in the scientific community for his work on software engineering and metrics. Experienced in data mining, he is a prolific researcher and writer who shares with his students his latest findings and views. Even though he was subsequently promoted to professor, his passion for research, writing, and publishing continues. Unfortunately, his research time was sharply reduced when he was selected (in addition to his regular duties) as the acting director of the MBA program and devoted countless hours to rebuilding this program after it had a substantial drop in enrollments. To remedy this, he participated with Betsy Mayotte in many recruiting presentations at four distant locations. In addition, his frequent travels included round trips between his home in Montgomery County and the site of his MBA office in downtown Baltimore. After (along with Betsy Mayotte) rejuvenating the MBA program in terms of quality in the classroom and increased numbers of qualified students, he also made arrangements for additional sections of MBA classes and the faculty to teach them. In keeping with the adage of "giving work to a busy person," he was selected during 2006 to be the acting co-director of the Graduate Division of Business and Management. In addition to his academic prowess, he is a two-sport college athlete, a former boxer, and an ardent O's Fan (per his "O's Fan" license plate) and tries to make most of the Hopkins LAX games. He also has a warm personality and a wonderful sense of humor.

Darlene Dixon—Before becoming a member of Hopkins, Dixon had five years' experience in the field of adult education. From 1989 to 1991, she was a staff assistant in the Financial Aid Office at Prince George's Community College, and from 1991 to 1993 she served as an administrative assistant in the History Department at Towson State University. Now in her 11th year at Hopkins, she has a total of 16 years of experience to offer.

Starting in the Department of Information Technology as a "temp" in January 1996, she established herself at Hopkins when she was hired on a full-time basis in April 1996 and has been in the same department ever since. Advancing through the system first as a program assistant and then as an education support services coordinator, she is currently an academic program coordinator. During a period of rapid change and expansion, she was part of the Department of Information Technology as it moved across the street from the original Baltimore Downtown Center Annex to the second floor of the Nation's Bank Building at 201 North Charles Street. She then accompanied her colleagues as they moved to the new Baltimore Downtown Center at 10 North Charles Street. Shortly after this move, they displaced again to the seventh floor of 100 North Charles Street. In 2003, however, they made their longest move, to the Montgomery County Campus. Finally, all of the members of the department were in the same location, when they moved from the main building to Building 3 at the Montgomery County Campus.

As might be expected, Dixon performed all manner of tasks in the day-to-day operation of the department, ranging from advising students and taking care of faculty to making sure the correct books are ordered (and arrive in time for the first night of class) and handling any concerns of faculty and students. Although she continues to jump in when necessary, she has focused lately as a special projects coordinator. In this role, she administratively organized a chief information officer (CIO) forum, in which a panel of CIOs discussed the latest developments in the industry as well as other contemporary topics. Furthermore, she organized the department's first executive seminar, conducted in 2005 at the Mount Washington Conference Center and the Baltimore Downtown Center. Although the academic offerings were led by Dr. Jay Liebowitz and Dr. William Agresti, Dixon's organization skills were evident in the excellent outcome of the executive seminar. She also administratively assisted Dr. Liebowitz in organizing a one-week Information Technology Summer Institute for high school students for the summer 2007 semester. Dixon also assists Dr. Jay Liebowitz in the administration connected with the Alpha Iota Mu National Honor Society for students in Information Systems. In addition, she also administratively supports Liebowitz in the selection of the winner of the annual Vargas Advanced Technologies Group (VATG) Award of Excellence in Information Technology.

Before Dixon arrived, Dr. Sarah Bryant, chair of the Finance Department, departed and was eventually replaced by Dr. Michael Prietula, who headed both Finance and Information Technology. In fact, Dixon recalls being a member of the Department of Commerce and Technology. Asked to recall a funny incident, Dixon remembered the time at a departmental meeting when Dr. Novitzki, chair of the department, told her that she is "the glue that holds this department together." Her response caused an outburst of laughter when she asked Dr. Novitzki, "Elmer's Glue or Crazy Glue?"[42]

G. Reza Djavanshir—Appointed assistant professor during August 2002 in the Department of Information Technology within the Business Division, Dr. Djavanshir teaches a wide range of courses in the area of information technology. Before coming to Hopkins, he was a member of the Products Development Division of BBN/GTE/Telenet Corporation. His background in the information technology field also includes experience as a senior technologist and as vice president of Citicorp's Global Information Systems; in addition, he applied established and new

---

42 Darlene Dixon completed her baccalaureate degree program and at the diploma ceremony in May 2008 received a BA in communications.

technology in a real-world setting as "a lead scientist in MITETEK where he worked on Business Process Re-engineering and Technology upgrades of the US Postal Services. [Furthermore,] he also worked on NASA Systems Engineering Projects" (http:// carey.jhu.edu/faculty, accessed April 6, 2007).

Dr. Djavanshir is actively involved in curriculum design for new initiatives in both credit and noncredit offerings in the Information Technology Department. In addition, he participates in the development of the necessary courses to support these new initiatives, including developing course objectives, selecting textbooks, writing syllabuses, and selecting new instructors. The caliber of his classes and team efforts with his peers add much to the activities of the Department of Information Technology. In addition, his pleasant outlook and good humor are most welcome.

Megan Glover—When Megan Glover started with the Graduate Division of Business and Management in November 2002, she worked half-time on admissions with Ms. Sabree Akinyele and half-time with the Department of Information Technology. Then, working full-time as an academic program coordinator in the Department of Information Technology, her efforts focused on cohort groups of students who were enrolled in a certificate program and/or graduate degree program sponsored by their employer. Two employers, the Department of Defense and Booz Allen Hamilton, became partners with Hopkins in an educational effort to offer a certificate program and/or graduate degree programs to some of their employees. As an academic program coordinator, Glover worked with her counterparts in these two organizations to ensure that students had favorable experiences in the programs. Consequently, she examined any complaint or recommendation and took action when appropriate. Countless sections of classes owe their favorable experiences to the diligence of Glover. Indeed, students and employers alike were so satisfied with the quality that many students who completed certificate programs enrolled further in a follow-on degree program. In addition to working with cohort groups, Glover helps Alisa Kinney with overall advising for the department.

Jay Liebowitz—Since arriving in August 2002, Dr. Jay Liebowitz looks to use his creativity in many ways. For example, he developed the first Executive Education course for the Graduate Business Division, the first CIO forum, the first Summer IT Institute for High School Students, and the graduate certificate in competitive intelligence. As an expert with an international reputation in knowledge management and intelligent systems, Liebowitz encourages faculty and students alike to become actively involved in research, writing, and publishing. He was recently ranked third in the world (out of 11,000 researchers/educators/practitioners) in knowledge management research productivity. In addition, he is the founder and editor in chief of the *Expert Systems with Applications* international journal (Elsevier), which was cited as the top-ranked journal in its field. He led the way in terms of numbers and quality of publications and presentations, and his initial appointment to professor was made shortly after his arrival. Beyond his own interests, he secured a five-year grant from the GEICO Philanthropic Foundation to finance the GEICO Scholarship in Discovery Informatics, as a result of which his students have published three articles to date as the lead authors in internationally refereed journals. He also has a Navy research project examining cross-generational knowledge flows in edge organizations.

In addition to his academic pursuits, Jay Liebowitz is known for his wit, humor, and love of people. Because of his interest in the human side of "working in the office," the Department of Information Technology participates in noontime walks and the occasional use of a conference room table for ping-pong.

Department of Management (during 2006)

Toni S. Ungaretti, chair—*See* Division of Undergraduate Studies

James R. Calvin—For the past 11 years, Dr. James Calvin has been the focal point for the Hopkins Leadership Development Program for Minority Managers. This program, known as the LDP, supports "the advancement of high potential minority managers by offering education in the latest management and leadership theories and applications" (*SPSBE Academic Catalog 2005–2006*, 2005, p. 112). Furthermore, this 15-credit program, when successfully completed, can be used as part of a subsequent graduate-level degree program. Developed and approved in 1990 and launched during the fall semester of 1991, the Leadership Development Program had been under way for about five years when James Calvin was appointed director and assistant professor in April 1996 (he was later promoted to associate professor). Carol Lyles (now Lyles-Shaw), appointed the initial director during 1990, was succeeded by Dr. Jo Ellen Gray. A major event during Jo Ellen Gray's administration is still talked about today: the winning of the National Black MBA Case Competition during September 1994 in San Francisco. This was the first time that the Hopkins LDP team participated in this nationwide annual competition, sponsored by the National Black MBA Association, and they developed and presented the winning solution to a real-world case involving a Procter & Gamble product. The team, coached by Christina Rodriguez, consisted of Jerome Alston, Helen Holton, and Blair Johnson.

During the past 11 years, under Calvin's stewardship, the Leadership Development Program matured and evolved into a nationally famous program with a strong group of faculty, students, and alumni. James Calvin can be proud of the accomplishments of LDP alumni in graduate-level degree programs and the workplace, as well as of the LDP case competition teams that consistently show in the top-tier second or third places of the annual National Black MBA Case Competition. Calvin's major challenge each year is recruiting the very best candidates for his program, and he partnered with business to develop and produce a high-quality recruiting video. Unlike most programs in the Graduate Division of Business and Management, in the LDP, students join cohort groups, so the challenge is to have a sizable cohort group of high-quality students ready to launch each fall at both the Washington DC Center and the Baltimore Downtown Center. Calvin is also active in many projects within the Department of Management. For example, for many years he has been involved in curriculum development and also as an adviser for Directed Field Work students. In fact, in recent years, he has been running the Directed Field Work program. Also, he is frequently called upon for academic committee participation at the department, division, school, and university levels.[43]

Capers W. McDonald—Capers McDonald earned the distinction of Executive in Residence by virtue of his remarkable success in business and the thoughtful work he accomplished for Johns Hopkins University during the past decade and a half. When he joined BioReliance in 1992 as their president and CEO, the operation was very small, unprofitable, and unfocused. Twelve years later, in 2004, the company was acquired for $500 million and valued at $48 per share, a 32-fold increase and a greater than 33% annual return for both investors and employees over these 12 years. In addition to the rigors at work, McDonald found time from 1993 to 1996 to interact with the Whiting School of Engineering around his prior work in the field of bioengineering. During January 1997 and January 1998 intersession classes in entrepreneurship, he participated as a panelist judging undergraduate students from the Krieger School of Arts and Sciences on the presentation of their business plans. Years later, during Academic Year 2003–2004, he offered his company as a real-world live case study for students taking their Capstone class during the summer, fall, and spring semesters. But in more than just another case study, he posed substantial questions for teams of students' research and response. The best teams in each semester battled it out to decide the best team in the MBA graduating class. To add realism to the exercise, he and key members of his staff were available to respond to what would normally be in-house questions. Consequently,

43 Calvin is currently chair of the Membership Committee at the Academy of Management and serves on the executive board of the Society for Advancement of Management.

students learned real-world lessons that were truly a Capstone to their MBA programs. It was at one of these Capstone presentations that Erik Gordon (acting associate dean and director of the Graduate Division of Business and Management) discussed the possibility of McDonald being an executive in residence. Gordon, who was interested in entrepreneurship and the applications of technology, had found a person with a full measure of experience and academic preparation in both areas.

As an executive in residence, McDonald taught and helped design a program leading to a joint certificate in Technical Innovation and New Ventures, involving both the School of Professional Studies and the Whiting School of Engineering. Then he helped develop an in-house MBA program for a corporate client. Unfortunately, a change in the client's leadership caused the client to be unable at the time to enter this venture. However, clear heads prevailed, and the effort was not in vain when it was further developed into a successful MBA Fellows program. McDonald taught in this program and has had an active role in the refinements in the program as it was implemented.

McDonald is an interesting individual with an outgoing leadership style that focuses on building trust and lasting relationships. For example, as new members were brought into the group of planners for the MBA Fellows program, he was a bit of the extrovert (or showman) when he dashed across the room and hugged another rather outgoing professor, greeting him as his long-lost friend. There was no doubt after this first session that this was going to be a fun group, with lots of openness in the way they operated. Indeed, with this transparency, they really got down to work as people working together. In fact, their accomplishments help prove that good, trusting relationships at work can pay off. Further demonstrating his interest in the human side of enterprise, McDonald and his wife have endowed awards for Excellence in Mentoring and Advising within the Schools of Engineering at Johns Hopkins, Duke, and MIT, and on a national basis through Tau Beta Pi, the engineering honor society.

Margaret L. Criscione—In August 1991, Margaret Criscione started her long association with Johns Hopkins University, working for human resources manager Edwin (Ed) Warfield as an administrative assistant in the Johns Hopkins University Human Resources Office located on the first floor of Garland Hall. Then, in the summer of 1992, she became a member of the School of Continuing Studies, working in Shaffer Hall half-time for Jon Heggan, Associate Dean for Administration and half-time for the school's incoming human resources manager, Alison Pullins. After 1½ years, Criscione departed on maternity leave and did not return on a full-time basis. However, during the first week of January 1995, she worked on a part-time basis for Pete Petersen typing a paper about W. Edwards Deming and formatting it into APA style within the week to meet the submission deadline of the Academy of Management. In the normal course of events, Petersen took advantage of having a capable individual available who could provide high-quality typing and editing. As Criscione worked additional hours, she was appointed to the position of Program Assistant I in 1996, working a steady 20 hours each week. At the time Criscione used an extra desk in the Business Division's office on the second floor of 201 North Charles near the Downtown Center, but she accomplished most of her work at home via personal computer. Her husband John received an MD from the School of Medicine and a PhD from the Whiting School of Engineering in 1999, and the family moved to San Diego, CA where Dr. John Criscione participated in a postdoctoral fellowship at the University of California San Diego.

In the closing years of the 1990s, telecommuting was one of the many subjects discussed in classes about contemporary management approaches. One could avoid the hassle of commuting and use a personal computer, phone, copier, and fax to turn out high-quality work at home. In reality, however, people like to cluster and socialize with others in the office and prefer to go to work in a more traditional way. Although Petersen valued having a part-time employee who produced quality work, it was unknown whether it could work out in a telecommuting format—could Petersen and Criscione handle that three-hour time difference between San Diego and Baltimore? This turned out to be a minor issue; a bigger challenge was the inability to talk face-to-face. At first Petersen made numerous phone calls, but there are limits to what a person working 20 hours a week can be expected to endure especially at odd hours. Consequently, the problem was solved by having this dialog on the personal computer, largely eliminating the inconvenience of differences in time zones. In addition, an attitude that nothing is a rush can go a long way in having a harmonious relationship.

When Petersen and Criscione started working together, the Crisciones had one child; now, they have seven, ranging in age from 14 years to two months. They currently homeschool the oldest four. The big surprise is that the working situation has worked so well. In the process, two books were produced, as well as about half of Petersen's 90 articles and published papers, in addition to syllabuses and daily class outlines for about five classes each term, as well as promotion packets, including curriculum vitae for almost every member of the Business Division's faculty who was promoted in the past decade.

Asked if she can recall any exciting (or perhaps crazy) moments, Criscione described a few occasions involving power outages that caused a scramble or two in saving material on the computer and meeting deadlines. She also recalls dealing with a very sophisticated and experienced editor of a prestigious press who was fanatical about not using the passive voice to the extent that he forbade the use of the words "is, was, and were"; indeed, some funny rewrites resulted in trying to implement this edict. Overall, for Criscione, this telecommuting experience has been fun, exciting, and rewarding.

Richard G. Milter—Director of the MBA Fellows program, interim chair of MBA programs, and Associate Professor of Management Dr. Rick Milter had his first association with the Graduate Division of Business and Management in February

2003 when he made a presentation to the faculty about the value of an alternative approach for conducting MBA programs.[44] In addition to the somewhat conventional MBA program, Milter saw a need for an approach that would be suitable for executives who did not have time to attend class on a routine and structured basis. Then, from September 2004 through December 2005, he worked as a two-to-four-day-per-month consultant, developing this innovative action learning approach for a Hopkins corporate client. Unfortunately, months later, the corporate client faced other commitments and could not implement the program. Clear heads prevailed; rather than abandon this approach, an MBA Fellows program emerged with a cohort group starting in November 2006. Promotional material introducing the Johns Hopkins MBA Fellows program captures the essence of this exciting approach for earning an MBA.

> Executives who race between Chicago, Atlanta, and Denver still have time to earn an MBA in Baltimore…. You can earn your degree in two years, and still accommodate career demands, business travel, and family life. Combining periodic short residencies, project collaboration, and the power of online learning, our program takes MBA study far beyond the ordinary classroom. (http://cte.jhu.edu/mbafellows, accessed April 19, 2007)

Having joined the division on a full-time basis in January 2006, Milter, who led this effort from the very start, now pursues the actual running of the MBA Fellows program with a similar passion. The program has attracted experienced executives who are comfortable operating online and in the classroom. Furthermore, they readily collaborate, learning from each other as well as from their experienced faculty, and participate in academic problem-solving situations that further enhance their teamwork and leadership skills. Based on the caliber of the students and this unique learning approach, it seems that the MBA Fellows program is now evolving into an Executive MBA program. Indeed, these are exciting times.

44 Promoted to professor on September 1, 2007.

Peter B. Petersen—*See* About the Author

Beverly A. Sauer—Before becoming Professor of Management in the Graduate Division of Business, Dr. Sauer taught professional writing and classical rhetoric as an Associate Professor of English and Rhetoric (with tenure) at Carnegie Mellon University. She was previously an Associate Professor of English (with tenure) at the University of Maine. At Johns Hopkins, Sauer taught risk communication, managerial communication, and cross-cultural communication. Supported by funding from five National Science Foundation grants, Sauer has written extensively on the subject of risk communication in difficult cross-cultural contexts. Her book, *The Rhetoric of Risk: Technical Documentation in Hazardous Environments* (2nd. ed., Routledge, 2002) is a significant contribution to the field. In 2003, *The Rhetoric of Risk* was awarded the prize for Best Book in Scientific and Technical Communication from the National Council of Teachers of English. Beyond the world of academia, Sauer is very much involved in applying her research to current problems in government, business, and industry. Her most recent research investigates worker–management communication in South African coal mine safety training programs. Sauer was consultant to the NASA Columbia Accident Investigation Board investigating communication and leadership in the Shuttle Challenger disaster and continues her work in communication and system health management with systems engineers in the Systems Engineering Education and Development (SEED) program at NASA–Goddard Space Flight Center. In January 2006, she served as a member of West Virginia Governor Manchin's Special Commission on the Sago Mine Disaster. Sauer currently serves as a panel member of the National Transportation Board of the National Academy of Sciences. She is currently Professor of Management Communication in the McDonough School of Business at Georgetown University.

Lindsay Thompson—Dr. Lindsay Thompson became a member of the Graduate Division of Business and Management in 2001 and, working with deans Fessler and de la Viña, developed an ethics component for the MBA curriculum. The initial version presented the subject in three one-credit courses spread throughout an MBA student's program. In time, however, these three courses were consolidated into one three-credit course presented in one semester. This case-based experiential course required instructors who could present this subject without going off on a theoretical tangent, so rather than selecting philosophy professors, Lindsay Thompson selected seasoned attorneys capable of interacting with MBA students, who then received a special orientation and a one-year apprenticeship with an attorney currently teaching the class. Consequently, the part-time instructors teaching this class engaged MBA students effectively and presented what could have been a dry subject in a compelling fashion. She also served for some time as the director of academic affairs for the division and then, in collaboration with the Division of Undergraduate Studies, became immersed in the Business Transition program.

Lawrence A. Waudby—Mr. Lawrence Waudby became a member of the Graduate Division of Business and Management during February 2003, working in the office of Dean Lynda de la Viña with Dr. Lindsay Thompson, who, at the time (as an additional function), was Director of Academic Affairs for the division. Detailed records for part-time faculty (including class evaluations) were established for the first time at the division level. During May 2004, he moved to the Department of Management OD/Strategic Human Resources. Since then, as a member of that department, he has acted in a number of capacities, including during a time when he was the only full-time person in the department. His functions included responding to questions and comments from perspective students; in conjunction with the Office of Admissions, helping prospective students in the department's programs through the admissions process; helping new students select their initial courses; helping students well into the program select and recruit research advisers; helping students complete their programs and prepare for graduation; responding to questions from part-time faculty and potential part-time faculty; and, finally, providing advice concerning the budget, course scheduling, and the part-time faculty needed to teach these courses.

Kenya White (formerly Kenya Crawford)—Kenya White became a member of the Graduate Division of Education in August 2003 and then transferred to the Graduate Division of Business and Management during January 2005. For the next 2½ years, she worked with students and instructors in the MBA program, including in her role as senior coordinator for the MBA program's Capstone course. In July 2007, she relocated to the state of Texas.

Department of Marketing (during 2006)

Toni S. Ungaretti, chair—*See* Division of Undergraduate Studies

Deborah A. Boyd—In November 1998, Debbie Boyd joined Dr. Carlos Rodriguez and Kathy Wilson as a member of the Department of Marketing. Then, following the departure of Dr. Rodriguez, she worked with Kathy Wilson for many years on the marketing program. During this time, the Master of Science in Marketing evolved and became one of the best graduate marketing programs in the mid-Atlantic region. Ms. Boyd also contributed to the overall effort by helping instructors, students, and prospective students. By working closely with instructors and students, Dr. Wilson and Ms. Boyd developed a cohesive group of instructors, students, and alumni. Consequently, they always looked forward to attending their annual pre-graduation celebration, during which the unveiling of a special framed poster containing the names of that year's graduates was met with cheers and celebration. They also added much to individual morale and the esprit de corps of the division by organizing and running informal office functions to celebrate birthdays, holidays, and events pertaining to many other occasions. In fact, those occasions added to the fun of working with colleagues.

Edward H. Weiss—As his lengthy career in the field of marketing advanced, Ed Weiss founded his own company, titled Weiss Strategic Marketing, to focus on branding for small and mid-sized businesses. Then, armed with extensive marketing experience, he started teaching with the Graduate Division of Business and Management in 1998 as a member of the practitioner faculty. As one of the students' favorite marketing instructors, he further increased his involvement with the Department of Marketing by guiding students in their marketing research and by advising them in a broad range of marketing subjects and approaches. Indeed, his experiences in the real world of marketing, combined with his understanding of sound academic theory, have provided students with a distinctive and valuable resource. In 2007, Weiss joined the department as its full-time Academic Adviser.

The dean who led the School of Professional Studies in Business and Education (SPSBE) and all of those in the SPSBE headquarters who supported the Business Division during 2006

Ralph Fessler, Dean, SPSBE—In 1983, when he was appointed director and professor in the Graduate Division of Education within the Evening College and Summer Session, Dr. Fessler's colleagues throughout the school soon viewed him as the authority on academic processes and protocols. He lived up to this reputation, placing the highest priority on using the best approaches to achieve quality in an academic setting. Indeed, his arrival served as a milestone in the school's journey from continuing education to the establishment of Schools of Business and Education. Instead of the folly connected with lobbying for Schools of Business and Education, his approach emphasized continuous quality improvement within the school. Thus the Graduate Division of Education achieved accreditation at the national level, recognizing its high-quality program beyond the level of many schools of education. The school was renamed the School of Continuing Studies a year after his arrival, and Fessler began the work of moving away from a focus on an evening college.

Fessler's drive for quality continued when he was appointed (as an additional function) associate dean of Academic Affairs from 1993 to 1999. In addition, the overall focus on the fields of business administration and education were reinforced on July 1, 1999, when the school was renamed the School of Professional Studies in Business and Education. Then, during September 1999, Ralph Fessler became acting dean, replacing the retiring Stanley C. Gabor. However, the following year Fessler was officially appointed dean of the School of Professional Studies in Business and Education. For the next six years, as members of the school became aware of the possibility of establishing a business school, Dean Fessler had the additional task of helping everyone deal with uncertainty. As it became much more apparent that this event would happen, he was faced with both uncertainty and a major change. Consequently, the 3 years 2004, 2005, and 2006 were a significant period in the history of SPSBE. In fact, during these three years, Fessler had his hands full in leading SPSBE as well as looking out for the interests of the Graduate Division of Business and Management, the Division of Undergraduate Studies, the Division of Public Safety Leadership, and his own Graduate Division of Education. This in particular was a time when a dean certainly earned his paycheck.[45]

Office of Dean (during 2006)

Amy Yerkes-Schmaljohn, Associate Dean for Academic Affairs—Amy Yerkes-Schmaljohn came to Johns Hopkins University in October 1997 to serve as executive assistant to then-dean of the School of Continuing Studies Stanley C. Gabor. Working with such an experienced leader in the field of continuing higher education, Yerkes-Schmaljohn was afforded

---

45 Under Fessler's leadership, the School of Education, established on January 1, 2007, was ranked 20th in the nation's schools of education by *US News & World Report* during spring 2008.

the opportunity to learn firsthand what is required of a successful leader in academia. Gabor set high standards for all who worked in the dean's office, especially when it came to written communications. He was famous for his markups of drafts with a blue felt-tip pen (years earlier it was green), one could only hope for the return of a paper with as few marks as possible. Dr. Yerkes-Schmaljohn, a skilled writer herself, pursuing a PhD in comparative literature, demonstrated her ability to write quickly and effectively. Furthermore, her diplomatic flair in both oral and written presentations has disarmed many an adversary.

In addition to communications, Dean Gabor expected and received much, much more. Indeed, the scope of Yerkes-Schmaljohn's position widened and became more complex as she served Dean Gabor and his successor, Dean Ralph Fessler (starting in September 1999) and earned her doctorate; she advanced from executive assistant to Associate Dean for Academic Affairs. Her contributions to the school and all its members consisted generally of five major functions.

Advocate for all—There was a flurry of activity that exceeded what one leader could handle during the final years of Gabor's long deanship and during Ralph Fessler's years as dean (1999–2006), leading up to the creation of the Carey Business School and School of Education. Consequently, members of the school sought out Dr. Yerkes-Schmaljohn in pressing situations. In many cases, she would resolve situations and later inform the dean or get the facts and parties together and subsequently meet with the dean. On many occasions, however, she would argue for a cause, recommend a solution, and receive a decision. Her timely arrival at proper solutions allowed the work of the school to proceed as smoothly as possible during times of considerable change.

Assist the dean—As the volume of the workload increased further and became more complex, she assisted the dean by accomplishing part of the work and by meeting with individuals unable to squeeze into the dean's overloaded calendar. She represented him on numerous occasions, ranging from meetings and ceremonial activities to social activities. As an external coordinator representing the dean in many meetings within the Hopkins community, she could be counted on to understand the situation, represent the school well, and follow through on actions required after the meeting. She also represented the dean beyond the Hopkins community, such as when she represented the school and Graduate Division of Business and Management with Booz Allen Hamilton in the development and implementation of graduate-level degree programs offered in-house for the large organization. Although this effort overlapped the succession of three directors of the division, it did not falter—because of her constant attention.

Chair of Academic Policy Committee and member of the Academic Council—During her tenure, the school's overall effort focused on increasing quality in all areas, ranging from recruitment of new students to what happens in the classroom and interactions with alumni. In addition, efforts increased to establish effective partnerships with business and industry; various organizations in the public, private, and not-for-profit sectors; and sister schools within Johns Hopkins University. Many of these efforts were fostered and developed during monthly Academic Policy Committee (APC) meetings. Concurrently, the development of many programs had their beginning in discussions at APC meetings and then grew to completion when they were presented and critiqued during a rigorous peer review. When finally approved by the APC (chaired by Yerkes-Schmaljohn) these new programs were reviewed by the dean and were forwarded to the school's Academic Council. At the Academic Council meeting (chaired by the JHU provost), Dr. Yerkes-Schmaljohn presented these proposed new programs for review and final approval.

Supporter of administrative personnel—Starting in 2002, she became increasingly involved with first-line staff and administrators. She met with these individuals, who normally didn't attend meetings but had a lot to offer about how to improve the system, and who were also unaware of or did not fully understand what was going on at various levels of their division and the school. This was particularly applicable in the Business Division, which, at the time, had a succession of nine directors in nine years. As might be expected, the new directors concentrated on putting out the largest "fires" first and never seemed to have time for extended discussions with first-line administrators. Good things were accomplished, and staff at all levels of the school found that they had a voice in the dean's office.

Faculty member—Dr. Yerkes-Schmaljohn taught in three of the school's four academic divisions: undergraduate, business, and education. She counts her work with returning adult undergraduates—who consistently demonstrated keen intellectual curiosity and brought rich life experiences to the classroom—as a highlight of her teaching career.

When asked for her reflections on the most pleasant moments at Hopkins, she described how she enjoyed chairing the Academic Policy Committee, interacting with enthusiastic people who proposed new programs and with others at the meetings who offered their thoughtful advice. In fact, she cites the day of the APC meeting as the best day of each month. She also recalled the diploma ceremony as the high point of the year, when hard-working students crossed the stage in their caps and gowns. In 2006, Yerkes-Schmaljohn accepted a position at Friends School of Baltimore, bringing together her spiritual life as a Quaker and her lifelong love of teaching.

Elizabeth K. Mayotte, Associate Dean for SPSBE Administrative Systems—Over the past 20 years, Betsy Mayotte has served in senior administrative roles in higher education and in senior executive roles in business. Mayotte earned the Master of Administrative Science degree at Johns Hopkins University in 1987. She joined the School of Continuing Studies in 1989 and the following year was appointed director of the Columbia Center. Beginning in 1990, she led a major facility design, construction, and relocation project to move the Columbia Center to its current location in the Gateway Corporate Park. She created the first School of Continuing Studies center-based advisory board of corporate leaders and led its outreach efforts in the mid-Maryland region. To enhance academic quality for Hopkins graduate students, Mayotte forged an active partnership with the Milton S. Eisenhower Library to bring library training and resources to the School of Continuing Studies faculty and students at off-campus sites. Mayotte represented the School of Continuing Studies on the university-wide strategic planning initiative Committee for the 21st Century, serving on the technology committee.

Promoted to the position of Assistant Dean Responsible for Electronic and Distance Education in the School of Professional Studies in 1997, she managed a corporate partnership that enabled SPSBE and the School of Medicine to jointly develop a new distributed learning model to deliver the Hopkins Business of Medicine certificate program nationwide. The program earned national recognition and awards for innovation in program delivery and the creation of strategic academic–corporate partnerships. Mayotte also led the multistate licensing and accreditation effort in order for Johns Hopkins University to deliver the program in 22 states.

In 2000 Mayotte moved to the corporate sector, recruited to the position of vice president at the Thomson-Prometric Corporation, a computer-based testing company. She served in both a client management and business development capacity, leading a business unit charged with managing the company's major academic client, Educational Testing Service (ETS). Her team also created and led a six-vendor partnership to design and deliver a workforce development solution for the state of Ohio, delivered through its network of community college campuses.

In 2002 Mayotte became more involved in her family's Ohio-based business, a steel fabricating and construction company known for half a century in the Midwest for many of the landmark buildings it erected and for the steel roller coasters it fabricated and installed all over the world. Unfortunately, the company was one of many in the Ohio steel industry that suffered a decline in 2002. Unable to effect a turnaround in operations, the company was forced to liquidate its hard assets in 2004. As president of the company, Mayotte works with other officers and the board of directors to wind down the business post-liquidation.

She returned to Johns Hopkins University in 2004, appointed Director of Recruiting and Business Outreach in the Graduate Division of Business and Management. Her responsibilities and commitment to the school have increased steadily as Mayotte was appointed Associate Dean for SPSBE Administrative Systems in 2006. Ending one era and beginning another, she was appointed associate dean and director of the Professional Schools Administration, established on January 1, 2007, to provide administrative services to the two new schools at Johns Hopkins University—the Carey Business School and the School of Education.

Kevin Crysler, Director, Development—Kevin Crysler joined the School of Professional Studies in Business and Education in January 2003 as assistant director reporting to Mr. Judson K. Crihfield, who was at that time Assistant Dean for Development and Alumni Relations. During January 2004, when Jud advanced in his career and became the Hopkins director for annual giving, Mr. Crysler was appointed Interim Director of Development, and Christina Godack was selected as Director of External Affairs and Alumni Relations. In a few months Crysler became Director of Development, a position he held until the organization of the Carey Business School and the School of Education when he joined the School of Education.

Although the top SPSBE development activity was the generous $50 million gift by trustee emeritus Mr. William P. Carey on December 5, 2006, Kevin Crysler also supported other development activities during this time. In July 2004, Mr. Edward

St. John donated the largest gift ever received to establish a named department within the Business Division; $5.9 million to establish the Edward St. John Department of Real Estate. Furthermore, many long-term relationships were established or maintained by Crysler during this four-year period prior to the establishment of the Carey Business School. For example, Clyde and Ruth Williams, along with William and Katherine Ginder, continue their most welcome and generous annual gifts. Both Clyde and Bill are members of Delta Sigma Pi (the business fraternity), an organization on behalf of which Crysler also spends considerable time and energy. In addition, the new presentation at the Passano Gallery about the history of the Charles Center brought together and continued the close relationship between SPSBE and members of the Greater Baltimore Committee. Kevin Crysler and Betsy Mayotte also maintain continuing relationships with the business community in the Baltimore–Washington area, the overall effort being partnerships for the greater good of the community and the university.

During this period, the advisory council and alumni group for the Leadership Development Program for Minority Managers also saw considerable activity. The time, personal energy, and generous contributions by Mr. John Hunter, senior vice president of QVC and a major force in the advisory council added substantially to the Leadership Development Program. During the past three years, a highly professional video about the Leadership Development Program was produced at QVC with the support of Hunter. As this program evolves further, much of its progress can be attributed to him.

When asked if he recalled any unusual experiences at Hopkins, Crysler had two immediate flashbacks. Both were similar experiences that represent a development person's nightmare— talking with a potential giver and getting ready to ask for a substantial donation when, out of the blue, a member of his own organization butted into the conversation and changed the subject. In the first story, Crysler was at a reception at the Hopkins

Club; while going for the big donation, he was interrupted by a colleague who noisily joined the conversation and jokingly said, "Kevin, I understand that you are the person to see if you need money." In the second story, a senior executive of a nationwide major company had just finished a lengthy presentation in a large auditorium near the Business Division's Washington DC Center. The plan was to build on the topic just presented and embraced by the speaker by asking for funds to make this dream happen. Unfortunately, just as the dialogue got productive, Crysler was interrupted by a colleague who handed the executive a typed proposal on a different subject and asked her to read and consider it as they stood near the stage. Fortunately for the school, on both occasions Crysler's quick thinking and experience helped him get the donation requests back on track.

Cathy Deyo Wilson—*See* Institutional Research and Assessment

Tylis B. Cooper—Tylis Cooper's first position in January 2000 at Johns Hopkins University was as a program assistant with the Department of Information Technology, then located on the second floor of 201 North Charles Street in downtown Baltimore. Working with Sabree Akinyele and Darlene Dixon, Cooper processed book order forms, instructor evaluations, and contracts for part-time instructors. If mishandled, an error in any one of these items could produce a problem that would surface in a few weeks or, in some cases, a month or two. Daniel EagleEye, then the Business Division's new Assistant Dean for Administration, centralized these activities for the entire Business Division and, noticing her good work, recruited Cooper to accomplish the same tasks for the entire division rather than for one department. Working with Joan Johnson, Assistant Director of Administration, she accomplished these three functions and also worked on the annual catalog and course schedules.

During the summer semester of 2003, Amy M. Yerkes, Associate Dean for Academic Affairs, asked Cooper to work with her and

Mort Grusky, Associate Dean for Financial Operations, equally splitting her time between them. On that occasion and, to a greater extent, later, after Grusky departed, Cooper coordinated activities in the dean's outer office and made guests feel comfortable and welcome. Then, in June 2006, her career advanced further when she was selected for a position as senior academic coordinator in the Department of Molecular Microbiology and Immunology in the Bloomberg School of Public Health. In this current role, she handles the department's administration for PhD students and related tasks for conducting their classes and also focuses on her own studies. (She earned a Bachelor of Arts degree in Communications and Interdisciplinary Studies at Johns Hopkins in 2005.)

Asked about an unforgettable event that she experienced in the School of Professional Studies, Cooper tells of a distraught woman who phoned, crying about a hold on her graduation caused because her tuition, usually furnished by her employer, had not been received. Cooper worked the matter out between Hopkins and the employer, much to the relief of the woman, who was eight months pregnant. A few days after graduation, Cooper received a card from the lady, expressing her appreciation; it made Cooper's day.

Financial Operations (during 2006)

Debbie H. Rice, Associate Dean for Financial Operations— Debbie Rice became a member of the School of Continuing Studies in December 1990 and worked on the fourth floor of Shaffer Hall as accounting supervisor. At the time, very basic electronic processes for accounting and budgeting had arrived as personal computers continued replacing IBM electric typewriters throughout the school. Initially, she worked directly for Barbara Plummer, who, in turn, reported to Dr. Jon Heggan, who led the school's efforts in financial matters. With the guidance and help of Plummer, whom Rice describes fondly as her mentor, she quickly adapted to the ever-changing accounting and budget systems. Around the same time, during the early 1990s, Sherri Wood, who headed the school's human resource management activities, eventually replaced the retiring Barbara Plummer. Consequently, Rice then reported to Wood, who had become Director of Business Services. Then, when Sherri Wood departed during 1995, Rice reported directly to Jon Heggan. As a person with an understanding of the details of the school's accounting and budgeting processes, she was in a position to assist Heggan as the application of information technology moved to a higher level and the school expanded, causing some financial operations to become more complex. Hard work and the ability to deal with ever-changing conditions propelled her career through a series of positions with ever-increasing amounts of responsibility. She became Assistant Director of Business Services, then Director of Business Services, then Director of Financial Operations, then Assistant Dean for Financial Operations, and, finally, Associate Dean for Financial Operations. Mort Grusky replaced Jon Heggan when he retired, and Debbie Rice replaced Grusky when he departed, about four years later. Until she left Hopkins in 2006, Amy M. Yerkes-Schmaljohn became Rice's mentor and confidante. In addition, Debbie Rice became a major associate of Dean Fessler as he led the initial transition of the school into the Carey Business School and the School of Education.

Asked about unforgettable moments, Rice related two recollections. She particularly enjoys helping out at graduation by escorting students to their seats and is thrilled when they smile and say thank you—"It gives me real goosebumps." Furthermore, she once had the misfortune of walking into Shaffer Hall one morning following a snowfall and having a section of snow slip off the roof and land directly on her. Maintenance workers continue to ask, "Are you the lady who got hit with that load of snow?" Rice offers this advice for anyone dealing with a bad budget year: Be flexible; consider your options; plan ahead; get everyone involved in the solution. She concludes, "These are exciting times, when two new schools will be successful and we will move on to the next chapter."

Suprena D. Williams, Associate Director of Financial Operations—Suprena Williams first joined Johns Hopkins University on October 31, 1991, as an accounts payable clerk in Garland Hall. She moved on to the Hopkins Press and then to the School of Hygiene and Public Health, where she was a support services coordinator. Then, as a member of JHPIEGO, she was located at their new office on Thames Street and subsequently moved back to the School of Hygiene and Public Health in 2000.

The experience Williams gained over this decade was welcome when she became Assistant Director of Administrative Services in the Graduate Division of Education, working with Paul Adams in Whitehead Hall starting October 2001. Then, in November 2003, she began working with Debbie Rice as associate director for Financial Operations, in which capacity she handled day-to-day operations from the office on the second floor of Shaffer Hall. When asked about memorable occasions, Williams reflects on those many occasions when she has been able to help unhappy and sometimes hostile people—for example, by rectifying a situation when someone has not been paid. Doing so often involves calling in favors to bend the regulations regarding how many days it takes to process this or that, but Williams is willing to go the extra mile to fix the problem.

Michelle J. Robinson—Michelle Robinson's first job at Hopkins was working on the Halstead Floor at Johns Hopkins Hospital during 1987 and 1988. Then, in 1990, after a two-year break, she became a member of Johns Hopkins University, working in Dave Binko's Homewood Academic Computing. However, her long association with the School of Continuing Studies and its successor organizations began during the spring semester of 1993, when she worked on the second floor of Shaffer Hall in the office of Business Services, then directed by Sherri Wood.

In time, the functions of business services and information technology were consolidated, and the office was renamed the Office of Business and Information Technology Services, also directed by Wood. Then, after Ron Hudson led this element for about 10 months, Brian Cooke became the director. During these many changes and adjustments, Robinson was responsible for software licensing and e-mail accounts for full- and part-time faculty, staff, and students. In addition, she worked on financial matters for the school, including the dean's budget and the school-wide technology and software budgets.

During Cooke's administration the office was further reorganized and titled the Office of Information Technology Systems and Support. Then, in August 2000, Philippe Homassel became director; during early 2002, the Office of Information Technology Systems and Support moved from Shaffer Hall to the seventh floor of 100 North Charles Street. After the move, Robinson continued with her tasks but acquired the additional responsibility of handling the financial matters for the Office of Marketing and Communications, then collated with Robinson on the seventh floor of 100 North Charles Street. In 2006, she returned to the second floor of Shaffer Hall on the Homewood campus, but on this occasion as a member of the Office for Financial Operations. Nevertheless, her functions were somewhat similar; she conducted budget analysis for the Graduate Division of Business and Management and the Division of Public Safety Leadership.

Asked if she recalled any memorable moments she described a situation on the seventh floor of 100 North Charles during a fire drill when she was locked in the ladies room for about 20 minutes. When the fire alarm was activated, a procedure used at the time prevented people from entering various floors by invalidating all key cards used to unlock doors. Unfortunately, this system also prevented entry and exit from the ladies' room. This mistake was corrected, but a month later there was a similar situation when flashing lights replaced audio alarms on the seventh floor. Unable to see the flashing lights from within the offices, and with no alarm going off, it took a while for everyone to discover that the building was evacuated because of a false fire alarm. Fortunately, changes have been made, and fire alarm procedures are now in good order at 100 North Charles.[46]

Helen D. Thornton—During March 1995, Helen Thornton became a member of the staff at Johns Hopkins University, working on the payroll for Kathy Graham in the School of Continuing Studies. At the time, Business Services conducted this work under the direction of Sherri Wood, who in turn reported to Jon Heggan. Their office on the second floor of Shaffer Hall moved to the fourth floor and then years later returned to the second floor. Starting around the year 2000, Thornton became part of the accounts payable process, ensuring that the school paid its bills on time and that members of the faculty and staff received their travel pay on a timely basis. Then, in 2004, she became an Accountant IV and handled the undertaking of budget reconciliation, which determined after the fact that all invoices were properly paid and that the school had received all that it was due, with receipts having been properly deposited. She currently performs these tasks as a budget specialist.[47]

Human Resources and Payroll (during 2006)

Connie M. Kinsley, Human Resource Manager—During April 2003, Connie Kinsley became the human resource manager of the School of Professional Studies in Business and Education. From her location in Shaffer Hall, Room 203, her actions as human resource manager played a key role in the effective establishment of the Carey Business School and the School of Education on the foundations of successful programs in the School of Professional Studies in Business and Education (SPSBE). Kinsley considers the past year to have been a time of great excitement and organizational growth for the school. When she arrived, and for the next three-and-a-half years, the possibility of a business school progressed

---

46 In 2008, Michelle Robinson continues as an employee of Johns Hopkins University as a financial analyst in the Carey Business School.

47 During April 2007, her office moved to the second floor of 6716 Alexander Bell Drive (next door to the Columbia Center), in a space also occupied by the Division of Public Safety Leadership.

from initial speculation to a decision by the Hopkins board of trustees on December 4, 2006, to establish two new schools within the university. Their decision came in response to the largest gift for business education in the history of the university. In addition, at the same time, the university was also implementing the first phases of an enterprise-wide reporting system that would for the first time bring a common system for human resources, financial transactions, and data archiving and reporting across the university. Kinsley readily embraced both changes, noting that with such sweeping positive change also come many challenges. After the decision on December 4, 2006, and also with the introduction of the new enterprise-wide reporting system, there was much uncertainty, and many questions emerged at a time when answers were not always readily available. Reassuring staff and communication across the school was crucial. At such times, the role of Human Resources becomes even more important. Kinsley was pleased to play an important role—built on trust established over the past three-and-a-half years—as a member of the leadership teams working to effect these organizational changes and make smooth transitions. Indeed, long after the establishment of the two schools, Kinsley will be remembered for her effective role in this major reorganization.

A lesson learned from all of this is the need for transparency in what is being accomplished and for frequent communication. Kinsley particularly values the willing professional collaboration and warmth from her colleagues at Johns Hopkins University and feels that those relationships are what truly distinguish her experience at Johns Hopkins University.

Peppi L. Faulk—On February 28, 2001, Peppi Faulk became a full-time member of the School of Professional Studies, working with Associate Dean Jon Heggan on the second floor of Shaffer Hall on the Homewood campus. As an administrative assistant within Heggan's office, she worked on a number of tasks pertaining to financial operations and information technology systems and support. After Dean Heggan's retirement at the end of 2001, Faulk joined the Human Resources element in January 2002 working with the human resources manager, Cherita Hobbs, and the human resource coordinator, Rosemary Okoye-Hartman. Faulk was promoted to payroll specialist in October 2006 working closely with Debbie Rice, Associate Dean for Financial Operations. Now Faulk works as the senior human resources coordinator with Connie Kinsley, the subsequent human resources manager. Determined to complete a bachelor's degree that she began many years ago, Faulk successfully graduated with a Bachelor of Science in Interdisciplinary Studies. Shortly thereafter, Faulk enrolled in the Master of Science in Education degree program with a concentration in School Administration and Supervision that she plans to use to "educate as many students as possible." She is also a proud member of the National Honor Society, Alpha Sigma Lambda Chapter, at Johns Hopkins University and is the mother of a Baltimore City police officer and a Rutgers law student.

Asked if she recalled a memorable occasion at Hopkins, Faulk responded that it was clearly her graduation day in May 2006. "I was asked by my adviser, Irene Edmond-Rosenberg, to be the class marshal, and it was an experience that I'll never forget," she said. Faulk recalls her father's amazement when he realized that she was leading her class and carrying the processional flag. "My dad has always been my biggest supporter, and I'm just thankful that he was there to witness that moment." Faulk finally completed her bachelor's degree after a nearly 30-year pursuit.

Kathryn L. Graham-Young—In March 1994, Kathy Graham became a member of Johns Hopkins University as a payroll assistant in the School of Continuing Studies, working for Sandy Davidson on the fourth floor of Shaffer Hall. Work on the payroll at the time was conducted within Business Services, directed by Sherri Wood. However, in April 1995 when Davidson departed Graham became the payroll coordinator for the school. Then, during 1998, she was appointed Budget Analyst III and charged with a portion of budget development in addition to working on the school's payroll, becoming a part of the process to forecast payroll costs for the following year's budget. Her career advanced further in 1999, when she was appointed payroll administrator, continuing with her work on the payroll and budget development. Years later, in November 2005, she transferred to the GWC Whiting School of Engineering, where she worked on the payroll, budget development, and grants management, but she has since returned to her old functions, working with the Division of Public Safety Leadership at 6716 Alexander Bell drive, located next door to the Columbia Center.

Asked if she recalled any unforgettable moments, she related a rather unusual story. Although in all walks of life people make mistakes, a payroll mistake that reduces someone's pay can cause quite a reaction. On one occasion, when she was sharing an office with Helen Thornton, an angry part-time instructor whom she never had seen called Graham, complaining about a payroll mistake—and, unfortunately, the caller became very confrontational. A few hours after this call, a huge man wearing a trench coat appeared unannounced and blocked the doorway. As he reached into his chest coat pocket, they thought he was going to pull out a pistol. Instead, he displayed an identification document identifying him as a member of the Defense Investigative Services, there to do a background check on someone who had applied for a sensitive position. Relieved that he was not the angry part-time instructor, both women howled with laughter.

Charlene Walizer—Prior to coming to Johns Hopkins University, Charlene Walizer did bookkeeping at home for her family business. Then, in January 2000, she was hired as a part-time employee at the School of Professional Studies Downtown Center in Baltimore. Working nights, Walizer helped operate the Downtown Center's reception desk and helped Sabrina Scarborough, then Noncredit Registrar, process registrations. In January 2001, when the new Downtown Center opened on the corner of Charles and Fayette Streets, Walizer was hired on a full-time basis as an education support service assistant.

In May 2004, she was asked to replace Tylis Cooper, who departed on maternity leave. In this capacity, she worked half-time for Amy Yerkes, Associate Dean for Academic Affairs, and half-time for Kevin Crysler, Director of Development; then, when Cooper returned, she worked full-time for Crysler for about a year. She advanced in her career in January 2006, when she was selected as a member of the SPSBE Payroll Office; she is presently a payroll specialist.[48]

Institutional Research and Assessment (during 2006)

Jason N. Adsit, Assistant Dean for Institutional Research and Assessment—Forming the first organization for institutional research for the school, Dr. Jason Adsit joined the School of Professional Studies in Business and Education in June 2006. In the past, deans and assistant deans have responded to questionnaires and surveys about the school and its various subordinate elements. For example, the director of the Division of Administration and Business responded annually to requests from Peterson's Guide over 25 years ago. This publication conducts surveys in an attempt to provide an accurate one-page summary of the characteristics of regionally accredited MBA and graduate degree programs. As the findings of these surveys become more important in attracting potential students and with the greater demand for public accountability by educational institutions, the information provided to the surveys has to be more meaningful and more accurate. In an attempt to reach these objectives, Adsit now directs this three-person Institutional Research unit. Overall, he sees his role as providing institutional research for external reporting and internal analysis. For example, for the Business Division, that means focusing on measuring student outcomes; for the Graduate Division of Education, concentrating on the accreditation process. Before coming to Hopkins, Adsit was an Assistant Professor of Education and Director of Standards, Policy and Assessments at Baldwin-Wallace College in Berea, Ohio. He

48 On July 1, 2007, she became payroll specialist for the Carey Business School. Upon her marriage on September 21, 2007, her name changed to Charlene Camponeschi.

firmly believes that by having the correct information in the right form when interacting with external elements, the school can shift from being on the defense to owning the debate.

Regarding an unforgettable experience, Adsit described an occasion when he canceled a voluminous and detailed report that he thought no one wanted. It turned out that people agreed with him—perhaps merely because they wanted to be agreeable. In what he calls the "fallacy of misplaced consensus," people agreed when they should have demanded a much less complicated report that provided the basic data they needed. He is currently meeting this need.

Hillary A. Hardt—Hillary Hardt's first association with Johns Hopkins University was as a temp during July 2005, working in the development office of the Zanvyl Krieger School of Arts and Sciences. Then, still as a temp, she started working in January 2006 in the Department of Counseling in the Graduate Division of Education in the School of Professional Studies. Finally, in April 2006, she started working on a full-time basis when she was employed by SPSBE's Student Services Office, located in Shaffer Hall. In September 2006, she advanced in her career when she was selected as the research coordinator for the newly formed Office of Institutional Research and Assessment. Hardt received a master's degree from Ohio State University in Educational Policy and Leadership and is currently enrolled in the Hopkins MBA program. In her current position, working with Dean Adsit and Cathy Wilson, Hardt will have an opportunity to apply her educational background and experience. Indeed, the three of them are the founders of this office and are committed to making it a success.[49]

Cathy Deyo Wilson—Cathy Deyo became a member of the admissions office of the Business Division in 1996, working with Susan Marzullo and Robin Reed, and later joined by Marnie

---

49 Then, in January 2008, Hillary Hardt became the manager of special events in the School of Education's Center for Summer Learning.

Fallon, in an annex to the original Downtown Center, located near the southwest corner of Charles and Saratoga Streets. After the termination of the lease on the Downtown Center annex in 1997, some of the occupants moved to 201 North Charles Street; others moved to the Columbia Center. During this adjustment, Cathy Deyo transferred to the Department of Management, which was part of the group moving to the Columbia Center. From 1997 to 2002, she worked with Cynthia Tucker in the suite of offices located on the first floor of the Columbia Center. With the transition of several directors in their department during this period, Deyo and Tucker conducted the department's day-to-day operations. Then, in 2002, the Department of Management returned to Baltimore; moving to the seventh floor of 100 North Charles Street, where Cathy Wilson (formerly Deyo) and Tucker continued to run the department. Although the management classes that were part of the Master of Science in Business program had most of the students, their attention focused mainly on behavioral classes and graduate behavioral degree programs. It seemed that students in behavioral programs needed more tending, and with Wilson and Tucker on the scene they were well cared for—as were the public and instructors in particular. Cool and responsive, they put irate callers at ease while appearing unflappable. Then in 2003, Wilson transferred to a position at the Hopkins Bayview Medical Center and subsequently decided to spend more time with her family. In September 2004, she returned to the School of Professional Studies, working in the Office of the Dean with Dr. Jason Adsit, Assistant Dean for Institutional Research. No matter the office, Cathy's expertise and finesse are always appreciated.

Office of External Affairs (during 2006)

Christina A. Godack, Assistant Dean for External Affairs— Christina Godack started at Hopkins during February 1983 in the Johns Hopkins University Office of News and Information, with an office in Homewood House on the Homewood Campus. As Assistant Director of News and Information, she focused her attention on undergraduate students and programs in the School of Arts and Sciences and covered a wide range of activities such as media relations, copywriting, and events. Departing in 1986, she added over a decade and a half's worth of experience in the field of communications by working for two Baltimore full-service advertising agencies, where she served as Vice President for Public Relations. In these capacities she conducted crisis communications for clients, developed strategic plans, wrote speeches and press releases, coordinated events, and served as a media spokesperson for some of her clients.

In March 2003, Godack rejoined Hopkins in the School of Professional Studies in Business and Education as Associate Director of Communications and Alumni Relations, reporting to Judson K. Crihfield, at that time Assistant Dean for Development and Alumni Relations. During January 2004, when Crihfield advanced in his career and became the Hopkins director for annual giving, Godack was selected as Director of External Affairs and Alumni Relations, and the school's marketing department also came under her charge. Over time, she gained a wider focus on all manner of communications as they pertain to faculty, staff, students, alumni, and the public in general. Her greatest challenge was to effectively market the school's four distinct divisions while maintaining an overall branding identify for the entire school. In August 2005, she advanced further to the position of Assistant Dean for External Affairs.

In reflecting on lessons learned, she urges that we listen to and know the audiences rather than make assumptions and respond with an "ivory tower" mentality. One of her favorite memories was when she approached the dean with the suggestion of using billboards. The initial response was, "I'm not comfortable with doing billboards. We don't do billboards." But after he was shown a media analysis, he reconsidered. "That was one of the strengths of our school and its leadership. When we had the data, we weren't afraid to take risks and work outside the box." In this case, the data showed that young professionals were too busy to read newspapers, and that they spent a great deal of time in their cars traveling to work. "Billboards were the best way to reach them, and it worked. We actually had people calling from car cell phones and requesting information to apply."

But, above all, a lesson to follow in communications is that honesty is the best policy—never craft a story instead of dealing openly with the facts. Godack comments, "Our students wanted to apply and register for courses online way before we were even thinking about it. Instead of giving excuses and putting it off, we simply admitted that they were ahead of us, and we worked quickly to respond to their needs. Our job is to serve our students and alumni, and it's important to have a healthy working relationship. Listening to students and being honest with them results in happy students, which in turn results in happy alumni."

Office of Marketing and Communications (during 2006)

Barbara J. Wallace, Director of Marketing and Communications—Barbara Wallace's association with Johns Hopkins University started in 1981 when she enrolled in the Master of Administrative Science program. From 1973 to 1984, she was a tenured assistant professor teaching writing and communications skills at Catonsville Community College, but by the time she graduated from Hopkins in 1985, she was employed by Westinghouse, where she would work for a total of 12 years. Working in the field of marketing and communications, she applied in a real-world setting the knowledge of communications she had gained from a bachelor's and a master's degree in English from the University of Michigan. Then, in 1996, she advanced further in her career by working in the field of marketing at the University of Maryland Medical System. In time, Wallace's boss, Susan Dyer, was hired for a position at the School of Continuing Studies as Director of Marketing and Communications. Dyer convinced Wallace to follow, and on November 30, 1998, Wallace became Associate Director of Marketing and Communications in the School of Continuing Studies. With the subsequent departure of Dyer from Hopkins in 2002, Wallace became the interim director and, a few months later, the Director of Marketing and Communications.

Wallace is quick to point out that there have been many exciting events and changes since her arrival in 1998—the name of the school changed; the MBA was introduced; the functions of Marketing and Communications became decentralized in 2002, giving substantial budget authority to the academic divisions, and then, about two years later, reverted to being centralized. Correspondingly, the title of her organization changed from the Office of Marketing and Communications (OMC) to the Office of Communications Services (OCS) before reverting to its original title. In addition, a trend that started long before her arrival but continued at a faster pace after she arrived was the increased focus on two academic disciplines, business and education, with the loss of the Master of Liberal Arts degree and similar programs.

Her most memorable experience is one that she continues to this day, the experience of working with a wonderful group of people. Her colleagues in the Office of Marketing and Communications are driven people who have a passion for their work. They are a cohesive group that has its good days and not-so-good days, but it seems as if adverse situations or an unusually short suspense date pulls them together rather than apart. Just as in the field of advertising, they need a thick skin to properly face critics of their creative products. As an example of their dedication and passion for their work, they stay late when needed and without being asked and show up back in the office after a retreat because they want to finish what they were doing.

Wallace made a real difference by reaching diverse audiences, building awareness of the school's many challenges, and successfully recruiting students. She and her colleagues have learned from one another and accomplished a lot together, and she has been a good problem solver and consensus builder. Her greatest pleasure has been to use her skills to attract students to a school that she knew would bring them enormous academic, professional, and personal benefits.

Andrew S. Blumberg—With more than a prior decade's experience in the field of marketing and communications, Andy spent a year with the School of Hygiene and Public Health (now the Bloomberg School of Public Health) before joining the School of Continuing Studies on May 1, 1995. What he particularly enjoys at Hopkins is the sense of working with truly creative people and being exposed to new ideas every day. Years earlier, he cut his teeth with a major Baltimore advertising agency for 2½ years and then spent 7½ years at Blue Cross and Blue Shield of Maryland. Then, advancing further in his career, he became assistant manager of marketing at Chase Bank of Maryland, a position that he held before joining Hopkins 3½ years later. As one of the marketing account representatives for the Business Division, his challenge is creating a compelling message that will motivate promising students to inquire about the school's programs and to enroll if qualified. Blumberg's daily work encounters two consistent challenges: the need to create an effective message using a limited budget and the scrutiny of his creative copy by experts and laymen alike, with feedback often requiring a rather thick skin.

Asked about an unforgettable experience, it seems to Blumberg that in his field, almost every day can be filled with drama and trauma—and that the fields of advertising and marketing are not usually for the faint of heart. But he loves it. He did offer an example of a bit of excitement that someone in his position may run into from time to time. He recently completed a fact sheet for the new Carey Business School that was one of the first pieces to be distributed about the new school. It met with everyone's approval, but fortunately, at the last moment, Blumberg spotted a misspelled word—it was "Krieger" as in the Zanvyl Krieger School of Arts and Sciences—and the fact sheet was corrected before being released for widespread distribution. There are several lessons to be learned in this situation, one of which is to pay attention to computerized spell-checking processes. Although proper names are often incorrectly identified as misspelled, users should be slower to click the "Ignore" box, instead personally double-checking the spelling of proper names.

Away from the office, Blumberg, who is involved with several local historical organizations, unwinds at the Baltimore Streetcar Museum, where he is a member of the board and performs the museum's marketing and public affairs tasks on a pro bono basis. But his big thrill, as a qualified streetcar motorman and conductor, is operating the streetcar full of guests, making the rounds in the vicinity of the Jones Falls Valley and ringing the very loud antique streetcar gong.[50]

Michael Brands—On October 15, 1997, Mike Brands became a member of Johns Hopkins University as an assistant graphic designer in the Office of Marketing and Communications, then under the direction of Nancy Grund. At the time, the development of effective graphic design solutions had to include using new technologies focusing on the Web as well as the latest applications for print media. During this period of rapid change, software advances allowed the integration of previously separate components, and desktop computer capabilities grew. As a result, advertising and collateral material could be produced more efficiently and could be integrated with the design of the school's Web presence (sometimes handled by outside firms).

Currently a senior graphic designer, Brands quickly adapts and embraces the ever-changing technology in his field. Asked if he recalled a funny story or situation in the office, Brands remembered an event that would amuse co-workers both uptown and downtown. After the office moved to the seventh floor of 100 North Charles, a well-equipped galley allowed him to cook complete meals for himself. But the earlier Homewood location was furnished only with a microwave and a typical coffeemaker with sealed burners, forcing Brands to be more creative. He put

---

50 On July 1, 2007, Andy Blumberg became the publications manager for the Carey Business School.

half a bagel on each burner and placed a pot of coffee on top of each to toast the bagel. One morning, going back to his desk while his bagels toasted, Brands overheard the remarks of the dean, who had noticed the unorthodox cooking method. Fortunately, the office moved downtown not long afterward, and Brands took this anecdote and his untoasted bagels with him.

Shannon Doolin—In December 2005, Shannon Doolin joined the Office of Marketing and Communications and became the marketing manager for the Graduate Division of Business and Management. A major effort during the year that followed was preparing for the disestablishment of the School of Professional Studies in Business and Education and the establishment of both the Carey Business School and the School of Education. Publications had to be rewritten and marketing approaches modified to reflect this new arrangement. Another effort in 2006 was the implementation of Content Management Systems, an approach to empower program coordinators with the authority to modify material about their programs on the Web site. Because they are their programs' experts, their involvement furnishes the latest information to those who use the Web site as their primary source of information. Doolin provides watch over this effort, allowing information technology personnel to work on other tasks. Training provided for program coordinators enables them to accomplish the task of having the Web site state what they want with the appearance that they want. For example, material for the Web site about Information Sessions for the Carey Business School is furnished by Robin Reed and Sarah Tennyson, and general information about the Carey Business School is provided by April Stanson.

Doolin enjoys the freedom to express herself creatively in the development of advertising copy. Recently, the collaboration of several folks within the Office of Management and Communications and the Business Division led to an alternative to the overuse of photos of students and faculty in advertisements both by Johns Hopkins and by competitors. The new approach consists of sketches of businesspeople at work (the boardroom and conference room) or traveling (sitting in an airport lounge). Accompanying the sketches are words about the program and the consistent tagline of "Talent, Teamwork, and Leadership." Although these sketches of people did not show details (faces for example), they did show laptop computers and related electronics, such as palm pilots used by businesspeople at work. Although reaction to these sketches was mixed, Doolin found that external audiences, such as potential students, generally liked the advertisements; the internal audience (faculty and staff) were less positive. Looking to the immediate future, there will be a need to find the best approach in the upcoming advertisements in order to be in step with the vision of the dean selected to lead the Carey Business School and his or her reflection of what it is. In fact, Doolin sees this task as a paramount challenge for the marketing and advertising folks.

John W. Robertson—John Robertson started as a temp in February 1999, working with Dr. Gene Swanson, the director of the emerging MBA program. Swanson, selected during 1998 to develop the long-awaited MBA, needed help before launching the MBA program during the summer semester of 1999. Working on the second floor of 201 North Charles, the office had a flurry of activity, and in June 1999, at the start of the summer semester, Robertson was selected as an Education Support Services Assistant II on a full-time basis. As the program gained momentum, he worked with Jeanine Corcoran, assistant director of the MBA program, to convert MSB alumni who desired to become MBA degree holders with additional coursework. Then, during January 2001, with the opening of the new Downtown Center on the corner of Charles and Fayette Streets, the MBA program office moved from 201 North Charles Street to the third floor of the new Downtown Center; in June 2001, Robertson was appointed to the role of Academic Program Coordinator II. He continued to work with the MBA program alongside Bernadine Johnson, who joined the MBA program to assist with the marketing and promotion of MBA cohorts, and also later, when she stepped in as interim director after Dr. Swanson's departure from Johns Hopkins. After Dr. Lynda de la Viña was appointed associate dean and director of the Business Division in September 2001, the approach (at her and others' recommendation) for marketing academic programs throughout the school shifted from centralized to decentralized; much of the budget for marketing the division's academic programs shifted from the Office of Marketing and Communications to the division. Maria Lopez led this marketing effort for the Business Division, and in June 2002, Robertson was appointed marketing coordinator. In this capacity, he, as a graphic designer, produced electronic and hard copy brochures and flyers as well as multimedia designs. Around the time of Dean de la Viña's departure, during January 2004, the marketing and communications functions reverted to centralized control, Lopez departed, and Robertson, the only remaining marketing person, assisted in the division's efforts by translating the newly approved Business identity into different media by creating graphics and PowerPoint presentations for internal communications, open houses, and information sessions, supplemented by material for many other occasions. Robertson standardized the format for flyers, handouts, and general information sheets by creating the "masthead" for the Business Division, thereby eliminating delays caused by format discussion and correction. The preprinted masthead let the division move quickly when generating information, allowing directors to concentrate on the message rather than on the design and maintaining a professional, unified look for the division. Robertson also supported the work being conducted at the school level by the Office of Marketing and Communications for the Business Division. During June 2005, he joined the Office of Marketing and Communications in Shaffer Hall, where, as marketing and communications coordinator, he develops electronic and printed communications material for the Business Division as well as for other divisions.

Asked about an unforgettable moment, Robertson recalls turning a current advertising campaign into an animated presentation for the Business Division information sessions. (Ad campaigns and business marketing materials had been separate designs up to that point.) Soon after the debut of the presentation, his focus changed to maintaining business design standards that ensured consistency across the division. This theme—about classes delivering both a full measure of theory and practice—continues at some level today. Posters contained a written discussion of this theme and photographs of both a full-time professor and a member of the practitioner faculty, along with their backgrounds, illustrating this integration of theory and practice. In his spare time, Robertson is rehabbing an 1890 row home and converting its carriage house into a studio where he hopes to create figurative steel sculpture and furniture. He is also certified in gas, MIG, and TIG welding.[51]

Sarah Tennyson—In December 1994, Sarah Tennyson joined the Office of Marketing and Communications as a fulfillment specialist. In this capacity, her task is to focus advertising on the most likely targets, soliciting those who will be most interested rather than wasting limited resources on mass mailings likely to be perceived as junk mail. No easy task, this effort requires constant updating and refinements to the lists of potential students. Tennyson needs to know what program directors have in mind for a target audience and what is needed to attract them. Furthermore, appropriate forms of advertising must be used; for instance, it could be that potential MBA students are not avid readers of newspapers but do see billboards while driving to and from the office or hear radio advertisements while stuck in heavy traffic. In trying to find potential graduate students interested in the field of finance, Tennyson might study, for example, the results of a potential student's self-reported interests revealed in questionnaires completed when taking the GMAT. In any event, the limited advertising budget has to be spent wisely. In addition, Tennyson manages the centralized distribution of marketing pieces to prevent simultaneous multiple mailings that might overload the interest of the potential recipient. She also pays attention to

---

51 In June 2007, John Robertson was promoted to senior graphic designer in the School of Education.

ideas generated by focus groups, the interests of employers, and the views of trade associations.

Asked if she recalled a memorable occasion Tennyson described a situation when she helped out working the graduation registration desk where graduates picked up the card they would hand to a person who would announce their name as they walked across the stage. When the graduation exercise was well under way, a late arrival appeared at her desk. This student had just been in a minor auto accident and was visibly shaken; however, Tennyson gave her the card needed for the announcer and helped her find her seat. After the ceremony, the graduate found her in the crowd and thanked Tennyson for her help.

Student and Alumni Relations (during 2006)

Jennifer A. Dotzenrod, Director of Student and Alumni Relations—Jennifer Dotzenrod became a member of Johns Hopkins University during April 2000 as the assistant director of the Columbia Center and subsequently advanced through a series of positions of increasing responsibility. In December 2000, Dotzenrod became director of the Columbia Center and in November 2003 became Director of Admissions for the School of Professional Studies in Business and Education. Then, during September 2005, she became Director of Student and Alumni Relations, dealing with constituents from their beginnings as students throughout the balance of their lives as alumni. This office has four major components, each with its own unique functions.

1. Career Services—Places an emphasis on the individual's entire career rather than performing the typical job search and résumé writing.

2. International Services—Serves our international students by helping them comply with the many requirements that have changed since 9/11.

3. Alumni Relations—As happy students become happy alumni, the task is helping them want to stay connected with the school.

4. Student Affairs—Informs students with a consistent point of focus; listens to their suggestions and views and, when appropriate, takes action. Administers Student Code of Conduct and addresses grievances.

Dotzenrod's philosophy is helping the busy person achieve balance and success in their lives at home, at work, and at Hopkins. Typical of the interesting activities now appearing is the newly organized Finance Club, advised by a full-time member of the faculty, Dr. Celso Brunetti; it has 70–80 active student and alumni members. The Marketing Club, advised by a member of the practitioner faculty, Anne Lauer, has just received an Alumni Association Community Service Grant for their work with the nonprofit organization Potomac River Keepers, where they are doing pro bono marketing work related to watershed issues.

Asked about an unforgettable moment, Dotzenrod described a quick recovery from a mishap at the graduation diploma ceremony during May 2006. Her role was obtaining 3×5 name cards from students about to graduate after they climbed the stairs on to the stage, and then giving them to an announcer who would read the name of the person to receive the degree as the graduate walked across the stage. As luck would have it, she dropped a card that fluttered to the grassy field below. Taking immediate action, she leaped off the stage, retrieved the card, and jumped back on the stage—not bad for a lady who had given birth three months earlier. All the faculty and staff on stage admired her quick thinking and showed their appreciation by smiling in her direction and silently applauding.

Elizabeth D. Emery—After a 10-year career in hotel marketing and sales and a seven-year hiatus to raise her three children, Betsy Emery started with Hopkins in 1998, working part-time with Jan Moylan, who was then director of the Columbia Center. Working on marketing projects for the center, Betsy Emery assisted Jan Moylan in developing relationships with various community and governmental groups, including the Chamber of Commerce, Howard County's Office of Economic Development, business corporations, and nonprofit groups. In many cases, having an element of Hopkins in Howard County was something these groups could talk about as they promoted their own activities, as the Office of Economic Development did. In time, Emery and Moylan, building on the prior work of earlier directors of the Columbia Center, such as Peggy Murphy and Betsy Mayotte, enabled the center to expand its presence and further the wide range of relationships in Howard County.

Starting in 2003, Emery was employed full-time at the Columbia Center with the added functions of registration and budgeting. Then, in 2004, in a major career shift, she became the school's Admissions Department supervisor; in this capacity, she trained members of the school's staff about Prospect Tracker and how it could be used as a marketing tool. Prospect Tracker enables the department to follow students in the admissions process, revealing (among many other things) where and when some of them decide not to continue in the admission process. Indeed, promising applicants can be identified and encouraged on an individual basis to finish the process. Furthermore, Prospect Tracker can pinpoint where in Maryland, Virginia, and the District of Columbia prospective students live and work. Subsequently, the marketing process can focus on where it can do the most good. Emery's career progressed further in September 2005, when she became Coordinator of Student and Alumni Relations, working with the school's student groups and international students.[52]

Adrienne Gilchrist Allen—Started at Johns Hopkins University in the School of Medicine in August 1994 and then became a member of the School of Professional Studies in Business and Education in November 1999. As Special Events and Alumni

---

52 Then, with the establishment of the two new schools (Business and Education), Betsy Emery became the Associate Director of Student and Alumni Relations for the School of Education.

Relations Coordinator, her job combines planning thrilling events and caring for alumni. She enjoys the excitement of her position and acknowledges that the quality of the final product is usually determined by planning efforts and good coordination. In caring for alumni she helps them become more connected with the school by doings things such as maneuvering around the school to get answers to questions and facilitating alumni requests, such as a desire to serve on an advisory board or to be a guest speaker in a class dealing with a certain professional expertise.

Gilchrist Allen collaborates with members of the Business Division in planning and coordinating the annual Ginder Lecture, as well as other special events. In addition, she works on the annual alumni reunion for the entire school, including planning and preparing for the dean's reception on Thursday night. This event includes interactions ahead of time with alumni about the time and the place, as well as arrangements for their special needs. Sending invitations and responding to a surge in the volume of phone calls immediately preceding the event are part of her routine.

For the Graduate Division of Education, Gilchrist Allen recalls a gathering of about 300 educators from throughout the State of Maryland that required prior coordination with numerous counties and independent organizations. Parking for many of the attendees was at Hopkins at Eastern, which entailed use of shuttle buses, including provisions during the day for transportation of those who had to leave early. Initial gatherings and smaller sessions were held in Hodson Hall, and lunch was served in the Glass Pavilion. Although the event had a lot of different simultaneous activities, the overall result was a day of productive experiences for the attendees.

Asked about unforgettable moments, Gilchrist Allen provided two examples. In the first, a larger-than-expected group arrived, resulting in about a third of them standing in the rear of the room. Taking immediate action, she recruited people on the spot to retrieve chairs, and subsequently everyone was seated. In a more stressful example, the caterer arrived at a wrong location not too far from the conference. Taking immediate action, she located the caterer, who started driving to the proper site, and concurrently got the speaker to start in on new material scheduled for the early afternoon. The caterer eventually arrived, lunch was served, and everything was back on track. Gilchrist Allen's advice? Stay calm and don't let them see you sweat.

Professional Career Services (during 2006)

Patrick Madsen, Director, Professional Career Services— Patrick Madsen became a member of Johns Hopkins University in December 2005 as SPSBE's Director of Professional Career Services, with prior experience in a similar position as the assistant director within Nova Southeastern University in Fort Lauderdale, Florida. Significant is that alumni now receive career services for life; the name of the function has changed from career services to professional career services. Although a solid program had existed at SPSBE for over a decade and a half, since Madsen's arrival there have been notable improvements. More specifically, in the past year there has been a 140% growth in the number of student appointments and a growth of 80% in the number of students registered for his programs. Furthermore, rather than focus on entry positions for MBA graduates, nearly 80% of the positions now posted are at the mid- to senior level. There has also been a 101% increase in the number of employers who have contacted the office, and the number of new organizations contacted has increased by 92%.

At SPSBE, approximately 45% of enrolled students contact professional career services. This reflects the hard work being done now that gives students the desire to return to this office. Indeed, students report that if it is worth their while, they will return. In addition, a recent MBA career fair in Washington DC, conducted jointly by Johns Hopkins University, American University, the University of Maryland, George Washington University, Georgetown University, George Mason University,

Howard University, and Wake-Forest University, attracted recruiters from 85 different companies, with the second-highest number of students attending from Hopkins. Asked if he could think of a particular memorable occasion, Madsen proudly described the accomplishments of one international student who attended every career development seminar, visited his office almost weekly, and participated in two internships, including one overseas. As a result of all this work by the student and members of Madsen's office, he landed a good position in Chicago with Ernst & Young immediately following his graduation with a Master of Science in Finance.

International Services (during 2006)

Ann M. Roeder—In July 1984, a few months after she graduated from high school, Ann Roeder (nee Dunn/Harrell) began her career at Johns Hopkins University working in Room 99 in the basement of Garland Hall. Roeder now speculates that the room was originally a hallway, but then, after a door was put at one end, it was used as the place to assemble publications for distribution. During the summer of 1985, Roeder and her co-workers, who reported directly to B. J. Norris, Vice President for Communications and Public Affairs, were fortunate to be moved to the second floor of Whitehead Hall. Then, she departed from Hopkins in May 1986 to attend college on a full-time basis. Unfortunately, this became financially impossible, so she returned to Hopkins in August 1986 as an employee of the School of Arts and Sciences, working in the Department of Chemistry in Remsen Hall.

In May 1994, Roeder departed from the Department of Chemistry and became a member of the School of Continuing Studies as a program assistant in the Career and Life Planning Center (CLPC), located on the second floor of the Columbia Center. Replacing Dorothy (Dottie) Wilson, who had been working half-time for Pete Petersen and half-time for the center, Roeder worked with the director of the center, Kathleen (Kathy) Bovard. Years later, in October 1998, the Office of Student Affairs was established with Kathy Bovard as the director, and Mary Somers replaced her as the new director of CLPC, at that time considered a subordinate unit of the Office of Student Affairs. Concurrently, Roeder's career advanced when she became the program coordinator of the Office of Student Affairs with the added tasks of disability support services and liaison with student organizations. Her responsibilities increased further in fall 2000 with the establishment of International Student Services. Then during spring 2001, Bovard who had been Director of Student Affairs, departed and was replaced by Michael Ward as Director of Student Affairs. Subsequently, when Ward became Senior Director of Student Services for SCS in fall 2003, Roeder became Assistant Director for International and Disability Services. In addition to moving forward in her career, Roeder accomplished her personal educational aims by earning a Bachelor of Science in psychology from the School of Continuing Studies in 1993.

Administrative Services (during 2006)

Paul L. Adams, Senior Director of Administrative Services— On May 1, 2000, Paul Adams joined the School of Professional Studies in Business and Education as Director of Administration in the Graduate Division of Education. Prior to coming to Hopkins, he held various academic and administrative positions at the University of North Carolina at Chapel Hill, City Colleges of Chicago–European Division, and the University of Washington. In his role at Hopkins, Adams managed the business, administrative, and financial management functions for the Graduate Division of Education. He developed and administered revenue, grant, and contract budgets; supervised financial planning, admissions and enrollment services, computer systems, facilities, and human resources; oversaw $6.3 million in expenses; and supervised five direct reports and fifteen indirect reports. Some of his selected contributions include

> Spearheaded development and execution of the SPSBE Data Integration Project and Data

Warehouse to collect, analyze, and report school data to aid in administrative decision making.

Developed and administrated all revenue and expense general funds and sponsored project budgets. Consistently exceeded projected revenue budget while controlling expenses.

Contributed to School's successful accreditation by the National Council for Accreditation of Teacher Education. Served as the chief information and reporting officer for the project.

Represented the University on Project SITE SUPPORT, a joint initiative of Johns Hopkins University, the University of Maryland, Baltimore County, Morgan State University, the Baltimore City Public School System, and numerous high-profile local businesses, as the team's chief budget officer and administrator to oversee a $12.7 million federal grant. Worked collaboratively with partners to create a program to recruit, train, support, and retain a new generation of teachers to meet the diverse learning needs of K–12 children in high-need urban schools.

In 2005, Adams was selected for the newly created SPSBE position of Senior Director of Administration to provide strategic, administrative, and organizational leadership for the offices of Enrollment Management, Information Technology Support Services, Student and Campus Services, and Facilities Management for the school. As senior director, Adams articulated and implemented a comprehensive strategic vision designed to maximize student recruitment and retention through the creation of an effective student services infrastructure. In addition, he oversaw information technology projects to enhance the student experience as well as to improve administrative operations. In collaboration with the Associate Dean for Financial Operations, he helped develop the annual course schedule, and, in coordination with the Office of External Affairs, helped create and maintain a comprehensive online presence and portal development plan.

Adams supervised four direct reports (including Director, ITSS; Director of Student and Campus Services; Director of Student Information Systems and Registrar; and Director of Financial Aid) and 80 indirect reports and administered a $7.3 million general fund budget. Some of his other contributions include supervising the design and renovation of a new Education Building—an $8 million project—oversight of system development and integration within the school for ISIS, the integrated student information system; introduction of "One-Stop Service Centers" across five campuses to provide students with greater access to service; and the implementation of the Student Service Advisors program and school-wide call center to coordinate services and improve operating efficiency by resolving student needs on first contact.

These strategic initiatives laid the foundation for the creation of the Professional Schools Administration. Adams values the many friendships and close associations that he has with members of the faculty and staff not only in the school but throughout Hopkins as well.[53]

Admissions and Registration (during 2006)

Twana Mason, Director of Admissions and Registration—In January 1995, Twana Mason became a member of the Johns Hopkins University School of Continuing Studies, working as a registration assistant for Peggy Flynn in Shaffer Hall, Room 204. In 1996, she was promoted to registration coordinator, and in 1998, to office supervisor for the registrar's office and the admissions office. In 1996, the office moved from Baltimore to 7150 Columbia Gateway Drive, a few blocks from the Columbia

---

53 On April 20, 2007, Adams was informed that his position as Senior Director of Administrative Services had been abolished because of organizational decisions that had been made as a result of the split of the School of Professional Studies in Business and Education into the Carey Business School, the School of Education, and the Professional Schools Administration.

Center; in 2000, she advanced to the position of Assistant Director of Admissions. Then, in 2002, the office moved to Suite 110 in the Columbia Center, at 6740 Alexander Bell Drive. In 2005, Mason was promoted again to Director of Admissions and Registration. Concurrent with these promotions to ever-increasing levels of authority, Mason's effective leadership enabled her staff to achieve their mission despite changes in location, procedures, and organizational structure.

Asked if she recalled a memorable occasion, Mason told an office story that improves with age as it is repeated and handed down to new members of the organization. It seems that members of the office who return from vacation usually bring something edible to share with their colleagues. It was no exception one day when one of their assistant directors, who had just returned from vacation, brought a very special bottle of hot sauce to the office along with a large bag of chips. Pouring the sauce out in a small bowl, he cautioned everyone, essentially, that it was the mother of all hot sauces. Consequently, only one small drop should be taken with each chip—or several chips. There was no disagreement with this statement as folks in the room tried the new product. In due time, everyone returned to work, and the chips and bowl of hot sauce were placed in the nearby office kitchen. One of their colleagues, who arrived late to work, slipped into the kitchen and grabbed a few chips and a good quantity of what he thought was a salsa dip. When he screamed, everyone ran into the kitchen to save him. The moral of the story? Try a tiny portion first before you gobble down free food in the office.

Assistant Director for Admissions—Position vacant in 2006

Admissions (during 2006)

Carol Herrmann—In November 2005, Carol Herrmann became a member of Johns Hopkins University, joining the admissions office for SPSBE with the major event of her office for the second half of 2006 the preparation for the split of SPSBE into the Carey

Business School and the School of Education. Although their admissions office continues to process applications for both schools, it is located temporarily on the third floor of the Columbia Center while their first floor office is being renovated. But beyond this major reorganization and the renovation of an office, another event will take center stage, involving the application of rapidly changing technology. Indeed, the students may be ahead of our current approach for processing applications for degree programs. However, it appears that online applications will become a reality for both schools in the later part of 2007. In fact, another office is currently processing applications online for the MBA Fellows program. The students submit their applications electronically and learn the school's decision in a similar fashion. Although it sounds simple, the process is complicated by the need for applicants to furnish a copy of all of their college transcripts, some of which arrive directly from the prior school's registrar's office. Procedures are currently being implemented to address these challenges. Amid so much change, Herrmann and her colleagues' hard work and flexible natures will enable the two schools to advance to a higher level.

Joyce Owings—In June 2006, Joyce Owings became a member of the School of Professional Studies in Business and Education at Johns Hopkins University. Working in the admissions office, located in the Columbia Center, she processes applications from potential students.

Theressa M. Rose—During January 1998, Theressa Rose's first job at Johns Hopkins University was in the Graduate Business Admissions office, working with Susan Shaffer, Robin Reed, and Kelly Williams in Suite 180 at the Columbia Center. After the new Baltimore Downtown Center opened in January 2001, at the corner of Charles and Fayette Streets, the Graduate Business Admissions office moved to the third floor of the Downtown Center. Then, in 2003, Rose transferred to the Office of International and Disability Services, located in Suite 150 at the Columbia Center. Having lived abroad for about 20 years,

Rose related well to international students and was very helpful in helping them become acclimated to their new environment and Hopkins' academic programs. However, in 2005, she returned to the Office of Admissions, working with student admissions for both Business and Education.

Rose's fond memories at Hopkins focus mainly on her interactions with international students. Some of them were real characters, such as a physician enrolled in the MBA program who, in spite of doing well, had concerns about his ability to do the work in the next course. So, at the start of each semester, after receiving the syllabus during the first class, he would visit Rose and declare, "Just kill me!" After several repetitions of this routine, Rose knew him as "Dr. Just Kill Me." Nevertheless, she rooted for them all— and the doctor received his MBA and moved on to prepare for tests allowing him to practice medicine in the United States.

Records and Registration (during 2006)

Margaret Flynn, Associate Director for Records and Registration—Peggy Flynn (formerly Peggy Swagger) started at Johns Hopkins University in August 1978. Working in the Evening College and Summer Session, she was located in Shaffer Hall, Room 103. This particular office was a combination of the dean's office, student services, and any other function higher than the academic division level. In a few years, her activities shifted from being a generalist to focusing on registration and graduation, and, by and large, her activities remain the same almost three decades later. In August 1997, she accompanied other members of Student Services in their move to a building located at 7150 Columbia Gateway Drive, several blocks from the Columbia Center on Alexander Bell Drive. Then, in 2002, she accompanied them again in a subsequent move to the Columbia Center.

Although registration for classes takes place generally throughout the year, her other task of getting ready for graduation involves a surge of activity. Most students follow the process of applying for graduation and tune in to the follow-on audit of their classes and grades. However, some fail to apply for graduation, show up at a few weeks prior to graduation (or later), and expect to graduate. On some occasions, the latecomers did not take the correct courses or submitted a graduate research project late. Significant stress for Flynn occurred when, for example, a student informed her that family and friends had bought nonrefundable tickets on a flight to Baltimore and attempted to shift the blame to Flynn and supposed bureaucratic red tape. Adding to Flynn's graduation activities is the need to provide complete lists of graduates and award recipients to the Hopkins Central Administration so that programs can be printed. Information technology has been helpful to registration and the process of getting ready for graduation, but there are limits to the advances in technology for helping the lost soul.

Asked for an unforgettable experience, Flynn mentioned being part of an effort to raise money for the Mary Levin Scholarship Fund by writing and selling a cookbook with Betty Sattler and her other colleagues, which garnered between $2,000 and $3,000:

> The cookbook was called "Cooking with Class" and came out when we were called the Evening College. The first chapter was called "Prerequisites"—in this section were recipes for different types of salads. The next chapter was called "Informal Courses" because that was what our noncredit courses use to be called. This was for different types of appetizers. The next one was "Core Courses" representing main foundation type of courses that students need to take. This would be main meals. The final chapter was called "Electives" for different types of desserts.
>
> Bev Kahler and I worked on this. Bev did the majority of the typing for the book. Some of the staff names in this book are Pat Gold, Teresa Schwartz, Larry

Larsen, Bev Kahler, Carol Janes, Sandy Molyneaux, Ruth Kerin, Gloria Martins, Marion Panyan, Alma McMahon, Ruth Scharfe, Betty Sattler, Betty Vaughn, Denny Mullins, Jeannette McGrew, Martha Hill, Elaine Davis, Gilbert Schiffman, Claire Hooper, Mildred Verhaalen, Debby Loomis, Lynn Fox, Shirley Belz, Claire Brown, Pam Carmen, Keith Glancy, and Peggy Taylor (personal e-mail from Flynn, May 3, 2007).

Probably her most memorable occasion was rehearsing and being part of the entertainment for a holiday party involving faculty and staff performing as a chorus line. Conducted in December 1981, it was intended to be a surprise for Dean Roman Verhaalen, who would retire six months later, on June 30, 1982. The faculty and staff rehearsed for weeks under the direction of Dr. Ronald (Ron) Berk and Dr. Margaret (Peggy) Murphy. Unknown to most participants, Berk was working secretly with Roman Verhaalen on a similar routine. The entertainment conducted on stage in Shriver Hall was followed by a buffet in the Clipper Room on the second floor. The chorus line was fun to be part of and funny to watch, but the big surprise came when Roman Verhaalen joined the last number, performed satisfactorily, and brought the house down with laughter and applause.

John Bates—In July 1992, John Bates became a member of Johns Hopkins University, working in the registrar's office in the basement of Garland Hall. In this capacity, he was the "transcript person" for the School of Arts and Sciences and the GWC Whiting School of Engineering until September 1997. Then he became a member of the School of Continuing Studies, working for Peggy Flynn on registrar's matters at 7150 Columbia Gateway Drive, several blocks from the Columbia Center on Alexander Bell Drive. In 2002, he accompanied his colleagues as they moved to more convenient quarters in the Columbia Center. Most members of the faculty know him as the person who receives the grade roster. In fact, if instructors don't turn in their grades on time, he is the person they have to deal with, particularly if the class is during the spring semester and the grades are needed to determine who will graduate. But grades are only a small portion of his job as manager of data operations of the registrar's office. Because this data becomes a component for many decisions and is part of the university's official record, its accuracy is essential, and he is responsible for checking for data errors as well as for missing and mismatched data. He also handles staff member requests for access to the Integrated Student Information System (ISIS). In fact, as of 2006, about 70% of his time was dedicated toward the implementation of ISIS.

Asked if he could think of a funny or odd situation, Bates recalled the many times that students have asked, "What are you going to do during the December break or the summer break?" In fact, the December break may be the time he spends the most considerable amounts of time attempting to get caught up, and during the summer, it is business as usual.

Dawn M. Kostik—Before coming to Hopkins, Dawn Kostik worked from 1995 to 1998 as an admissions counselor at the College of Notre Dame of Maryland. In June 2001, Dawn Kostik joined Johns Hopkins University as an Assistant Director of Graduate Business Admissions and Advising, working for Kelly Williams. She divided her time between Baltimore and Columbia, meeting with students on the first floor of the Downtown Center and the first floor of the Columbia Center. Then, in June 2003, she departed from Hopkins and worked at Walden University for about two years. Returning in October 2005, she became a member of the Office of Records and Registration, working for Peggy Flynn. Ironically, the office that she now occupies is the same one she started in back in 2001. When asked about memorable occasions, Kostik described the good work accomplished by working with Dr. Gene Swanson in taking care of MBA students. As the first director of the MBA program, he was notified that some MBA students received excellent out-of-town job offers that they could not refuse. Apparently, the good work these students were doing at Hopkins was making them more attractive as candidates for excellent jobs; unfortunately, accepting these offers meant that students who were about 90% through the program would be unable to finish their degree programs. Swanson, working with the advising team, solved the problem by working individually with each student to establish independent research projects and elective courses that could be completed from their new locations. Indeed, it was a win–win solution for both the program and the new employer.

Crystal N. Robertson—Before becoming a member of Johns Hopkins University, Crystal Robertson worked as a program assistant at the National Foundation for the Improvement of Education. As one of her last activities there, she was part of an effort to award grants for the application of technology in the classroom to 30 outstanding teachers. When Robertson joined the Records and Registration Office at the School of Continuing Studies, it was directed by Peggy Flynn (the current director) and located at 7150 Columbia Gateway Drive, several blocks from the Columbia Center. However, in 2002, she accompanied members of her office to their current location at the Columbia Center.

As Coordinator of Transcripts and Records, Robertson focuses solely on internal documents generated by Hopkins. In addition, she handles veterans certification, which is required for students seeking education benefits from the Veterans Administration. Asked if she recalled any unusual events, Robertson described an unusual request from a student who wanted to receive his diploma via e-mail.

Financial Aid (during 2006)

Laura M. Donnelly, Director, Financial Aid—On May 19, 1997, she began working in the School of Continuing Studies in the Office of Financial Aid, located in Shaffer Hall on the Homewood Campus. Then, during August 1997, the Office of Financial Aid moved to a building at 7150 Columbia Gateway Drive, a few blocks from the Columbia Center in order to be centrally located in relation to all campuses. Finally, in 2002, the office moved to Suite 110 in the Columbia Center itself and continues to operate there, in close proximity to students. In addition to serving all of the students in the School of Professional Studies in Business and Education, Donnelly and her staff respond to financial aid questions from faculty members and staff concerning actions they are about to take at other institutions for their own children. Asked if she recalled any humorous incident, Donnelly recollected the time when a middle-aged man checked the wrong box on a form concerning his marital status. Instead of checking the box marked "Married," he checked "Separated." "When this was discovered, she and her co-workers asked him, "Does your wife know that?" and added that they'd tell her if he wasn't cooperative. He laughed and jokingly responded, "Oh, don't do that!" For some time, they continued to joke about it when he came by. It seems that getting to know students and building helpful relationships over the years is one of the joys of working in the financial aid office.[54]

Maria Izquierdo-Whitaker, Associate Director, Financial Aid—Before joining the Office of Financial Aid in the School of Continuing Studies at Hopkins on October 1, 1998, Maria Izquierdo-Whitaker had 10 years' experience working in the field of financial aid at the Pontifical Catholic University of Puerto Rico. Since her arrival at Hopkins, she has assisted the director, Laura M. Donnelly,[55] in the ever-changing field of financial aid and the application of technology to improve the system to help students. In addition to performing all of the functions related to assisting a director, she writes publications for the office, such as one titled *Frequently Asked Questions*, and prepares the information on the financial aid Web site. She also speaks at numerous information sessions informing potential students how to obtain financial

---

54 With the establishment of the Carey Business School and the School of Education, Donnelly became the Director of Financial Aid for both schools; her office is called OneStop Financial Aid.
55 During April 2007, Maria Izquierdo-Whitaker was promoted from assistant director to associate director of the Office of Financial Aid as it serves both the Carey Business School and the School of Education.

aid. Asked about an unforgettable experience, she related the happenings of a most unusual event.

Early one morning, during the spring semester of 2004, she called a student, who happened to be a police officer, to request some documents he needed to submit. While speaking to him, his speech sounded slurred to Izquierdo-Whitaker's ears, and the student stopped talking midway through the conversation. She quickly sought help for the unresponsive student by calling his police precinct and may have ultimately saved his life; officers who rushed to the scene found him unconscious. The student, who recovered and graduated with his master's degree, is just one of many who has benefited from the care and concern shown by the staff in the Office of Financial Aid.

As a member of the Hopkins Diversity Leadership Council and the School of Professional Studies Committee on Diversity and Civility and as a person who does uncalculated amounts of pro bono work, Maria Izquierdo-Whitaker is a credit to herself and a genuine treasure to the Hopkins community and beyond. She conducts bilingual presentations to middle school and high school students stressing the need for education and achievement, as well as bilingual workshops on how to pay for college, throughout the continental United States and Puerto Rico. Izquierdo-Whitaker is a recipient of numerous awards, such as the Johns Hopkins University Diversity Leadership Council Inaugural Award of 2003. But more important to her than awards are the comments from parents and students at graduation. Comments such as "We couldn't have made it without your help" bring tears to her eyes.

Monette Chambers—During February 1997, Monette Chambers started at Hopkins as a temp in the Office of Financial Aid in the School of Continuing Studies. She had previously been a research clerk in the banking industry. Then, in August 1997, based on her excellent performance, she was selected as a member of the Financial Aid team. She was part of the team that moved from Shaffer Hall to a building at 7150 Columbia Gateway Drive in Columbia in August 1997 and then moved again in 2002 to the Columbia Center, located on Alexander Bell Drive. As she manages day-to-day electronic processes, she is a key member of the Financial Aid office, where members conduct most of their transactions electronically. In addition to working on electronic processes, Monette enjoys working with students.

Monica B. Hudson—Before becoming a member of the Office of Financial Aid in October 2006, Monica Hudson worked for six years at the Young School Early Education program, a preschool serving two- to four-year-olds. In her prior role, she became a senior instructor and eventually one of the directors. Now, in the Financial Aid Office, she does a wide range of counseling and takes care of students in the Division of Public Safety Leadership. Hudson's sister, who formerly worked in the Office of Financial Aid for many years, recommended her for the job. As might be expected, Monica Hudson is outgoing and enjoys working and interacting with people of all ages.

Regina E. Roberts—Working previously in the Finance Office at Howard Community College, Regina Roberts joined the Financial Aid Office at the Johns Hopkins University School of Professional Studies in Business and Education in October 2006. Within the office, her work focuses on financial aid from the state of Maryland. In these cases, students deal directly with the state of Maryland, and the state deals directly with Regina Roberts. This procedural system goes smoothly if it is followed, but troubles ensue if the procedures are circumvented or if an action is processed at the last moment. Working well with everyone, Roberts makes sure that the system is in fact moving smoothly and that students are taken care of in a timely fashion. Recently, the director of the Office of Financial Aid received a compliment about Roberts from a Hopkins student who is also a Hopkins employee in another Hopkins school. Roberts had provided accurate assistance in a professional manner, and the student appreciated it and said so.[56]

56 Regina Roberts recently returned to Howard Community College and is currently a career programs administrative associate in the Office of Continuing Education and Workforce Development.

Student Accounts (during 2006)

Angela L. Banks-Smith, Manager, Student Accounts—Angie Banks-Smith started her long career at Johns Hopkins University in the School of Continuing Studies (SCS) during February 1989 as a member of Business Services, reporting to Debbie Rice, who reported to Barbara Plummer (who was later followed by Sherri Wood). Then, in 1994, she departed from SCS, joining the Homewood School's Student Accounts Office, where she worked on third-party billing, billing employers for tuition remission for their employees. She also acted as an assistant to Beth Bishop, the manager of the Student Accounts Office, and filled in for her during her absence. During May 1998, when SCS decided to do their own student account activities, Angie Banks-Smith returned to SCS, joining the Enrollment Management Office, located at 7150 Columbia Gateway Drive. In 2002, she moved with her colleagues to the Columbia Center building on Alexander Bell Drive. She is now in Suite 140 of the Columbia Center as the manager of student accounts, and her office receives and bills for all student-related tuition and fee charges; collects and processes all payments, including JHU tuition remission, third-party billing, registration payments, student invoice payments, financial aid payments, collection agency payments, and monthly installment payments from an outside payment plan agency; and monitors and places aging accounts with a collection agency and issues refunds to students with credit balances on their account.

Towanda Gardner—On April 28, 2003, she became a member of the staff at Johns Hopkins University as a front desk receptionist at the School of Professional Studies Columbia Center. She worked from 11:00 AM until 7:00 p.m., primarily taking care of students attending the late afternoon classes and those attending the first evening session. Although the center remained open until 10:00 p.m., most of the activity subsided by the time Gardner departed at 7:00 p.m. About a year later, her work schedule changed to 8:30 AM to 5:00 p.m., and she focused on daytime classes and preparation for late afternoon classes. Then, in March 2006, her career progressed when she was appointed a student accounts assistant and later became a student accounts coordinator in the Office of Student Accounts, where she was responsible for cohort billing and other student account activities. Gardner fondly recalls the warm feelings she had when students expressed their gratitude for the way she handled their accounts. In some of these cases, students had difficulty in meeting their financial obligations and Gardner was able to find an approach that would meet their needs.

Patricia A. Robinson—During November 1998, Patricia Robinson became a member of Johns Hopkins University, working in the Student Accounts Office in the School of Continuing Studies. Before coming to Hopkins, she worked as an account clerk at the University of Maryland at Baltimore. When she began at Hopkins, she was located initially at 7150 Columbia Gateway Drive, and she moved with her colleagues when the office relocated to the Columbia Center at 6740 Alexander Bell Drive. Starting out as a student accounts assistant, Patricia Robinson was promoted in January 2004 to student accounts coordinator. Unlike yesteryear, when tuition was paid at the time of registration, students can now register and opt to receive an invoice allowing them to pay their bill by mail, in person, or electronically. Consequently, Patricia Robinson's job is to assist students by processing their payments for tuition and fees. This can be stressful when students are overdue with their payments or do not understand the charges. However, Patricia Robinson appreciates when students thank her for going out of her way to solve a complex financial problem.

M. Jan Suter—Before being employed by Johns Hopkins University, M. Jan Suter worked for CSX Transportation for 20 years and then was hired as a budget analyst in March 1995 by the Peabody Institute. In December 1998, she became a member of the School of Continuing Studies as a student account assistant. She is currently the school's senior coordinator of student accounts. Although much of the collection of tuition payments is outsourced as payment plans operate online, her office comes into play when there are exceptional cases or when students need special guidance and direction.

Reflecting on her 12 years at Hopkins and 9 years at SPSBE, Suter comments about the substantial number of changes but also recognizes that "at Johns Hopkins University, we are a close knit group with a family-like atmosphere that is hard to find today in the corporate world."

Information Technology Systems and Support (during 2006)

Philippe D. Homassel, Director, Information Technology Systems and Support—Philippe Homassel began his association with Johns Hopkins University in October 1993 as a member of the staff at Homewood Academic Computing, where he administrated two IBM RS/6000—AIX systems and developed the Student Information System for the Homewood Schools. He also taught related workshops for Hopkins employees. Before coming to Hopkins, Homassel had been employed by the Mindbank Consulting Group in Vienna, Virginia, where he developed a management reporting system for Perdue Farms and a new data entry correcting system for the American Postal Workers' Union. Leaving Homewood Academic Computing in April 1998, he joined the School of Continuing Studies as project manager for the Data Warehouse. His office was located at the time in Shaffer Hall, and he reported to Brian Cooke, Director of Information Technology Systems and Support. Then, in August 2000, Homassel assumed his current position of Director of Information Technology Systems and Support. In 2002, about a year after the new Downtown Center opened during January 2001, his office moved from Shaffer Hall to the seventh floor of 100 North Charles Street.

As the field of information technology evolved and expanded, his organization adjusted accordingly, and operations are now conducted by three major subordinate leaders—Bonnie J. Woods, Web Project Manager; Kevin M. McIntyre, Manager Network/

Technology Services; and Mindi B. Shephard, Project Manager, Student Information Systems. In essence, Homassel is charged with developing and running the school's Web, managing the network (including technology services at all locations), and developing and operating administrative and academic systems.

Asked if he recalled a memorable occasion, Homassel described the time when there was a fire in the basement at 100 North Charles Street that shut down his server. Oddly enough, the server had been located to this building because it was a place that had access to three power grids in Baltimore. Unfortunately, the power transformer for the building had burned, and consequently it rendered the server inoperable. Luckily, the fire occurred on a Friday, and everything was back to normal in 48 hours.

Web and Portal Development (during 2006)

Bonnie J. Woods, Web Project Manager—Before her association with Johns Hopkins University, Bonnie Woods majored in journalism at Virginia Tech, located in Blacksburg, Virginia, receiving a Bachelor of Arts in Communication Studies. Subsequently, she taught remedial English grammar at Baltimore City Community College. Then, in August 1992, she started her long association with Johns Hopkins University, like many other members of the staff, as a Kelly temporary employee. As she worked in the Business Division's Office of Admissions, it did not take the director, Susan Marzullo (later Susan Shaffer), very long to recognize her talents and to hire her on a full-time basis starting in October 1992. During the next 15 years, her career was part of the fairly rapid evolution of the application of information technology in the School of Continuing Studies (SCS), later the School of Professional Studies in Business and Education (SPSBE).

From its beginnings in 1916, administrators of the teaching of Business Administration at Johns Hopkins University were interested in the number of students who were accepted into programs and the number of students enrolled in classes. As might be expected, success was measured in part by these statistics, comparing them to prior years and other programs. When Woods began in the Office of Admissions, there was an interest in applying information technology to compile this data in a quick and reliable format that could be used for sound planning and budgeting. This search for reliable data on a timely basis continues in academia today. During her three years in the Office of Admissions, Woods worked on an admissions database and rebuilt the system so that admissions and enrollment figures could be compared with prior figures. Furthermore, she was part of the effort to convert the DOS database to a Windows operating system, in which the mouse replaced key strokes, simplifying use of the personal computer. It is interesting to note that during this time, Brian Cooke (one of the founding fathers of the application of Information Technology in the SCS) was a work-study student from the School of Arts and Sciences who worked on similar efforts at the SCS level with Dr. Jon Heggan.

In 1995, Woods became a user systems specialist at the Business Division level, reporting to Ann Thomasson, the Director of Administration for the division, then located in the second floor annex of the original Downtown Center, at the southwest corner of Charles and Saratoga Streets. In this role, she facilitated the further introduction of information technology throughout the Business Division, including training members of the division during 1995 on the use of Windows-based e-mail. During this time, she also worked with Tom Wojeck, an SCS-level database developer who created the Credit Course Scheduling System (CCSS) used to generate the academic year printed catalog. Even though the catalog is now in an electronic form, it continues to use CCSS to generate content, and until JHU launches its university-wide registration system, this system also serves as the back-end course schedule for the school's Web sites. Woods also joined her colleagues when the Business Division moved across the street to the second floor of 201 North Charles.

From January to September 1997, she had the position of programmer/data analyst, remaining in the Business Division and continuing to report to Ann Thomasson, Director for Administration. She also became webmaster for the division, creating the first Division of Business Web site. In addition, working with Carol Keyser (who, among many other functions, directed noncredit information technology courses), Woods posted pages for graduate-level Capstone courses on the Web and also worked with Susan Rubb, the school's data warehouse developer, preparing computer-generated reports for the Business Division. Then, in September 1997, she moved from the Business Division to the SCS level, replacing Tom Wojeck as database developer for the school. In this capacity, Woods worked for Sherri Wood, Director of Business Services, who reported to Jon Heggan. Although Wojeck had developed the Credit Course Scheduling System, she enhanced it commensurate with changing requirements and advances in technology. As Systems Development Administrator, from September 1997 to April 2001, she worked with Colleen Hughes, the database manager, and embarked on numerous projects. Significant at this time was the development of custom databases as many new academic programs were introduced and the directors of existing programs sought custom databases. Also during this period, Woods honed her skills as a project manager, working with end users to determine system requirements and usability needs for CCSS. In fact, some of her fondest memories reflect on the days working as project manager with end users and having representatives from centers such as Jackie Deyo and from every academic division gather together for the purpose of improving the system. Indeed, their involvement made it much easier to implement their findings throughout the school.

In April 2001, Woods advanced further in her career by being appointed Web project manager for the School of Professional Studies in Business and Education. A major challenge for organizations, including SPSBE, continues to be how to best represent themselves on the Web. Accordingly, Woods made considerable improvements in this area, as well as in the development or expansion of more than eight Web sites. Then, as the application of information technology matured, emphasis turned toward maintenance and enhancements, as well as continued improvement of the actual content. A major task accomplished by Woods occurred during 2006, when plans had to be made for the creation of two new schools—the Carey Business School and the School of Education. In a two-month period, Woods and her staff converted Web sites from the SPSBE to the two new schools. Indeed, her current task as Web project manager provides the very best representation on the Internet for both schools. Also noteworthy is the fact that during seven years, Woods, as a part-time student, earned a Master of Liberal Arts degree in 1996 and a Master of Science in Information and Telecommunication Systems for Business degree in 1999. When asked if she recalled any unusual happenings, she indicated that she was amazed that about 40 children overall were born during the past few years to members of the organization, a number oftentimes aided by multiple births.

Janine E. Harig—In August 1991, she was hired as a program assistant by Becky Strang, the director of career services at the Downtown Center. Two weeks later, Kathy Bovard was interviewed and accepted the position of assistant director. Within a month of their arrival, Strang departed. Until then, the Office of Career and Life Planning was focused on presenting noncredit courses and providing individual career counseling to people in the community. In 1992, the focus shifted to providing career services to students and alumni. In 1994, the Career and Life Planning Center moved to the second floor of the Columbia Center. As use of the Internet became popular during the 1990s, Harig spent a good bit of her time helping students use the Internet for career and job searches and was promoted to career information specialist. A little-known fact is that Harig's development of a Web site for Career and Life Planning marked the first Web site developed for the School of Continuing Studies; she partnered with Maureen Beck in the MSE Library to launch the Web site.

Harig feels strongly that Kathy Bovard, her supervisor, colleague, and friend, made a significant impact on her career. It seems that being exposed to such a professional as Bovard led Harig to believe that she learned as much as she gave to that job. "Indeed, she took an interest in my career development and was the best supervisor I'll ever have. In fact, I attribute most of my success at Hopkins to her influence."

Building on her information technology skills, Harig made a lateral move in 1999 to the Office of Information Technology Systems and Support. In this new position, she became a Web development specialist, with an office on the fourth floor of Shaffer Hall. In 2003, she joined her colleagues as they moved to the seventh floor of 100 North Charles Street. Currently a Web development programmer, she is now at the senior staff level in the university. Plans for 2007 include a move of their office to the Columbia Center.

From a human interest point of view, Harig recalls the time when she was working on the fourth floor of Shaffer Hall and a squirrel became trapped in the attic above their peaked ceiling and was running back and forth just above the ceiling tiles overhead. An environmentally friendly squirrel catcher was called to the rescue and, with little effort, he caught the animal and then freed the lucky squirrel outside.

Network/Technology Services (during 2006)

Kevin M. McIntyre, Manager—Kevin McIntyre's first association with Johns Hopkins University was in 1994, as a technician working in Garland Hall for Joseph (Vince) Lamonte, Director of Microcomputing Services, an element of Art Heigl's Office of Administrative Computing for Johns Hopkins University. Then, in August 1996, McIntyre became a member of the School of Continuing Studies (SCS) and moved from Garland Hall's basement to the fourth floor of Shaffer Hall, sometimes referred to as "the penthouse." There, he reported to Brian Cooke, Director of

Information Technology Systems and Support, who was replaced in August 2000 by the current director, Philippe D. Homassel. In this new role, McIntyre repaired SCS computers and printers at all of the center locations and the Homewood Campus; however, most of his activities were at the Homewood Campus and the Montgomery County Campus. About two years later, Associate Dean Jon P. Heggan centralized the leadership, under Cooke, of all computer/audiovisual personnel previously directed by each center director. In 2000, McIntyre became the manager of all computer/audiovisual personnel. In large part because of the centralized reporting structure, the quality of all computer operations has improved, becoming uniform and easier to serve.

Asked about an unforgettable moment, McIntyre described an occasion in early 1999 when the Business Division moved from the original Downtown Center Annex, located near Charles and Saratoga Streets, to the second floor of 201 North Charles Street. Long before January 2001, when the Downtown Center itself displaced to the southwest corner of Charles and Fayette Streets, an incident occurred when a lease was terminated because of a leaking waste water system and the Business Division moved with little advance preparation. Business Division and support personnel such as McIntyre pulled together by moving across the street while continuing to be operational and supporting classes in progress. He continues to marvel how the school has the ability to act on a moment's notice and is more than ready to roll with the punches.

Homewood Campus

Timothy C. Reiss—During May 1991, Timothy Reiss started his long association with Johns Hopkins University in the basement of Garland Hall, working for Murry Ryan, director of the Telecommunications Department. In this capacity, Reiss was part of the effort to install all of the AT&T phones on campus, including student phones. He also laid cable and programmed the installation of phones. Then, in 1998, he became a member of the School of Continuing Studies (SCS) as a microcomputer technology specialist. His initial tasks were providing computer support to SCS elements on the Homewood Campus, to SCS elements at the Montgomery County Campus, and for all computers at the Washington DC Center. He now focuses on Shaffer Hall, the Education Building (formerly Seton Hall), and the SPSBE staff located at the Montgomery County Campus. Currently network administrator, he uses Altiris software to install other software electronically to computers at the Montgomery County Campus, thereby relieving him from making round trips to the distant campus. Furthermore, at the Education Building, he provides two mobile computer labs consisting of carts with 20 wireless computer laptops.

Asked if he could recall a heartwarming situation, he described how he keeps in touch with former work-study students from the Krieger School of Arts and Sciences and the Whiting School of Engineering. Many of these students who had worked with him for years have moved on to graduate school and great careers. He describes them as being very bright and "so leading edge." Indeed, his heart goes out to them.

Downtown Center

Susan R. Gilden, Center Technology Manager—Susan Gilden's association with Johns Hopkins University began over a quarter of a century ago. Like many other Hopkins employees Susan Gilden has been with different portions of the university. She started out as a cataloger with the MSE Library in 1981 and 1982 and then returned to Hopkins, working in the School of Hygiene and Public Health from 1986 to 1990, when she concurrently earned a Master of Administrative Science degree in the School of Continuing Studies. Finally, in 1999, she became a member of the newly designated School of Professional Studies in Business and Education, where for the past eight years she has been responsible for the operation of information systems and electronic audiovisual support of classes in Baltimore's Downtown Center.

As office computer systems matured during the early 1990s, one might hope that after everyone had a workable computer, Gilden's activities would settle down and be reduced to routine upgrades and day-to-day operations. Unfortunately, this was not to be, as many of the members of the Business Division changed buildings when the offices of some portions of the Business Division, located at 201 North Charles, moved to the seventh floor of 100 North Charles Street; other portions moved to the third floor of the new Downtown Center, at 10 North Charles. In addition, occupants of the old Downtown Center moved one block in January 2001, requiring the establishment of new electronic audiovisual systems in every classroom. As the person to call when things go wrong (or seem to go wrong) Susan Gilden is a popular person who is usually greeted at the start of the day with troubles from the night before and then computer-related activities throughout the day, with the addition of classroom activities during the day that pick up in the late afternoon. From time to time, challenges at work seem to follow her when she leaves the office. Several years ago, when she was a member of a nearby health club, she was paged while cleaning up after a workout. Waiting in the lobby of the health club were two members of the Downtown Center staff who were very concerned about a malfunctioning computer lab. Returning to the Downtown Center, Susan Gilden remedied the problem and the class continued. Quick on her feet and possessed of a good sense of humor, Gilden is a valued member of the team.

Keith Michie—Like many Hopkins part-timers, Keith Michie has been with Hopkins for over a decade. Working full-time at the Greater Baltimore Medical Center, Michie has been a member of the Downtown Center staff since June 1996. Working every Saturday from 8:00 AM to 5:00 p.m. as an audiovisual and computer technician, he recalls being hired by Scott Kelsey, one of the founding fathers of the Downtown Center computer techies. At the time, Jan Moylan directed the center, then located near the southwest corner of Saratoga and Charles Streets. On some occasions, Michie fills in for others at night during the week, but, by and large, his work is limited to Saturdays. What he likes the most about working on Saturday is the feeling of independence when he is alone, more or less, with the instructors and students he serves. Asked about his most unusual experiences, he responds that most of the computer and audiovisual stoppages in the classroom are caused by operator errors, such as equipment not being plugged in or not being turned on. Compared with yesteryear, Michie responds, "I used to have to move equipment from room to room, but now it is so much easier because it is built into each classroom."[57]

Columbia Center

Jacob P. Aierstock—Jacob Aierstock started at Johns Hopkins University as a microcomputer services technician during March 1999, as the name of the school was about to change from the School of Continuing Studies to the School of Professional Studies in Business and Education. Earlier, he was employed in the information technology field by the United States Naval Academy, from 1995 to 1997, and Air Canada, from 1997 to 1999. In fact, Aierstock claims that his job at an airline ticket counter taught him how to deal with unhappy (and sometimes angry) people, a quality that can come in handy for microcomputer technicians.

Starting out working in the evening at the Columbia Center, he shifted to working full-time and is now the microcomputer services coordinator for the center. Since 1999, he has seen and been part of the evolution of the application of information technology in an academic setting. In fact, he feels strongly that he is making a real contribution in his job and has a good feeling about how the Columbia Center is progressing.

Christopher Crabb—Chris Crabb had worked for Dell in Austin, Texas, prior to relocating to the Eastern Shore of Maryland to work for a small company providing computer support to homes and small- to mid-size businesses. Then he became a member

---

57 Michie reports that he is "currently getting a lot of requests to configure the students' laptop computers now that we have wireless technology in place."

of Johns Hopkins University in November 2006, working as a Microcomputer Services Technician IV at the SPSBE Columbia Center. There he provides computer support to faculty, staff, and students, helping with the day-to-day operation of computer labs and offices as well as furnishing personal computers with updates and the latest antivirus software.

Montgomery County Campus

Timothy C. Reiss—In addition to his role at the Homewood campus as network administrator, Tim Reiss is responsible for providing computer support for SPSBE full-time faculty and staff located at the Montgomery County Campus. This is assisted in no small measure by the use of Altiris software, which enables him to install other software electronically from afar.

Washington DC Center

Gary Robinson, Center Technology Manager—Gary Robinson's association with Hopkins for over a decade started in October 1996, when he worked with Hedy A. Schaedel, the registrar, whose office is located in the basement of Garland Hall. As a programmer and information technology support person, Robinson was the coordinator of student data operations and, when needed, could interact with the mainframe and produce reports furnishing requested data and statistics. Then, during April 1999, he became a member of the Graduate Division of Education's Center for Technology in Education (CTE), working with their director, Dr. Jackie Nunn. While courting his wife to be, he traveled frequently between Baltimore and the Washington DC area, where she lived. After they married in June 2003, he joined her in Washington DC. Finally, he transferred from CTE to another element of SPSBE by becoming the Washington DC Center technology specialist, who sees that the center's technology needs are met by tending to all of the technology in the center, including that used by students, staff, and faculty. He also purchases needed equipment and software and sees that the center's technology is properly maintained and protected.

Asked if he recalled a significant event at Hopkins, he related an embarrassing moment. Late one afternoon, while alighting from the basement of Garland Hall after a rainstorm, he ran across Garland field toward his parked car. Although part of the field was flooded, he ran on the limited dry space but almost collided with a parked helicopter. Surprised, as he ran, he said out loud to himself, "Who the heck put a helicopter here?" The voice of a future mayor of the City of New York answered, "That is my helicopter." Recognizing that this was certainly not the time to get into a discussion of right-of-way, Robinson excused himself as diplomatically as possible and quickly moved on.

Student Information Systems (during 2006)

Mindi B. Shephard, Project Manager, Student Information Systems—Before coming to Johns Hopkins University, Mindi Shephard worked in her first job after college as a computer programmer/analyst for Piedmont Airlines (a subsidiary of US Air at the time), supporting systems relating to aircraft maintenance and parts inventories. As an employee, she welcomed the perk of being able to fly free whenever and wherever she wanted on US Air. Moving on in her career, she leaped from the aviation industry to the world of academia, joining Hopkins in 1995 as an applications developer working in Homewood Academic Computing, primarily supporting a budget and accounting system and a help desk system. She subsequently became the database administrator and then the database and applications development manager for Homewood Academic Computing.

In November 2000, Shephard was hired by the School of Professional Studies in Business and Education (SPSBE) as a project manager for student information systems. Her first major project was the EPIC project, where she managed the implementation of the Exeter SMS off-the-shelf admissions module for the three part-time schools of the university (SPSBE, Part-time Engineering, and Part-time Arts and Sciences). It was during the EPIC project implementation that she was recruited to manage the Applications Development Group of the ITSS Unit. This unit supported internal SPSBE systems, such as the Credit Course Scheduling System, Prospect Tracker, SchedulerPlus, Finance System, and the Affiliate Instructor Payroll System.

Other major projects that Shephard managed for SPSBE include

1. The SPSBE Data Integration Project, with the scope of

> Identifying key data elements that reside within SPSBE and university-wide databases that will help the SPSBE divisions answer questions regarding their students, faculty, and programs.

> Populating the identified data elements into a central repository (enhanced SPSBE Data Warehouse).

> Creating a user-friendly Web front end to the SPSBE Data Warehouse to facilitate accurate queries and reports for analyzing data.

> Ensuring that information queried from any of Hopkins' different systems yields the same results.

Phase I of this project was given a six-month time frame, and the tasks were driven by the Graduate Division of Education for the purpose of meeting NCATE accreditation requirements. Although the focus was on the Education Division, the results benefited all divisions within SPSBE.

2. The Integrated Student Information System (ISIS)

This is Hopkins' first university-wide, Web-based, integrated student information system with SPSBE participating in all modules of the implementation, including Admissions (for SPSBE this was an upgrade of the software used for the EPIC project), Student Billing, Financial Aid, and Records and Registration.

Asked if she could recall a memorable or unusual occasion, Shephard remembered the time when, many years ago, the Applications Development Team had a team-building opportunity. After brainstorming and much debate, the group selected a golf outing at a nearby golf course. This was not a miniature putt-putt golf course, but the real thing. With only one or two members of the team having had prior golf experience, this was quite an event. At the golf course, all six of them golfed together, rather than the customary foursome. As the six golfers hacked their way around the course, they had loads of fun learning the game, riding the golf carts, and scaring the other players with their wild hooks and slices. This adventure is now part of the organization's folklore and grows with age as it is retold to new members.

Roderick Garza—Roderick Garza was initially hired as a contract employee in November 2001 and then joined Hopkins as a full-time employee in May 2002. Working for Mindi Shephard, project manager for Student Information Systems, Garza plunged into the development of the Data Warehouse with his job title clearly stating his function—database applications developer. For years, members of the faculty and staff had talked about the creation of a data warehouse that would fulfill everyone's need for accurate information. Now, with the four-person team of Mindi Shephard, Jennifer Parks, Ralph Rizza, and Rod Garza, this wish would come true. More complex than people imagined, the development of the Data Warehouse involved standardizing definitions, terms, and processes that differed from user to user. As the project was being developed, short suspense dates, driven by the NCATE accreditation process, added to the urgency of completing the mission, including a seven-day work week and work on Christmas Eve and New Year's Day. Then, as the stress continued to increase, the team finally completed its project. However, as more questions were answered by the data warehouse, more questions were asked, and more requirements were placed on the product. Garza is currently providing technical support to the Data Warehouse Online System, as well as supporting the ISIS Financial Aid and Billing modules. Asked if he recalled any momentous occasions, he was quick to recap his discussion about the data warehouse and the tremendous good feeling he had when it had been completed.

Jennifer Parks—In January 2002, Jennifer Parks joined Johns Hopkins University as a database developer working toward the creation of an integrated student information system. This system needed to be user-friendly, to furnish what users needed, and to consolidate redundant reporting. In some cases, this redundant information occurred because a wide range of users were not being provided with what they wanted. A lack of consistent definitions for variables such as classes and students added to the complexity of this effort. Because classes can differ in length and magnitude, and because full-time and part-time students do not enroll in the same number of classes, a common set of definitions was needed. Much progress has been made, but work continues on this overall effort.

Parks was most helpful in developing a "real-world" application to enable students to be tracked and served according to their needs at a particular time. An example of a successful application is the tracking of graduate-level teacher preparation interns as they complete their internships. Their activities and ratings become part of the database, as well as part of their own electronic portfolios.

Thinking back on memorable occasions, Parks recalls the time when three departments of the Business Division (Marketing and Communications, Information Technology Systems and Support, and the academic Marketing department) were located on the seventh floor of 100 North Charles. When all these people were together on the same floor, Parks, Debbie Boyd, Michelle Robinson, Mike Brands, and Page Barnes would make arrangements for office parties in honor of springtime,

Halloween, Thanksgiving, the December holidays, and nearly any other worthy event. The December holiday party included the furnishing of toys, clothing, and money to a needy family, an idea which originated with the collaboration of Christine Brodax (now Valeriann), Sarah Tennyson, and Mike Brands. Brodax brought this idea with her from her days working at the Post Office, where employees answered letters from needy families. Brodax, Tennyson, and Brands worked together to screen several letters and determine a family to support. On some occasions, they supported several of them. Then the family or families would be contacted to learn of their major needs as well as the specific ages and wishes of the children. Parks recalls the joy of wrapping presents in the conference room and their subsequent delivery by Brands and others. On a more humorous note, Parks recollects when the Office of Marketing and Communications moved to Shaffer Hall and the remaining staff held a farewell party for them. The party theme was one of mourning, and the crew even had a cemetery cake and played a special version of Pictionary that had two themes, SPSBE and movies and books with death references in their title. It seems that these informal moments add much to the morale and esprit de corps of the office.

Polina Mogilevich—Polina Mogilevich came to the United States from Kiev in the Ukraine 17 years ago and has been a member of the staff at Johns Hopkins University since November 15, 2004, working with Mindi Shephard, project manager for Student Information Systems. In this capacity, Mogilevich worked with her teammates on information technology applications for course scheduling, financial systems, and Prospect Tracker and is currently working on the Integrated Student Information System (ISIS). In mid-July, current plans call for the Department of Information Technology Systems and Support to move to the Columbia Center from the seventh floor of 100 North Charles in the heart of Baltimore. In looking toward the future, Mogilevich visualizes that "the Web will have it all"—data analysis, information, and learning. In fact, as it is for some today, much of the learning of tomorrow will be accomplished on the Web. Mogilevich is especially thankful for her working environment, where she feels surrounded by "really caring friends, ready to help in any situation. And for me as a person from a different country this is very important."

Campus Services (during 2006)

Blanca Poteat, Director of Student and Campus Services—In August 1998 Blanca Poteat started at Johns Hopkins University, following Rosel Halle as director of the School of Continuing Studies (SCS) activities at the university's Montgomery County Campus. In 2002, she became Director of Washington Region Centers, consisting of activities at the Montgomery County Campus and the Washington DC Center for what was then the School of Professional Studies in Business and Education (SPSBE). At this same time, Eva Lane, director of the Downtown Baltimore Center, became Director of Baltimore Region Centers, including the centers in Downtown, Homewood, and Columbia. In 2006, Poteat became Director of Student and Campus Services with oversight of all five center locations, working with center managers at each location.

When she first joined the effort at the Hopkins Montgomery County Campus, enrollments in SCS programs had declined, the SCS Business Division's Information Technology Department (because of a shortage of space) conducted classes several blocks away in rented space at the Bechtel Building, and potential relationships with the local business community languished. The Education Division continued to build solid relationships with Montgomery County Public Schools, bringing in former principals and teachers to grow its teacher training programs.

The construction of a second building on the Montgomery County Campus relieved the shortage of classroom and office space and allowed Business Information Technology programs to return to the campus. When the new MBA program was launched in 1999, interest and enrollments grew at all center locations, and Poteat, Lane, and others worked with faculty to increase business community interactions and to explore possible expansion initiatives.

Each of the campus centers is different, with a unique portfolio of programs, course offerings, students, faculty, services, and facilities. The Homewood Center, situated on the Johns Hopkins University Homewood Campus, reflects the diversity of the university environment. The Downtown Center offers a unique urban setting for business programs and partnerships. The Columbia Center is an academic and administrative hub shared by business and education programs. The Montgomery County campus, unlike the other four SPSBE centers, is managed by the university provost's office and offers, in addition to business and education programs, graduate studies of Krieger School of Arts and Sciences, Whiting School of Engineering, and Bloomberg School of Public Health. The Washington DC Center offers business programs in the nation's capital on the same downtown block with the university's Krieger School of Arts and Sciences and the School of Advanced International Studies.[58]

Homewood Campus

Sabrina Scarborough, Campus Operations Manager—Sabrina Scarborough became a member of Johns Hopkins University in September 1997 as the noncredit registration coordinator for the School of Continuing Studies. Then, after being located at the Downtown Center for about five years, she accompanied her office as it moved to Shaffer Hall on the Homewood Campus and became part of the Division of Undergraduate Studies. At that time, noncredit offerings consisted mainly of Information Technology and Odyssey courses. Then, in 2003, she became the campus center coordinator for the Homewood Campus,

---

58 In January 2007, when the School of Professional Studies became the School of Education, the Carey Business School, and the Professional Schools Administration (PSA), Poteat continued her role as Director of Student and Campus Services, serving the two new schools through the PSA. In late 2007, she joined the staff of the Carey Business School, representing the school and MBA programs for the Montgomery County Campus.

and from October 2006 to March 2007, she was the operations manager for both the Homewood campus and the Downtown Center. Currently, she is the campus operations manager for the Homewood Campus.

Scarborough enjoys working with students and gets a great deal of satisfaction in talking with them when they graduate or when they return to offer thanks for her assistance. Asked for a significant event, she told a story that grows with age and that is repeated when the "old-timers" in her office meet with new members of the staff—the story about the time that Scarborough almost burned down the original Downtown Center, located near the southwest corner of Charles and Saratoga Streets. On that fateful day, she placed a frozen chicken potpie in the toaster oven and went back to her desk. Returning to the galley, she was surprised to find the toaster oven and surrounding area ablaze. She tried to grab the fire extinguisher but could not remove it from the wall and then, in an act of desperation, threw water on the electrical toaster, causing the flames to subside and subsequently extinguish. Jackie Deyo and Emily Nehring were present during this calamity and were later joined by Eva Lane. Many claimed that Scarborough could have been electrocuted, but since that time she has been banned from using a toaster oven under any circumstances.

Wendi Hairfield—During fall 2005, Wendi Hairfield became a member of Johns Hopkins University in the School of Professional Studies, working with Peggy Flynn in the SPSBE registrar's office located at the Columbia Center. In this capacity, she helped with a wide range of functions, ranging from registration to preparation for the diploma ceremony in May. While in the registrar's office, she visited various centers to train student service advisers on the latest registration approaches. At the Homewood Campus the last member of the existing team was departing, and Hairfield was selected in October 2006 to fill the gap. Concurrently, Sabrina Scarborough, who was then center operations manager of the Downtown Center, pitched in and helped get the Homewood campus operational. Scarborough, who became the campus operations manager, and Hairfield, who became the student services specialist, work side by side, operating the Homewood Center, which consists of the Education Building and Shaffer Hall.[59] As her career at Hopkins continues, Hairfield is also enrolled in a graduate program in the School of Education leading to a Master of Science in Organizational Counseling.

When asked to describe any unusual events on the job, Hairfield discussed how she enjoys helping students. She also mentions an occurrence that so far "has been a career highlight." During a major event at the Education Building (formerly Seton Hall) attended by the president and provost of Hopkins and other distinguished guests, Hairfield stood at the front door and welcomed the guests, and President Brody then shook her hand before moving on with the activities. It was a memorable reward for the hard work put forth to ensure the success of the event.

Downtown Center

Samartha Phifer, Center Operations Manager—Samartha Phifer, started working Fridays each week in December 1995 on student services activities in Shaffer Hall, Room 103, on the Homewood Campus. Then, in April 1996, she began working full-time in the same office as an education support services assistant. In 1997, Phifer progressed further in her career when she was selected for the position of Noncredit Registrar where she worked from 1997 to 1999 with Tom Crain on Odyssey course registrations and with Carol Keyser and Lucy Cooper on Information Technology and Personal Computer registrations. It was during this period that she moved from Shaffer Hall to the Downtown Center Annex. In November 1999 she departed Hopkins and became a compliance assistant at the Bank of America and in 2003 an operations manager at the University of Maryland School of Pharmacy. Phifer returned to Hopkins in September 2003 as an administrative assistant in the School of

59 With the creation of the two new schools, Wendi Hairfield's functions have evolved to meet changing needs, and she now works mainly at the Education Building.

Medicine, working with the director of the Center for Innovation in Quality Patient Care. Then, in March 2006, she returned to the Downtown Center in Baltimore as a student services adviser and in March 2007 moved up to the position of center operations manager for the Downtown Center.

She had some difficulty in recalling her most unforgettable moment at Hopkins but eventually related a story that could pass for a skit on *Saturday Night Live*. It seems that a task for the person scheduled to arrive early and open up the office was to make a pot of coffee for the dean, who had an office on the other side of the wall. It may sound easy enough, but her co-workers reminded her not to forget or goof it up. She put their minds at ease and made the coffee as scheduled early the next morning and carried on with her other tasks. However, as a non–coffee drinker, she used a full measure of water but very little coffee. Consequently, what she produced at the time was coffee so weak that you could see through it. When the dean took a sip of the coffee he inquired, "Who made this coffee?" Now, years later, she has acquired the taste for coffee and can brew it satisfactorily, but on a few occasions while making coffee, she thinks back to that time she brewed a horrible pot of coffee.

Robin H. Cook—In 1986, Robin Cook worked with Jan Moylan at Maryland Cup, in the vicinity of what is now Ravens Stadium. During 1986, when the company was acquired by Fort Howard Paper Company, located in Owings Mills, Jan Moylan joined the Hopkins team at the Downtown Center in Baltimore; shortly thereafter, Robin Cook accompanied her. At the time, Cook had given birth to her daughter and was willing to work only on Saturdays, so she started at the Downtown Center in the beginning of 1987 and has worked there just about every Saturday from 8:00 AM until 5:00 p.m. ever since. When she started, Judi Broida was the director and Jan Moylan the assistant director, and construction of the center had been completed. Classes started in early January 1987, and the dedication of this new facility was conducted on April 22, 1987. What Cook remembers most about those early days was Moylan's focus on service and the on staff having a customer orientation. At the time, total quality management was the rage in business and industry, but many in the academic world throughout the nation had some difficulty seeing students as customers. But that was not the way at the Downtown Center, where professionalism reigned, and everyone was treated with dignity and respect. Indeed, Robin Cook continues today to emphasize those qualities stressed by Jan Moylan and supported by Judi Broida.

Marcus Jackson—In 1985, Marcus Jackson started his long association with Hopkins, working for Broadway Services as the night security supervisor at the Peabody Institute. No stranger to security work, he had been employed before then as the operations manager of Northwest Investigations. Then, in 1992, he became a member of the School of Continuing Studies and part of the team at the Downtown Center in Baltimore. At the time, Jan Moylan was the director of the center, Eva Lane the assistant director, and Jackie Deyo the person who handled day-to-day operations. Asked to recall any unforgettable moments, Marcus Jackson is quick to describe activities at the tow away zone in front of the building each weekday from 4:30 to 6:30 p.m. On some occasions, drivers appreciate warnings about the possibility of having to pay over $200 in towing charges and a fine. But other drivers don't want to be told what to do and continue to park, or grumble as they drive away. Unfortunately for those who stay, independent tow truck operators, paid on a commission, circle the block, competing with each other, and are quick to pounce on their prey. Thinking of a more academic unforgettable moment, Jackson recalled the time Dr. W. Edwards Deming (famous for assisting the Japanese with their industrial renaissance) spoke in the Berman Auditorium on September 23, 1992, and, at age 92, would not climb the seven or eight stairs leading up to the stage necessary for using the newly purchased high-tech projector and screen; instead he prepared to go home. Hopkins trustees, who had been invited, as well as other distinguished guests, were waiting in the lobby, and there was a tense moment when the evening's event was about to be a flop. Coming to the rescue, Marcus assisted Eva Lane and Jackie Deyo, who were very much involved, by grabbing an overhead projector and screen from one of the classrooms and setting them up at floor level. The Deming lecture succeeded, the guests were satisfied, and the event made the *Washington Post* and *Baltimore Sun* the next morning.

Irish T. Jones—Irish Jones began her association with Johns Hopkins University as a campus police officer in June 2001. Assisting Harry Williams, she has an obviously outgoing personality and loves dealing with people. Similar to Officer Williams, she finds that people in general passing by on Charles and Fayette Streets are a sight to behold and a source of interest as the day progresses.

Harry Williams—Harry Williams became a member of Johns Hopkins University on February 27, 1995, as a campus police officer at the original Baltimore Downtown Center, located near the southwest corner of Charles and Saratoga Streets. For the past 12 years, he has seen countless members of faculty, staff, students, and passersby in general come and go. In fact, Williams is often the first person many people see when they begin a long-term relationship with Johns Hopkins University. After unlocking the building in the morning and turning off the alarm, he greets people with a smile and a cheery comment until he is relieved by fellow campus police officer Marcus Jackson in mid-afternoon. Very important, however, he adds to the area's overall security by stopping people who have no business in the building and sending them on their way. As a related task, he also serves as a source of information for disoriented pedestrians and insists that his job is never boring because of the unusual and sometimes peculiar people walking by on Charles and Fayette Streets.

Columbia Center

Jacqueline M. Deyo, Director, Columbia Center—The Deyo family has been active in the Evening College, the School of

Continuing Studies, and the School of Professional Studies. In fact, Robert (Bob) Deyo started teaching at Hopkins in October 1987 after he finished the Master of Administrative Science program. He also taught noncredit courses in personal computer troubleshooting and software courses such as WordPerfect and Lotus 123. Then, in 1998, he started as a faculty adviser in the Information Technology Capstone program and occasionally acted as an evaluator of MBA Capstone projects. The Deyo family contributed greatly to the 2001 opening of the Downtown Center in Baltimore as their son Rob did some contract work in the network area and their daughters Cathy (now Cathy Deyo Wilson) and Megan helped at the affair while Jackie was the assistant director of the Downtown Center. Bob is currently involved in the HopkinsOne SAP project.

Jackie started at Hopkins in November 1987 as a part-time staff member at the old Downtown Center in Baltimore, near the southwest corner of Charles and Saratoga Streets, and then became a full-time member of the staff in 1991. As assistant director of the Downtown Center, Jackie worked with members of the construction project for the new Downtown Center, completed in January 2001, which included the move of a portion of the Business Division from 201 North Charles Street to the third floor of the new Downtown Center. Then, in November 2003, she was promoted to director of the Columbia Center. At the moment, Jackie is involved in renovating the building at 6740 Alexander Bell Drive to accommodate new configurations of the elements formerly in the School of Professional Studies. As the teaching of business at Hopkins continues to adapt and evolve, the Deyo family can be counted on to provide much support and experience.

Hope Grandel—Now in her 23rd year, Hope Grandel started in 1984, just after the center had moved to Twin Knolls from Joseph's Square, and at the time when the Evening College and Summer Session became the School of Continuing Studies. Asked if she recalled any interesting stories, Grandel, who worked several nights each week, had a few reminiscences. Long before the advent of today's online registration, lines of students at registration snaked all around the center and out the front door as programs became more popular. To remedy the situation, numbers were distributed (she recalls over 300 on one night), and students no longer had to stand while waiting. Although most people who staff the reception desks and answer the phones recall the flurry of phone calls each winter, asking, "Are classes canceled for tonight?" after the sighting of the first snowflake, Grandel has a new twist to the story. It seems that at the Columbia Center, there were office pools in guessing the number of such calls. Each person answering the phones maintained a tally, which was totaled at the end of the evening.

Grandel also mentioned the need to schedule the use of the videocassette players and monitors, because on some evenings instructors requested more of them than were available. On occasions, one instructor would use the device longer than scheduled, cutting into time scheduled for the use of another. Grandel's experiences conducting equipment negotiations between pairs of unhappy instructors continued over the years, with the added challenge of personal computers being shared between several classes. Fortunately, for the most part, these challenges do not exist today, because each classroom is equipped with the necessary equipment. Grandel also recalls collating by hand papers to be handed out in class because the machine they were using didn't have the capability to collate. In addition, Grandel marveled at the instructors' abilities to jam the duplicating machines in the rush to copy material just before class. She gladly assisted them in fixing the machines and helped them get back on track while observing their futile efforts with the machines. Nevertheless, she has a high regard for the instructors and can even recall when a few of them were students.

Robert Hartge—On September 14, 1991, Robert Hartge started working on a full-time basis during the evenings and weekends at the reception desk (usually referred to as the front desk) at the

Columbia Center (located at the time at Twin Knolls). Then, in 1998, he shifted to working on a part-time basis from 5:30 p.m. to 10:00 p.m., Monday through Thursday, and also as needed on Saturday and Sunday. Working now at least 18 hours each week as a part-time employee, he has fond memories of the many instructors and students that he has become acquainted with during the past 16 years.

Always pleasant, Hartge is most helpful as he simultaneously answers a phone while trying to help an instructor in front of him find an audio and video specialist to care for an inoperable DVD player, also noting comments from a hurried instructor briskly walking by call out a change in schedule. These peak activities, just before early and late classes, repeat themselves twice each evening, and Hartge is far from surprised at any new event that occurs on his watch. Reflecting back on unusual events at the reception desk, Robert recalls something that happened years ago, on a Sunday afternoon, after the departure of an Applied Behavioral Science Fellows group that had finished their seminar, when he and Ret Robertson heard what seemed to be voices coming from the wall. Alone in the center, they thought it must be their imaginations until after considerable time it became evident that a man's voice kept yelling "Robert—Robert—Robert." After some time, they recalled that they had complained earlier that day to the property manager at Manekin about a faulty elevator, and (you guessed it) Tucker Davis, the ever-responsive property manager, stuck in the elevator between the second and third floors, had been investigating the problem that Sunday afternoon. Tucker Davis, Robert Hartge, and the late Ret Robertson chuckled about that eventful Sunday for years to come.

After a full measure of work during his "day job," one might wonder how Robert Hartge is able to maintain his composure in the evening. Perhaps it's because of the lull in the storm after the two peaks of activities each evening. Indeed, it's during these quiet moments that acquaintances get to know Robert Hartge as he talks about the weather, his favorite topic. One of his good friends and colleagues at the front desk will chime in from time to time, saying, "Don't get him talking about the weather." But his insight is enjoyed, and as a member of the team who backs up and helps students and instructors alike, Robert Hartge's presence is much appreciated.

Michael Houck—Like many other members of the Hopkins team, Michael Houck recalls the date he started working at the School of Continuing Studies; in fact, starting March 18, 1996, he worked part-time, teaching faculty, staff, and students how to access material from the library via personal computer. By 1996, most of these individuals were familiar with operating personal computers, so much of his time was spent on training them how to use a personal computer to deal with the library. Indeed, a challenge at the time for the Business Division was that their classes were conducted mainly at four off-campus sites, and there was a lack of library facilities at these locations. Although there had been attempts to gather books for each site, the task of replicating the MSE Libraries holdings of relevant Business Administration books and journals was not possible. Fortunately, off-campus library services improved greatly as Houck instructed faculty, staff, and students in the evenings and Saturdays on how to communicate electronically with the MSE Library.

As the various programs in the school evolved and matured, the use of library facilities by people located at off-campus sites became more extensive, responsive, and sophisticated. Now students can receive hard-copy documents from the MSE Library in a timely fashion, as well as material via interlibrary loan. Along with this increased use of library resources, faculty, staff, and students also seek Mike Houck's instruction to properly accomplish day-to-day academic work.

Consequently, starting January 6, 2003, Houck was appointed on a full-time basis the regional center librarian for Baltimore's Downtown Center and the Columbia Center. Currently, he spends most of his time helping students, teaching computer classes each week, and conducting refresher classes on research methods for Capstone students. He also teaches an undergraduate class about three times a year on research methods for the Division of Public Safety Leadership. Indeed, Mike Houck is a key aide for students engaged in research who need guidance on a specific approach or method.

Charles Lambdin—In 1993, Chuck Lambdin became a member of Johns Hopkins University as a campus police officer on the Homewood Campus; in 1995, he was selected as a campus police officer for the Columbia Center. Before working at Hopkins, he had three years' experience with the first mass transit police officers on the Baltimore subway and, later, 7 years' experience as a plant protection officer in the special police at the Westinghouse plant, then located near the BWI Airport. Ever willing to help students and faculty, he has changed tires and stayed with people after closing who were waiting for their ride in front of the Columbia Center; indeed, several members of the staff call him "the legend." Lambdin gained this nickname by coming to the rescue when audiovisual personnel are not available. He is quick to lend a hand in any situation that arises and is a valued member of the team.

Barbara C. Pair—Barbara Pair became a member of the Hopkins security effort during October 2005 as a campus police officer. Located at the Columbia Center, she enjoys interacting with students and instructors during her work hours of 2:00 to 10:00 p.m. When asked about any unforgettable experiences, Officer Pair commented about the high volume of items mistakenly left behind by students and faculty. Keys seem to be the most popular item overlooked, with laptop computers coming in second. Although keys are usually discovered missing when the person attempts to unlock his or her car, laptop computers are usually not missed until the person arrives home and takes things in from the car. Then a frantic call to the front desk informs security, and Officer Pair retrieves the item and places it in the safe overnight. Officer Pair enjoys interacting with these busy folks and is glad to lend a hand when they sometimes misplace their belongings.

John Whitehead—John Whitehead became a member of Hopkins in the School of Professional Studies during January 2000, in the Office of Financial Aid. There, Whitehead worked on the "front line," interacting with students on the phone and face-to-face in the office. Then, in October 2000, he transferred to the SPSBE registrar's office, where he continued to interact with students, faculty, and alumni but in a wider scope of activities, including the computation of class standings, the generation of grade rosters by computer, and preparation for the annual diploma ceremony. After receiving a full orientation and the experience at Hopkins as a beginning administrator in academia, Whitehead became a member of the administrative staff at George Washington University in August 2005, where he worked on George Washington University's graduation exercise. Then, after seven months, in March 2006, he returned to SPSBE as a student services specialist interacting with students at the Columbia Center. With his increased skills as an academic administrator, Whitehead helped establish the call center, continued expanding his skills in dealing with walk-ins, and went out of his way to focus on customer service.

Asked if he recalled any unusual events, Whitehead described the situation one day when a student arrived at 4:45 p.m. and asked an endless stream of questions about applying for a program and then, as the conversation concluded, embarked on an additional set of questions for a friend. Nevertheless, this two-hour discussion led to the enrollment of two qualified students. As Whitehead says, "walk-ins as you are ready to go home come with the territory."

Pamela J. Young—Pam Young began her career with Hopkins at the Applied Physics Laboratory for 2½ years (December 1996–April 1999) as an educational outreach coordinator in the Space Department. Then, in January 2000, she became a member of SPSBE as an educational support services coordinator at the Columbia Center. In an earlier portion of her career, she taught school for two decades at every level from fifth grade to the second year of college. From teaching in Maryland's affluent

Montgomery County, she significantly shifted her school setting, when she accompanied her husband (a PhD environmentalist) to the Mississippi Delta and taught there for six years in a rural public high school. She also accompanied her husband to Central America, where they lived on Barro Colorado Island, a Smithsonian Research station in the Panama Canal, while he tracked troops of howler monkeys to determine whether an outbreak of yellow fever would render them extinct.[60] Her husband is now retired from his position with the U.S. Department of Agriculture. Young enjoys her work in helping students at Hopkins and appreciates her home's convenient location near the Columbia Center, which alleviates having to fight the area traffic.

Montgomery County Campus

Janee McFadden, Campus Operations Manager—Janee McFadden recalls the date she started at Johns Hopkins University as April 24, 2006; as a member of SPSBE, McFadden was assigned to the Montgomery County Campus as the campus operations manager/senior student services adviser. Unlike other campuses, the Montgomery County Campus has degree programs from other Hopkins Schools in addition to SPSBE. In taking care of SPSBE students, it seems that about 60% are seeking a graduate education degree, and the remaining 40% are working toward a graduate degree offered by the Graduate Division of Business and Management. McFadden and her staff advise potential students, help them enroll if they are qualified, support them throughout their programs, and then assist them with graduation.

With the new Carey Business School and the School of Education, McFadden and her staff provide support for students in both schools. When asked if she recalled a memorable occasion, McFadden indicated that she has a wonderful feeling every time she or members of her staff receive thank you e-mails or face-to-face compliments.

---

60 The outbreak spared the island, sparing the troops of howler monkeys.

Carlene Charles-James—Originally from Trinidad and Tobago, Libby Charles-James was employed for six years by the Greater Baltimore Medical Center before becoming a member of Johns Hopkins University during October 2003. Starting at the Homewood Campus she worked for the Homewood schools as a Clinical Assistant IV in the Counseling Department, located in Garland Hall. After she got married in August 2004, she accompanied her husband to Montgomery County, but after many long commutes to Baltimore, she discovered that Johns Hopkins University had a facility much closer to her home. Charles-James began working in October 2004 at SPSBE's Montgomery County Campus, providing educational support services.

She arrives early at the Montgomery County Campus and, as academic services assistant, reviews material from Sharada Murthy, the evening person for the office, who records significant events and recommends action to be taken. Charles-James then reviews completed registration material, scans the mail, and resolves situations within the scope of her responsibilities. In thinking of memorable occasions, she recalls a part-time instructor who brought in flowers for her at the conclusion of her classes, thanking her for helping during the semester. In addition, Charles-James appreciates the good feeling she gets when students thank her for helping them beyond what might be expected. In one situation, she knew that a student needed and wanted a particular course; thanks, in large part, to her efforts, he was able to register for the last space available.

Preamela Minix—Originally from Kuala Lumpur, Malaysia, Preamela Minix started at Johns Hopkins University in the SPSBE office at the Montgomery County Campus as a Kelly temporary employee in December 2000. Shortly thereafter, in March 2001, Minix was hired on a full-time basis as an administrative assistant to respond to all manner of questions from callers pertaining to programs, courses, and registration. In addition, Minix is able to tell applicants to degree programs the status of their application, including the receipt of transcripts and letters of recommendation. She also tells callers how to find information on the Web that is relative to their interests and provides callers with contact information for their adviser. Now an academic services specialist, Minix reflects on her start seven years ago working on room scheduling and particularly enjoys her encounters with students and instructors over the years.

Asked if she recalled any unusual experiences, Minix described the time she was in a local hospital, right after she gave birth to twins, when she was recognized by a lady down the hall who was a current student. The student then bombarded her with questions about registration dates and the offering of classes. It was quite a memorable day for Minix.

Sharada S. Murthy—Sharada Murthy became a member of the Johns Hopkins University School of Continuing Studies (SCS) in September 1998, working as the receptionist/senior typist Monday–Thursday evenings and on Saturday representing the school at the Montgomery County Campus. Then, in April 2001, she became an educational support services assistant continuing to be located in the office used by the School of Professional Studies in Business and Education (SPSBE) element during the day. Although two additional buildings have been constructed since Murthy arrived, the location of the SPSBE office remains the same. During the past decade, she has become skilled in registration matters and also proctors examinations for instructors, returns graded examinations and term papers to students, and helps students use the school's information networks to find answers about their status on a wide range of issues. In fact, Murthy effectively fills the gap between the daytime staff and the students who take evening classes.

Asked if she could recall a memorable occasion, Murthy described how as part of her job she had taken care of the class registrations for one particular student each semester and was surprised and honored when at the time of graduation he gave her a brownie. He said, "My wife baked these, and I would like you to have one."

Murthy added, "It's situations like this that add to the reasons I love my job."

Washington DC Center

Robert R. Kavalek, Center Operations Manager—Robert Kavalek became a member of Johns Hopkins University during October 1999 as the education support services coordinator at the Washington DC Center. These were particularly exciting times, following the introduction of the MBA during the summer of 1999 and the change of the name of the school on July 1, 1999, from the School of Continuing Studies to the School of Professional Studies in Business and Education. Then, almost two years later, during July 2001, when the School of Hygiene and Public Health shared the Washington DC Center with the School of Professional Studies, the center's leadership passed to the provost's office, with a leadership arrangement similar to that of the Montgomery County Campus. As a result, Kavalek's job title changed to campus services coordinator, and he reported directly to the provost's office. In the normal course of events, the new MBA program caused graduate business enrollments to swell and subsequently use about 85% of the classrooms; the School of Hygiene and Public Health did not have a similar enrollment increase. With the subsequent departure of what is now the Bloomberg School of Public Health, the leadership of the center reverted to the School of Professional Studies, with Kavalek becoming assistant director of the Washington DC Center. During these successive periods of leadership, although he continued to be the senior person on site, it appeared to the casual observer that he was second-in-charge, working for someone else on site. A new job title on January 1, 2007, corrected this impression by naming him the center operations manager. However, it should be noted that several command arrangements had been tried for the purpose of simplifying the reporting of five directors to a higher level. The approach that finally emerged was to have one person, the Director of Student and Campus Services, handle the consolidated redundant administrative functions of all of the centers and speak as one voice for all the centers while a manager at each of the centers handled day-to-day operations.

Asked if he recalled any memorable occasions, Kavalek recalled two events: one an accomplishment and the other a funny situation. He feels that the efficiency of the center's operations has improved over the years, making it able to accomplish more with less people. Furthermore, the establishment of one person to speak for all the centers enabled their collective voices to connect with top leadership and consequently garner an appropriate response for all centers.

At the time of the anthrax scare, the Washington DC Center received an envelope addressed in a very sloppy fashion apparently written by a drunk or a deranged writer. Furthermore, the envelope lacked a return address. After an inspection by the Metropolitan Police Department and approval to open the envelope, its contents caused quite a chuckle in the office—and the situation remains part of the folklore of the Washington DC Center. The envelope contained a handwritten letter, written in a similar fashion, with an attached résumé, also handwritten. The writer was requesting an appointment as a part-time instructor in the MBA program. When he called a few days later, he was informed, correctly, that there were no openings.

Lawrence Swann—Lawrence Swann started working at Johns Hopkins University in June 1995 as a receptionist in the School of Continuing Studies Washington DC Center, eventually becoming campus coordinator for this center. In this capacity, he interacts with faculty, staff, students, and the general public. In addition, he schedules classrooms, troubleshoots electronic equipment in the classrooms, orders supplies, and handles day-to-day operations, including running the library. On occasion, Swann relates, it can get very busy when there is a sighting of the first snowflake and about 40 phone calls an hour deal with the question, "Are classes for tonight canceled?"

Asked if he recalled any memorable occasions, Swann described his friendships and acquaintances among students and faculty during the past 12 years. In fact, some people he has known as students have gone on to become instructors. It is a real pleasure for him to see people mature and advance in their careers.

Charles A. Underwood, Jr.—On September 11, 2002, Chip Underwood became a member of the staff at Johns Hopkins University, working as an admissions assistant at the School of Professional Studies in Business and Education center located in Washington DC. Then, in October 2005, he was promoted to educational support services coordinator; he is currently an academic services specialist. Since his arrival, he has taken on an ever-increasing number of tasks, such as interacting with potential students and, for those qualified, overseeing the process for admission to one of Hopkins' programs. In addition, he advises students and assists them with financial aid and student accounts. He also schedules classrooms and arranges for visits by the traveling bookstore. Underwood particularly enjoys seeing students successfully complete their programs and empathizes with the adult learner who has to balance a full-time job with earning a degree.[61]

Center for Teaching and Learning (during 2006)

Shelley A. Chapman, Director, Center for Teaching and Learning—Starting in August 2000 as the program director of what was then called the Academic Support and Testing Center, Dr. Chapman spent the next seven years helping the Business Division move to a higher level in terms of how the overall curriculum was developed and its classes taught. The Business Division's mostly part-time faculty had challenges in consistently presenting high-quality courses; in addition, the need to apply new technology in the classroom during the late 1980s through

---

61 During the diploma ceremony on May 17, 2007, Chip Underwood received a Bachelor of Science in Business Administration. He had completed all 120 credits for this degree as a part-time student since his first classes during the spring semester of 2003.

the 1990s presented an even greater challenge. Nevertheless, the Business Division muddled its way through the process and by the year 2000 was presenting high-quality classes. The subsequent efforts of Chapman and her colleagues led to even greater accomplishments and gains in professionalism.[62]

Although the need to carefully administer and evaluate technology and writing examinations during 2000 was the Academic Support and Testing Center's initial focus, the organization evolved in about a year into the Academic Resource Center. The electronic educational approach titled Blackboard was coming of age in 2002, and all instructors and students who had not previously mastered its use in teaching classes had to quickly get with the program. With Chapman's leadership, the Center for Teaching and Learning was organized during Academic Year 2002–2003, offering "programs and services that help build community and discourse for significant and transformative learning experiences for students, faculty and staff" (Center for Teaching and Learning brochure, 2006, p. 1).

> 1. Teaching Dialogues—Volunteer faculty, both part-time and full-time come together to read and discuss a book or set of articles over a period of about eight weeks.
>
> 2. Curriculum Design and Redesign Course— Through a hybrid format, in which faculty meet, faculty learn how to design or redesign a course or program focusing on deep understanding, assessment for learning, evidence-based learning, and significant learning experiences.
>
> 3. Technology for Learning—Small group and individual consultations assist faculty in deciding when and why to use certain tools.

---

62 On July 1, 2007, Dr. Chapman was appointed Vice President for Academic Services at Southern Wesleyan University in Central, South Carolina.

4. Class Visitation and Consultation—At the invitation of the faculty member being visited, a low-stakes, nonevaluative classroom visitation is conducted for formative feedback.

5. Individual Consultations—The Center for Teaching and Learning staff meet with individuals to help them in different ways such as orientation of new faculty, interpretation of course evaluations, exploration of new ways to create significant learning experiences, and brainstorming for solutions to classroom problems.

6. Resources—The Center for Teaching and Learning has a lending library with excellent resources on how people learn, how to design significant learning experiences, and strategies for teaching and learning (extracted in bits and pieces from the above reference, pp. 1–2).[63]

Natalie Hannon, Assistant Director, Center for Teaching and Learning—Natalie Hannon started with the School of Continuing Studies on July 13, 1998, and, while located initially with a portion of the Business Division on the second floor of 201 North Charles, spent much of her time working directly with the associate dean of the school, Dr. Jon P. Heggan. With the job title instructional designer, she focused on how emerging technology could be used for teaching. As the application of this technology for learning evolved, use of the electronic educational approach titled Blackboard created a substantial demand for classes to

---

63 Further information on how the Center for Teaching and Learning helped the Business Division is contained in a chapter in an edited book of readings titled *Leadership in Place: How Academic Professionals Can Find Their Leadership Voice* (JB—Anker Series), edited by Jon F. Wergin. The chapter pertaining to the Department of Management, written by Dr. Shelley A Chapman and Dr. Linda M. Randall, discusses how a graduate degree in the department was totally revamped and subsequently became a model for the revamping process. More specifically, the chapter describes a case in which part-time faculty were empowered to lead their department in the development of a new master's degree program. During this process, Dr. Randall was the chair of the Department of Management.

teach faculty about using this resource. Consequently, Hannon transferred to the Center for Teaching and Learning during the summer of 2002 and became immersed in learning about many of these new learning technologies and sharing information with others. As assistant director, she backed up Shelley Chapman in the flurry of activities that arose.

Sara Hill—Upon joining the Center for Teaching and Learning as a curriculum designer during August 2003, Hill taught numerous workshops to help the faculty with their approaches to develop or revise their curriculum and in turn develop high-quality classes. Concurrently, as the demand for sessions on Blackboard became more pressing, she taught countless group and individual sessions to both faculty and students. Ever patient and understanding, she dealt with faculty and students who had delayed their instruction to the last moment, often to the point of panic. Furthermore, as the subject of hybrid classes emerged, she was the focal point for instruction and coaching to faculty volunteers who attempted this approach.[64]

Jennifer Smith—Jennifer Smith became a member of the Academic Support and Testing Center during October 2000, shortly after the arrival of Shelley Chapman. Like Dr. Chapman, she was with the unit for the past seven years as it evolved from testing to a center of teaching and learning. As coordinator, she controlled a variety of activities in the ever-expanding center. Initially, Smith administrated the waiver examinations and then ran a tutor referral network for students. She also coordinated technology and writing workshops for incoming MBA students and recruited and hired a variety of instructors to help incoming graduate students obtain the skills required for success in the new MBA program. Smith provided oversight for the overall operations of the Center for Teaching and Learning, ensuring

---

64 During September 2007, Sara Hill departed from the Carey Business School and is now a member of the Hopkins Bloomberg School of Public Health. She reports, "Although I am very happy with my new position, I continue to miss my colleagues from the Carey Business School and those SPSBE days."

that faculty and students alike received the resources and support necessary to assure significant learning experiences across the Business programs.

Appendix R
Advisory Boards and Faculty
Listings (AY 2005–2006)

Division of Undergraduate Studies*

ADVISORY BOARD

Mary Pat Clarke
Baltimore City Council
Member
City Council of Baltimore

Colene Daniel
President and Chief Executive
Officer
Maryland General Hospital

William Phillip, Jr.
Associate Executive Director
NAFSA Association of
International Educators

Mark Pollitt
President
Digital Evidence Professional
Services, Inc.

Lois Shofer
Retired Professor
Community Colleges of
Baltimore County

O. James Talbott
Chairman, President and CEO
Farmers and Mechanics Bank

FACULTY

John Baker, Sr., MAS
Director, Technology Programs

* SPSBE Academic Year Catalog
2005–2006, pp. 360–364.

429

Linda Cortez, JD
*Director, Business and
Management*

Thomas A. Crain, MA
*Director, Interdisciplinary
Studies*

Toni Ungaretti, PhD
Assistant Dean and Director

Amy M. Yerkes, PhD
*Associate Dean, Academic
Affairs
School of Professional Studies
in Business and Education*

Faculty Associates

Peter D. Adams, MA
*Professor
Community Colleges of
Baltimore County, Essex*

Richard Albert, JD
*Hearing Examiner
Department of Labor, Licensing
& Regulation*

Richard P. Allen, PhD
*Director and Assistant
Professor of Neurology
School of Medicine
Johns Hopkins University*

David Ashley, MBA
*Program Adviser
Department of Homeland
Security*

Ross Ballard, MEd
*President
MountainWhispers.com
Audiobooks*

David Baron, MBA
*Senior Information Technology
Auditor
Office of Internal Audits
Johns Hopkins University*

Jack Bayer, MBA
*International Business
Development Manager
NOVA Services, Inc.*

C. Edwin Becraft, MD
*Chief of Medical Services
Maryland State Highway
Administration*

Phyllis Berger, MFA
*Director Photography
Programs, Homewood Art
Workshops
Johns Hopkins University*

Peter W. Bergstrom
*Fishery Biologist
National Oceanic and
Atmospheric Administration*

David M. Biddinger, MS
Faculty Associate
Division of Undergraduate
Studies

Joseph M. Bishop, PhD
Director, Office of Research &
Technology
National Oceanic and
Atmospheric Administration

T. Michael Blair, JD
Program Director
SRI International

Wesley D. Blakeslee, JD
Associate General Counsel
Johns Hopkins University

Travis Bonfigli, BA
Principal Engineer
US Internetworking, Inc.

Leonard Bowman, PhD, M Div
Faculty Associate
Division of Undergraduate
Studies

Georgia Brady, JD
Administrative Law Judge
Maryland Office of
Administrative Hearings

Scott Brainard, MA
Faculty Associate
Division of Undergraduate
Studies

James Breiner, MA
President and Publisher
Baltimore Business Journal

Cathy Buckman, MS
Faculty Associate
Division of Undergraduate
Studies

Art Buist, JD
Faculty Associate
Division of Undergraduate
Studies

Carl Burnett, MS
Faculty Associate
Division of Undergraduate
Studies

Jennifer Campbell, PhD
President
J. Blakely Campbell &
Associates, LLC

Michael Carlis, JD
Administrative Law Judge
Maryland Office of
Administrative Hearings

Shelley A. Chapman, MA
Director, Center for Teaching
and Learning
School of Professional Studies
in Business and Education

Mary Pat Clarke, MA
Baltimore City Council
Member
City Council of Baltimore

Lawrence M. Cohen, MBA
Director, Membership
Technology Integration
American Association of
Retired Persons

Emried D. Cole, JD
Partner
Venable, Baetjer and Howard,
LLP

Barbara Crain, MS, MEd, MA
Faculty Recruitment Overseas
Specialist
University of Maryland
University College

Mark Croatti, MA
Faculty Associate
Division of Undergraduate
Studies

Colene Daniel, MS
President and Chief Executive
Officer
Maryland General Hospital

Curtis G. Davis, BS
Instructor
Community College of
Baltimore County

Conan Dickson, MPH, PhD
Senior Researcher
Johns Hopkins Center for
Innovations in Quality
Patient Care

Ted Doederlein, MS
Faculty Associate
Division of Undergraduate
Studies

Ted Donnelly, PhD
Director of Research
Baltimore Research

Richard Dunfee, PhD
Lecturer
Whiting School of Engineering
Johns Hopkins University

Mia Emerson, MA
Senior Consultant
Booz Allen Hamilton

Katharine Fernstrom, PhD
Faculty Associate
Division of Undergraduate
Studies

Sheldon Fishman, MS
Internet Applications
Specialist/Webmaster
Swidler, Bevlin, LLP

David Fohrman, DTL, MLA
Rabbi, Resident Scholar
Hoffberger Institute for Torah
Studies

Ann Christine Frankowski,
PhD
Adjunct Assistant Professor
Department of Sociology/
Anthropology
University of Maryland
Baltimore County

Stanley C. Gabor, JD
Dean Emeritus
School of Professional Studies
in Business and Education

Lori Gillespie, MS
Curriculum Manager
American Red Cross

Alex S. Gogue, MGA
Senior Systems Analyst
Johns Hopkins University

Silvia B. Golombek, PhD
Vice President of Programs
Youth Service America

Martin Gordon, PhD
Chief Historian
National Imagery and
Mapping Agency

Kenneth Grant, MS
Vice President, General
Services
Johns Hopkins Health System

Christine R. Gray, PhD
Associate Professor of English
Community College of
Baltimore County

Michael J. Grieco, MS
Senior Program Manager
Lockheed-Martin Corporation

Karen Henderson, MEd
Consultant
Cruse Consulting

Leroy Hewitt Jr., MSE
Director
Hewitt Engineering

Sara Hill, MA
Curriculum Designer
School of Professional Studies
in Business and Education

David Hillman, MS
Faculty Associate
Division of Undergraduate
Studies

Theresa Hodge, MS
Senior Laboratory Instructor
Goucher College

Philippe Homassel, MS
Director, Information Technology
School of Professional Studies in Business and Education

David P. Hopkins, PhD
School Psychologist/Specialist
Baltimore County Public Schools

Ailish Hopper, MFA
Faculty Associate
Division of Undergraduate Studies

Linda D. Hummel, MA, MS
Faculty Associate
Division of Undergraduate Studies

Laurence A. Jarvik, PhD
Proprietor
The Idler

Suzette S. Johnson, MS
Senior Systems Engineer
Essex Corporation

Walter L. Jones, MS
Deputy Director/Management and Diversity
National Institutes of Health Clinical Center

Peter M. Joyce, PhD
Professor of Mathematics
Community College of Baltimore County–Catonsville

Kathryn H. Kavanagh, PhD
Assistant Professor
University of Maryland

Sean P. Keller, MS
Vice President and Chief Operating Officer
SAGE Management Enterprises, LLC

Wanda King, MS
Manager, Management and Staff Development Programs
Johns Hopkins University

Rita R. Kolb, PhD
Associate Professor
Community College of Baltimore County–Catonsville

Richard L. Konigsberg, CPA
Faculty Associate
Division of Undergraduate Studies

Anthony C. Kouzis, PhD
Assistant Professor
Bloomberg School of Public Health

Ruth Kremer, BA
Marketing Director
MedStar Health

Michael Kubik, MBA
Analyst
T. Rowe Price Associates, Inc.

Michael A. Kulansky, MBA, MEd
Faculty Associate
Division of Undergraduate Studies

Darren Lacey, JD
Chief Information Security Officer
Johns Hopkins University

E. Joseph Lamp, PhD
Professor and Chair, Speech Department
Anne Arundel Community College

Kevin Lanagan, MBA
Project Officer
Social Security Administration

Edwin E. Lewis Jr., MS
Technical Director, Healthcare Counseling
Force3 Inc.

Steven Libowitz, MA
Director, Health Publishing Business Group
School of Medicine
Johns Hopkins University

Win G. Liu, PhD
President
Sharp Vision Software

Pat Lovenhart, MBA
President
Lovenhart Research & Consulting

Beverly Magda, MS
Information Technology Manager
Johns Hopkins University

John Martin, JD
Faculty Associate
Division of Undergraduate Studies

R. Donald McDaniel, MBA
Vice President, Insurance Solutions
Injured Workers Insurance Fund

William C. McDaniel, MA
Faculty Associate
Division of Undergraduate Studies

Elizabeth Melia, PhD
Faculty Associate
Division of Undergraduate
Studies

Greg Metcalf, PhD
Faculty Associate
Division of Undergraduate
Studies

Tanya T. Minkovsky, MS
System Analyst
Johns Hopkins University

Kathleen Minnix, PhD
Faculty Associate
Division of Undergraduate
Studies

Elizabeth Minthorne, MS
Principal and Consultant
Center for Leadership
Excellence

Richard B. Minthorne, MBA
Co-Founder
Center for Leadership
Excellence

Edward Mitchell, BA
Faculty Associate
Division of Undergraduate
Studies

Michele L. Moore, MS
President
SW Complete, Inc.

Daniel Morris, MS
Associate
Booz Allen Hamilton, Inc.

Susan Mrozowski, MS, MPA
Instructional Designer
School of Medicine
Johns Hopkins University

James T. Murray, JD
Administrative Law Judge
Maryland Office of
Administrative Hearings

Nancy R. Norris-Kniffen, PhD
Director Emeritus, MLA
Program
Krieger School of Arts and
Sciences
Johns Hopkins University

Stephanie Ogle, MS
Manager
Booz, Allen Hamilton, Inc.

Edwin C. Oliver, PhD
Psychologist
Baltimore Lab School

Christopher Olsen, PhD
Faculty Associate
Division of Undergraduate
Studies

Maxwell Oppenheimer, JD
General Counsel
Cell Works, Inc.

Edward C. Papenfuse, PhD
Archivist, Commissioner of
Land Patents
State of Maryland

Bradley Parish, MS
Senior Financial Analyst
US Postal Service—Contractor
Consultant

Karri H. Paul, MFA
Faculty Associate
Division of Undergraduate
Studies

Edward G. Piper, MS
Senior Consultant
Piper Group

Mark Pollitt, MS
President
Digital Evidence Professional
Services, Inc.

George D. Rahal, MBA
Director, Procurement & Risk
Management
Constellation New Energy

Jignasa Rami, MSE
Assistant Professor
Community College of
Baltimore County

Jana K. Rehak, MFA
Adjunct Faculty
Department of Anthropology
American University

Joseph Reinsel, MFA
Faculty Associate
Division of Undergraduate
Studies

Kimberly P. Riley, PhD
Senior Faculty Associate
Division of Undergraduate
Studies

Allan Rivlin, MBA
Partner
Peter D. Hart Research
Associates, Inc.

Ash Rofail, PhD
Chief Technology Officer
Santeon, Inc.

Robert G. Roop, PhD
Vice President, Human
Resources and Education
Humane Society of the United
States

Dianne Scheper, PhD
Faculty Associate
Division of Undergraduate
Studies

George L. Scheper, PhD
Professor Emeritus
Community Colleges of
Baltimore County, Essex

Sonja Schmitz, PhD
Faculty Associate
Division of Undergraduate
Studies

Carolyn Schoenian, MAS
Faculty Associate
Division of Undergraduate
Studies

Mark Seaman, MA
Faculty Associate
Division of Undergraduate
Studies

Kenneth Seidl, MS
National Sales Training
Manager
United Parcel Service

Paul Shibelski, MS
Faculty Associate
Division of Undergraduate
Studies

Mary K. Shock, JD
Administrative Law Judge
Maryland Office of
Administrative Hearings

Irving H. Smith, PhD
Faculty Associate
Division of Undergraduate
Studies

Stephen M. Smith, MBA
President/CEO
Naviance LLC

Karen Spencer, EdD
President
Purposeful Development
Associates

Roger Staiger, MBA
Chief Financial Officer
Caruso Homes, Inc.

Stephen Steele, PhD
Professor
Anne Arundel Community
College

Charles J. Stine, SCD, MLA
Faculty Associate
Division of Undergraduate
Studies

Dalton Tong, MBA, CPA
President and Chief Executive
Officer
Tong and Associates
Healthcare Management
Consultants

Paul Totaro, BS
Faculty Associate
Division of Undergraduate
Studies

Michael S. Tumbarello, MS,
MBA
President
First Service Financial Group,
Inc.

William T. U'Ren, MA
Faculty Associate
Division of Undergraduate
Studies

Edwin E. Urie, MS
Senior Program Manager
Northrop Grumman
Information Technology

Thomas A. Vadakkeveetil, PhD
Independent Consultant
Alexander Consulting

Raymond P. Villard, MS
Public Information Manager
Space Telescope Science
Institute
Johns Hopkins University

Lamont Wells, MS
Senior Vice President,
Corporate Development
American Systems Corp.

Christine Weston-Lyons, MS
Business Development
AT&T

Amity Willenborg, MBA
Faculty Associate
Division of Undergraduate
Studies

Charles Willenborg, MS
Technology Liaison/ Computer
Instructor
Baltimore County Public
Schools

Katherine N. Wilson, MSEd,
MBA
Interim Chair, Department of
Marketing
Graduate Division of Business
and Management

Joan M. Worthington, MBA
Director, Internet Services
System Source

Graduate Division of Business and Management*

ADVISORY BOARD
BUSINESS DIVISION

Emried D. Cole, JD
Venable, Baetjer and Howard, LLP

Greg Conderacci
Consultant, Good Ground Consulting

Stephen Cooper
Harry B. Cooper & Associates

Donna C. Easton
President, Easton Communication Group

Douglass W. List
President, List & Company

Laurence M. Merlis
President and Chief Executive Officer
Greater Baltimore Medical Center

Claudia Pleasants
President, Suburban Properties, Inc.

Christina Rodriguez
Chief Financial Officer and

General Counsel
SAGE Dining Services

LEADERSHIP DEVELOPMENT
PROGRAM ADVISORY BOARD

John Hunter
Senior Vice President, Customer Services/QVC, Inc.

James R. Calvin
Associate Professor and Director, Leadership Development Program

Hilda Crespo
Vice President for Public Policy, Aspira Association

A. E. Edwards
Division Manager, NISRD AT&T Government Markets

Edward Fujimoto
Management Consultant

Ernest Green
Senior Managing Director, Lehman Bros. Inc.

Blair Johnson
Vice President, Lincoln National Corporation

Floretta Dukes McKenzie
President, The Mckenzie Group Inc.

* SPSBE Academic Year Catalog 2005–2006, pp. 160–173.

Oral Muir
Director, E-commerce
Opportunity Evaluations
Marriott International

Alfred Ramirez
President, National
Community for Latino
Leadership Inc.

Richard Rowe
RAISE, Baltimore Mentoring
Institute

Gene Spencer
Vice President, Investor
Relations, Fannie Mae

EDWARD ST. JOHN
DEPARTMENT OF REAL ESTATE
PARTNERSHIP MEMBERS

Research Members

William J. Armstrong
Maryland Association of
Realtors

David M. Cohen
Linowes and Blocher LLP

Daniel Colhoun III
Medical Office Properties, Inc.

Jeffrey Kanne
NEBF Investments

John P. Kyle
Bethesda, Maryland

Harold Manekin
The Manekin Corporation

Ronald Racster
Home Hoyt Institute

Robert J. Robidoux
Maryland Chapter of the
Appraisal Institute

Thomas Robinson
Legg Mason Wood Walker

Ellen Roche
National Association of
Realtors.

Edward St. John
MIE Properties, Inc.

Dean Wilson
Wood Partners

Program Members

Chris Holt
Susquehanna Bank

John Macsherry
Nottingham Properties

Eric G. Regelin
Atlantic Builders Group, Inc.

Corporate Members

Ballard Spahr Andrews &
Ingersoll LLP
Morton P. Fisher Jr.

Building Owners and
Managers Association
(BOMA)

Colliers Pinkard
Terry R. Dunkin

Consolidated Engineering
Services, Inc.
Phillip Rogers

CORFAC
Thomas Bennett

Hines Interests LP
Howard Riker

Hughes & Associates LLC
F. Patrick Hughes

National Multi-Housing
Council
Douglas M. Bibby

Opus East LLC
James J. Lee

James W. Todd
McLean, Virginia

Individual Members

Don Ashbaugh
NVR, Inc.

John Blumer
CB Richard Ellis

Lewis Bolan
Bolan Smart Associates, Inc.

Robert F. Bradley
Baldwin, Maryland

M. J. Brodie
*Baltimore Development
Corporation*

Joe Callanan
Trammell Crow Company

Priscilla Carroll
*Whiteford Taylor and Preston
LLP*

J. Joseph Casey (lifetime
member)
Trammell Crow Company

Dan Colhoun
*HealthCare Financial Parters
REIT*

R. Clayton Emory
*Emory Hill Real Estate
Services, Inc.*

Crispin Etherington
Ashbourne Properties Limited

Jim Fergatter
Association of Foreign Investors in Real Estate (AFIRE)

Julian A. Josephs
Madison Marquette

Dan Kohlhepp
Crescents Resources LLC

Henry Kornblatt
The Kornblatt Company

Shawn Krantz
Mortgage Bankers Association

David Mayhood
The Mayhood Company

Martin L. Millspaugh
The Enterprise Development Company

William Morrill
Brown Investment Advisory & Trust

Patrick Phillips
Economic Research Associates

Claudia F. Pleasants
Suburban Properties, Inc.

Robert Rajewski
Building Investment Trust

Patricia T. Ralston
General Services Administration

Coleman Rector
The Rector Companies

T. Edgie Russell III
Partners Management Company

Eric Smart
Bolan Smart Associates, Inc.

Carl Struever
Streuver Brothers Eccles & Rouse, Inc.

Linda Veach
Bob Ward Homes

Michael C. Weitzmann
Weitzmann Associates, Inc.

David L. Winstead
Holland & Knight LLP

FACULTY

William Agresti, PhD
Interim MBA Director, Professor, Department of Information Technology

Michael A. Anikeeff, PhD
*Professor and Chair, Edward
St. John
Department of Real Estate*

Celso A. Brunetti, PhD
*Assistant Professor,
Department of Finance*

James R. Calvin, PhD
*Associate Professor,
Department of Management,
Director, Leadership
Development Program*

Kwang Soo Cheong, PhD
*Associate Professor,
Department of Finance*

Reza G. Djavanshir, DSc
*Assistant Professor,
Department of Information
Technology*

Erik M. Gordon, JD
*Assistant Professor,
Department of Marketing*

Douglas E. Hough, PhD
*Associate Professor and Chair,
Department of The Business of
Health*

Jay Liebowitz, DSc
*Professor, Department of
Information Technology*

Michael G. McMillan, PhD,
CFA, CIC
*Instructor, Department of
Finance*

Isaac F. Megbolugbe, PhD
*Associate Professor, Director
of Community Development
Program, Edward St. John
Department of Real Estate*

James E. Novitzki, PhD
*Associate Professor and Chair,
Department of
Information Technology*

Peter B. Petersen, DBA
*Interim Dean and Division
Director
Professor and Interim Chair,
Department of Management*

Beverly A. Sauer, PhD
*Professor, Department of
Management*

Lindsay J. Thompson, PhD
*Assistant Professor,
Department of Management*

Ken Yook, PhD
*Chair and Director, Associate
Professor, Department of
Finance*

444

Toby A. Gordon, ScD
Associate Professor
Vice President, Strategic
Planning and Market Research
Johns Hopkins Medicine

PRACTITIONER FACULTY

Zayd Abdul-Karim, EdD
President
Development Training Systems,
LLC

Fredric Abramson, PhD
President and Chief Executive
Officer
Alphagenics, Inc.

Jonathan I. Ahn, JD
Principal
Semmes, Bowem & Semmes
P.C.

Jerome Alston, MS
Consultant
Alston Consulting

William E. Althoff, MS
Task Leader
Booz Allen & Hamilton

Raj Ananthanpillai, MSE, MS
Partner
The MIRA Group, LLC

Gary D. Anderson, PhD
Vice President
TEC

Lawrence B. Aronhime, MBA,
MS
Lecturer
Johns Hopkins University

Cyrus H. Azani, SCD
Senior Technical Staff
TRW

John G. Bacher, MPA, JD
Vice President, Business
Development
AmeriChoice

John G. Bacot, MBA
Regional Sales Manager
Marquip Ward United, Inc.

James A. Baisey, MA, CPA
Practitioner Faculty
SPSBE Graduate Division of
Business and Management

Ross Ballard, MEd
President
MountainWhispers.com
Audiobooks

Alfred W. Barry III, BS
President
AB Associates

Ada-Helen Bayer Volentine, PhD
President
Performance Development, Inc.

Ademar Bechtold, PhD
Associate Professor
College of Notre Dame of Maryland

William R. Bitman, MS
Senior Systems Analyst
JHU Applied Physics Laboratory

Mark Bittle, MBA
Administrator for Ambulatory Operations
Johns Hopkins Hospital

Carol Bloomberg, MBA
President and Chief Executive Officer
Bloomberg & Associates

Lewis Bolan, MCP
Principal
Bolan Smart Associates, Inc.

Dina Boogaard, PhD
Organizational Consultant
Boogaard Consulting

Ra'id I. Breiwish, PhD
Senior Transportation Engineer
Science Applications International Corporation (SAIC)

James A. Brenton, MBA
Principal Network Security Program Manager Sprint Corporate Security

David M. Brickman, MPA
Director of Pricing, Costing and Quantitative Financial Analysis, Multifamily Division Freddie Mac

M.J. (Jay) Brodie, MA
President
Baltimore Development Corporation

Anthony J. Brooks, MBA
Technical Training Program Manager
NuTek 2000 Inc

Ronald G. Brunner, MS
President and Owner
Ronald G. Brunner and Associates

Michael D. Bulley, MBA
Vice President Research & Development
Steben & Company, Inc.

Terence E. Burns, MBA, CFA
Senior Vice President and
Portfolio Manager
Bank of America

Charles Butler, MA
Director, Network Operations
Advertising.com

Neil J. Campbell, MBA, MA
Chairman and Chief Executive
Officer
Mosaigen, Inc.

Robert W. Cannon, LLB
Partner
Saul Ewing LLP

Leonardo A. Canseco, MS,
CPA
Consultant
Comprehensive Business
Services, Inc.

Todd A. Canter, MBA
Senior Vice President
LaSalle Investment
Management Securities

Martha L. Carter, PhD
Senior Vice President and
Director, U.S. Research
Institutional Shareholder
Services

Anthony J. Castellano, MS
Director
General Services
Administration

Tsze H. Chan, PhD
Principal Research Analyst
American Institutes for
Research

Shelley A. Chapman, MA
Director, Center for Teaching
and Learning
School of Professional Studies
in Business and Education

Lea S. Chartock, MA
Lecturer
University of Maryland

Man Cho, PhD
Director, Credit Pricing and
Analysis
Federal National Mortgage
Association (Fannie
Mae)

J. Joseph Clarke, MLA, MAS
President
JJ Clarke Enterprises

Melinda Clem, MBA
Principal Consultant
Clementine Group

Traci E. Clemons, PhD
Biostatistician
EMMES Corporation

Charles L. Cochran, PhD
Professor
US Naval Academy

H. Susie Coddington, PhD
Consultant
Coddington Learning Co.

Cecelia G. Coffin, EdD
Staff Development Facilitator
Howard County Public School
System

David M. Cohen, JD
Partner
Linowes & Blocher LLP

Joseph A. Colantuoni, PhD
Senior Financial Economist
Federal Deposit Insurance
Corporation

Emried D. Cole, JD
Partner
Venable, LLP

Jack Cole, PhD
Executive Director
American Council for Adjunct
Faculty

James Cole, MBA
Program Analyst

US Environmental Protection
Agency

Pierre A. Colombel, Sr., EdD
Organization Development &
Training Specialist
Coldon & Associates, Inc.

Robert Comment, PhD
Principal
FinancialEcon.com

Greg Conderacci, MS
President
Good Ground Consulting LLC

Anthony A. Connelly, MS
Software Project Manager
PB Farradyne

Alicia D. Cooper, PhD
Assistant Professor of
Marketing
Morgan State University

Steven Coppel, MAS
Systems Engineer
Cisco Systems

Thomas A. Crain, AM
Director, Interdisciplinary
Studies
Division of Undergraduate
Studies

Sandra J. Crowley, EdD
President and Principal
ERIS Enterprises, Inc.

Stanley Dambroski, PhD
Adjunct Associate Professor
University of Maryland

Richard O. Davis, EDM, PhD
Executive Director
Johns Hopkins Medicine
Ambulatory Operations
and Practice Management

Victoria Davis, MBA, MSE
President
Mid City Urban, LLC

Melvin B. deGuzman, PhD
President
Systems Management
International, LLC

Joan DeSimone, PhD
Instructor
Division of Public Safety
Leadership

Marc DeSimone, Sr., PhD
Lead Consultant and Partner
ILDC Inc.

Robert A. Deyo, MAS
SAP Development Specialist
Northrop Grumman

Debra J. Diamond, MBA, CFA,
CIC
Principal
Debra Diamond and
Associates, Inc.

Conan Dickson, MPH, PhD
Senior Researcher
Johns Hopkins Center for
Innovations in Quality
Patient Care

Diane L. Dixon, EdD
Consultant, Writer and
Teacher/Leadership and
Organization Development
D. Dixon & Associates, LLC

Michael R. Doerrer, MA
Writer-Editor
U.S. Department of Agriculture

Christopher Dreisbach, PhD
Assistant Professor
Division of Public Safety
Leadership

Charles B. Duff, Jr., MCP
President and Executive
Director
Jubilee Baltimore, Inc.

Lydia B. Duff, JD
Senior Environmental Counsel
WR Grace & Company

Paul J. Duffy, PhD
President
Marketing Directions, Inc

Jeffrey Dunaway, MAS
Senior Vice President & Chief
Operating Officer
Ameritrial OTC Research, Inc.

Terry R. Dunkin, MS
Vice President/Principal
Colliers Pinkard

Dawn Edmiston, MBA
Marketing Director
The Tribune-Democrat

Kenneth J. Egan, MS
President
Mid-Atlantic Group, Inc.

Edward Ely
Vice President and Director
Rouse Company

Paul M. Ertz, MA
Senior Manager
Titan Systems Corporation

Victor A. Espitia, MBA
North America Process Leader
Honeywell, Inc.

M. B. Fardanesh, PhD
Practitioner Faculty
Graduate Division of Business
and Management

Soheila K. Fardanesh, MA
Lecturer
Towson University

James R. Farnum, Jr., MBA
COO
Brooks Financial Group, Inc.

Cynthia A. Femano, MS
Principal Consultant
Sybase, Inc.

Frank E. Ferrante, MS
Co-Founder, Executive Vice
President
FEF Group LLC

Frank D. Ferris, DPA
National Executive Vice
President
National Treasury Employees
Union

David Fick, MBA
Vice President–Real Estate
Analyst
Legg Mason Wood Walker, Inc.

Karen S. Fireman, MBA, MS
Practitioner Faculty
Graduate Division of Business
and Management

Eric Fishman, PhD, JD
Lawyer
Holland & Knight LLP

Patrice Flynn, PhD, MA, MSW
Economist
Flynn Research

Frederic C. Foley, MS, MBA
Certified Federal Enterprise IT
Architect
US Office of Personnel
Management

Charles C. Freitag, MBA, CPA
Chief Financial Officer
Data Trace Publishing
Company

Stephen Frempong, PhD
Assistant Professor
Baltimore County Community
College

Arthur R. Freidman, MS, BA
Division Chief
Department of Defense

Lynn Friedman, PhD
Clinical Psychologist/
Organizational Consultant
Consultant

Michael Friedman, MS
Management Analyst
National Institutes of Health

Edward K. Fujimoto, PhD
Director of Business
Management
Knowledge Advantage, Inc.

Frank B. Fulton, MS
Strategic Planner
Maryland Mass Transit
Administration

Donald A. Gabriel, JD
Chief Appraiser
Baltimore County Government

Eloy B. Garcia, MA
Treasurer
Inter-American Development
Bank

James G. Gatto, JD
Partner
Pillsbury Winthrop

Pamela Gerhardt, MFA
Freelance Writer
The Washington Post

Arefaine Ghebre-Yohannes,
PhD
Financial Advisor
HD Vest Advisory Services

Nicholas J. Giampetro, JD,
MBA
Attorney
Nicholas J. Giampetro, Esquire

Steven Gibson, PhD
Assistant Professor,
Department of Information
Sciences and Systems
Morgan State University

Daniel E. Gilbert, PhD
*Joint Strike Fighter
International Program
Manager
Northrop Grumman*

Lori Gillespie, MS
*Curriculum Manager
American Red Cross*

Caryn F. Ginsberg, MBA
*Strategic Idealist
Priority Ventures Group*

William Giuffre, JD
*Assistant Public Defender
Office of the Public Defender*

Alex S. Gogue, MGA
*Senior Systems Analyst
Johns Hopkins University*

Paula D. Gordon, PhD
*Practitioner Faculty
School of Professional Studies
in Business and Education*

Christopher P. Gorton, MD
*Health Management
Consultant*

Jay Gouline, MBA
*President
Springlake Corporation*

Vincent Grano, PhD
*Chief Systems Engineer
NOAA/NESDIS/IPO*

Steven L. Grant, MA
*Manager, Branding & Message
Development
National Education
Association*

Cheryl Gray, MS
*Consultant
Cheryl Gray and Associates*

Dale A. Gray, MBA
*Director of Technical Product
Management and
Development
Community of Science, Inc.*

Bruce D. Gregoire, MS
*Founder and President
Desktop Marketing Solutions
Inc*

Eric F. Grosse, Jr., EdD
*Dean, Division of Business and
Management
Prince George's Community
College*

Ann-Michele Gundlach, PhD
*President
AMG Consulting*

Paul Gurny, MBA, MS
Consultant
Gurny and Associates

Stanley J. Haavik, MBA, MS
HIPAA Practice Manager
Internet Commerce Corp

Ali Habib, MS
Practitioner Faculty
*Graduate Division of Business
and Management*

Michael S. Haigh, PhD
Senior Financial Economist
*Commodity Futures Trading
Commission*

John A. Halkias, PhD
*System Operations and
Management Team Leader*
*Federal Highway
Administration*

Griff Hall, MSB
Executive Director
Leadership Anne Arundel

Nancy H. Hall, MBA
Director of Finance
*Maryland Association of
Nonprofit Organizations*

David Harper, MS
Project Manager
*JHU Applied Physics
Laboratory*

Oliver O. Harris, MS
Loan Officer
CWCapital LLC

Diane L. Hartley, MBA
Managing Director
Clark Education

Raza Hasan, MIS
Instructor
University of Baltimore

Jon E. Hass, Sr., MBA
*Director, Real Estate
Investments*
Madison Capital Advisers Inc

Mark S. Hassinger, MCP
Senior Vice President
WestDulles Properties, LLC

Thomas A. Hauser, JD
Partner
*Ballard Spahr Andrews &
Ingersoll, LLP*

Rosa Heckle, MS
Adjunct Faculty
University of Maryland

Eric C. Helfers, MS
SeniorCost Analyst-Key
BAE Systems

Christopher T. Helmrath, MBA
Managing Director, Corporate Finance
American Express Tax and Business Services Inc

Karen Henderson, MEd
Consultant
Cruse Consulting

Lenneal Henderson, PhD, MA
Distinguished Professor
University of Baltimore

Catherine A. Heslep, MA
Director
Share Our Strength

Vicki T. Hess, MS
Consultant
Catalyst Consulting, LLC

Diane Hetherington, MS
Executive Coach/Organization Development
Consultant
Diane Hetherington Associates

Leroy Hewitt Jr., MSE
Director
Hewitt Engineering

Lolita L. Hickman, MS
President
Organizational Resource Group, Inc.

Sara Hill, MA
Curriculum Designer
School of Professional Studies in Business and Education

Terry A. Hinch, PhD
Multimedia Analyst
U.S. Postal Service

Loretta M. Hobbs, MS
President
ONeal-Hobbs Associates

Barbara S. Hoffman, MBA
Project Director
Council for Affordable Quality Healthcare

Jack C. Holleran, MA
Principal Partner
Halleran Associates

Harry W. Holt, Jr., ABD, MBA
Managing Director
Inroads/Greater-Washington

Robert C. Horn, EdD
President
Premier Consulting Service

Marvin Horowitz, PhD
President
Demand Research

Hsiaosu Hsiung, MS
Principal Engineer
The Mitre Corporation

Andrew R. Iserson, MS
Director of Systems Development
PB Farradyne

Alex C. Isherwood, PhD
President
Strategic Horizons Ltd

Mark T. Jacobson, MS
Consultant
Jackson Consulting

Craig A. Janus, MS
Vice President, Center for Information Systems
Mitretek Systems, Inc.

Laurence A. Jarvik, PhD
Proprietor
The Idler

Jean-Marie Jean-Pierre, PhD, MBA
Customer Relations Manager
NASA Goddard Space Flight Center

Kenneth Y. Jo, PhD
Staff Member
Satellite Communications Division

Blair Johnson, MS
Vice President, Corporate Planning and Development
Lincoln National Corporation

Quincey R. Johnson, MA, JD
Lawyer and Owner
Law Offices of Quincey R. Johnson

Suzette S. Johnson, MS
Project Manager
Northrop Grumman

Alfred Johnson Jr.
President
Johnson Management Services Corp.

Keith B. Johnston, MS
Director of Information Systems
The Analysis Corporation

Gary F. Jonas, MBA
Managing Partner, Chief Executive Officer
Strategic Philanthropic Advisors

Julian A. Josephs, MBA
Senior Vice President
Madison Marquette

Matthias A. Joyce, MS
Senior Information Security Engineer
Northrop Grumman

David P. Kaplan, JD
President
LECG

John A. Karikari, PhD
Assistant Director
US General Accountability
Office

Fred A. Katz, MBA
Practitioner Faculty
Graduate Division of Business
and Management

Kimberly Keating, MBA
Partner/Consultant
KLC Group

William W. Keating III, MBA
Vice President
AmeriChoice Health Services

William W. Keating, Jr., MBA
Practitioner Faculty
Graduate Division of Business
and Management

Anil Khatri, PhD
Computer Scientist
Department of Commerce

Mehrdad Khoshand, MS
Project Lead
NIC Commerce

Louis O. Kiang, MBA
Vice President
Townsend Capital

Michael Kim, MS
Manager of Business
Development
SAIC

Marsha King, PhD
Director of Human Resources
Capital One Financial

Stephen B. King, PhD
Chief of Learning
Constellation Energy Group

Mark D. Knobloch, MS
President
RSMK, LLC

Jon-David W. Knode, EdD
Lecturer in Reading, Special
Education, and
Technology
Towson University

Robert Kociemba
Senior Information Assurance
Engineer
Scientific Engineering Solutions
Group

Michael Kociemba, MS
Principal—Information
Assurance
Van Dyke Technology Group

Martin B. Kormanik, EdD
President and CEO
OD Systems, Inc.

M. Shawn Krantz, MBA
Principal
Brownstone Capital, LLC

Gary S. Lachman, JD
International Real Estate
Portfolio Manager
Office of Overseas Buildings
Operations
US Department of State

Jon M. Laria, JD
Partner
Ballard Spahr Andrews &
Ingersoll

Martin J. Lattman, MBA
VP of Marketing and Sales
Systems Plus, Inc.

Anne Lauer, MS, MA
Practitioner Faculty
Graduate Division of Business
and Management

Denise Lee, MS
Project Manager
Edurech Ltd

Michael Nicholas Lee, MBA,
CFA
Financial Markets Expert in
Residence
US Department of Labor

Paul Lee, MS
Lead, Data Analyst Group
Space Telescope Science
Institute

Waldon Lee, MBA
General Manager
Construction Technology
Associates

Won C. Lee, PhD
Associate Director
Aht Associates, Inc.

Harold Lehmann, PhD, MD
Associate Professor
School of Medicine, Johns
Hopkins University

Sande Lehrer, PhD
Chief, Performance and Career
Development
Branch
US Office of Personnel
Management

Paul G. Leiman, JD
Principal
KeyWitness

Andrew C. Lemer, PhD
Principal
The MATRIX Group, LLC

Gilbert B. Lessenco, JD
Of Counsel
Thompson Hine LLP

Ori Lev, MA
Lecturer
Institute for Policy Studies,
Johns Hopkins
University

Bernard (Bob) Lewis, PhD
Chief Technologist for
Knowledge Management
Integrated Systems & Solutions,
Lockheed Martin

Edwin E. Lewis Jr., MS
Technical Director, Healthcare
Consulting
Force3 Inc

Cheryl R. Lieberman, MS
Senior IA Consultant
EDS, Inc

Vaughan Limbrick, MS
President
Success Accelerators, Inc.

Aline Lin, MA
Chief Executive Officer
Link Studio, LLC

David Lingelbach, MS
Chairman and Chief Executive
Officer
Hilltop Global Advisors, LLC

Simon Y. Liu, PhD
Director, Information Systems
National Library of Medicine
National Institutes of Health

Win G. Liu, PhD
President
Sharp Visions Software

Adrian E. Long, MD
Chief Medical Officer
St. Agnes Healthcare

Paul S. Lowengrub, PhD
Economist and Financial
Manager
CAP Analysis

Jonathan P. Luckett, MS
Practitioner Faculty
Graduate Division of Business
and Management

Daniel J. Lund, MBA
President
Gateway Development Group

Frank V. Maisano, MBA
Director, Strategic
Communications
Bracewell & Patterson, LLP

Saundra R. Maley, PhD, MA
Adjunct Assistant Professor
George Washington University

Robert A. Manekin, JD
Principal
Robert Manekin Partners LLC

William C. Manion, MBA
Principal
O'Neil & Manion Architects,
PA

Joan E. Marshall, MS
Executive Director
College Savings Plans of
Maryland

Scott A. Mason, DPA
Managing Partner
SKM Enterprises, LLC

Maureen L. McAvey, MBA
Senior Research Fellow
Urban Land Institute

William E. McCaffrey, MBA
Adjunct Assistant Professor
University of Maryland
University College

R. Donald McDaniel, MBA
Vice President, Insurance
Solutions
IWIF

Capers R. McDonald, MBA
President and Chief Executive
Officer
BioReliance Corporation

Donna H. McKalip, MS
Practitioner Faculty
Graduate Division of Business
and Management

Peter McKenney, MBA
CEO
Cipher

William McNaught, PhD
Assistant Director, Center for
Economics
US General Accounting Office

Yesook Merrill, PhD
Assistant Director, Center for
Economics
US General Accounting Office

Leigh B. Middleditch, MBA
Chief Information Officer
Office of the Governor

John P. Milatzo, PhD
Consultant
Independent Consultant

Bruce M. Miller, MS, MSBA,
ABD
Program Manager
The Mitre Corporation

Lee Miller, MS, MSBA
Program Development Officer
Walter Reed Army Hospital

Matt Minahan, EdD
Principal
M&M Associates

Tanya T. Minkovsky, MS
System Analyst
Johns Hopkins University

Richard B. Minthorne, MBA
President/Chief Executive
Officer
Network Analytics and
Telecommunications

Charlene Mollison, MA
Vice President
Constituency Services Group,
Council on
Foundations

Jennifer J. Monteith, MS
President
Monteith Business Solutions,
Inc.

Catherine J. Morrison, JD
Consultant
Morrison Associates

David Morrocco, EdD
Professional Development
Facilitator
Howard County Public School
System

Charles J. Morton, Jr., JD
Partner
Venable, Baetjer and Howard,
LLP

Debra J. Moser, MS
Executive Director
Rockville ARTS

Deanna Mummert, MA
Executive Director, Generation
Strategy
Constellation Energy Group

Anne Murphy, JD
Attorney, Civil Division,
Appellate Staff
U.S. Department of Justice

Gregg Nass, MBA
Business and Operations
Manager
Center for Technology in
Education
Johns Hopkins University

Thomas Naugler, MBA
Practitioner Faculty
Graduate Division of Business
and Management

David E. Nelson, MBA
Senior Vice President, Portfolio
Manager
Legg Mason Wood Walker, Inc.

Ronald Newcomer, MS
Manager
Qwest Communications

Alvin Officer, PhD
Program Manager
Graduate School USDA

Lisa K. Olson, PhD, MBA
Executive Director
Heart Rhythm Foundation

James A. Overdahl, PhD
Senior Financial Economist
Office of the Comptroller of the
Currency

Katherine Paal, MBA
Financial Advisor
Heritage Financial Consultants

Chul W. Park, PhD
Financial Economist
Commodity Futures Trading
Commission

Pamela Paulk, MSW, MBA
Vice President, Human
Resources
Johns Hopkins Hospital

Alfred P. Pavot, MBA, CPA
Assistant Chief Accountant
US Securities and Exchange
Commission

Robert Pernick, PhD
HRD and OD Consultant
Amherst Group

Robert E. Perry, MBA
Controller and Operational
Manager
Rose Financial Services

James Peter, MS
Information Systems
Engineering
Johns Hopkins Applied Physics
Laboratory

Frank Piff, MBA
President and CEO
Behavioral Dynamics LLC

Jo Ann Pina, PhD, MA
President
InspirAction

Edward G. Piper, MS
Senior Consultant
Piper Group

Morris A. Pondfield, MS
President
BiggerNET LLC

Douglas Porter
President
Growth Management Institute

Surya S. Prasad, PhD
President and Chief Executive Officer
Applied Technical Services Corporation

Carolyn W. Price, MBA
President
IMPACT Marketing & Public Relations, Inc.

John R. Pugh, Jr., MA, CFA
President
Insight Wealth Management, Inc.

Robert T. Rajewski, MS
Asset Manager
AFLCIO–Building Investment Trust

Patricia T. Ralston, MS
Vice President
General Services Administration

Abdul H. Rana, PhD
Vice President, Engineering and Operations
Arrowhead Global Solutions

Gale E. Rasin
Associate Judge
District Court for Baltimore City

Coleman G. Rector, MS
President
Rector Construction

Frederick F. Repetti, JD, CPA
Practitioner Faculty
Graduate Division of Business and Management

Robert K. Richardson, MAS
Vice President
Destiny Management Services, LLC

Jay S. Richman, MS, MAS
Staff Project Manager
Qwest Communications

Margery Ritchie, MAS
Independent Consultant
Ritchie & Associates

Christopher J. Ritz, PhD
Practitioner Faculty
Graduate Division of Business and Management

Bonnie L. Robeson, PhD
President
Spectrum Bio Sciences, Inc.

Christina Rodriguez, JD
CFO and General Counsel
Sage Dining Services

Toni D. Rosen, MS
President
TRG Networking Inc

Ed Rudden, MSITS
Chief Executive Officer
Accordia Consulting, LLC

John P. Sagi, PhD
Associate Professor of Business
and Computer
Studies
Anne Arundel Community
College

Dominador D. Sanchez, MS
Chief Information Security
Officer
The Architect of the Capitol

Stephen R. Sandler, MA
Partner
Sandler-Innocenzi, Inc.

Tara A. Scanlon, JD
Partner
Holland & Knight, LLP

Janis B. Schiff, JD
Partner
Holland & Knight LLP

Walter G. Schneider, PhD
President
Lighthouse Consulting, Inc.

Bradley C. Schoener, PhD
OD Manager
University of Maryland
Medical System

Steven Schulman, MBA
Web Architect Engineer
Lockheed Martin

H. Michael M. Schwartzman,
MS
Vice President and Director of
Development
Ross Development &
Investments

Herman M. Scott, MA
President
Response Group

David Scribner, Jr., PhD
President
Scribner & Partners, Inc.

William Segal, PhD, CFA
Assistant Director, Risk
Modeling
Federal Housing Finance Board

David J. Segmiller, MS
Senior Vice President
Cochran Stephenson &
Donkervoet, Inc.

Moe Shahdad, PhD
Professor
Strayer University

Stephen M. Smith, MBA
President/CEO
Naviance LLC

Karl N. Snow, PhD
Senior Economist
Welch Consulting

Richard E. Solli, MBA
Senior Marketing Manager
Maryland Mass Transit
Administration

Marina P. Somers, MBA
Senior Programmer/Analyst
Johns Hopkins University

Mary Somers, MS
Faculty Associate
Division of Graduate
Education

Pamela B. Sorota, JD
Attorney
Law Office of Pamela B. Sorota

Richard O. Spence, MS
Director Engineering Systems
Verizon Global Networks

Mitchell G. Spiegel, MS
President
VIZ Corporation

Vanessa K. Spiller, MS
Practitioner Faculty
Graduate Division of Business
and Management

Bellur N. Srikar, PhD
Senior Program Manager
Intelsat Corporation

Thomas F. Staffa, JD
Chief Compliance Officer
Johns Hopkins Health System

Stephen Steele, PhD
Professor
Anne Arundel Community
College

Jennifer P. Streaks, JD, MBA
Attorney Consultant
US Treasury Department,
President's Commission on the
US Postal Service

John D. Sullivan, PhD
Executive Director
Center for International
Private Enterprise

Derk Swain, PhD
Practitioner Faculty
Graduate Division of Business
and Management

Kathleen K. Swanson, JD
*Coordinator for Planning and
Council Services
Archdiocese of Baltimore*

Wendy S. Swire, MA
*President
Swire Solutions*

Mark Tabisz, MS
*Management Assistant II
Baltimore County Government
(Bureau of Utilities)*

John J. Tamer, MBA
*Area Manager, General
Accounting Systems Support
Johns Hopkins Applied Physics
Laboratory*

Alex P. Tang, PhD, CFA
*Professor
Morgan State University*

Joyce O. Taylor, MBA
*President
SWATH Leadership, Inc.*

Percy Thomas, SCD
*Chief of Training Division
National Weather Service*

Mark J. Thronson, JD
*Attorney
Dickstein Shapiro Moran &
Oshinsky LLP*

Dalton Tong, MBA, CPA
*President and CEO
Tong and Associates
Healthcare Management
Consultants*

Chamesou Toure, MBA
*Practitioner Faculty
Graduate Division of Business
and Management*

Raymond Truitt, JD
*Partner
Ballard Spahr Andrews &
Ingesoll*

Francois O. Tuamokumo, PhD
*Statistician
Walter Reed Army Medical
Center*

Michael S. Tumbarello, MS,
MBA
*President
First Service Financial Group,
Inc.*

Jeffrey D. Turner, MS, MBA
*Vice President
Brailsford & Dunlavey*

Thomas A. Vadakkeveetil, PhD
*Independent Consultant
Alexander Consulting*

Emily J. Vaias, JD
Partner
Linowes & Blocher LLP

Alan P. Vollmann, JD
Partner
Holland & Knight LLP

John M. Volpe, PhD
Principal
Volpe & Associates

Christine V. Walters, JD, MS
Independent Consultant
FiveL Company

Sabrina L. Warren Bush, MS
Partner
Carl Warren & Associates, LLC

Elizabeth Watson, MBA
Executive Vice President
National Government
Properties, LLC

Angela Watts, MS
President
Annapolis Professional
Resources, Inc.

James P. Wayne, MBA
Dean, Workforce Development
Community College of
Baltimore County

Charles A. Weber, PhD
Project Manager
Institute for Defense Analysis

Edward H. Weiss, MS
Director of Marketing
ADS Retail

Frederick Wheeler, MBA
Practitioner Faculty
Graduate Division of Business
and Management

Paul R. Willging, PhD
Practitioner Faculty
Graduate Division of Business
and Management

Barney M. Wilson, EdD
President
Wilson's Services

Jeffery D. Wilson, MS
Assistant Program Manager for
Radio Systems
Marine Corps Systems
Command

Katherine N. Wilson, MSEd,
MBA
Interim Chair, Department of
Marketing
Graduate Division of Business
and Management

Landon A. Wilson, MBA
Senior Project Manager
Otsuka America
Pharmaceutical, Inc.

Ira Winakur, PhD
Director
Center for Economic
Understanding

Michael S. Winett, JD
Attorney
The Law Office of Michael S.
Winett

Steven M. Worth, MA
President
Plexus Consulting Group

James Wynn, MA
Instructor
University of Maryland

John W. Yates, MBA
Senior Partner, Management
Consulting Services
Focus Group Corporation

Robert A. Younglove, MA
Performance Coach
PATH Associates

Appendix S
Inaugural Dean Appointed for
Carey Business School

1. Announcement from President Brody to Faculty, Staff, and Students: Carey Business School Dean Appointed (e-mail message dated October 28, 2007).

2. Carey Business School Names First Dean: Article by Dennis O'Shea in *The JHU Gazette*, the newspaper of the Johns Hopkins University (October 29, 2007/Vol. 37, No. 9).

3. Getting Down to Business: Yash Gupta, Dean of Carey School, lays out vision for first year ... Article by Greg Rienzi in *The JHU Gazette*, the newspaper of the Johns Hopkins University (January 7, 2008/Vol. 37, No. 16).

Subject: Carey Business School dean appointed
Date: Sun, 28 Oct 2007 13:49:51 -0400
From: JHBroadcast <JHBroadcast@jhu.edu>
To: recipients@listproc.hcf.jhu.edu

October 28, 2007

Dear Faculty, Staff and Students:

I am pleased to announce that the board of trustees voted today to accept my recommendation that Yash P. Gupta be appointed the inaugural dean of the Carey Business School, effective Jan. 1.

Dr. Gupta is an experienced, innovative and dynamic leader in business education who has served as dean at three prominent business schools, most recently the Marshall School of Business at the University of Southern California.

He is a visionary academic leader. He is a creative and resourceful strategic planner. He is a scholar and a teacher. And he has been a builder of close and meaningful relationships, within schools, within universities, and between the university and business communities.

All these characteristics will stand Dean-designate Gupta in good stead at Johns Hopkins. Building on our strong tradition of business education dating back to 1916 and on our thriving interdisciplinary MBA and other graduate business programs, he will lead us in breaking the business school mold.

There are many business schools across this country, and a number of great ones. Were we to have no aspiration higher than to replicate what exists elsewhere, there would have been no good reason for Johns Hopkins to establish a stand-alone school of business.

But we do have higher aspirations. We intend to create a world-class business school, a school for the future.

Under Yash Gupta's leadership, and in collaboration with other Johns Hopkins divisions, the Carey Business School will educate broadly prepared leaders in finance, industry and entrepreneurship.

Those leaders will be distinguished from their peers by their ability to draw not only on specialized business skills but also on critical cross-disciplinary knowledge from other Johns Hopkins programs.

Yash's track record as dean at USC, the University of Washington and the University of Colorado at Denver confirms that he has the imagination, the energy and the skill to build the Carey Business School into one of the nation's most innovative and respected.

I want to reiterate here what I said in December when I announced the establishment of the Carey Business School: Trustee Emeritus William Polk Carey has made this moment possible. I commend him for his vision. He will long be remembered for his generosity.

I also want to thank Vice Provost Pamela Cranston, who has served as interim dean since the school was born on Jan. 1. Her hard work, and the talent and devotion of the entire faculty and staff, has gotten the Carey School off to a tremendous start.

Thanks as well to the search committee that led the recruitment of our new dean, ably led by Dr. David Nichols and Dr. Edgar Roulhac.

I know that all of you join me in offering congratulations to Yash Gupta and look forward, as I do, to working with him. Hang on tight; we're in for an exciting ride.

More information about Dr. Gupta is available in this week's edition of the Gazette, or in the story that is online now at http://www.jhu.edu/gazette/2007/29oct07/29gupta.html

Sincerely,

Bill Brody

Carey Business School
Names First Dean

Yash P. Gupta chosen to reinvent
the model of business education

By Dennis O'Shea
Homewood

The goal: audacious. The challenge:
daunting. The dean: ready.

Yash P. Gupta wants to help make
Johns Hopkins' new Carey Business
School one of the most innovative
and most prominent schools of
business in the world.

After 14 years at the helm of
three prominent, established
business schools, Yash P. Gupta
(photographed here at the
University of Southern California)
says that being involved with a
startup 'is a great opportunity.'

"This is a great opportunity to create
a world-class business school in a
world-class university," said Gupta,
appointed by the board of trustees Sunday to serve as the school's
first dean.

The university aims to build a school that purposefully teaches
students not only business skills but also critical cross-disciplinary
knowledge taught in other Johns Hopkins divisions.

It wants to prepare business students broadly, to arm them with
all the skills they need to lead companies and organizations in
emerging industries.

In other words, the university wants to reinvent the model of
business education.

473

A worthy goal. But why would someone who has already spent 14 years as dean of three prominent, established business schools want to involve himself with a startup?

"It's a great opportunity," Gupta said. "If there is no risk, there is no reward. In this case, the reward is creating a business school that is one of the leading business schools in the world; truly the most innovative business school in the country."

Gupta, who most recently served as dean of the University of Southern California's Marshall School of Business from 2004 to 2006, will begin in his new position Jan. 1.

"Yash is a visionary academic leader," said university President William R. Brody, who recommended Gupta to the trustees. "He is a creative and resourceful strategic planner. He is a scholar and a teacher. And he has been a builder of close and meaningful relationships, within schools, within universities and between the university and business communities.

"He has the imagination, the energy and the skill to build the Carey Business School into one of the nation's most innovative and respected," Brody said.

"Dr. Gupta is an energetic leader with a great appetite for work," said Kristina M. Johnson, provost and senior vice president for academic affairs. "He will build relationships across Johns Hopkins, establishing programs of 'selective excellence,' thus distinguishing the Carey Business School and deepening the Johns Hopkins brand."

The school, built on a tradition of business education at Johns Hopkins that dates to 1916, was launched last January on the strength of a $50 million gift from trustee emeritus William Polk Carey through his W.P. Carey Foundation. The new school already collaborates with other Johns Hopkins divisions to offer, for instance, joint master's/MBA programs in biotechnology, nursing,

474

public health, communication, information and telecommunications systems, and government.

"We have a strong base to leverage from to create a new kind of business school," Gupta said. The first priority, he said, is to form even stronger working relationships with other Johns Hopkins schools, where faculty and students are hatching new ideas in science, health, technology, international relations and other fields.

"The issue is one of innovation," he said. "The business schools that can teach students how to be innovative and how to understand the process of innovation will be the anchor points for the evolution of new businesses."

Other key tasks in building the new school, Gupta said, include making program and curriculum decisions, establishing partnerships with the business community, the critical undertaking of faculty recruitment and "the mother of all, if you like, fund raising."

John J. Fernandes, president and chief executive officer of the Association to Advance Collegiate Schools of Business, said he has followed many dean searches. Johns Hopkins, he said, has chosen well.

"I said that Johns Hopkins is going to need someone who is going to put heart and soul into the job, someone who knows curriculum, a successful innovator, a relationship builder and a prolific fundraiser," Fernandes said, "someone who will work tirelessly, who has the vision, the energy and the human relations skills.

"Yash has been successful in all those areas," he said. "This situation requires someone who can go in a lot of directions, the right way, at a hundred miles an hour. I think you've got the right person."

Gupta has been dean at the University of Colorado at Denver, the University of Washington and, most recently, USC, where he led the creation of a new five-year strategic plan. During his tenure, USC's Marshall School raised more than $55 million; expanded its faculty; increased emphasis on faculty research; created research centers focused on such areas as global business, bio-business, sports business and brand management; reorganized the job placement center for students and alumni; and developed a new innovation-focused MBA curriculum.

Gupta was dean of the University of Washington Business School from 1999 to 2004, a period in which its endowment grew from $44 million to $82 million, the MBA program was redesigned to enhance students' global perspective, and the school's entire curriculum was re-examined. The school also established a technology management MBA for scientists and engineers.

Gupta also headed the College of Business and Administration at the University of Colorado at Denver from 1992 to 1999, doubling the number of research grants, expanding the faculty and student body, establishing mentoring programs and setting up a program where teams of graduate students and faculty provided consulting for local businesses.

Gupta said he looks forward to meeting and working with the current faculty and staff of the Carey School. "I really believe that they have an opportunity to be a part of a great school in the making," he said. "What a sense of pride you can have that you are the builders, the creators."

A widely published scholar in operations management, Gupta served before he became a dean on the faculties of the University of Louisville, University of Manitoba and Memorial University of Newfoundland. He is a 1973 graduate of Panjab University in India, holds a master's degree in production management earned in 1974 from Brunel University, West London, and earned a PhD in management sciences in 1976 from the University of Bradford in England.

Gupta is married with two sons. One is participating in the Teach for America program, and the other is a senior at the University of Washington.

Office of News and Information
Johns Hopkins University
901 South Bond Street, Suite 540
Baltimore, Maryland 21231
Phone: 443-287-9960 | Fax: 443-287-9920

October 29, 2007
FOR IMMEDIATE RELEASE
CONTACT: Dennis O'Shea
443-287-9960
dro@jhu.edu

Getting Down to Business

Yash Gupta, dean of Carey School, lays out vision for first year

By Greg Rienzi
The Gazette

Yash Gupta says he doesn't play basketball, but he understands teamwork and chemistry.

In his first week on the job, Yash Gupta tours the Homewood campus with new JHU colleagues Pam Cranston, Sally O'Brien and Page Barnes (rear).
Photo by Jay VanRensselaer / HIPS

Sitting in his office in Homewood's Shaffer Hall on day one of his tenure as inaugural dean of the new <u>Carey Business School</u>, Gupta rhetorically asks why it is that a team wins one day and loses the next against the same opponent?

"Chemistry. They just didn't have it. You need to create a rhythm and keep it going," says Gupta, a man who exudes both enthusiasm and optimism.

He was talking about how to manage people in a business, but he just as easily could be referring to the daunting task that lies before him: taking the helm of a startup and turning it into one of the most innovative and prominent schools of business in the world.

How does one start this process? He listens, a lot.

Gupta's appointment calendar for the next two months is already bursting with meetings with students, faculty, directors and deans. He says he wants feedback to help shape the school's curriculum and guide what he calls "the planning process," a period of four to five months that will ultimately result in a mission statement. This statement, he says, will clearly articulate the vision for the new school and a strategy for reaching milestones.

"I want to be able to communicate what the school will look like, what form it will take," says Gupta, who before joining Johns Hopkins spent 14 years as dean of three prominent, established business schools. He most recently served as dean of the University of Southern California's Marshall School of Business, from 2004 to 2006. Gupta also headed the University of Washington Business School and the College of Business and Administration at the University of Colorado at Denver.

Gupta's first week at Johns Hopkins, not unexpectedly, was a hectic one. He attended dozens of meetings, all amid "housekeeping" matters such as getting his J-Card and going over his university benefits with a human resources representative. There was also an informal welcome breakfast—a chance to meet and greet Carey Business School staff in Shaffer Hall—and a condensed tour of the Homewood campus.

The Carey Business School, built on a tradition of business education at Johns Hopkins that dates to 1916, was launched last January on the strength of a $50 million gift from trustee emeritus William Polk Carey through his W.P. Carey Foundation. The new school already collaborates with other Johns Hopkins divisions to offer, for instance, joint master's/MBA programs in biotechnology; nursing; public health; communication, information and telecommunications systems; and government.

Gupta anticipates more such collaboration in the future and is eager to start building relationships with other deans and directors. He says the university aims to build a school that purposefully teaches students not only business skills but also critical cross-disciplinary knowledge taught in other Johns Hopkins divisions.

"I want to see what we can do together," Gupta says. "These are top-notch schools, so why wouldn't we want to hitch our car to their wagon? We are the new kids on the block, and we need help from these schools. From liberal arts here we can learn mental flexibility, from engineering we can gain technical understanding, and from medicine we can get health care knowledge. I see us building upon the strengths at Johns Hopkins to create something unique, not copying what others have done."

Gupta says that year one of his tenure will focus heavily on recruiting world-class faculty, a process that has already begun.

"Our faculty must reflect Johns Hopkins' quality and support the brand," he says. "We must be outstanding in this regard, and I'm dedicated to this goal."

Gupta also wants to help recruit an "outstanding" advisory board that will include luminaries from the business world.

"I see this as very critical to our future and success," he says. "These will be people who will help provide leadership and vision."

In terms of curriculum, Gupta says his meetings with faculty and students will start to bring into focus what elements need to stay, what need to go and what need to be added.

He did say, however, that the curriculum would likely reflect what he describes as three major trends in business education: globalization, the business of knowledge/innovation and changes in world demographics.

He points to the year 2050, when the world population is expected to reach 9.5 billion people.

"How will we deal with this large workforce, and provide services for this number of customers, the majority of which will be outside the United States? These are questions we need to be asking," he says. "And innovation is very important. How can we take new ideas and make the most of them? How do you perpetuate innovation? This is some of what we need to be teaching."

Gupta says that he realizes much work lies ahead to get where the school wants to go. Asked if people should be patient, Gupta laughs and says he would never ask that. "No, we're in a hurry," he says. "Well, as much in a hurry as you can be in academia."

Appendix T
Index

Joseph's Square 9, 36, 37, 182
Joyce
  Matthias A 455
  Peter M 434

K

Kahler 381
Kanne 441
Kaplan 455
Karikari 456
Karpinski 78, 177
Katana 246
Katz 456
Kavalek 422
Kavanagh 434
Keating
  Kimberly 456
  William W 456
Keating, Jr.
  William W. 456
Keller 434
Kelly 310
Kelsey 398
Kerin 382
Keyser 393, 409
Khatri 456
Khoshand 456
Kiang 456
Kilian 308
Killingsworth 56, 57
Kim 456
King
  Marsha 456
  Stephen B 456
  Wanda 434
Kinsley 353, 354, 355
Klein 39, 177
Knobloch 456
Knode 456
Knott 246
Kobler 82
Kociemba
  Michael 456
  Robert 456
Kohlhepp 443

Kolb
  Nicholas E 38, 39
  Rita R 434
Konigsberg 434
Kormanik 456
Kornblatt 443
Kostik 383
Kouzis 434
Krantz 443, 457
Kremer 435
Krieger School of Arts and Sciences
        xi, xv, 15, 41, 69, 111, 150,
        240, 297, 312, 332, 358, 363,
        397, 407
Kubik 435
Kulansky 435
Kyle 246, 441

L

Lacey 435
Lachman 457
Lambdin 417
Lamonte 395
Lamp 435
Lampkin 40
Lanagan 435
Lancaster
  H. C. 277
  Louise 306
Lane 307, 308, 406, 408, 411, 412
Laria 457
Larsen 382
LaSalle 110
Lattman 457
Lauer 457
Lavarello xii, 70, 84
Leadership Development Program for
        Minority Managers 11, 91, 97,
        98, 99, 110, 111, 112, 115, 118,
        119, 305, 331, 347
Lee
  Denise 457
  F. E. 158
  James J 442
  Michael 457

494

R

Racster 441
Radcliffe 262
Rahal 437
Rajewski 443, 462
Ralston 443, 462
Rami 437
Ramirez 441
Ramsen 271, 274
Rana 462
Randall 46, 426
Ranum 78, 80, 183, 206, 208, 210
Rasin 462
Real Estate Department 98, 103, 317
Rector 443, 462
Reed 291, 303, 310, 311, 358, 365,
    379
Regelin 441
Rehak 437
Reiley 40
Reinsel 437
Reiss 396, 400
Remsen 24, 28
Repetti 462
Reynolds 55, 56, 57
Rice 245, 349, 351, 355, 388
Rich 292
Richardson 462
Richman 462
Riker 442
Riley 437
Ritchie 462
Ritz 462
Rivlin 437
Rizza 403
Robbins 38, 40, 182
Roberts
  Janet 297
  Regina 387
Robertson
  Crystal 384
  John 366
  Ret 415
Robeson 462

Robidoux 441
Robinson
  Gary 400
  Michelle 351, 352, 404
  Patricia 389
  Thomas 441
Roche 441
Rodriguez
  Carlos 46, 101, 102, 302, 339
  Christina 97, 331, 440, 462
Roeder 374
Rofail 437
Rogers 248, 442
Rome 318
Roop 437
Rose 291, 380
Roseman 287
Rosen 463
Roulhac 86, 291, 471
Roulston 276, 277
Rourke 18, 19, 20, 21, 72, 129, 179,
    186, 187, 206
Rowe 441
Roy xii, 1, 2, 9, 16, 21, 168, 173, 181,
    182, 183
Rubb 393
Rudden 463
Russell III 443
Ryan 396

S

Sadowski 46, 103, 109
Sagi 463
Sanchez 463
Sandler 463
Sattler 40, 381, 382
Sauer 46, 337, 444
Scanlon 463
Scarborough 356, 407, 408
Schaedel 400
Scharfe 382
Scheper
  Dianne 437
  George 438
Schiff 463

About the Author

Dr. Pete Petersen, the senior professor of the business faculty at Johns Hopkins University, spent 26½ years at Hopkins before being appointed professor emeritus in 2006. At Hopkins, he taught between 5,000–6,000 MBA students and also, as part of an overall Hopkins effort, conducted numerous executive leadership seminars for U.S. federal organizations (such as the Secret Service and the Bureau of Alcohol, Tobacco, Firearms, and Explosives) with a particular emphasis on teams, teamwork, and leadership. Keenly interested in crisis management, he completed the book The Great Baltimore Fire (now in its second printing) just in time for the 100th anniversary of the conflagration, which took place February 7–8, 1904. Also the author of an earlier book and more than 90 articles and published papers, he received the John F. Mee Prize and the Richard D. Irwin Award for his work on management history.

As an infantry officer before joining Johns Hopkins University in 1979, Petersen helped establish the first Special Forces operational base in Vietnam during 1962 and, years later, commanded an 814-man infantry battalion for 210 days in combat. His awards include two silver stars and a bronze star for valor, but his career later as a colonel involved the further drama and trauma of being a bureaucrat in Washington DC, dealing with real-world planning, programming, and budgeting.

Dr. Petersen is also a master parachutist with 80 parachute jumps, has traveled to Antarctica and Tibet, and, at age 65, reached the summit of Mount Kilimanjaro. Beyond all this, he enjoyed the excitement of interacting with executives in the classroom. Now retired from both Hopkins and the Army, he lives in Vero Beach, Florida, where he completed this book.

Printed in the United States
140644LV00005B/1/P